*B*enjamin
Franklin's
Printing
Network

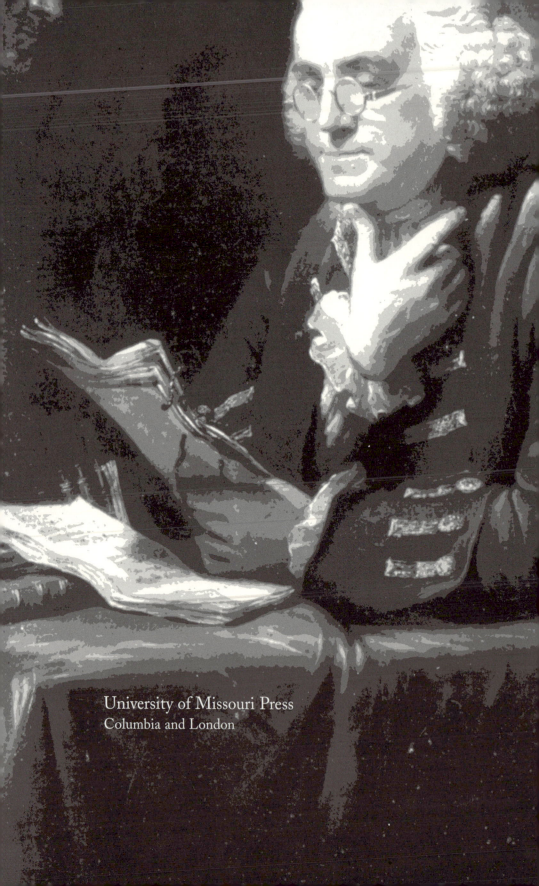

University of Missouri Press

Columbia and London

Benjamin Franklin's Printing Network

Disseminating Virtue in Early America

Ralph Frasca

Library of Congress Cataloging-in-Publication Data

Frasca, Ralph, 1962–
　　Benjamin Franklin's printing network : disseminating virtue in early America / Ralph
Frasca.
　　　　p.　　cm.
　　Summary: "Explores Benjamin Franklin's network of partnerships and business relation-
ships with printers. His network altered practices in both European and American colonial
printing trades by providing capital and political influence to set up working partnerships
with James Parker, Francis Childs, Benjamin Mecom, Benjamin Franklin Bache, David
Hall, Anthony Armbruster, and others"—Provided by publisher.
　　Includes bibliographical references (p.　) and index.
　　ISBN-13: 978-0-8262-1614-4 (alk. paper)
　　ISBN-10: 0-8262-1614-5 (alk. paper)
　　1. Franklin, Benjamin, 1706–1790—Career in printing. 2. Franklin, Benjamin, 1706–
1790—Friends and associates. 3. Business networks—United States—History—18th
century. 4. Printing industry—United States—History—18th century. 5. Printers—United
States—Political activity—History—18th century. 6. Printing—Social aspects—United
States—History—18th century.　I. Title.
　　Z232.F8F83 2006
　　686.2'092—dc22

　　　　　　　　　　　　　　　　　　　　　　　　　　　　　　　　2005027403

Designer: Jennifer Cropp
Typesetter: Crane Composition, Inc.
Printer and binder: Thomson-Shore, Inc.
Typefaces: Caslon and Apple Chancery

Contents

Preface

"Historians relate, not so much what is done, as what they would have be-lieved," Benjamin Franklin suggested to readers of his *Poor Richard's Almanack* in 1739.[1] Franklin's view, although characteristically cynical, underscores the historian's important role of "interpreter." When there is dis-agreement on the "truth" of what happened in the past, historians propound their theories, which compete for acceptance and validation in the Miltonian free marketplace of ideas. Even more subject to interpretation is the question of why something happened. Seldom can absolute truth be located in this search, which is why "why" is the historian's most challenging question.

This book addresses both the "why" and the "what" of Franklin's printing network, as in "What form did it take?" and "Why did he create it?" Franklin himself offers only a few vague allusions to his printing network, which has contributed to the minimal acknowledgement of its existence in the volumi-nous literature about Franklin. Thus, my task here has been to reconstruct an organization from inference, by piecing shards of information together to suggest the structure and functions of a printing network that served vari-ously as an economic investment, political force, mechanism of press growth, and means for Franklin to attain his ideological ambitions.

The abundance of Franklin scholarship and primary-source materials pre-sents the omnipresent temptation to say everything about Franklin, or at least everything about his printing career. I make no attempt at comprehen-siveness here, for such an effort would be redundant in light of the numerous lengthy treatments of the subject. Consequently, the interesting stories of Franklin's apprenticeship in Boston, his service as a journeyman in London and Philadelphia, the British influences on his writing, and his career as printer of the *Pennsylvania Gazette* are treated in a cursory manner, as are his numerous political posts.

This book is not a history of Franklin's journalism career, but rather an analysis of his methods—and particularly, his motivations—for establishing business and personal relations with other printers of the era. They range from the Job-like James Parker to the cunning Francis Childs, the loyal Timothy family to the firebrand Benjamin Franklin Bache, and the steadfast David Hall to the disturbed Benjamin Mecom. With these and many other printers, Franklin fashioned an informal network of affiliated partners, relatives, and allies that not only proved essential to the development of the early American press, but served to disseminate Franklin's views of hard work, character, and virtue to a mass audience.

In the interests of historical accuracy, I have quoted correspondence and printed matter precisely, resisting the convention of modernizing spelling or grammar. Most colonial writers, like Franklin, capitalized their nouns. The reason was that capital letters gave emphasis to the word and variation to the arrangement of words on the page. "I have minutely followed my old Rule of capitalizing all Substantives," Samuel Davies informed Franklin network printer John Holt in 1761, upon submitting a religious sermon for publication.[2] The practice of capitalizing nouns faded late in the century, however. "This Method has, by the Fancy of Printers, of late Years been laid aside, from an Idea, that suppressing the Capitals shows the Character to greater Advantage," Franklin wrote to editor and lexicographer Noah Webster in 1789. Franklin equated such "pretended Improvement" in the language to "paring all Men's Noses," which "might smooth and level their Faces, but would render their Physiognomies less distinguishable."[3]

In keeping with the policy of strict grammatical accuracy, I use emphasis in quotations only when placed there by the original authors, in published and unpublished writings. The sole exception to my policy is the substitution of periods for dashes, which some eighteenth-century writers used in private correspondence to indicate the end of a sentence.

The research for this project has involved extensive use of more than twenty historical archives and university libraries. These archives and libraries are repositories of thousands of personal letters, business records, and eighteenth-century newspapers that provided vital evidence for the contentions and conclusions I advance herein.

"If you wou'd not be forgotten As soon as you are dead and rotten, Either write things worth reading, Or do things worth the writing," "Poor Richard" advised his readers in 1738.[4] During his lifetime, Franklin accomplished both; I am content merely to strive for the former. Numerous people have aided my effort to write something "worth reading." I am indebted to the library staffs of the various archives listed in the "Abbreviations" section. Plaudits are also due to the library staffs at the University of Iowa and Marymount University. I am grateful for funding from the University of Iowa and from the John Carter Brown Library. Portions of this book appeared in earlier versions. I thank editors of the following publications for permission to use them here: *American Journalism, Connecticut History, Fides et Historia, Michigan Academician, New Jersey History, Pennsylvania History,* and *The Pennsylvania Magazine of History and Biography.*

I particularly appreciate the contributions of numerous individuals. Marita Schmidt provided German translations. Scholars Jeffery A. Smith, Barry Markovsky, and the late Sydney V. James furnished beneficial guidance. Most of all, I am grateful for the extremely valuable counsel and assistance of my wife and best friend, Clare Frasca, to whom this work is dedicated. Lastly, heinous gaffes or glaring omissions in this book will be cheerfully blamed on my computer.

$\mathcal{B}$enjamin Franklin's Printing Network

Introduction

The Challenge of Franklin's Printing Network

Three forces have influenced understandings of eighteenth-century press freedom: printers' impartiality and concomitant hesitation to offend readers, their reliance on subsidy in the form of printing contracts, and the public's desire for an activist press to represent the populace in the political process.[1]

Many scholars have considered legal limitations and political ramifications of an increasingly aggressive press, but few have considered labor economics and relations, the judicious management of affairs, and the financial ability to set up and maintain a printing shop in early America. The sources of press freedom and income have been studied extensively, but there has been scant examination of economic and organizational factors, such as partnerships and the apprenticeship system. These elements made it possible for the press not only to survive but to grow, while serving, in the words of attorney Andrew Hamilton during the Zenger trial, "publicly to remonstrate the abuses of power in the strongest terms, to put their neighbors upon their guard against the craft or open violence of men in authority."[2]

Though the early American press may have been observed remonstrating against authority by its outside world of the public, its inner world of economics, alliances, and norms of conduct were mostly hidden. Although seldom mentioned, even in private correspondence, these business, economic, and organizational factors shaped the press's development. The early American press was characterized by interconnections, within which was a pattern of activity, rather than an agglomeration of isolated, idiosyncratic behavior. For many printers, economic survival depended on connections with other printers. These linkages were the building blocks of informal and loosely structured—yet powerful—trade affiliations, or printing "networks." Most printing networks in early America were family-based, with assistance and training passed from one generation and one relative to another.

However, the largest and most influential of the early American printing networks was primarily non-familial, established by Benjamin Franklin. It represented one of Franklin's major contributions to American journalism, because through it he financed and assisted some of the most important printers of the era and helped lay the foundation for an increasingly free press. His network also served as a mechanism of press growth and—most importantly to Franklin—a means by which he could disseminate his conceptions of virtue and morality to a mass audience.

Of all those who plied the early American printing trade, Franklin was the most renowned and successful. Born when only one newspaper was printed in North America, and that under the ponderous hand of colonial authority, he lived long enough to see and contribute to the spread of a vigorous and instructive press throughout America's eastern seaboard. Franklin's life has been recounted in myriad biographies, and most facets of his literary and journalistic career have been dutifully chronicled. He has been lavished with hagiographic encomiums as the "Franklin myth" he helped create pervaded historiography, causing recent biographers to identify Franklin as "The First American" and "the founding father who winks at us."[3]

However, others have sought to find ignoble motives in his conduct and to dismiss his writings and printing career as self-serving and pecuniary. Surveying some of the articles and books about Franklin's writings, one reviewer noted, "So complex has this 'simple' man become in recent years that it is now difficult to say for certain what he had in mind in his supposedly straightforward autobiography and in his purportedly light bagatelles."[4]

Franklin's dual organizational and ideological influences on the early American press have been cursorily considered since the early twentieth century, but explorations of it as a factual entity have been rare. Little attention has been paid to its genesis and structure, or Franklin's aspirations for it.[5]

Much may be learned about the operations, relationships, freedoms, and constraints of the early American press by examining the Franklin network. However, studying it presents an immediate conceptual problem: Did it actually exist? No writings or business records of the day explicitly acknowledge its existence. The clearest reference is a 1785 letter to printer Francis Childs, in which Franklin listed ten "young printers of good character" whom he had set up in business.[6] Indeed, the passage of time has created considerable difficulties for studying the Franklin network. Correspondence and other forms of contact occurred among network members, but relatively little evidence of it has survived from the eighteenth century to the present.

Because their existence must be constructed from inference, early American printing networks are relatively unmined veins of press history. Some evidence exists suggesting one network printer's relationship to another, but no primary source conclusively links any number of them, and no study of eighteenth-century press practices explores printing networks in a systematic and detailed manner.

Thus, the network concept is imposed here upon these relationships as an organizing metaphor to orchestrate the qualitative data about the indeterminate group of printers aligned with Franklin. Just as it contributes little to study one person in an effort to understand a society, examining a single printer offers limited insight into the early American press. It is more instructive to study groups, because linkages among individuals evident in the human social environment can reveal much about relations, processes, and roles. Franklin acknowledged this in his *Autobiography*, repeatedly observing how his reputation and business opportunities improved as he became acquainted with "many principal People of the Province" and made "some very ingenious Acquaintance whose Conversation was of great Advantage to me."[7]

It is easy to define the general concept of a printing network—an informal yet influential interconnection of printers who were business partners, trade associates, and/or family members. However, any analysis of printing networks must begin by considering the concept of a network as a field of social interaction, a "community" linked not by geographic boundaries but by associational ones.

To explore networks, one must initially make four assumptions about social interaction. First, and most fundamental, is that people inevitably associate in groups. This interdependence has been repeatedly expounded in the literary world. Several generations before Franklin's birth, poet John Donne wrote, "No man is an Iland, intire of it selfe." One of the chief influences on Franklin's ideology of public service, Cotton Mather, underscored this theme while exhorting colonists to the service of others. He wrote in 1701, "a man cannot live without the Help of other men. But how can a man Reasonably look for the Help of other men, if he be not in some Calling Helpful to other men?"[8]

Second, social networks are not ochlocratic but are structured in the sense that people interact with each other via certain points of reference, such as the common pursuit of a particular trade or goal.[9]

Third, these interactions take place through the forms of communication available at the time. For printers in the Franklin network, this included face-to-face conversations, correspondence, and communication through third parties.

The fourth assumption is that relationships among people form observable yet ambiguous networks. Since individuals interact with other individuals, and these interact with still others—some of whom have relationships with the first and some not—then these interconnections form networks, which rely on available channels of communication for their cohesion.

Social networks were common in early America, taking the form of networks within communities, colonies, and the nation. Examining them is like archaeology in that it involves the systematic recovery of an organizational and cultural reality; but it is meaning, rather than material evidence, which is reconstructed, using the data of human communication. This reconstructive process most commonly depends upon verbal reports from and cognizable behavior of living people. In studying social interaction, it is essential "to render observable, explicit and quantitative that which was previously only inferred, implicitly assumed or qualitatively described," a sociologist wrote. An early behaviorist argued that "real advance" in studying social interaction "is contingent upon the accumulation of a body of scientific knowledge based upon controlled experimentation."[10]

Network theory most commonly relies on observable behavior, verbal reports, and recent data, none of which are available to historians who study early America. This fact deters scrutiny of organizational networks from that era. Thus, examining Franklin's printing network presents enormous methodological problems, because the behavior of its actors cannot be viewed, the actors cannot respond to questions, and their verbal exchanges with each other are lost. All that remains is the small percentage of surviving published reminiscences, business records, and private correspondence.

While it is impossible to recover printers' conversations with each other and their thoughts when they read each other's publications, and while most business records and correspondence were not preserved, it is possible to form inferences about printing networks through the use of historical data. Such inferences can expand modern understanding of the forces that forged the content and workings of the press in a vital period of history.

Printing networks in general, and Franklin's in particular, are important to study on three fronts—economic, prudential, and legal. If a printer lacks start-up costs and sufficient ongoing financial support, that printer will likely fail economically. The eighteenth-century printer required capital to purchase printing materials, rent a shop, and hire employees. This financial backing sometimes came from an established printer who used his influence and capital in exchange for a percentage of the profits. Franklin was proficient at orchestrating these relationships with his network members so that all parties usually benefited. He was instrumental in the growth of the eighteenth-century press through his financial investments, which he used to set up some of the key early American printers, including David Hall, Peter Timothy, and James Parker. Once they were in business, Franklin aided their operations by serving as a reliable supplier of printing materials who had an economic interest in their success.

Affiliation with other printers was also important for those who sought to market certain products or supplies. For instance, Franklin used his network to distribute his *Poor Richard's Almanack* through many colonial printers.[11]

The prudential elements of the network were also beneficial to all parties, as Franklin occasionally provided instructions to network printers that shaped their editorial content and helped them cope with social and political problems. Franklin and most of his network members espoused republican ideology, with its inherent view that capable, civic-minded leaders and a vigilant press were the best safeguards of individual rights and social order. As Franklin noted, printing "diffuses so general a light, augmenting with the growing day, and of so penetrating a nature" on public affairs "that arbitrary governments are likely to become more mild and reasonable, and to expire by degrees, giving place to more equitable forms."[12] These views were central to the emergence and eventual Constitutional guarantee of press freedom. That so many of Franklin's associates adhered to republicanism was not coincidental—Franklin carefully selected them, and subsequently aided or sanctioned them, based in part on their political, economic, social, and moral beliefs and actions.

The third consideration meriting study pertains to press freedom, which can mean more than simply the workings of courts or government. In fact, how closely one examines these "official" sources as opposed to other sources will play a role in how much freedom one believes existed in the eighteenth century. Those who place greater emphasis on government and court activities may be more inclined to contend that little press freedom existed, while others who focus less on law and more on practice have claimed press freedom may not have been evident in official records, but was a national reality.[13] To take the argument a step farther, some have argued that laws are not inherently powerful and influential. Extra-legal groups, like trade associations and networks, are often more effective at molding behavior than civil laws.

Indeed, these institutions sometimes subvert the law. Groups and often networks administer their own rules and apply their own sanctions to those who come under their jurisdiction.[14]

Networks were integral to the success of the early American press, both as a means of providing economic assistance to printing operations and as a mechanism by which the press grew, not only in geographic and numerical scope but also in social importance. The Franklin network functioned as a vital mechanism of press growth, a source of wealth, and a means by which Franklin disseminated his ideology of virtue to a mass audience, indelibly stamping his mark on the American consciousness.

The first four chapters of this study identify the formation of Franklin's moral thinking and its manifestation in his journalism. The middle four delineate successes and failures of some major partnerships at expanding Franklin's network and promoting virtue among diverse audiences. The final four chapters examine the network's disintegration and revival amid turbulent business alliances, the American Revolution, the new nation, and an increasingly unrestrained press. Cumulatively, this book traces and evaluates the origins, progression, and impact of the Franklin printing network and its mission of teaching virtue to Americans—the higher purpose of Franklin's journalism career and the principal motivation for his printing partnerships. Franklin was determined to demonstrate what he described, at age twenty-three, as his "Zeal for the Publick Good."[15]

1

The Art of Virtue and the Virtue of the Art

Upon his return to Philadelphia in 1785 after nine years of diplomatic service in France, Benjamin Franklin learned that a new state had been named for him. The fledgling state's Congressional delegate, William Cocke, informed Franklin that "as a testimony of the high esteem they have for the many important and faithful services you have rendered to your country," the region's denizens "have called the name of their State after you." Franklin responded, "It is a very great Honour indeed, that its Inhabitants have done me, and I should be happy if it were in my Power to show how sensible I am of it, by something more essential than my Wishes for their Prosperity."[1]

During his lifetime and for every generation since, Franklin's name has been appropriated by schools, commercial establishments, cultural societies, and philanthropic organizations to honor him and associate themselves with his legend. This practice has been most often employed in naming municipalities and children. Nearly every state has at least one town or county named for Franklin, owing in large measure to his being perceived as "the perfect civic leader" by settlers of interior lands in the late eighteenth century and throughout the nineteenth century.[2] During the same period, thousands of children have been named for him, and of those who were not, some of the most public-spirited have been bestowed with Franklinesque nicknames, such as *Kentucky Gazette* printer John Bradford, whose fellow Lexingtonians dubbed "The Benjamin Franklin of the West." One Philadelphia newspaper noted in 1780, "The name of Franklin is sufficiently celebrated that one may glory in bearing it," adding that the French were contending with the

English for the right to claim "having given birth to the ancestors of a man who has rendered that name so famous."[3]

In the Revolution and the new republic it spawned, Franklin symbolized the distinctly American character. Bourgeoisie and craftsmen alike celebrated him, both groups regarding him as one of their own. "Dr. Franklin is a very popular character in every part of America," Benjamin Rush observed in 1774, predicting he would be "handed down to posterity among the first and greatest characters of the world." Some of these encomiums came to Franklin's attention. "I never see any Boston newspapers," he told his sister Jane. "You mention there being often something in them to do me honour. I am obliged to them." Although Franklin had become one of the wealthiest men in the new nation, more than half a century removed from his plebeian origins, artisans and mechanics quaffed toasts to Franklin's health and, beginning in 1790, his memory, every Independence Day.[4]

Franklin was even more lionized after his death. Despite some posthumous character assaults launched by William Cobbett, John Adams, and others, Franklin's self-styled reputation not only survived, but exceeded his expectations.[5]

Franklin was posthumously showered with lavish praise in the American press as a literary giant, ingenious inventor, crafty sage, dedicated public servant, and sterling example of the fruits that industry, virtue, and hard work might bear. A Vermont newspaper proclaimed in 1792 that Franklin "will shine with distinguished lustre in the page of history," while a book six years later described him as "the Ornament of Genius, the Patron of Science, and the Boast of Man."[6] Such publications not only enhanced Franklin's reputation, both in America and abroad, but more importantly, indicated that the process of constructing Franklin's enduring legend was well under way.

More than two centuries after his death, the Franklin legend thrives. A 2002 Act of Congress created the Benjamin Franklin Tercentenary Commission to commemorate the 300th anniversary of his birth in 2006, with President George W. Bush serving as honorary chairman. A United States Senate bill commemorating the bicentennial of Franklin's death described him as "the epitome of all that America was to become" and noted, "for as George Washington is remembered as the Father of our great Nation, Ben Franklin might well be the grandfather." This was not the first time Franklin and Washington had been elevated to a special place of honor. As Thomas Jefferson asserted, "the world had drawn so broad a line between [Washington] & Dr. Franklin, on the one side, and the residue of mankind, on the other."[7]

Many qualities would be ascribed to Franklin—some more deservedly than others, John Adams noted. Adams feared his vital contributions to the American Revolution would be obscured by Franklin's larger-than-life image. Writing two weeks before Franklin's death that "The history of our Revolution will be one continued Lye from one end to the other," Adams decried that history books would certify *that Dr. Franklins electrical rod, smote the Earth and out sprung General Washington. That Franklin electrified him with his rod—and thence forward these two conducted all the Policy, Negotiations, Legislatures and War.*" During their diplomatic service in France, Adams was appalled by Franklin's growing fame and willingness to be credited with achievements that were, in part or whole, the work of others. "He has a Passion for Reputation and Fame, as strong as you can imagine, and his Time and Thoughts are chiefly employed to obtain it, and to set Tongues and Pens male and female, to celebrating him," a resentful Adams wrote of Franklin. "Painters, Statuaries, Sculptors, China Potters, and all are set to work for this End."[8]

The two men were allies and leading lights in the Independence movement, helping to shape public opinion during the Revolution with their political screeds in newspapers and pamphlets. In 1756 the twenty-year-old Adams had praised Franklin as "a prodigious Genius cultivated with prodigious industry." However, their relationship soured when they were sent to France on diplomatic service for their new country. "Franklin is a Wit and a Humorist, I know," Adams wrote to Thomas McKean. "He may be a Philosopher, for what I know, but he is not a sufficient Statesman, he knows too little of American Affairs or the Politicks of Europe, and takes too little Pains to inform himself of Either."[9] Franklin was aware of such criticism, but tried not to let it bother him. "I have long been accustomed to receive more blame, as well as more praise, than I have deserved," he wrote. "It is the lot of every public man, and I leave one account to balance the other."[10]

That his glowing reputation has endured and become part of American folklore, such attacks notwithstanding, has much to do with the fact that Franklin, better than any other early American figure, carefully crafted a public image of himself during his own lifetime. His voluminous correspondence and his *Autobiography* were parts of a brilliantly successful effort to shape opinion about his character and achievements, as well as to encourage others to follow his example.[11]

Franklin enjoyed the project, telling a French correspondent in 1788 that he was "writing my own History, which calling past Transactions to Remembrance makes it seem a little like living one's Life over again." He was careful about what to include, though, omitting stories that did not promote virtue and including those that did. He assured one friend his memoirs "will contain a Number of Precepts . . . all exemplified by the Effects of their Practice in my own Affairs." When Franklin included tales of his own wrongs, they were intended to aid readers in "avoiding the errors which were prejudicial to me."[12]

Franklin wrote the *Autobiography* in four parts, initially in the form of a letter to his son William, from whom he later became estranged. In it, Franklin cast himself as a multifaceted character, alternating among the roles of civic philanthropist, moral philosopher, and common tradesman on a pilgrimage through life. The latter role seems to have best suited his inspirational purposes, and it is the one upon which he chiefly relied to advance the narrative. Borrowing from the classical epic writings like *The Iliad* and *Beowulf,* Franklin found it conveniently self-effacing to depict himself as a well-meaning young provincial swept up on a whirlwind voyage, in search of fulfillment and virtue. Brother James Franklin and Governor William Keith made early appearances as villains, printer Samuel Keimer served as a vainglorious bumbler, businessmen William Coleman and Robert Grace surfaced as benefactors, and assorted "low women" took turns playing the siren, with Deborah Read as the true love. The hero in this epic, armed with his code of virtuous living, overcame myriad obstacles in the quest for prominence, wealth, and respect while beckoning others to follow his path. He stated this clearly at the beginning of his *Autobiography.* "Having emerg'd from the Poverty & Obscurity in which I was born & bred, to a State of Affluence & some Degree of Reputation in the World, and having gone so far thro' Life with a considerable Share of Felicity, the conducing Means I made use of, which, with the Blessing of God, so well succeeded, my Posterity may like to know, as they may find some of them suitable to their own Situations, & therefore fit to be imitated," he wrote.[13]

Franklin's *Autobiography* led one recent historian to laud "the nice mix of cleverness and morality" that helped "aspiring tradesmen become more diligent, and thus more able to be useful and virtuous citizens." Another hailed his efforts to "foster altruistic impulses and to channel selfish ones into useful activities."[14] More skeptical historians have read into it "a careful contrivance of masks and *personae* arranged to make himself seem the benevolent friend of humanity" and claimed that it "deliberately fabricates an identity, purporting to be that of Franklin as a boy and man." The confusion over Franklin's intent may have been due to his dexterity at "blending fact and fancy so that in the end neither reader nor author could be sure of truth," one biographer noted.[15]

Whatever the degree of truth in the memoirs, Franklin's stated intention was that the work be "entertaining, interesting, and useful" in educating readers about his virtue-driven "modes of conduct."[16]

Writing the *Autobiography* in stages between 1771 and his death in 1790, Franklin sought to influence public opinion about himself, both among his contemporaries and for posterity. He crafted it as a literary work in which he as the central character is the protagonist, rather than a narrator strictly recounting factual historical occurrences. In this aim he was enormously successful, as his modern reputation as a superior moralist and belletrist augments his fame as a statesman, inventor, scientist, patriot, and philanthropist. The most instructive portion of the work is the brief Part II, which he wrote in France in 1784, at the urging of friends Abel James and Benjamin Vaughan. The former had besought him "to promote a greater Spirit of Industry & early Attention to Business, Frugality and Temperance with the American Youth," while the latter claimed that Franklin's memoirs would serve as a literary map that others could use to achieve greatness. Even those who lacked the fundamental wisdom necessary to achieve eminence may benefit, Vaughan suggested, for Franklin's moral instruction would offer the prospect of "improving the features of private character, and consequently for aiding all happiness, both public and private."[17]

In Part II, Franklin described his efforts to bring order to the moral chaos that permeated his early life. He attributed his recalcitrance to the effects of "Natural Inclination, Custom, or Company," and sought to cultivate a more restrained and benevolent character. His detailed plan, which he called a "bold and arduous Project of arriving at moral Perfection," took the form of a calendar, wherein he listed thirteen virtues—including Industry, Frugality, Chastity, and Moderation—and tallied his success in maintaining them each day. He defined these narrowly, believing they would be easier to conquer by using "rather more Names with fewer Ideas annex'd to each." In addition to general maintenance of the virtues, he "determined to give a Week's strict Attention to each of the Virtues successively. Thus in the first Week my great Guard was to avoid even the least Offence against Temperance, leaving the other Virtues to their ordinary Chance." With each succeeding week he expanded his focus to a new virtue, so that he could complete the cycle in thirteen weeks, four times per year.[18]

This plan represented his effort to devise a uniform and structured method of coping with the unpredictability of life and the irrationality of human nature, which had vexed him since childhood. Franklin described this plan for governing his "future Conduct in Life" metaphorically, "like him who having a Garden to weed, does not attempt to eradicate all the bad herbs at once, which would exceed his Reach and his Strength, but works on one of the

Beds at a time, & having accomplish'd the first proceeds to a second." By adhering to this design, Franklin hoped to have "the encouraging Pleasure of seeing on my Pages the Progress I made in Virtue, by clearing successively my Lines of their Spots, till in the End by a Number of Courses, I should be happy in viewing a clean Book after a thirteen Weeks daily Examination."[19]

Franklin's intent was to live sinlessly, "without committing any Fault at any time." Despite his desire for moral perfection, he repeatedly fell prey to passion and committed "errata." His efforts to govern his own conduct fell far short of perfection, forcing him to conclude that sincerely intending to do good is easier than consistently doing it. He ultimately rationalized his moral flaws, jocularly noting "that a perfect Character might be attended with the Inconvenience of being envied and hated; and that a benevolent Man should allow a few faults in himself, to keep his Friends in Countenance."[20]

Having segmented virtue into its component parts and achieved some mastery of each through diligence and repetition, Franklin encouraged others to do the same. He believed most people could be trained to behave virtuously through incremental implementation of his plan. "Men don't become very good or very bad in an Instant, both vicious and virtuous Habits being acquired by Length of Time and repeated Acts," he wrote. Foreshadowing behaviorism, Franklin was more concerned with modifying external conduct, implicitly rejecting the Aristotelian notion of virtuous sentiments as a prerequisite for virtuous actions.[21]

Franklin thus conceived of virtue as action rather than intention, of doing good rather than contemplating goodness. He was more concerned with demonstrable benefaction, believing that "the most acceptable Service of God was the doing Good to Man; that our Souls are immortal; and that all Crime will be punished & Virtue rewarded either here or hereafter." He once advised a minister that true religion consists of "real Good Works, Works of Kindness, Charity, Mercy, and Publick Spirit; not Holiday-keeping, Sermon-Reading or Hearing, performing Church Ceremonies, or making long Prayers, fill'd with Flatteries and Compliments." Buttressing his argument with Biblical examples, he added that God "prefer'd the Doers of the Word to the meer Hearers." Frustrated with his inability to consistently act in strict accordance with his intentions, and disappointed by some people's willingness to make promises they did not intend to keep, he concluded that evidence, not intent, was the most accurate gauge of human virtue.[22]

Like the scientist he was to become, Franklin began placing his faith in the observable and factual at an early age. He never adequately resolved the relationship between good deeds and the spiritual beneficence that impels them.

Instead, he hoped inner change would result from outer change, in contrast to most religious and ethical teachings. In one such teaching, Jesus cautioned, "if your uprightness does not surpass that of the scribes and Pharisees, you will never get into the kingdom of Heaven." To clarify that "uprightness" referred to intent, not merely action, Jesus added that not only is the act of adultery wrong, but "if a man looks at a woman lustfully, he has already committed adultery with her in his heart."[23]

For others to effect outer change through his plan, Franklin recognized they would need a motive to behave virtuously. They would be loathe to do it, he thought, without the lure of self-interest, and he ruefully noted "how great a Proportion of Mankind consists of weak and ignorant Men and Women, and of inexperienc'd and inconsiderate Youth of both Sexes." He envisioned material gain as this motive, preaching in *Poor Richard's Almanack*, "Industry, Perseverance, and Frugality, make Fortune Yield."[24] The glorification of acquiring wealth and property was a theme present in many of his writings throughout his lifetime—for Franklin, merit yielded possessions and riches.

Franklin best articulated this view in his famous "The Way to Wealth" essay in 1758, which consisted of about one hundred aphorisms and maxims that had previously appeared in his almanac, woven into a speech by his character "Father Abraham." Franklin's message was that hard work, thrift, and careful attention to business were the means to a successful and comfortable life, as well as the keys to salvation. However, Father Abraham's teachings, like those of some Christian ministers, failed to inspire. "The People heard it and approved the Doctrine, and immediately practised the contrary, just as if it had been a common sermon," Father Abraham lamented.[25]

Nonetheless, Franklin remained firmly committed to his method of encouraging virtuous conduct among the early American populace by emphasizing that, aside from whatever inherent spiritual benefits it yielded, it also paid earthly dividends. In 1729, under the name "Busy-Body," the idealistic twenty-three-year-old Franklin emphasized the public approbation one might merit, remarking that "*Virtue alone is sufficient to make a Man Great, Glorious and Happy*," for "we should become really Great by being Good." He mildly reproved those who sought other attainments, querying, "what is Wit, or Wealth, or Form, or Learning when compar'd with Virtue? 'Tis true, we love the handsome, we applaud the Learned, and we fear the Rich and Powerful; but we even Worship and adore the Virtuous."[26]

Although the prospect of social esteem might induce some to virtue, Franklin later became convinced that the most persuasive method of encouraging goodness was a direct appeal to material wealth. Noting there is "Nothing so likely to make a Man's Fortune as Virtue," Franklin wrote in his memoirs that it was in everyone's "Interest to be Virtuous, who wish'd to be happy in this World," and "no Qualities were so likely to make a poor Man's Fortune as those of Probity & Integrity."[27]

He saw nothing wrong with emphasizing wealth, suggesting that the desire for luxuries leads to hard work. "Is not the Hope of one day being able to purchase and enjoy Luxuries a great Spur to Labor and Industry?" he inquired rhetorically in 1784. "May not Luxury, therefore, produce more than it consumes, if without such a Spur People would be, as they are naturally enough inclined to be, lazy and indolent?" This philosophy contrasted with the views of others, particularly Bostonians, who perceived luxury as the greatest danger to virtue in the post-Revolution new nation.[28]

Franklin's efforts to demonstrate the earthly rewards of virtue represented a partial repudiation of the Judeo-Christian belief in celestial happiness through worldly holiness. He had been deeply affected by evidence of this belief. In the 1770s, he vividly recalled that fifty years earlier he had become acquainted with "a Maiden Lady of 70." A Roman Catholic, she lived a spartan existence by choice, giving most of her money to charity and eating only boiled gruel in the garret of Franklin's boarding house. "She look'd pale, but was never sick, and I give it as another Instance on how small an Income Life & Health may be supported."[29] Despite his approval of this example, Franklin saw no conflict in trumpeting material success more prominently than the attainment of Heaven, perceiving the former to be more tangible and persuasive in encouraging people to meet the needs of the human community.

To Franklin, the acquisition of wealth became central to virtuous conduct, for he doubted people could be charitable without financial security. As "Poor Richard," he wrote, "it is hard for an empty Sack to stand upright." Sometimes, Franklin was pessimistic about people's wisdom in handling financial security. He expressed sadness at their "Pursuit of Wealth to no End," instead of using some of it for the "Publick Good." He grew disenchanted with the multitudes that became slaves to their economic self-interest. "The Love of Money is not a Thing of certain Measure, so as that it may be easily filled and satisfied," he wrote to one correspondent.[30]

As a tradesman concerned about his own financial security, Franklin felt obliged to pay close attention to his public image, admitting that he practiced his virtues as much to be seen doing so as to please himself or God. By wearing plain clothes and being "seen at no Places of idle Diversion," Franklin became "esteem'd an industrious thriving young Man." In his *Autobiography*, he confessed further that he struggled with his own humility, but did not let others know. "I cannot boast of much Success in acquiring the Reality of this Virtue; but I had a good deal with regard to the Appearance of it," he wrote.[31]

Franklin had intended to elaborate on his concepts of virtue and success in a book, "The Art of Virtue," which he first planned in 1732 and nursed for more than half a century. He never found time to write it, though, due to "the necessary close Attention to private Business in the earlier part of Life, and public Business since." His ambition was to accompany the list with "a little Comment on each Virtue" that would reveal both "the Advantages of possessing it, & the Mischiefs attending its opposite Vice."[32]

Franklin's motivation for conceiving the book and going so far as to outline it in his *Autobiography* was characteristic of the man: part sincere altruism and part ostentatious didacticism. According to Franklin, the proposed book "would have shown the *Means & Manner* of obtaining Virtue; which would have distinguish'd it from the mere Exhortation to be good, that does not instruct & indicate the Means." As he wrote to the Scottish philosopher Lord Henry Kames, "Many People lead bad Lives that would gladly lead good ones, but know not *how* to make the Change. They have frequently *resolv'd* and *endeavour'd* it; but in vain, because their Endeavours have not been properly conducted." Franklin revealed his proposed book to Kames, assuring his friend it would not merely admonish people to be virtuous, but would demonstrate "*how* they shall *become* so."[33]

Franklin's advocacy of his plan for promoting virtuous conduct suggests he felt confident in his understanding of what virtue was and in his ability to judge it. Franklin regarded it as a compilation of ethical and moral actions, propounding variously that it was "to act always honestly," or that it consisted of "Truth, Sincerity & Integrity in Dealings between Man & Man." Others also ascribed traits to virtue. One pseudonymous essayist viewed it as "love of the republic, its nature, principles, and laws." Physician and Declaration of Independence signer Benjamin Rush asserted it includes "bravery, humanity, and magnanimity." John Adams wrote that reaching the pinnacle of virtue required possessing "The Wisdom of Solomon, the Meekness of Moses, and the Patience of Job, all united in one Character." Franklin's one-time friend (and later enemy) William Smith taught rhetoric students at the College of Philadelphia that the virtuous speaker is "honest, prudent, benevolent, impartial, disinterested, and thoroughly possessed of his Subject from a real Conviction of its being just, honourable and of public Utility."[34]

There is irony in Franklin's resolute belief in his suitability to provide moral instruction, considering his own lapses. His efforts to maintain the virtue of "chastity" had been confounded by "that hard-to-be-govern'd Passion of Youth" that "had hurried me frequently into Intrigues with low Women that fell in my Way, which were attended with some Expence & great Inconvenience, besides a continual Risque to my Health." He also "attempted Familiarities" with a friend's mistress and fathered at least one child out of wedlock.[35] Franklin's determination to practice the virtue of "justice" was called into question during a heated 1764 political contest, when the matter of the identity of his son William's mother arose. Pamphleteer Hugh Williamson identified her as Barbara, a maidservant in Franklin's household, and accused Franklin of having "cruelly suffered her TO STARVE" and later burying her "Without a *Tomb*, or even A *Monumental Inscription*," never having allowed her the benefits of marriage or motherhood. The accuracy of this partisan attack is at least partially confirmed by the son of one of Franklin's friends, who wrote in 1763 about William, "tis generally Known here his Birth is illegitimate and his Mother not in good Circumstances . . . I understand some small provision is made by him for her, but her being none of the most agreeable of Women prevents particular Notice being shown, or the Father and Son acknowledging any Connection with her."[36]

Franklin's reference to Pennsylvania Germans as "Palatine Boors" who were being allowed "to swarm into our Settlements and by herding together establish their Language and Manners, to the Exclusion of ours" was not characteristic of "moderation," and despite telling Kames and Vaughn of his intentions to write "The Art of Virtue," Franklin failed, violating his own credo of "resolution," which he defined, "Perform without fail what you resolve." As for "frugality," the virtue represented by the admonition "Make no Expence but to do good to others or yourself: i.e. Waste nothing," the already wealthy Franklin confessed to his mother in 1750, "I intend to spend what little I have, my self; if it please God that I live long enough." Franklin's avaricious inclinations prompted him to break off a "serious Courtship" with a young woman whom he conceded was "very deserving" when her parents declined to mortgage their house to pay off Franklin's debts.[37] Early in life Franklin even repudiated any distinction between virtue and vice, claiming that it is not the presence of morality, but rather a desire to be free of physical or emotional pain (which he called "Uneasiness"), that motivates human action.[38]

Despite these character traits, Franklin envisioned himself qualified to be a "Censor Morum," or moral critic, under the guise of his pseudonym "The Busy-Body." Influenced by such British satirical journals as *The Spectator*,

Franklin whimsically commented on social mores for Andrew Bradford's *American Weekly Mercury* readers "out of Zeal for the Publick Good." Franklin even betrayed a hint of smugness, giving further evidence of his difficulties with the virtue of humility, noting, "as most People delight in Censure when they themselves are not the Objects of it, if any are offended at my publickly exposing their private Vices, I promise they shall have the Satisfaction, in a very little Time, of seeing their good Friends and Neighbours in the same Circumstances."[39]

Franklin believed moral superiority would result from an accretion of rational deliberation, sincere thrift, industrious labor, and disciplined behavior. These qualities were prized in republican thought, wherein character, spirit, and public virtue were essential to effective government and social harmony.[40] However, he clearly understood from his own experiences that these were acquired, rather than innate, skills. To embrace virtue, people must learn "the Principles of the Art, be shewn all the Methods of Working, and how to acquire the *Habits* of using properly all the Instruments; and thus regularly and gradually" arrive "by Practice at some Perfection in the Art," Franklin asserted.[41]

Thus, Franklin viewed it as one of his life's duties to teach people the "art" of virtuous conduct and show them how to practice it daily. To accomplish this task, he used the existing organs of mass communication. In addition to his *Autobiography* and pamphlets, Franklin employed his annual *Poor Richard's Almanack* and newspapers—both his own, the weekly *Pennsylvania Gazette,* and those published by others—to convey his ideology of virtue to the masses.

In doing so, Franklin was employing one "art" to convey another. Printing had long been esteemed as an art, requiring special skills and knowledge beyond the grasp of the ordinary person. Early American writers celebrated printing as "the art which gives universality to and perpetuates every other art and improvement," and "the ingenious ART" which is "held in the highest Veneration and Esteem by the most knowing and civiliz'd Nations of the Universe." Another essayist gushed, "The Art of Printing is one of the greatest benefits which human ingenuity has introduced into the world."[42]

Although he abandoned his cherished "The Art of Virtue," Franklin trumpeted virtue through "the art." In his continuing mission to enlighten the masses, he submitted his trove of moral maxims to the public through his journalism. He filled his almanac with what he called "proverbial Sentences, chiefly such as inculcated Industry and Frugality, as the Means of procuring

Wealth and thereby securing Virtue." In Franklin's estimation, wealth was useful because poverty often creates a barrier to moral rectitude. One way to minimize pecuniary wants was to save part of one's earnings. As Franklin's "Poor Richard" noted, "Industry's bounteous hand may Plenty bring, But wanting frugal Care, 'twill soon take wing."[43]

Franklin viewed his almanac "as a proper Vehicle for conveying Instruction among the common People, who bought scarce any other Books." His sprightly wit served him well, as his amusing and laconic writing style made moral teachings more accessible and appealing to the populace. This had been his design all along. As "The Busy-Body," he admitted his desire "to inculcate the noble Principles of Virtue, and depreciate Vice of every kind." However, he recognized that the more conventional means of moral education—religious sermons and nondenominational but nonetheless lofty exegeses—lacked both levity and brevity. He acknowledged, "as I know the Mob hate Instruction, and the Generality would never read beyond the first Line of my Lectures, if they were usually fill'd with nothing but wholesome Precepts and Advice; I must therefore sometimes humour them in their own Way." One of these methods was satire. "There are a Set of Great Names in the Province, who are the common Objects of Popular Dislike," Franklin's "Busy-Body" wrote. "If I can now and then overcome my Reluctance, and prevail with my self to Satyrize a little, one of these Gentlemen," this "will induce many to read me through."[44]

Franklin utilized the *Pennsylvania Gazette* in the same educational manner, recalling, "I consider'd my Newspaper also as another Means of communicating Instruction, & in that View frequently reprinted in it Extracts from the Spectator and other moral Writers, and sometimes publish'd little Pieces of my own," which he had first auditioned for the Junto, a group of intelligent young Philadelphia men dedicated to self-improvement. Throughout his life, Franklin viewed these published moral lessons as a service to humanity, and therefore to God. Citing the Book of Matthew chapter 25, Franklin commented in a 1738 letter to his parents that he wished to serve God through his virtuous deeds. "Scripture assures me, that at the last Day, we shall not be examin'd what we *thought*, but what we *did*; and our Recommendation will not be that we said *Lord, Lord*, but that we did GOOD to our Fellow Creatures." Nine years later, he advised readers of his almanac, "What is Serving God? 'Tis doing Good to Man."[45]

Not everyone agreed with this practice, though. Thomas Jefferson told a relative that people should not presume to offer behavioral counseling, for

"The man who undertakes the Quixotism of reforming all his neighbors and acquaintances, will do them no good, and much harm to himself."[46]

Such sentiments notwithstanding, Franklin sought to lend a moral superiority to the early American press. He vigorously advocated that journalism should be a beneficial social force, both "agreeable and useful" to its readers. Subsequent printers concurred, intending their newspapers to be "independent of Party, upon Principles of Public Utility" and "entertaining, pure and instructive." Printer William Goddard observed that "A Public Paper, well conducted, is allowed by the most sensible People to be very serviceable to a community" as "the easiest and cheapest Path to the Knowledge of Mankind, and so suitable for the Instruction of Youth, as well as for the Satisfaction of the Mature." Newspapers were, in fact, one of the chief agents of education in early America. Because of their pervasiveness, social prominence, relatively easy accessibility, and presentation of some of the most important thinking of the era, newspapers encouraged literacy and political participation.[47]

Envisioning the press as the optimal means to convey his moral instruction and believing it to be truly beneficial to the improvement of colonial society, Franklin commenced a practice of forming printing partnerships. His first was a short-lived arrangement with Hugh Meredith in Philadelphia, but Franklin soon fashioned a plan to create a chain of partnerships in other cities. These alliances, forged with explicit written contracts, became the foundation upon which Franklin constructed a printing network that grew to be the largest, most powerful, prominent, and geographically extensive of the early American printing organizations. Composed of Franklin's business partners, trade associates, and family members, the network lasted from the 1720s to the 1790s, stretched from New England to the West Indies, and comprised more than two dozen printers. As an economic entity and source of mutual support, Franklin's network was integral to the success of many eighteenth-century printers and played a key role in the development of American journalism.[48]

The standard partnership with Franklin began with him identifying a large community that either had no printer or had room for competition with existing printing houses. Once he identified a likely site, Franklin offered a partnership to a printer, often one who worked for him as an apprentice or journeyman and whose character, skill, and work ethic impressed him. Franklin then supplied the press and types and, in some cases, used his capacity as deputy postmaster-general for North America to arrange for the partner to serve as a local postmaster. These postmasterships provided the printers with additional income and free mailing privileges, while allowing them to be the first in their locations to receive information and newspapers from other colonies and abroad. It also encouraged them to publish newspapers and communicate more with Franklin, because letters and printed matter to and from the deputy postmaster-general traveled free of cost.[49]

In the six-year partnership contract, Franklin shared the cost of materials, used the printer as a distributor of *Poor Richard's Almanack,* and received one-third of the profits. However, he stipulated that the printer must use only the types and press he provided, effectively prohibiting expansion. After the contract expired, the printer could continue the arrangement or buy Franklin's press and types. Franklin recalled that most were "enabled at the End of our Term, Six Years, to purchase the Types of me." These contracts were remarkably similar, in which Franklin took great pride.[50]

Franklin's preparation of worthy apprentices and journeymen for their own printing houses represented a substantial departure from the European system, also practiced in colonial America, in which master craftsmen used apprenticeships to limit the growth of their trades. By substituting apprentices for journeymen and other hired help, these masters spared themselves the journeymen's wages and thereby prevented many journeymen from raising enough capital to open their own shops.[51]

Instead, Franklin—alone and in tandem with partner James Parker—used apprentices and journeymen alike to *expand* the printing trade through his peculiar practice of franchising. He benefited financially from this expansion of the trade in many ways, as it afforded him more markets for which he could act as a distributor of printing supplies and made him a prominent entrepreneur. Of course, part of his success in establishing this web of printers was his knack of working with and setting up printers he could trust, most notably David Hall in Philadelphia, the Timothys in Charles Town, and James Parker in New York, New Haven, Connecticut, and Woodbridge, New Jersey. Isaiah Thomas and others emulated this practice later in the century.[52]

As Franklin trained many early American printers in his own shop, having the opportunity to impress his beliefs upon them and school them in the ways of proper conduct as much as in the art of printing, and setting up some in partnerships or maintaining other affiliations with them, he helped establish a distinctly American character of public service for the American press. This public-service ideology and its relationship to press freedom elevated printer-publishers from tradesmen of modest social status to recognition as prominent and respected leaders of public opinion. This harbinger of press professionalization led to Constitutional recognition and protection of journalism's social and political utility.

The network Franklin and his associates crafted served to enlarge the scope of the early American printing trade, hasten the dissemination of information and opinion to a mass audience, and impress the importance of journalism upon the collective consciousness of eighteenth-century America, thereby playing a central role in establishing the legacy of social importance that the press has enjoyed to the present day.

2

From Apprentice to Journeyman to Master Printer

While apprenticed to Benjamin Franklin's grandson, Philadelphia printer Benjamin Franklin Bache, David Chambers confessed to his father in 1796 that his health was failing due to the long hours, hard work, and nominal diet, which consisted of "bread & Tea for breakfast & Supper." "[B]utter is forbidden fruit here," Chambers wrote. "Mr. Bache tells the prentices that Dr. Franklin used to say butter blinded printers."[1] His concerned father responded, "If your health should not permit a proper attendance to business it might be proper for you" to leave Bache's shop. "Your determination in the City must depend entirely on the state of health you may attain together with your own inclination."[2] Chambers persevered, though, graduating from his apprenticeship to become a master printer in the new state of Ohio. He later used his journalistic prominence as a springboard to politics, gaining election as a state senator and later a U.S. Representative from Ohio.[3]

Although Chambers endured, the grueling life of an apprentice proved to be more than many eighteenth-century boys could abide. Franklin was one who could not, abandoning his own printing apprenticeship in 1723. The apprenticeship, in printing and many other trades, was a well-established social custom for conveying vocational training to youths in the American colonies and abroad. It originated in medieval England, where governments assumed responsibility for regulating commerce and ensuring a sufficient workforce. Beginning at a young age, apprentices served up to ten years as contractually bound, unpaid laborers. They made written promises not to gamble, marry, fornicate, patronize taverns, buy and sell without the master's permission, or divulge business secrets. They worked long hours six days per week, performed menial tasks, and suffered punishments, all without pay, because the profit from their labors belonged to their masters. Yet apprentices endured the arduous life because it promised eventual self-employment. They sought to learn a craft they could practice after their apprenticeships expired, hoping to reap the wealth that Bache's journeymen wistfully told Chambers awaited early America's master printers.[4]

The fact that apprentices were unfree laborers bound by one-sided contracts and possessing few rights made them easy targets. The British Council for Trade received a petition in 1661 to stop "the great abuse that is, dayly used, by forcible takeing up and spiriting of children, Apprentices, and servants, and transporting them into Virginia, Barbadoes, and other forreigne ports beyond the Seas, without their owne, their parents, or their Masters privety or consent."[5]

The apprenticeship system experienced little change for centuries, on either side of the Atlantic. Apprentices performed duties intended to teach them a job, thus insuring an adequate supply of skilled labor within the trade. For boys, those crafts ranged from bookselling, glazing, and sailing to silversmithing, cobbling, and weaving, while girls usually secured apprenticeships cooking, cleaning, and sewing. The terms of the agreement were typically enumerated by filling in the blank spaces on pre-printed forms. Thus, Gardhill Darling's shoemaking and tanning apprenticeship extracts from him and his master, William Moulton, promises similar to those required of printing apprentice James Franklin Jr. and his master, Benjamin Franklin, more than half a century earlier.[6]

The apprenticeship system was essential to the growth of early American trades. Apprenticeships were means of vocational education through which the "art" (special skill) and the "mystery" (special knowledge) of the craft were passed from one generation to the next.[7] Securing a printing apprenticeship was especially desirable because of the trade's potential earning power and its emerging social prominence. By the Revolution, printing had ascended to the top of the craft hierarchy. Growing populations, increased literacy, and expanded commerce gave the colonial printer a thriving market. So, too, did maturing societal organizations. In Boston, for example, religious groups issued numerous publications, providing a substantial income for printers.[8]

In printing and other trades, apprentices usually lived in the master's home and worked closely with each other and the master, in contrast to the work settings of modern industry, which emphasize hierarchical organization and impersonal control. Apprentices, indentured servants, and slaves became appendages of the family structure in colonial America. They ate, worked, and attended church and schools together, all under the care and direction of the paterfamilias.

Sometimes these relationships turned sour, though, due to the master's cruelty, the apprentice's slothfulness, or both. In one such instance, printer James Parker, an integral member of Franklin's network, took on Benjamin Mecom as an apprentice in 1745 when Mecom, the son of Franklin's sister Jane Mecom, was about twelve years old. The relationship was a stormy one, and Mecom wrote bitterly to his mother and uncle about Parker's poor treatment of him. Mecom complained of inadequate clothing, "the bad attendance afforded him in the smallpox," and the beatings he received. Parker, on the other hand, objected to Mecom's habits of staying out all night and "refusing to give an account where he spends his time, or in what company." Mecom tried to run away by enlisting on a privateer, but he was caught. Franklin had little sympathy for his nephew, calling Mecom's actions "the high road to destruction" and noting of the beatings, "I think the correction very light, and not likely to be very effectual, if the strokes left no marks."[9]

Other apprenticeships fared equally poorly. Joseph Belknap's apprenticeship to Philadelphia printer Robert Aitken in 1783 began smoothly. A family friend wrote Belknap's father, Jeremy, that "From what I hear I believe Josey will not disappoint your Expectation; he appears to be perfectly Satisfied, & I think I can see that Mrs. A. has adopted him as her Son." Aitken also painted a picture of felicity, informing the elder Belknap, "we are very happy with him, he is a good natured pleasant Boy." Aitken placed Joseph with the bookbinders in his shop, "his Education in its present state somewhat imperfect for the printing business." Aitken planned to remedy this shortcoming by sending Joseph "to an Evening school to learn Eng[lish] gram[mar] & Writing & spelling with some more practice in reading."[10]

However, several years later Joseph's relationship with Aitken had deteriorated. Letters from each led Jeremy Belknap to conclude, "the breach is grown so wide that they *both* desire a Seperation. A. by *his own* acco[unt] has made a very free use of 'the Fist' and the 'knotted Cord' both very bad instruments of reformation. . . . Master Bob's mode of Correction has entirely disgusted Jo & alienated his affections."[11]

While the custom's primary purpose was to impart vocational skills, another function of the apprenticeship in Europe and America was subtler—it reaffirmed social class hierarchy. Masters in the most attractive trades sometimes demanded fees to accept apprentices. As impoverished parents could seldom afford this payment, their children were rarely apprenticed in trades offering the chance to ascend the social ladder.

Fees were less common in America than in Europe, yet even Franklin's father faced this obstacle. The expectation of payment prompted Josiah Franklin to remove twelve-year-old Benjamin from an apprenticeship to a Boston cutler, cousin Samuel Franklin, and instead place him in the printing trade with brother James Franklin, who agreed not to charge a fee. Samuel Franklin's "Expectations of a Fee with me displeasing my Father, I was taken home again," Benjamin Franklin wrote, where his father "at length determin'd . . . to make me a Printer."[12] One of Benjamin Franklin's partners, Peter Timothy, also expected fees for accepting apprentices. He expressed this desire by seeking boys who could be "well recommended." In one newspaper advertisement, Timothy announced, "The printer of this paper will take an apprentice, provided he be well recommended." In another he noted, "The printer of this paper wants a sober lad as an apprentice, who must be well-recommended."[13]

Not only did apprentices replenish the ranks of paid labor by graduating to journeymen and some ultimately to masters of their own shops, they also enabled their masters to hire fewer journeymen. Because the prospect of economic gain dictated freedom of movement in colonial America, journeymen were often transient. As the term implies, journeymen tended to move from city to city in search of higher wages, bringing them closer to their goal of saving enough capital to open their own shops.[14] Records of a 1730s London printing house indicate a small group of workers stayed for a year or longer, while the rest were transient, working a few weeks or months before departing. Some returned, presumably after failing to find more lucrative work.[15]

Most journeymen in colonial America had little trouble securing steady work, though, due to the growth of the printing trade. However, for masters to maintain some continuity in their work force, as well as to counter the spiraling wage demands of journeymen, many relied heavily on apprentices. Apprentices cost little more than food and a room in the house, were usually bound for at least seven years, and could be trained to perform many of the journeymen's duties. This arrangement allowed printers to hire fewer journeymen and thus pay fewer—and lower—wages.[16]

Reliance on apprentices came at a price. If they mastered the trade too soon, they could run away. Franklin did, and so did one of his closest associates and network members, James Parker. On January 1, 1726, Parker, at about age eleven, signed an apprenticeship indenture with New York printer William Bradford for a term of eight years.[17] In exchange, Bradford would teach Parker printing and bookbinding; provide him with food, drink, apparel, and lodging; and supply him two sets of clothes at the end of his apprenticeship. Parker ran away before he finished it, though. He fled Bradford's shop May 17, 1733, and traveled south to Philadelphia, believing his printing skills were already superior to his master's and thus deciding Bradford had nothing more to teach him. Parker's talent offered him the prospect of earning a living on his own, which he preferred over an apprenticeship that restrained him and afforded him no opportunity to improve in his craft. Decades later, Parker boasted of his youthful talent. "Forty Years ago when a Boy . . . I was the first that brought the printing Art into any Credit here [New York City]," he wrote.[18]

Bradford advertised for Parker's return, describing him as "an Apprentice lad . . . by trade a Printer, aged about 19 years; he is of a fresh Complexion, with short yellowish Hair" and offering twenty shillings for his return, doubling the sum a month later. Probably at the urging of Franklin, who had taken in the runaway and presumably permitted him to work in the Philadelphia shop as a journeyman, Parker served the duration of his apprenticeship, plus a penalty of additional service for running away.[19]

Franklin's reason for urging Parker to return to Bradford may have been his own imprudence a decade earlier. At age twelve in 1718, Franklin had been apprenticed to his older brother James, the printer of the *New-England Courant*, until he turned twenty-one (effectively, for a period of more than eight years). The indenture included an unusual clause—during his final year, Benjamin would receive journeyman's wages. "In a little time I made great Proficiency in the Business, and became a useful Hand to my Brother," he wrote.[20]

However, after repeated quarrels with his brother, who "was passionate & had often beaten me," Benjamin ran away in 1723 and offered his services to the four other Boston printers. None would employ him, though, for James "took care to prevent my getting Employment in any other Printing-House of the Town, by going round & speaking to every Master, who accordingly refus'd to give me Work."[21] James's ability to prevent his brother from securing work demonstrates the structural solidarity within the printing trade that later characterized networks.

Stymied in his efforts locally and trying to avoid his family, whom he thought would prevent his departure, Benjamin Franklin arranged to board a New York–bound ship covertly, under the guise that he "had got a naughty Girl with Child, whose Friends would compel me to marry her." Finding no work there, he traveled to Philadelphia and passed himself off as a journeyman, eventually securing employment with both of that city's printers, first Andrew Bradford on a sporadic basis and then Samuel Keimer full-time.[22]

Had he been in England instead of America, Franklin would not have succeeded in billing himself as a journeyman. England's eighteenth-century guild jurisdiction was so powerful that he probably would have failed to find work because his credentials would have been thoroughly investigated. Had he been discovered as a runaway apprentice, he could have been prosecuted. However, because there were no guilds in colonial America, a capable boy like Franklin could simply move to a different colony and claim journeyman status. The legal penalties for runaway apprentices differed from colony to colony and did not extend across colonial borders. Also, neither printers nor government authorities normally kept records certifying completion of apprenticeships. A high demand for skilled workers in the more prestigious crafts gave the colonial printing apprentice an excellent chance of finding employment.[23]

Despite the unkindness with which his brother had treated him, Franklin later expressed regret for his action. Returning to New England in 1733, ten years after he had fled, Franklin visited his estranged brother, who had moved to Rhode Island, and made amends. Franklin wrote, "In returning I call'd at Newport, to see my Brother there with his Printing-House. Our former differences were forgotten, and our Meeting was very cordial and affectionate." In failing health and anticipating death, James asked Benjamin to accept his son, James Franklin Jr., as an apprentice. The Philadelphian agreed, later noting, "Thus it was that I made my Brother ample Amends for the Service I had depriv'd him of by leaving him so early."[24] Franklin was probably never completely contrite, though, as he was by this time in charge of his own Philadelphia printing house and had fared as well or better than if he had remained under James's tutelage for the duration of his indenture.

The omnipresent temptation to run away must have seemed even more attractive to boys like Parker and Franklin, who were confident of their printing skills, because of the relative ease of traveling to another colony and seeking employment as journeymen. When apprentices ran away, they hurt the businesses of many colonial printers, who needed all available workers. Printers frequently published notices offering rewards for the return of their footloose apprentices. Andrew Bradford advertised in his *American Weekly Mercury* for the return of apprentice Nicholas Classon. In his *Virginia Gazette,* William Parks warned colonists that one of his runaways was adept at making and picking locks. *Maryland Gazette* printer Joseph Royle sought the return of one apprentice, whom he described as "very thick, stoops much, and has a down look; he is a little Pock-pitted, has a Scar on one of his Temples, is much addicted to Liquor, very talkative when drunk and remarkably stupid." Despite this unflattering portrayal, Royle offered the hefty sum of five pounds sterling for the young man's return. Apparently content to be rid of him, James Franklin advertised for Benjamin's replacement rather than his return. He simply informed his *New-England Courant* readers, "James Franklin, Printer in Queen Street, wants a likely lad for an apprentice."[25]

After securing employment with Keimer in Philadelphia, Franklin met Pennsylvania Governor William Keith. Opining that "The Printers at Philadelphia were wretched ones" and esteeming the eighteen-year-old Franklin to be "a young Man of promising Parts," Keith vowed to finance Franklin and make him the province's official printer, thereby ensuring him considerable work and income. Franklin was elated. "Yet unsolicited as he was by me, how could I think his generous Offers insincere? I believ'd him one of the best Men in the World."[26]

At Keith's request, Franklin traveled to London in 1724 to establish business relationships with suppliers of books and stationery and secure the needed printing materials, including a press and types. He was to purchase these with letters of credit Keith promised to send aboard Franklin's ship, but the governor never furnished them. Franklin later learned from an acquaintance in London, merchant Thomas Denham, "there was not the least Probability that he had written any Letters for me, that no one who knew him had the smallest Dependance on him," and that Keith's promise to give Franklin letters of credit was amusing, for Keith had "no Credit to give." Years later, Franklin chose to view Keith's reprehensible conduct in the most charitable light, writing that the governor "wish'd to please every body; and having little to give, he gave Expectations."[27]

His own expectations shattered, and without money to pay for return passage, Franklin secured work in London as a journeyman printer, first with Samuel Palmer and then John Watts. While employed in their shops, Franklin became disenchanted with the behavior and rituals of the apprentices and journeymen with whom he worked.[28]

For example, the businesslike Franklin deplored their practice of drinking on the job. "I drank only water; the other Workmen, near 50 in number, were great Guzzlers of Beer," he recalled. Laughed at as "the Water-American," Franklin impressed his colleagues by regularly carrying a large form of type in each hand, while the others, who drank "*strong* beer that [they] might be *strong* to labour," could carry only one form at a time. Franklin explained to them the strength beer afforded was only proportional to the flour of the barley it contained, and that more flour could be found in a piece of bread, which was much less expensive. Most ignored his persuasive attempt, though, and "continu'd sotting with Beer all day." Sometimes the workers failed to show up for work due to drunkenness, claiming they had observed a "St. Monday" holiday, which Franklin proudly noted he had never taken. Each week Franklin witnessed them squandering their wages "for that muddling Liquor," compelling him to conclude with a mixture of pity and censure, "And thus these poor Devils keep themselves always under."[29]

Franklin formed a similar opinion about others addicted to alcohol—his childhood friend John Collins and the Carlisle Indian tribe with whom Franklin negotiated a treaty. Franklin recalled Collins had "a wonderful Genius for Mathematical Learning in which he far outstript me." Accordingly, Collins "was much respected for his Learning by several of the Clergy & other Gentlemen, & seem'd to promise making a good Figure in Life." However, Collins fell prey to liquor, soon lost his money on brandy and gambling, became unruly and obstinate, and was evicted from his residence. He traveled to Philadelphia with Franklin, where he failed to secure employment, likely because prospective employers "discover'd his Dramming by his Breath, or by his Behaviour." The Native American Indians also became fractious when intoxicated, Franklin observed. He witnessed them commence "quarreling and fighting. Their dark-colour'd Bodies, half naked, seen only by the gloomy Light of the Bonfire, running after and beating one another with Firebrands, accompanied by their horrid Yellings, form'd a Scene the most resembling our Ideas of Hell that could well be imagin'd." Repulsed by how "those People are extreamly apt to get drunk," Franklin noted, "if it be the Design of Providence to extirpate these Savages in order to make room for Cultivators of the Earth, it seems not improbable that Rum may be the appointed Means." His experiences with alcoholics led Franklin to dismiss excessive drinking as "a detestable Custom."[30]

In London, Franklin was soon promoted from the press room to the composing room, where he was expected to pay the newcomer's fee of five shillings for beer. Franklin refused, having paid the fee while a pressman. "I had thought it an Imposition, as I had paid below," Franklin wrote. "The Master thought so too, and forbad my paying it." Franklin held out for two or three weeks and "was accordingly considered as an Excommunicate." Franklin's refusal to pay twice for beer he did not consume angered the compositors, who performed "so many little Pieces of private Mischief," including "mixing my Sorts, transposing my Pages, breaking my Matter, &c. &c. if I were ever so little out of the Room," he wrote. He eventually paid, having become "convinc'd of the Folly of being on ill Terms with those one is to live with continually."[31]

After about eighteen months, Franklin had "grown tired of London, remember'd with Pleasure the happy Months I had spent in Pennsylvania, and wish'd again to see it." So when Denham informed Franklin he intended to return to Philadelphia and open a mercantile business, offering to employ the young man as a clerk, Franklin agreed and "took Leave of Printing, as I thought for ever."[32]

They sailed for America July 23, 1726, and during the nearly twelve-week journey, Franklin ruminated on the disturbing character traits he had observed in others—and himself. Governor Keith had betrayed him. Franklin's London print-shop colleagues displayed indolence, carelessness, and wastefulness. Also in England, he had seen his friend James Ralph abandon his wife and child and take a mistress, "Mrs. T," who "lost her Friends & Business" and "was often in Distresses" because of Ralph. Franklin was no more faithful than Ralph. After having "interchang'd some promises" with his Philadelphia sweetheart, Deborah Read, Franklin virtually ignored her once he arrived in England. "I never wrote more than one Letter, that was to let her know I was not likely soon to return," he recalled. With Ralph out of town, Franklin often visited Mrs. T, whom he esteemed as "sensible & lively, & of most pleasing Conversation." Having become "fond of her Company, and being at this time under no Religious Restraints," Franklin "attempted Familiarities" with her, which she repelled.[33]

Franklin also found financial matters nettlesome. He collected a debt for acquaintance Samuel Vernon, but instead of relinquishing the money, he kept it. Even so, Franklin found that his funds were dwindling because he spent much of it on entertainment. Although Ralph had no income, he and Franklin were boon companions, and they dissipated Franklin's money "in going to Plays & other Places of Amusement." Ralph owed Franklin about twenty-seven pounds sterling, but he refused to pay it once he learned of Franklin's attempted seduction of his mistress. Because of these judgment errors, Franklin was never able to save enough for return passage to Philadelphia, and he resigned himself to a daily grind in which he "just rubb'd on from hand to mouth" until Denham paid his passage.[34]

The cerebral Franklin reflected on these and other "great Errata of my Life" during the America-bound ocean voyage. He had nearly three months to scrutinize his own moral arsenal, and concluded it was little better than those of the deceptive Keith or the malfeasant London printers. Impelled by his rueful evaluation of the darker hues of his own character that he exhibited in London, the twenty-year-old Franklin formulated a "Plan of Conduct" to govern the duration of his life. He explained this intention by confessing in 1726, "I have never fixed a regular design in life; by which means it has been a confused variety of different scenes." The plan had four main resolutions: frugality until debts are repaid, truthfulness and sincerity, patient dedication to hard work, and refusal to defame others. In time, this plan evolved into his "Project of arriving at moral Perfection," in which his tenets of belief were expanded to thirteen virtues.[35]

His London experiences inspired some of these virtues. His recognition of alcohol's destructive influence on the London printing workers evolved into the virtue of Temperance, accompanied by the exhortation, "Drink not to Elevation." The lessons he learned from Keith's falsehood became the virtues of Justice and Sincerity, with the respective admonitions that one should "Wrong none, by doing Injuries or omitting the Benefits that are your Duty" and "Use no hurtful Deceit." His aspiration to avoid "Intrigues with low Women" yielded the virtue of Chastity, with the accompanying desire to avoid "the Injury of your own or another's Peace or Reputation." The work ethic that Ralph, the printing-house workers, and others seemed to lack received particular attention in Franklin's menu, as he partitioned the concept into the virtues of Order ("Let each Part of your Business have its Time"), Resolution ("Perform without fail what you resolve"), and Industry ("Be always employ'd in something useful"). Forty-five years later, Franklin regarded his plan as "the more remarkable, as being form'd when I was so young, and yet being pretty faithfully adhered to quite thro' to old Age."[36]

Franklin's emerging code of moral conduct was influenced as much by his positive London role models as by his negative ones. In the midst of his feckless London revelries, Franklin wrote his first pamphlet, *A Dissertation on Liberty and Necessity, Pleasure and Pain,* to justify self-indulgence. His "little metaphysical Piece" contended, "nothing could possibly be wrong in the World, & that Vice & Virtue were empty Distinctions, no such Things existing." He inscribed it to his fellow merrymaker Ralph and printed it. However, his employer Samuel Palmer "seriously expostulated with me upon the Principles of my Pamphlet which to him appear'd abominable," Franklin related. After some reflection, Franklin concluded that Palmer was correct to criticize the pamphlet's hedonistic premise, for despite its superficial logic, it advocated wanton conduct that was "perverted" and "not very useful."[37]

Franklin learned about thrift from the elderly Catholic woman in his London boarding house and from Denham. Franklin affectionately recalled that Denham once fell into debt, but several years later, after "a close Application to Business," he invited his creditors to dinner, where they found bank drafts for full repayment, plus interest, under their plates.[38]

When they arrived in Philadelphia, Franklin and Denham opened a dry-goods store on Water Street and commenced their own close application to business, but several months later Denham became ill and died, and his heirs closed the shop. Again forced to seek employment, Franklin returned to the trade he knew best, printing, and entertained another offer from Keimer. Keimer's establishment had fallen into disarray, and he enlisted Franklin to manage the shop and train the five workers.[39]

Franklin found as much disorder in Keimer's shop as in the London printing houses. Three workers—pressman Hugh Meredith, bookbinder Stephen Potts, and apprentice David Harry—had farming backgrounds. The other two, George Webb and another named John, were indentured servants obligated to work four years for Keimer because he had paid their passage from England and Ireland, respectively. Franklin esteemed the workers as "raw cheap Hands" who were ill-suited to their jobs and possessed of dubious character. Meredith was "a poor Pressman, & seldom sober," John was "wild" and soon ran away without serving his time, and Webb, an erstwhile "Oxford Scholar," was "idle, thoughtless & imprudent to the last Degree." The paucity of reliable help was common in the early eighteenth century, before printing became a high-status trade, James Parker recalled. He wrote that printers were often "obliged to take of the lowest People" for apprentices and journeymen, because no family "of Substance would ever put their Sons to such an Art."[40]

However, Franklin's most censorious recollections were of Keimer, whom he described as an ersatz intellectual and scheming eccentric. Franklin recalled him as "an odd Fish, ignorant of common Life, fond of rudely opposing receiv'd Opinions, slovenly to extream dirtiness, enthusiastic in some Points of Religion, and a little Knavish withal." He was also "a great Glutton" who once ate an entire roast pig that he was to have shared with Franklin and two women. Predictably, Keimer's shop was "in great Confusion."[41]

Franklin soon realized that Keimer desired his services only until he organized the business and taught the other workers. This apprehension, plus his growing desire to fully implement his Plan of Conduct by escaping the imprudent influence of others, inspired him to contemplate founding his own business. Thus, when Franklin resigned after arguing with Keimer, Meredith proposed a partnership and Franklin accepted. Financed by Meredith's father, Franklin and Meredith opened their own printing shop, the third in Philadelphia, in 1728.[42]

The partners quickly received job-printing work and decided to publish a newspaper to compete with Andrew Bradford's *American Weekly Mercury*, which Franklin regarded as "a paltry thing, wretchedly manag'd, no way entertaining." The fact that such a newspaper was lucrative was additional incentive for Franklin, who reasoned that "a good Paper could scarcely fail of good Encouragem[en]t." Franklin confided his intention to his quondam co-worker Webb, who violated Franklin's trust by informing Keimer. Keimer immediately announced plans to begin a newspaper, and he published the first number of the *Universal Instructor in all Arts and Sciences; and Pennsylvania Gazette* on December 24, 1728. "I resented this," Franklin recalled in his *Autobiography,* "and to counteract them, as I could not yet begin our Paper, I wrote several Pieces of Entertainm[en]t for Bradford's Paper" that "burlesqu'd & ridicul'd" Keimer. The first two assailed Keimer's decision to reprint an essay on abortion from an encyclopedia. Writing under the guise of "Martha Careful," he warned Keimer that aggrieved Philadelphia women aspired to seize him "by the Beard, at the next Place we meet him, and make an Example of him for his Immodesty." In another letter in the same issue, Franklin's "Caelia Shortface" claimed to speak for "all the Modest and Virtuous Women in Pensilvania." She threatened, "if thou proceed any further in that Scandalous manner, we intend very soon to have thy right Ear for it," and suggested that if the newspaper's content did not improve, Keimer should stop publishing it.[43]

The following week, Franklin and friend Joseph Breintnal commenced the "Busy-Body" series of essays in Bradford's newspaper, which took swipes at Keimer as "crafty, but far from being Wise" and suggested his workers serve him "rather thro' Fear of the Harm thou may'st do to them, than out of Gratitude." Not knowing Franklin was the writer, Keimer rebuked the pseudonymous author for using "gross Descriptions" that have an "ill Effect." Later he called the series "a confounded Noise and Racket" that wove bad moralizing among plagiarized writings.[44] The series of published thrusts and parries between the "Busy-Body" and Keimer found the latter overmatched by Franklin's and Breintnal's satirical skill. With impatient creditors and no more than ninety subscribers, Keimer was compelled to sell the *Universal Instructor.* He offered it to his apprentice, David Harry, who declined, and was ultimately forced to peddle it to Franklin and Meredith "for a Trifle."[45]

Franklin and Meredith shortened the newspaper's name to the *Pennsylvania Gazette* and changed both content and appearance. They unveiled a revised product with the issue of October 2, 1729. In the process, they took a jab at competitor Bradford's paper. "There are many who have long desired to see a good News-paper in Pennsylvania," they noted in their first issue. The redesign and shift in content from publishing dictionary excerpts, which would require "fifty Years before the Whole can be gone thro' in this Manner of Publication," to making the newspaper "as agreeable and useful an Enter-

Eighteenth-century Printing Press

This printing press that Franklin used is in the Division of Graphic Arts of the Smithsonian Institution.

tainment as the nature of the Thing will allow," succeeded immediately. Just three weeks later, Franklin and Meredith informed readers that they were "meeting with considerable Encouragement." Franklin later recalled that his newspaper "prov'd in a few Years extreamly profitable to me."[46]

Franklin had risen from runaway apprentice to successful master printer, taking charge of one of only seven newspapers in the American colonies, and he had done it by circumventing the labor hierarchy present in most early American trades. Printing houses relied on apprentices as an inexpensive yet essential source of labor, and in exchange, offered vocational education. These apprentices aspired to master their craft well enough to work as journeymen, and as such were the beneficiaries of training programs designed to fill the ranks of their craft. The instruction of colonial youths through the apprenticeship system was essential to the stability and continuity of the printing trade while it provided an unpaid work force that enabled the fledgling American press to survive and expand.

The confident and rebellious Franklin spurned this system and made his own way into the upper ranks of the colonial printing trade, setting an example that may have inspired many boys who ran away from their own apprenticeships, intent on seeking the same adventures and success Franklin found. His fortune was unique, though. In the decade between the commencement of his apprenticeship and the formation of his first partnership, Franklin experienced a broader spectrum of life than his ordinary Boston upbringing amid a large Puritan family would have suggested. He had joined his brother in waging a journalistic war against government and religious authorities over smallpox inoculation, abrogated his legal obligations by fleeing his apprenticeship, lied his way into employment in Philadelphia printing houses, and been tricked into traversing the Atlantic Ocean. However, he was perhaps most deeply affected by witnessing characters in various stages of squandering their wealth and potential while neglecting their responsibilities.

These experiences and observations of drunkenness, imprudence, and self-gratification—both in others and himself—left a lasting impression on Franklin. Once he attained a position of responsibility and authority, he vowed to avoid knowingly employing indolent and alcoholic workers. Having formulated a code of moral behavior by which to conduct his life, he resolved to surround himself with others of similar inclinations as apprentices, journeymen, and partners, and to impart his values to a vice-ridden society through the available channels of mass communication.

3

The Moral Foundations of Franklin's Journalism

Benjamin Franklin's religious beliefs confused many observers. John Adams wrote disparagingly, "the Catholics thought him almost a Catholic. The Church of England claimed him as one of them. The Presbyterians thought him half a Presbyterian, and the Friends believed him a wet Quaker. Indeed, all Sects considered him, and I believe justly, a friend to unlimited toleration in matters of religion."[1] Adams himself decided that Franklin was properly situated among "Atheists, Deists, and Libertines."[2] University of Edinburgh director William Robertson put his views of Franklin's religion more charitably, informing a mutual friend that "Theology I believe is of all the Sciences the only one in which I suspect he is not perfectly sound."[3]

Adams and some other contemporaries viewed Franklin's religious convictions as superficial and ill-formed, and Franklin conceded that he flirted with deism during his youth. He read several books assailing it, but he found himself swayed more by the deistic arguments than their refutations. "I soon became a thorough Deist," Franklin recalled in his memoirs. He became so convinced of this stance that he persuaded several of his friends and in 1725 published as a pamphlet his *A Dissertation on Liberty and Necessity, Pleasure and Pain,* which asserted that vice and virtue were empty distinctions. However, he soon saw the bad effects of deism in the conduct of his deistic friends, who injured Franklin without remorse. He also observed that his own character had veered toward selfishness and deceit. As a result, Franklin began to wonder "whether some Error had not insinuated itself unperceiv'd, into my Argument, so as to infect all that follow'd, as is common in metaphysical Reasonings." Franklin eventually recanted his deistic beliefs and embraced a practical though neither deep nor denominationally bound Christianity. For this conversion he credited "the kind hand of Providence, or some guardian Angel" for preserving him "thro' this dangerous Time of Youth & the hazardous Situations I was sometimes in among Strangers, remote from the Eye & Advice of my Father."[4]

In March 1790, Franklin answered a friend's inquiry into his religious beliefs with a surprising response. "It is the first time I have been questioned upon it," Franklin wrote, and happily provided his views. He acknowledged God's providence, the immortality of souls, the existence of Heaven, and the importance of doing good to others while on earth. Franklin acknowledged Jesus' "System of Morals and his Religion, as he left them to us, the best the World ever saw or is likely to see; but I apprehend it has received various corrupting Changes." Franklin admitted wrestling with Jesus' divinity, but confessed he had never studied the matter "and think it needless to busy myself with it now, when I expect soon an Opportunity of knowing the Truth with less Trouble." He found out less than six weeks later.[5]

Franklin's youthful embrace of deism and the derisive opinions of Adams and others have led to a popular myth that Franklin was a lifelong deist or even atheist. One Franklin biographer, a philosophy professor who studies deism, argued that Franklin "was a disbeliever in Christianity—or, what often amounted to the same thing in the judgment of eighteenth-century minds, an out-and-out atheist."[6] While not a vigorous exponent of any particular denomination, Franklin's religious beliefs were nonetheless inextricably intertwined with his utilitarian conception of virtue. As such, Christianity influenced his writings and the publications that emerged from his printing presses. Franklin tailored his teachings to his audience, occasionally advocating religion as a means of securing virtue. Echoing Biblical themes, Franklin taught that virtue would bring happiness in the forms of material rewards and public respect, while folly would produce ruin and scorn. One of his best-known "Poor Richard" maxims, "Virtue and a trade are a child's best portion," resembles the Biblical proverb "Give a lad training suitable to his character and, even when old, he will not go back on it." Another, "The noblest question in the world is *What Good may I do in it?*" echoes one of Franklin's favorite Bible verses, "It is by my deeds that I will show you my faith."[7]

These writings represent a marked change in Franklin's thinking from his *A Dissertation on Liberty and Necessity*. In maturity, he returned to the religious values with which he was reared. Despite the apparent flaws they possessed under the scrutiny of metaphysical logic, those values were the keys to contentment. Reflecting on his young adulthood, Franklin acknowledged this maturation process. "I grew convinc'd that *Truth, Sincerity & Integrity* in Dealings between Man & Man, were of the utmost Importance to the Felicity of Life," he wrote.[8]

Before Franklin became theologically confusing to contemporaries and historians, he spent his youth immersed in the philosophy of American Puritanism. Just as earthly success connoted winning favor with God, American Puritans customarily concluded that unfortunate occurrences were examples of God's direct punishment of the wicked, and that it was appropriate to communicate tales of misfortune via print as exhortations to repentance. A 1722 Boston newspaper reported that one youth died and others were injured when the ice on which they were skating cracked. Noting that this incident occurred on Sunday, the Puritan newspaper correspondent moralized about sabbatarian expectations, "it may be a fair warning to them and all others not so prophanely to abuse the Lord's Day, in turning it into a Day of Sport and Diversion as these did." Eight years later, Massachusetts Governor Jonathan Belcher banned game-playing and cursing on Sundays, and he ordered residents "to attend the publick Worship of GOD on every LORD'S DAY."[9]

Because of such irreverence, natural disasters and tragedies were often ascribed to God's wrath. Puritan minister Cotton Mather attributed the "Growth of many Miscarriages" to God's anger at impious people, and an essayist attributed an earthquake that struck Boston to the "special Influence and Direction . . . of our heavenly Father."[10] Because they believed the meaning of an event could be ascertained by placing it in a theological context, Puritan leaders such as Increase Mather and his son Cotton regarded the reporting of "shipwrecks, preservations, thunder and lightning, tempests, witches and demons, and deformities" as an important task, for these events "were merely the latest recurrences of types that fit into the larger pattern of God's work in history," a historian wrote. Franklin came from this Puritan stock. His maternal grandfather, Peter Folger, wrote a 1675 broadside claiming that "the Indian Wars & other Distresses, that had befallen the Country" were "Judgments of God" punishing them for religious persecution of Quakers and Baptists.[11]

Franklin had wrestled with his Puritan upbringing early in life, and doubted whether God visited direct punishment upon the sinful. He also was frustrated that Christianity seemed to rely too much on faith and ritual, and not enough on deeds that manifest the Christian doctrine. "I wish it were more productive of Good Works than I have generally seen it," Franklin wrote to a correspondent about faith. "I mean real good Works, Works of Kindness, Charity, Mercy, and Publick Spirit."[12]

In a youthful effort to display the "Good Works" doctrine he advocated and confound the religious leaders he viewed as excessively dogmatic, the teenaged Franklin gladly aided his brother's crusade against the Mathers and other Puritan leaders during the 1721 controversy surrounding smallpox inoculation.[13] The resulting battle for public support led Cotton Mather to fume, "The Town is become almost an Hell upon Earth, a City full of Lies, and Murders, and Blasphemies, as far as Wishes and Speeches can render it so; Satan seems to take a strange Possession of it." Mather fixed blame for Boston's turmoil upon James and Benjamin Franklin and their coterie of inflammatory writers, branded by detractors with the name of an outlawed English satanic cult, the "Hell-Fire Club." Referring to James, Benjamin, and other members of the Hell-Fire Club, the clergyman noted in his diary, "warnings are to be given unto the wicked Printer, and his Accomplices, who every week publish a vile Paper to lessen and blacken the Ministers of the Town, and render their Ministry ineffectual. A Wickedness never parallel'd any where upon the Face of the Earth!"[14]

Despite this tussle for popular opinion, Franklin respected and benefited from Mather. As a boy with a "Bookish Inclination," he read Mather's *Essays to Do Good*, "which perhaps gave me a Turn of Thinking that had an Influence on some of the principal future Events of my Life," Franklin wrote in his *Autobiography*. Franklin was thus inspired at an early age to work for civic improvement, despite his one effort to block it by dissuading the public against the use of smallpox vaccinations—a cause Mather championed.[15]

The minister did not hold the teenager's impudence against him, though, later accepting a visit from Franklin. Franklin recalled,

He received me in his library, and on my taking leave showed me a shorter way out of the house through a narrow passage, which was crossed by a beam over head. We were still talking as I withdrew, he accompanying me behind, and I turning partly towards him, when he said hastily, "*Stoop, stoop!*" I did not understand him, till I felt my head hit against the beam. He was a man that never missed any occasion of giving instruction, and upon this he said to me, "*You are young, and have the world before you; STOOP as you go through it, and you will miss many hard thumps.*" This advice, thus beat into my head, has frequently been of use to me.[16]

Mather's influence remained with Franklin his entire life. Nearly seventy years after first reading Mather's *Essays*, Franklin told the reverend's son Samuel that the book had given him "such a turn of thinking, as to have an influence on my conduct through life; for I have always set a greater value on the character of a *doer of good*, than on any other kind of reputation; and if I have been, as you seem to think, a useful citizen, the public owes the advantage of it to that book."[17]

Franklin had inherited the philosophy of good works from Mather, less as evidence of Puritan affiliation than as agreement with the belief. Despite being raised a Puritan of the Congregationalist stripe by his parents, who "brought me through my Childhood piously in the Dissenting Way," Franklin recalled, he abandoned that denomination, briefly embraced deism, and finally became a non-denominational Protestant Christian. He attended some Presbyterian services in the 1730s, but rarely attended church. "Tho' I seldom attended any Public Worship, I had still an Opinion of its Propriety, and of its Utility, when rightly conducted, and I regularly paid my annual Subscription for the Support of the only Presbyterian Minister or Meeting we had in Philadelphia," Franklin noted.[18]

Although sharing the Puritan disdain for many ceremonial aspects of organized religion, Franklin was more Christian than deist, agnostic, or atheist. He believed in the divine providence of God, acknowledged the power of prayer, tried to imitate the humility of Jesus, and envisioned the existence of Heaven as "a State of Happiness, infinite in Degree, and eternal in Duration," which he did not believe people could earn solely by their actions.[19] However, through good works people could exhibit gratitude to God for His blessings and, with faith, recommend themselves to God's wisdom. Discussing his "Notion of Good Works," Franklin told a correspondent "that I am far from expecting (as you suppose) that I shall merit Heaven by them," adding that God's grace was also required, but the following year he counseled readers of his almanac, "Learning to the Studious; Riches to the Careful; Power to the Bold; Heaven to the Virtuous."[20] Comforting a relative grieving over the death of Franklin's brother John, he expressed his belief that temporal existence is fleeting and deceptive. "We are spirits," Franklin wrote. "That bodies should be lent us, while they can afford us pleasure, assist us in acquiring knowledge, or doing good to our fellow creatures, is a kind and benevolent act of God." He concluded his letter by asserting John had gone to Heaven, so "why should you and I be grieved at this, since we are soon to follow, and we know where to find him."[21]

Franklin had always disliked religious dogma, viewing it as excessively concerned with technicalities at the expense of teaching the fundamental concepts. He recalled once attending church services for five successive Sundays, but stopped because the minister's "Discourses were chiefly either polemic,

Arguments, or Explications of the peculiar Doctrines of our Sect, and were all to me very dry, uninteresting and unedifying, since not a single moral Principle was inculcated or enforc'd, their Aim seeming to be rather to make us Presbyterians than good Citizens." He once found a minister he liked, Samuel Hemphill, whose sermons appealed to Franklin because "they had little of the dogmatical kind, but inculcated strongly the Practice of Virtue, or what in the religious Stile are called Good Works." When members of the congregation who "disapprov'd his Doctrine" sought to have Hemphill dismissed, Franklin wrote and printed three pamphlets and a newspaper essay to defend him in the press. These efforts to save his pulpit were unsuccessful.[22]

Although he disliked many of the frustratingly human facets of organized religion, Franklin "had still an Opinion of its Propriety," and took to heart the Christian ethic of good works, believing that Jesus Christ "prefer'd the Doers of the Word to the meer Hearers." Those who merely hear and pray, without actions, are "as if a Tree should value itself on being water'd and putting forth Leaves, tho' it never produc'd any Fruit," he wrote. Like many of Franklin's exhortations, these assertions are adapted from the Bible. The apostle James told the Jews to "do what the Word tells you and not just listen to it and deceive yourselves." In a parable about sinners, Jesus cautioned that trees bearing no fruit may be judged useless and cut down.[23]

Franklin understood that the greatest good he could do for others was to lead them, by example and rational appeals, to virtuous conduct. To set the example in his own life, he crafted a personal code by which he might live virtuously. The process of persuading others to do the same was another matter entirely. Franklin had never conceived of himself as a dynamic speaker or writer, noting that in youth "I fell far short in elegance of Expression, in Method and in Perspicuity." In adulthood, he was still "but a bad Speaker, never eloquent, subject to much hesitation in my choice of Words, hardly correct in Language," yet he recalled, "I generally carried my Points."[24]

Despite his modest oratorical skills, Franklin was a gifted writer and skillful printer who believed the talents he developed and opportunities to use them were attributable to God's "kind Providence." Influenced by Mather's teachings, Franklin determined that God was best repaid by doing good for others, and he used his abilities to serve and instruct the masses. Upon replacing his brother at the helm of the *New-England Courant* in 1723, he insisted that one of his main functions would be "to fill up these Papers with a grateful Interspersion of more serious Morals" mixed with stories of "the most comical and diverting Incidents of Humane Life." He brought this blend of tutelage and amusement to the *Pennsylvania Gazette*, in which he advised potential contributors that wit exercised "for meer Ostentation of Parts" and not "aimed at the Good of others" is contemptible. To be acceptable, Franklin mandated that editorial submissions must benefit the reader by *"improving his Virtue or his Knowledge."*[25]

In using his press to do good by guiding readers to virtuous conduct, Franklin did not follow the path of moral leaders like Jonathan Edwards, who sought to inspire virtue by emphasizing the dire punishment that would be administered to the unregenerate by a fearsome God.[26] Instead, Franklin's early exhortations to rectitude revolved around the simplistic notion that all human action is motivated by the desire for pleasure and the prevention of pain. Thus, virtue would yield pleasure and avoid pain, he wrote in a 1725 pamphlet.[27] He later repudiated this view, but never completely abdicated its basic premise, suggesting nearly sixty years later that the pleasure derived from material goods was more beneficial than harmful, for it served as "a great Spur to Labour and Industry." This virtue was particularly important in early America, Franklin noted scornfully, because people "are naturally enough inclined to be, lazy and indolent."[28]

Franklin publicly advocated egalitarianism, but privately never shed his nagging pessimism and frustration with people of all stripes. He loathed arbitrary power, but viewed ordinary people as "viciously and corruptly educated," and thus unable to establish for themselves the enlightened society that European philosophers such as Rousseau, Voltaire, and Hume had envisioned, and of which Franklin secretly dreamed. While a delegate to the Constitutional Convention, he predicted dire consequences for the country if government leaders were paid. In his speech, he noted "there are two Passions which have a powerful Influence in the Affairs of Men. These are *Ambition* and *Avarice;* the Love of Power and the Love of Money." Jointly, these lures will attract to public office "the Bold and the Violent, the men of strong Passion and indefatigable Activity in their selfish Pursuits."[29]

Indeed, Franklin's cynicism about the moral bankruptcy of human nature at times seemed boundless. In 1764 he wrote to a physician friend,

Do you please yourself with the Fancy that you are doing Good? You are mistaken. Half the Lives you save are not worth saving, as being useless; and almost the other Half ought not to be sav'd, as being mischievous. Does your Conscience never hint to you the Impiety of being in constant Warfare against the Plans of Providence? Disease was intended as the Punishment of Intemperance, Sloth and other Vices; and the Example of that Punishment was intended to promote and strengthen the opposite

Virtues. But here you step in officiously with your Art, disappoint those wise Intentions of Nature, and make Men safe in their Excesses.[30]

Franklin compared the doctor's labors to those of a government official, "who out of the great Benevolence of his Heart should procure Pardons for all criminals that apply'd to him. Only think of the Consequences!"[31]

Despite his disdainful opinion that the masses yielded too readily to vice and were motivated chiefly by selfish ambition, Franklin assumed responsibility to lead them to upright conduct. This task derived from his "Notion of Good Works," which formed the foundation of his theology and inspired many of his actions. He regarded the duty as a repayment for human favors and a sign of gratitude for Divine mercy and benefaction.[32]

Early in his printing career, Franklin struggled with the ethical question of how to balance his faith convictions with periodic requests to write and publish religious polemics. He confronted this question in 1731 after being criticized for publishing an advertisement ridiculing the Anglican clergy. Franklin responded to the criticism by composing one of his most famous writings, the "Apology for Printers." It asserted that printers are motivated chiefly by revenue, without regard to its source. "Printers are educated in the Belief, that when Men differ in Opinion, both Sides ought equally to have the Advantage of being heard by the Publick," he wrote. Printers therefore "chearfully serve all contending Writers that pay them well, without regarding on which side they are of the Question in Dispute." He was careful to note, though, that his neutrality did not extend to publishing "Party or Personal Reflections" or corrupting public morals. "Printers do continually discourage the Printing of great Numbers of bad things, and stifle them in the Birth," he informed *Pennsylvania Gazette* readers. "I my self have constantly refused to print any thing that might countenance Vice, or promote Immorality."[33]

He later changed his mind about the impartiality of printers serving whoever paid them, deciding that this pecuniary rationale did not reconcile with his moral ideology and belief that printing should promote virtue. As he wrote in a newspaper essay, "nothing is more likely to endanger the liberty of the press, than the abuse of that liberty, by employing it in personal accusation, detraction, and calumny." Franklin therefore compromised his stance and resolved to consign writings "full of Spleen and Animosity" to pamphlets, rather than letting them dominate the pages of his newspaper. Matters of sectarian religious doctrine, like personal attacks, did not strike him as appropriate or effective topics of moral education.[34]

He occasionally made exceptions, such as letting his friend Ebenezer

Kinnersley, a lay preacher, attack the Philadelphia Baptist church and its minister for barring him from the pulpit. Just as he had initially rationalized the anti-clergy advertisement in the "Apology for Printers," Franklin justified his editorial decision using a Miltonian "free marketplace of ideas" appeal. "It is a Principle among Printers, that when truth has fair Play, it will always prevail over Falshood," Franklin wrote, "therefore, though they have an undoubted Property in their own Press, yet they willingly allow, that any one is entitled to the Use of it, who thinks it necessary to offer his Sentiments on disputable Points to the Publick, and will be at the Expense of it."[35]

Despite the occasional deviation, throughout his career as a master printer Franklin was reluctant to print personal attacks in his newspaper and almanac, desiring instead to make those publications entertaining in a more wholesome sense. Although alleging that scandal and insults are popular reading fare because "good things are not encouraged," he nonetheless perceived that he had "contracted with my Subscribers to furnish them with what might be either useful or entertaining." He instructed potential contributors *That no Piece can properly be called good, and well written, which is void of any Tendency to benefit the Reader, either by improving his Virtue or his Knowledge.* Thus, essays containing "Libelling and Personal Abuse" would do his audience "manifest Injustice."[36] This was consistent with the moral beliefs he formulated early in life, when he resolved to "speak ill of no man whatever, not even in a matter of truth," and regularly prayed for God's assistance, "That I may refrain from Calumny and Detraction." Franklin also advocated this view to others. "Let it lie by you at least a Twelvemonth," he told one correspondent who had sent Franklin the draft of an essay intended to defame an adversary. "Such personal public Attacks are never forgiven."[37] Franklin's business ethic prompted "a Reader" to comment, "Tho' your News-paper is sometimes as empty as those of others, yet I think you have for the most part . . . had the Modesty to keep it pretty clear of SCANDAL, a Subject that others delight to wallow in. These People, probably from some Corruption in themselves, and possibly from their own Stench, seem to think every thing around them tainted."[38]

Motivated by both economics and conscience, Franklin mostly avoided a scurrilous tone in his journalism. Although he could occasionally be moved to editorial vituperation, as in the Hemphill affair, Franklin decided that giving offense to as few as possible was the most pragmatic and profitable approach.[39] It was a lesson he learned while maturing as a printer. During his apprenticeship, Franklin witnessed his master and brother James imprisoned after offending the Massachusetts Assembly. To retaliate, Franklin reprinted

Cato's essay on "Freedom of Speech" and criticized government officials in the *New-England Courant.* However, he found this vengeful conduct disadvantageous, for "others began to consider me in an unfavourable Light, as a young Genius that had a Turn for Libelling & Satyr." Benjamin later emulated his brother's editorial conduct, which became more circumspect after his prison term. During public debates on the controversial plan to inoculate Bostonians against smallpox, James deflected criticism by claiming his newspaper was not a tool of any faction, and that "both Inoculators and Anti-Inoculators are welcome to speak their Minds in it." From these episodes, Benjamin learned which battles were worth fighting. He learned when to stand up, and when he should heed Cotton Mather's admonition to "STOOP."[40]

Throughout his life, Franklin possessed dichotomous views about journalism's social utility. A month after the Treaty of Peace with Great Britain brought to a conclusion that empire's claim on North America, Franklin viewed the press as an integral partner in the Revolution. He told a correspondent that printing was so powerful it could bring down monarchies and foster democracy.[41] However, as party factionalism threatened to rend the new nation that Franklin and others had fashioned, he feared that emerging journalistic tendencies toward scandal and defamation would make the United States appear divided and vulnerable to attack. Seven months before his death, Franklin lamented that press freedom in the infant country had come to mean "the Liberty of affronting, calumniating, and defaming one another." This freedom from restraint during the early years of the republic had corrupted the average printer, who "besides tearing your private character to flitters, marks you out as an *enemy to the liberty of the press.*" Franklin noted ruefully that people who "have not been mended by religion, nor improved by good education," and who delight in seeing others debased sustain such presses.[42]

Franklin disdained printers' penchant for detraction and scurrility at the expense of individual reputations. Having seen a vituperative partisan press assail the character of public figures (including his own) during the formulation and ratification of the Constitution, Franklin complained in 1788 that printers motivated by sensationalism knowingly published false accusations and caused duels. This practice, "so disgraceful to our Country," motivated him to discourage printers from the practice, offering his successful life as an incentive to moral conduct. Discussing how he discouraged many requests to print defamatory writings, Franklin admitted that he made particular mention of his journalistic values in his *Autobiography* to impart his values to printers so that "they may see by my Example" that virtuous conduct has its own reward.[43] Franklin argued that printers need not appeal to the plebeian instincts of the masses in order to thrive. By heeding his calls to hard work, thriftiness, modesty, and prudence, his journalistic heirs would be free to conduct a socially beneficial press while also attaining wealth and prominence. Virtuous conduct was the key element. As Franklin noted, profit without virtue is "not worth a farto."[44]

Franklin was not only unwilling to flay the reputations of others, he was concerned about his own reputation. In the small sphere of early eighteenth-century Philadelphia printing, reputation was more likely to attract or repel trade than any other factor. He had learned this lesson when townsfolk canceled their subscriptions and threatened to boycott the *Pennsylvania Gazette* because of the 1731 advertisement banning Anglican clergy from a ship. Franklin therefore was particularly careful to avoid defamation, for fear it would jeopardize his own reputation in the community. Throughout a seven-week trip to visit his family in Boston, he worried so much about the editorial decisions his workers might make in his absence that upon returning, he printed a blanket apology for "any passages [that] have appeared in the Gazette, that may be construed into Personal Reflection," attributing them 'to the Inadvertence' of his employees."[45] He also reminded his readers to be tolerant of his errors, promising "That whoever accustoms himself to pass over in Silence the Faults of his Neighbours, shall meet with much better Quarter from the World when he happens to fall into a Mistake himself."[46]

Teaching, learning, and promoting moral virtue became integral to Franklin's character and his journalism as he relinquished his flirtation with deism and adopted the Christian ethic of good works. His first plan, devised in 1731, involved the formation of "a united Party for Virtue," in which upright citizens of all nations would band together to promote the public good. The plan was catalyzed by his pessimistic conclusion from reading history that "few in Public Affairs act from a meer View of the Good of their Country," and even fewer "act with a View to the Good of Mankind." Franklin intended to call this organization "The Society of the Free and Easy." It would travel throughout the colonies and abroad, creating private libraries, chartering local chapters, and coalescing "Virtuous Men in all parts, who shall have an universal Correspondence and unite to support and encourage Virtue and Liberty and Knowledge," according to Franklin. The society's members would initially be limited to young unmarried men who would be governed by a theology-based creed recognizing God's providence and emphasizing good works. The "most acceptable Service of God is doing Good to Man," Franklin wrote in the articles of belief. Such benevolence would be ultimately repaid.

"God will certainly reward Virtue and punish Vice either here or hereafter," Franklin asserted.[47]

The proposed society was essentially an outgrowth of the "Junto," the club Franklin founded in 1727 to surround himself with industrious and intelligent people. It met weekly, usually at a tavern, for intellectual stimulation and fellowship, and its members discussed morals, philosophy, and politics in a structured and informed manner, "in the sincere Spirit of Enquiry after Truth, without fondness for Dispute, or Desire of Victory," he recalled. He later described it as "the best School of Philosophy, Morals & Politics that then existed in the Province." The members began each meeting with "Queries" to stimulate discussion, including "Do you know of any deserving young beginner . . . whom it lies in the power of the Junto in any way to encourage?"[48]

Franklin's plan for the society of virtue never came to fruition, causing Franklin to lament late in life that his initial lack of wealth and the demands of his printing affairs caused him to delay its implementation for so long that "I have no longer Strength or Activity left sufficient for such an Enterprize."[49]

Although his absorption in printing affairs compelled Franklin to indefinitely postpone the founding of his international philanthropic fraternity, the barrier to one of his lofty plans of moral instruction proved to be the means by which another was effected. The printing trade offered Franklin a pragmatic—and lucrative—opportunity to communicate virtue to a wide audience through his *Pennsylvania Gazette,* almanac, and other products of his press.

4

Communicating Instruction in Philadelphia

"The Author of a Gazette (in the Opinion of the Learned) ought to be qualified with an extensive Acquaintance with Languages, a great Easiness and Command of Writing and Relating Things clearly and intelligibly, and in a few Words," Franklin wrote in the *Pennsylvania Gazette*'s first issue under his ownership. To hold such a post of public responsibility and importance, the early American printer-editor "should be able to speak of War both by Land and Sea; be well acquainted with Geography, with the history of the Time, with the several Interests of Princes and States, the Secrets of Courts, and the Manners and Customs of all Nations."[1]

While self-deprecatingly noting he was deficient in some of these areas, and thus hopeful his readers would contribute informative essays, Franklin at age twenty-three thought himself sufficiently countenanced in the inaugural statement to assume control of one of only seven newspapers in the American colonies. He knew from the outset his partnership with Hugh Meredith would be an unequal one, with Franklin providing most of the vision, guile, and talent. He was unfazed by this responsibility, though, and in fact had relished the opportunity to control since his youth. He proudly observed in his autobiography, "when in a Boat or Canoe with other Boys I was commonly allow'd to govern, especially in any case of Difficulty; and upon other Occasions I was generally a Leader among the Boys." He viewed the Meredith partnership not as an equal sharing of duties, but as a pragmatic necessity: he had borrowed considerably from Meredith's father Simon to purchase the newspaper and acquire needed supplies. In the bargain, Franklin hoped Hugh Meredith would relieve him of some of the tedious mechanical chores, like composing and typesetting, freeing him to write.[2]

The *Pennsylvania Gazette*'s success and survival depended on Franklin's writing talents. It faced formidable competition from Andrew Bradford's *American Weekly Mercury*. Bradford's newspaper had been in existence for ten years, and he held the colony's printing contracts.[3] Other newspapers were situated in Boston, New York, and Annapolis, and all were widely circulated. In fact, it was this distinct lack of provinciality among the earliest American newspapers that helped make competition keen. Franklin had commenced his journalistic venture only a few years after his brother James ignored friends' admonitions and started the *New-England Courant*. "I remember his being dissuaded by some of his Friends from the Undertaking, as not likely to suc-ceed, one Newspaper being in their Judgment enough for America," Franklin recalled.[4]

Another obstacle to the *Pennsylvania Gazette*'s success was public apathy for early efforts at colonial newspaper journalism, despite high literacy rates. About half of the New England males could read and write in the 1620s, and by 1710, the rate had escalated to seventy percent. Nonetheless, colonial America of the seventeenth and early eighteenth centuries was a predomi-nantly oral culture, with printing used for preserving religious sermons and recording official government acts. Just 325 broadsides were published in Massachusetts between 1639 and 1710—an average of fewer than five per year. The transition from this oral culture to a print one occurred in the early eigh-teenth century through broadside ballads, which recounted individual episodes in verse.[5] Franklin dabbled in this form of reporting while an apprentice. He composed for his brother and master James "two occasional Ballads," one about a drowning and the other about the capture of a notorious pirate, which he described as "wretched Stuff, in the Grubstreet Ballad Stile." Franklin peddled his poetry in the streets of Boston and found that the first "sold wonderfully, the Event being recent, having made a great Noise." Its success "flatter'd my Vanity," Franklin noted, but added with relief that he was dis-couraged from further balladeering by his father, who ridiculed his work and said it would result in poverty and disreputability.[6]

As a vehicle for information and ideas, the early American press got off to a discouraging start, chiefly due to anxiety in seventeenth-century England that it would reduce American subservience to English rule. In 1662, two years after the restoration of the monarchy, Parliament passed another in a series of licensing acts that limited the number of printers and restricted their right and ability to print.[7] Intent on controlling free expression in the colonies,

King Charles II sent commissioners to Massachusetts in 1664 "to remove all jealousies and misunderstandings, which might [adversely affect] the loyalty and affeccon of Our good Subjects in those parts," to counter "insinuacons and representacons of those, whose businesse it is to foment jealousies," and to "disappoint all the designes of such wicked and seditious persons" in the colonies. Such persons, the king told Massachusetts governor John Endecott, "do not submitt to Our government, but looke upon themselves as independant upon Us and Our Laws."[8]

The commissioners interpreted the king's edict to include restrictions on printing and free speech. Endecott viewed these strictures as heavy-handed. Shortly after the commissioners' arrival in his colony, Endecott complained to British chancellor Edward Hyde that their conduct is "altogither inconsistant with the charter & priviledges, which his ma[jes]ty hath been graciously pleased in his severall letters to promise not in the least to violate or infringe," and he sought the commissioners' removal because their presence "doth greatly discourage and trouble his Ma[jes]ties poor Subjetts in this remote corner of the world." Confessing "we were equally amazed to find that you demanded a revocation of the Commission and Commissioners," Hyde retorted that the officials were present to safeguard loyal colonists against seditious speech and writings, and thus, "it will be absolutely necessary that you perform and pay all that sebordnece and obedience w[hi]ch is due from Subjects to their King, and which his Ma[jes]ty will exact from you."[9]

Forty years earlier, the House of Commons had expressed similar concern over the corrupting influence of published opinion. In a petition to the king decrying the spread of Catholicism, the House members ruefully noted that some "ill-affected persons" had "taken the boldness to divulge and disperse sundry popish, seditious, and pestilent Books and Pamphlets throughout all the parts of this your Kingdom." The goal, they feared, was "to corrupt the youth of this realm, to deprave and scandalize the true religion here established, and to advance the power and authority of the see of Rome."[10]

The licensing law remained until 1695, when it was allowed to expire.[11] Another means of restraining and regulating the press involved prosecutions for seditious libel or criminally defaming government and thus lowering it in the public's esteem or breaching public peace. In several extreme examples, writings perceived to suggest the king's death were found treasonable, and their authors or printers punished accordingly. For printing a 1663 tract contending people possessed the right to revolt against bad rulers, John Twyn was sentenced to be hanged, yet cut down while still alive, and then castrated, disemboweled, quartered, and finally beheaded. Algernon Sidney also paid with his life twenty years later when English officials found an unpublished inflammatory writing in his study.[12]

Punishments in America were not so drastic, but they did exist. After reading criticism that they failed to suppress Mohawk Indian raids in Maine, and a report that French King Louis XIV committed incest with his daughter-in-law, Massachusetts authorities suppressed Benjamin Harris's *Publick Occurrences, Both Forreign and Domestick* in 1690 after only one issue for violating licensing edicts.[13] As judge and governor's council member Samuel Sewall recorded in his diary, "A printed sheet entitled publick Occurrences comes out, which gives much distaste because not Licensed; and because of the passage referring to the French King and the Maquas."[14]

Colonial governors received instructions from London "to provide by all necessary orders that no person KEEP any press for printing, NOR that any book, pamphlet, or other matters whatsoever be printed without your especial leave and license first obtained."[15] In Massachusetts, the governor's council delegated this authority to the municipal magistrate, from whom Sewall sought permission to operate a printing press in Boston in 1681. Conceding that Sewall's press could operate "to the accomodation of the Publique," the magistrate approved the request, noting, "none may presume to set up any other Press, without the like liberty first granted."[16]

Licensing mandates were partly responsible for the tardy development of a colonial press, and they thus served to reinforce government authority against the dangers that mass dissemination of information and opinion represented. "I thank God, there are no free-schools, nor printing; and I hope we shall not have, these hundred years," Virginia governor William Berkeley gleefully wrote to his administrative superiors in 1671. "For learning has brought disobedience and heresy, and sects into the world, and printing has divulged them and libels against the best government: God keep us from both!"[17]

The American colonies did not have a lawful and continuously published newspaper until 1704, when postmaster John Campbell's *Boston News-Letter* appeared. He reprinted news from the London press for the benefit of colonists who lacked the English connections to get overseas newspapers. The *News-Letter* was "Printed by Authority," which meant its content was subject to prior approval by the royal government. Campbell also had no desire to be controversial. Referring to himself in the third person, Campbell stated his editorial policy had "always been to give no offence, not meddling with things out of his Province."[18] As such, the paper contained little that was seditious or controversial. This pleased authorities, but bored the public.

Circulation rarely exceeded three hundred, despite the *News-Letter*'s fifteen-year newspaper monopoly on the continent and Campbell's use of his post-mastership privilege to mail his paper free to distant regions. Many of Campbell's readers failed to pay, prompting him to complain of his debts even though he provided his "Labour for nothing."[19]

However, as colonial society made the transition from an oral to literate culture, the public warmed to the notion of a domestic press and welcomed newspapers into other cities, although continuing to view their purpose more as collectors and distributors of European news than American news. This underscored colonists' self-perception as English subjects, comparatively disinterested in the events of other North American communities. Campbell's newspaper was the only one on the continent until 1719, when new postmaster William Brooker commenced the rival *Boston Gazette* and Andrew Bradford established the *American Weekly Mercury* in Philadelphia. Several other newspapers sprang up in Boston as well. In fact, it was about 1720 that journalism blossomed on both sides of the Atlantic, due in part to an increased availability of type.[20] But with the exception of James Franklin's paper, which was sometimes rebellious, the earliest newspapers were lackluster and subservient, bowing to official pressure despite repeal of the licensing law in 1695.[21]

Early printers clearly understood royal power to silence or intimidate printers. In addition to suppressing Harris, government officials jailed and fined James Franklin and repeatedly subjected Andrew Bradford's father, William, to government prosecutions, first for violating the licensing law and later for seditious libel. Even after licensing's demise, authorities could regulate the press via threats of jail and fines for seditious libel, as well as their power to award government printing contracts, a vital source of income for early American printers.[22]

Under these prudential constraints, expansion of early colonial printing was slow and uncertain. The press growth that did occur transpired within family networks. These, coupled with the apprenticeship system, formed the foundation of the printing trade at the time. The most prominent of the "family dynasties" was the Green family, which stemmed from Samuel Green, who operated a printing press in Cambridge, Massachusetts, as early as 1649. His descendants who carried on the trade were numerous and prominent in American printing during the seventeenth and eighteenth centuries. As his great-grandson Timothy Green recalled, Samuel "had a numerous Family—his sons Samuel, Bartholemew, and Timothy set up the same business in Boston; but my Grandfather who was his youngest Son, removed to New London, in the Year 1714, if I mistake not."[23]

Within the Green clan and other printing families, sons and nephews received printing apprenticeships and journeyman posts, and later, their own shops. They went on to contract strategic marriages to make allies of rivals and perpetuate the family business. Other notable printing families in early America included the Fowles, the Kneelands, the Sauers, and the Bradfords.[24]

The social and political environment in the early eighteenth century was not conducive to rapid press growth, and prospects seemed gloomy for Franklin, a runaway apprentice whose debut had been orchestrated neither within a family network nor under the aegis of a powerful government official. Amid these unfavorable circumstances Franklin and Meredith commenced their newspaper in 1729, inheriting Keimer's paltry circulation. One reason Keimer's newspaper met with such a cool public reception lay in the attitude reflected by the first portion of its title: *The Universal Instructor in all Arts and Sciences.* Keimer used his newspaper to play the sage, imparting knowledge and wisdom to the callow masses. The partners believed such an overt focus on instruction, which Franklin observed was part of Keimer's character, was misguided. Franklin wanted to educate and inform his readership—but his newspaper experience taught him to do it more subtly, emphasizing recent events. Accordingly, Franklin and Meredith changed the name to the *Pennsylvania Gazette,* a title more evocative of recording events than educating the ignorant.[25]

The partners also replaced Keimer's serialization of an encyclopedia (his last eleven issues had devoted more than half their editorial content to the subject of "air") with news. Most of the *Pennsylvania Gazette's* content dealt chiefly with Western European affairs, thereby providing readers access to much of the same news contained in the London press, but it also included many local items. Franklin and Meredith published stories reprinted from other newspapers, and news events they personally witnessed or learned about by engaging in rudimentary reporting. They also relied on correspondence from others, a common newspaper practice of the time. Bartholemew Green advertised for correspondents in 1723, announcing that "he Desires of all Ingenious Gentlemen, in every part of the Country, to communicate the Remarkable Things they observe; and he Desires them to send their Accounts Post-Free, and nothing but what they assuredly know; and they shall be very gratefully Receiv'd and Publish'd." Franklin and Meredith likewise utilized correspondents to augment their editorial content, inviting "Gentlemen who are able" to contribute essays.[26]

Their increased dissemination of local news, which served to unite members of a society under the umbrella of shared interests and shared identity, suggests Franklin and Meredith were clearly endeavoring to ingratiate themselves with their principal audience—Pennsylvanians. Their reports were chiefly secular, reflecting Franklin's religious inclinations at the time; mercantile, acknowledging the vocational composition of much of their readership; and event-oriented, rather than analytical or historical.

Indeed, the partners claimed their newspaper contained "the Freshest Advices Foreign and Domestick," an advertising claim made by other printers of the era. This, of course, was relative. The fastest transmission of information from England to the American colonies in the early eighteenth century, under optimum sailing conditions, took about seven weeks. More often, European news was about three months old by the time it reached American readers.[27]

In addition to local news, the *Pennsylvania Gazette* revealed the commodity prices and ship schedules vital to its commercial readership. Much of the other information was gleaned from newspapers in London or Boston, or from ship captains interviewed along the wharf, especially those who had just arrived from Europe. This constituted another bond between British and American citizenry. Ship captains, and in turn newspapers, served as communication links between parent and offspring, emphasizing the dependence of the latter on the former. Concomitantly, this underscored the subservience of the American press to that of the British.[28]

However, Franklin and Meredith sometimes found that the arrival of news from London or Boston was sporadic. The primitive news-gathering apparati of colonial printers depended largely on transportation and chance. Faced with deadlines and too few of the "Freshest Advices," Franklin sometimes filled the space himself, adhering to his own admonition that good writing should be "smooth, clear and short." He commonly used pseudonyms, both to mask his own identity and hide his dearth of correspondents, as he wrote fictitious letters to the editor or spun yarns with a message. He was undaunted by the task, having developed in youth a "Stock of Words or a Readiness in recollecting & using them" and a "Method in the Arrangement of Thoughts" by emulating the writing style of Joseph Addison and Richard Steele in the *Spectator*.[29]

Franklin's engaging prose widened the appeal of his fledgling weekly. To build readership while imparting virtuous teachings, Franklin regularly crafted moral essays carefully ensconced in satire and farce, and pragmatic instruction designed to appeal to the universal quest for wealth. Franklin made sport of Philadelphia frivolities, to the gratification of his growing audience, while showing the way to wealth and felicity through virtue.

In his writings, Franklin emphasized that virtue took many forms, ranging

from "a prudent management of ourselves in Affairs and Conversation" to comforting the ill; from exhibiting industry by working long hours to promptly
repaying creditors. However, Franklin knew that performance of good works
for the exclusive benefit of others would attract few readers to upright conduct. Thus, to further encourage good deeds, Franklin emphasized the rewards they might expect, noting it was in people's "Interest to be virtuous,"
for the most likely qualities to yield a fortune were "Probity & Integrity." The
dividend for honesty was freedom from the fear of contradicting oneself and
being discovered as a liar; for industry, it was the acquisition of esteem, and
thus greater trade, in the community. In recompense for diligent repayment
of debts, one "may at any Time, and on any Occasion, raise all the Money his
Friends can spare. This is sometimes of great Use." Concluding an essay on
comforting the sick, Franklin wrote, "If the Considerations of Religion and
Humanity have not the Effect they ought to have on the Minds of some,
perhaps this Observation, which generally holds true, may have its weight
with the Self-interested, That there are no Kindnesses done by one Man to
another, which are remembered so long, and so frequently return'd with
Gratitude, as those received in Sickness."[30]

Among his most popular writings were hoaxes and satires.[31] Many were
designed to communicate moral lessons or to ridicule certain disdainful behavior, but in a manner more likely to find an audience, and prove memorable to it, than prudish exegeses. He ridiculed Puritan mystical beliefs in "A
Witch Trial at Mount Holly," with accused witches tossed into a pond with
hands and feet bound to see if they floated, which they did. "The more thinking Part of the Spectators were of the Opinion, that any Person so bound and
plac'd in the Water (unless they were mere Skin and Bones) would swim till
their Breath was gone, and their Lungs fill'd with Water," Franklin commented. In another he lampooned physical beauty, noting that the lone flaw
of "the prettiest Creature in this Place" was conceit. The following week, he
concocted reader replies. "Since your last Week's Paper I have look'd in my
Glass a thousand Times, I believe, in one Day," one responded, "and if it was
not for the Charge of Affectation I might, without Partiality, believe myself
the Person meant."[32]

Franklin's intent was to show readers the error of imprudent conduct.
However, he understood that "the Mob hate instruction," particularly "Lectures . . . fill'd with nothing but wholesome Precepts and Advice," and that
his guidance would be most successful if he could "humour them in their
own Way." This included farce, a device he recognized could "induce many to
read me through." Accordingly, his hoaxes and satires succeeded because he

made their characters seem absurd. Satirizing censure, Franklin had Alice Addertongue, "a young Girl of about thirty-five," continually find fault in others because of her childhood "Inclination to be ever talking in my own Praise."[33]

Two Franklin contemporaries took opposing stances on this practice. Historian Samuel Miller wrote in 1803 that fictitious accounts are "one of the most powerful means of exciting curiosity, of awakening sympathy, and of impressing the understanding and the heart." Perhaps thinking of Franklin, Miller noted that "some of the wisest human teachers have used the vehicle of lively and interesting fiction, known to be such at the time, for insinuating into the mind moral and religious lessons, which, in a different form, might not so readily have gained admittance." Conversely, Thomas Jefferson complained of the effects of fictive prose on a susceptible public. "When this poison infects the mind, it destroys its tone and revolts it against wholesome reading. Reason and fact, plain and unadorned, are rejected. Nothing can engage attention unless dressed in all the figments of fancy, and nothing so bedecked comes amiss. The result is a bloated imagination, sickly judgment, and disgust towards all the real businesses of life."[34]

Paradoxically, it was these ailments of the human character Franklin sought to overcome with his literary concoctions. He was seldom optimistic regarding his success, though, viewing people "to be a Sort of Beings very badly constructed, as they are generally more easily provok'd than reconcil'd, more disposed to do Mischief to each other than to make Reparation, [and] much more easily deceiv'd than undeceiv'd."[35]

Although they entertained and instructed readers, Franklin's literary contrivances betrayed his private view of humanity as vain and avaricious. In another of his hoaxes, "The Speech of Miss Polly Baker," he has a strumpet deliver a humorous but wildly improbable courtroom speech justifying fornication and the production of illegitimate children. Her syllogistic reasoning, dogged defense of a preposterous position, and ultimate vanity are amusing, yet subtly skeptical. Amid the absurdity of his hoaxes lurks Franklin's cynicism—his belief that, although the characters Polly Baker, Alice Addertongue, and the Mount Holly accusers are caricatures drawn with bold strokes, between the lines exist dark shadows of accuracy about human nature.[36]

Despite his skeptical view of humanity, Franklin commenced another publication of instruction in 1733, his annual *Poor Richard's Almanack*. Almanacs were widely read, particularly by the middle and lower classes, which comprised the people Franklin most desired to reach with his message of virtue. Part of the allure of almanacs, which dated to the sixteenth century, was their turbulent contents. English almanacs had been fractious and bawdy publications that included the controversial use of astrology charts to make predictions, although this practice was discouraged in Puritan New England. It was ironic that Franklin, the rational scientist, would dally with such hokum as stargazing, but he used the literary genre to burlesque the form. For instance, in 1739 "Poor Richard" answered the "Ignorant Men [who] wonder how we Astrologers foretell the Weather so exactly, unless we deal with the old black Devil." He replied that forecasts of wind and thunder are possible by peering "at the Heavens thro' a long Glass" and seeing Taurus stamping and bellowing. April showers are predicted by seeing Virgo "crouching down gently, with her Hands on her Knees."[37]

Franklin sought to use the public affinity for almanacs as another avenue for spreading his message. He self-deprecatingly asked the indulgence of his readership for "scattering here and there some instructive Hints in matters of Morality and Religion" amid the entertainment, for "the Vain Youth that reads my Almanack for the sake of an idle Joke, will perhaps meet with a serious Reflection, that he may ever after be the better for."[38] Intending to make his almanac serve "as a proper Vehicle for conveying Instruction among the common People, who bought scarce any other Books," Franklin acknowledged that he "endeavor'd to make it both entertaining and useful" by filling it with "Proverbial Sentences, chiefly such as inculcated Industry and Frugality, as the Means of procuring Wealth and thereby securing Virtue, it being more difficult for a Man in Want to act always honestly."[39]

Franklin edited and wrote the almanac for twenty-eight years, enjoying sales of ten thousand or more for each edition. He filled his annual with pithy, clever statements of common sense. They clearly support Franklin's efforts to educate the masses to live virtuously and strive for moral improvement—activities Franklin regarded as primarily solitary.

"Poor Richard's" epigrams exhorted readers to various types of virtue. They included "Eat to live, and not live to eat," "The worst wheel of the cart makes the most noise," and "Seek Virtue, and of that possest, To Providence, resign the rest."[40] To his gratification, Franklin observed that the almanac "was generally read, scarce any Neighbourhood in the Province being without it." Despite its extensive circulation, he was not always convinced of its success, complaining that although "Virtue is really the true Interest of all Men," and that "the SCIENCE OF VIRTUE is of more worth" than any other form of knowledge, people may choose to remain ignorant and selfish despite abundant opportunities for moral instruction.[41]

Franklin designed his aphorisms to achieve his ideological ends and fulfill his promise to the public that his writings would be "as agreeable and useful an Entertainment as the Nature of the Thing will allow." Indeed, he suggested in the *Pennsylvania Gazette* that the only submissions he desired from his readers were those conveying knowledge or promoting virtue.[42]

By offering such heterogeneous literary content, Franklin and his journalism appealed to diverse audiences—Christians, who viewed many of his writings as supplementing the exhortations of their church leaders; merchants, who applauded his pragmatic advice for business success; politicians, who were seldom made uneasy by seditious antigovernment screeds from his pen; and all who enjoyed the jocular wit, graceful yet accessible style, and utilitarian message.

Franklin's efforts to spread moral instruction were not new. Printers of newspapers, books, almanacs, and ballads in sixteenth- and seventeenth-century England trafficked in religious and behavioral admonitions. The products of their presses were implicit guides to earning God's graces, which could manifest themselves as wealth, possessions, and power. This Puritan conception of divine providence dated to the sixteenth century, and it influenced early American journalism, including Franklin's.[43]

To enhance his reputation in Philadelphia and offset the bad impression Meredith's drinking and carousing were giving the firm, Franklin made sure he was seen working late in the shop and toting supplies through the city streets. "In order to secure my Credit and Character as a Tradesmen, I took care not only to be in *reality* Industrious & frugal, but to avoid all *Appearances* of the Contrary," he wrote in his memoirs. His strategy paid off. Civic leaders saw a newspaper in the hands of a conscientious, prudent, and hardworking young man who could wield a pen with wit and style—an important attribute in an era of transition from an oral to a literate culture.[44]

During the first year of their partnership, Franklin decided Meredith was dead weight. He found Meredith's presswork and composing skills inferior and his sobriety infrequent. Some of his allies agreed. "My friends lamented my Connection with him," he recalled. When Meredith's father Simon was unable to advance enough money to cover the loans on the printing house, two of Franklin's friends, William Coleman and Robert Grace, agreed to loan him the requisite sum, provided Franklin sever his partnership with Meredith, whom the financiers "had often seen drunk in the Streets, & playing at low Games in Alehouses, much to our Discredit," Franklin wrote.[45]

Franklin offered Meredith ownership of the shop, but he declined, confessing to Franklin that printing "is a Business I am not fit for." Meredith announced his plan to buy North Carolina farmland and volunteered to quit the partnership if Franklin would repay Simon Meredith, cover Meredith's personal debts (which may have included gambling losses), and give him thirty pounds and a saddle. Franklin and Meredith thus amicably dissolved their partnership in 1730, with Franklin buying out Meredith's share and consequently plunging into debt. Meredith later wrote a lengthy description of the North Carolina soil and climate for *Pennsylvania Gazette* readers and served as a book distributor for Franklin, but he may have failed to remit the money he collected, according to Franklin's business records.[46]

Meredith's departure left Franklin seeking assistance for his burgeoning business. He offered a partnership to David Harry, a former Keimer apprentice, partly as a tactical move. "I was at first apprehensive of a powerful Rival in Harry, as his Friends were very able, & he had a good deal of Interest," Franklin remembered. However, Harry "rejected with Scorn" any thoughts of alliance and set up on his own, which Franklin later regarded as fortunate. Harry's lavish lifestyle and poor financial management soon thereafter compelled him to relocate to Barbados, where he hired as an employee the two men's former master, Samuel Keimer.[47]

Franklin was on his own at twenty-four years old, after being disappointed by his first partnership and jilted in his efforts to forge a second one. Saddled with substantial debt, he was for the first time forced to accept the full responsibility of a master printer. He had no choice but to risk everything on his business, trusting that diligence and acumen would eventually provide ample rewards. Or, as he imparted to almanac readers, "Keep thy shop, and thy shop will keep thee."[48] One of his most important decisions was to surround himself with people he trusted. He engaged Thomas Whitmarsh, whom he had known during his London printing days, as a journeyman, and Joseph Rose, the son of Andrew Bradford's former employee Aquila Rose, as an apprentice. Aquila Rose was "an ingenious young Man of excellent Character much respected in the Town, Clerk of the Assembly, & a pretty Poet," Franklin recalled. Aquila's early death in 1723 created the vacancy in Andrew Bradford's shop that drew Franklin from New York to Philadelphia.[49]

Another key to Franklin's success as sole proprietor of the printing shop was his wife Deborah, who "prov'd a good & faithful Helpmate [and] assisted me much by attending the Shop," Franklin wrote in his memoirs. As a result, "we throve together, and have ever mutually endeavour'd to make each other happy."[50] Their common-law marriage was occasioned as much by Franklin's pity for her and his guilt after leaving her in Philadelphia while he sought his fortune in England as it was by love. Indeed, the Franklins seemed a peculiar pairing—she never shared his literary skills, social pursuits, and intellectual inclinations; he was content to be absent from her on government business for years at a time, including fifteen of the last eighteen years of her life. Nonetheless, Franklin gave her a share of the credit for his accomplishments because she exhibited the work ethic he expected of himself and admired in others. More importantly, Deborah freed him from many domestic duties and aided him in the daily cares of his printing business, enabling him to become politically active and create his printing network. He admitted he was fortunate to have a wife "as much dispos'd to Industry & Frugality as my self. She assisted me chearfully in my Business, folding & stitching Pamphlets, tending Shop, purchasing old Linen Rags for the Paper-Makers, &c &c."[51]

Although of starkly disparate intellectual capacities, Franklin often sought Deborah's judgment on personal and business affairs because her intuition was sometimes superior to his logic. "All inferior Animals, put together, do not commit as many mistakes in the course of a Year as a single Man within a Month, even though this Man pretends he is guided by Reason," he wrote to a friend after Deborah's death. "This is why, as long as I was Fortunate enough to have a Wife, I had adopted the habit of letting myself be guided by her opinion on difficult Matters, for Women, I believe, have a certain feel, especially of Tact, that is better than our Reasonings."[52]

Characteristically, Franklin found the greatest virtue in the pragmatic aspects of marriage, rather than the romantic ones. He delighted in learning of weddings, for "I love to hear of every thing that tends to increase the Number of good People," he wrote to Deborah.[53] Women, Franklin thought, were particularly adept at saving money. "I and thousands more know very well that we could never thrive till we were married," he wrote in a 1735 newspaper essay. "What we get, the Women save." Nearly fifty years later, his opinion was unchanged. "Frugality is an enriching Virtue," he told a correspondent, "a Virtue I never could acquire in my self: but I was once lucky enough to find it in a Wife, who thereby became a Fortune to me."[54]

Franklin regarded marriage as the most useful and natural state of human affairs. "The married State is, after all our Jokes, the happiest, being conformable to our Natures," he wrote to London merchant John Sargent. "Man & Woman have each of them Qualities & Tempers, in which the other is deficient, and which in Union contribute to the common Felicity." To London brewer Thomas Jordan, Franklin wrote, "wedlock is the natural state of man. A bachelor is not a complete human being. He is like the odd half of a pair of scissors, which has not yet found its fellow, and therefore is not even half so useful as they might be together."[55]

Outside the home and shop, Franklin found friendship, intellectual stimulation, and business alliances amid the Junto, a club of young tradesmen he established for social and cerebral pursuits. Through his contacts in the Junto, his circle of contacts with prominent people widened as his printing business thrived. Franklin recalled in his autobiography that "the leading Men, seeing a News Paper now in the hands of one who could also handle a Pen, thought it convenient to oblige & encourage me" with subscriptions to the *Pennsylvania Gazette* and assorted printing jobs. This augmented trade "was one of the first good Effects of my having learnt a little to scribble," Franklin noted modestly.[56]

Franklin's writing skills helped him be named printer to the New Jersey Assembly. While in Burlington seeking the appointment, several legislators asked him to draft a response to a bitter diatribe against the Assembly written by Governor Lewis Morris. As Founding Father John Jay recalled the story Franklin told him, "tho they were Men of good understanding and respectable, yet there was not one among them capable of writing a proper answer to the Message." Franklin agreed, composed a witty retort, and "In Consideration of the Aid he gave them in that way and afterwards, they made him their Printer."[57] Franklin benefited again from his literary skills by writing a pamphlet advocating the adoption of a paper currency, a measure that eventually passed the Pennsylvania Assembly. As a result, "My Friends there, who conceiv'd I had been of Service, thought fit to reward me, by employing me in printing the Money, a very profitable Jobb, and a great Help to me." This, he recalled, "was another Advantage gain'd by my being able to write."[58]

To further ingratiate himself with "the principal People" in Pennsylvania and snatch a lucrative contract from rival Andrew Bradford, Franklin brazenly reprinted "elegantly & correctly" an address from the Pennsylvania Assembly to the governor, which Bradford had previously published "in a coarse blundering manner," Franklin claimed, and sent a copy to each legislator. Franklin was subsequently named printer for the Assembly the following year. Bradford retaliated with a series of essays vilifying Assembly speaker Andrew Hamilton, who had helped Franklin secure the public printing. This elicited a counterattack from the *Pennsylvania Gazette*. These episodes fueled a bitter rivalry between the two men, the genesis of which preceded Franklin's assumption of the *Pennsylvania Gazette*'s reins. While Franklin was writing his "Busy-Body" series for Bradford's *American Weekly Mercury*, Bradford suppressed an installment of it supporting the adoption of paper currency, viewing it as seditious.[59]

Thus, although Bradford had helped Franklin become established in Philadelphia, and even lodged him in his home, they became ardent adversaries. After Bradford secured the Philadelphia postmastership in 1728 and set up the post office in his home, he used the mail carriers to distribute his newspaper free of charge. However, he refused to permit Franklin's newspaper access to the mails. To distribute the *Pennsylvania Gazette* outside the city, Franklin was forced to bribe the post riders. This ended in 1737, when Deputy Postmaster General Alexander Spotswood, annoyed that Bradford

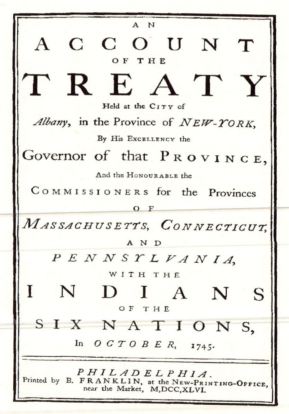

Example of Franklin's Publications

In addition to his Pennsylvania Gazette *and his* Poor Richard's Almanack, *Franklin periodically published pamphlets on his Philadelphia press. An important 1745 publication set forth terms of the treaty between colonists and the Indians of the Six Nations.*

had neglected to provide financial records, appointed Franklin to replace Bradford as postmaster. The change induced the two printers to fire a volley of published accusations at each other.[60]

The rivals also published competing almanacs and raced to issue the first American magazine. Bradford's *American Magazine* was first issued February 13, 1741, beating Franklin's *General Magazine* by three days. Embittered, Franklin ridiculed Bradford's publication by mocking his opponent's manner of speech. Both publications died in infancy, with Bradford's entry lasting only three months and Franklin's just six. Decades later, Franklin retained his animus toward Bradford, remembering him in 1771 as "very illiterate" and "poorly qualified."[61]

By the early 1730s, Franklin had become one of the stars in the constellation of Philadelphia commerce. His mode of ascendancy had been his printing press, which allowed him to be at the vortex of public opinion. Via his printing shop he formed his early allegiances with the powerful of Philadelphia and disseminated his ideology of virtue to Philadelphians and other readers in the middle colonies.

The establishment of his almanac and magazine demonstrates Franklin's recognition that people receive information from a variety of sources, including books, magazines, newspapers, pamphlets, signs, letters, and oral discourse. Thus, he sought to improve his own deficiencies, such as his ability to orally converse and persuade, to better extend his influence and communication of moral instruction through multiple channels.[62]

Although his business was thriving, his notoriety was growing, and his brand of journalism was being warmly received, his audience was still primarily provincial. In the years that followed, Franklin came to embrace the idea of expanding his power to communicate not only across media but also across geography. Accordingly, he crafted a means by which to extend the reach of his message while encouraging the growth of his trade—his printing network.

5

Spreading Virtue to South Carolina

Although he owed much of his wealth, fame, and influence to his printing career, Benjamin Franklin was sometimes critical of journalism's deleterious influence upon society. He recognized that while the demise of licensing laws enhanced colonists' liberty of discussion and the free flow of information, it also allowed for greater frequency and severity of personal defamation. While eighteenth-century Americans were reaping the benefits of knowledge that printing afforded, they were also developing a taste for scurrility and scandal.[1]

Early in his printing career, Franklin recognized both the blessings and dangers of a free press that could assail individuals' reputations. To convey the two sides, he invented an amusing hoax expressing the beneficial and detrimental sides of personal condemnation. In a 1732 essay on "Censure or Backbiting," he observed that public scrutiny "is frequently the Means of preventing powerful, politick, ill-designing Men, from growing too popular for the Safety of a State." He suggested to his readers that censure, "with her hundred Eyes and her thousand Tongues," is "a bright, shining, solid Virtue," for it "greatly assists our otherwise weak Resolutions of living virtuously."[2] Franklin had learned this lesson while apprenticed to his brother James on the *New-England Courant,* and he put it into practice after the Massachusetts assembly imprisoned his brother James for insinuating the government was lax in its pursuit of coastal pirates. "During my Brother's Confinement," Franklin recalled in his *Autobiography,* "I had the Management of the Paper, and I made bold to give our Rulers some Rubs."[3]

Despite his talent for censure, Franklin did not believe all criticism was

beneficial. He felt compelled to instruct his readers on the difference between character assassination and surveillance of public officials' conduct.
Having learned that the most effective way to instruct the populace was to
coat the lessons with humor, he created a loutish character to personify pur-
veyors of defamation. His invention, the preposterous and prating "Alice
Addertongue," responded to the "Censure or Backbiting" essay in the *Pennsylvania Gazette*'s next issue. She applauded "last Week's Paper upon
SCANDAL" as sanctioning slander. Alice claimed it was her "Duty as well
as inclination, to exercise my Talent at CENSURE, for the Good of my
Country folks," and offered to share her stock of gossip with the printer, including tales of "drub'd Wives" and "Henpeck'd Husbands." She advised, "I
have long thought that if you would make your Paper a Vehicle of Scandal,
you would double the Number of your Subscribers."[4]

Franklin's enthusiasm for journalism's influence on society waxed and waned
throughout his life, depending to some extent on whether its conductors
sought to garrote or laud his reputation. Learning from his sister that some
Boston newspapers had published flattering articles about him, Franklin expressed his gratitude, but he used the opportunity to share a truism about
public life. "On the other hand, some of our papers here are endeavouring to
disgrace me," Franklin wrote from Philadelphia. "I have long been accustomed to receive more blame, as well as more praise, than I have deserved. It
is the lot of every public man, and I leave one account to balance the other."[5]

His perception of the press also depended on whether he viewed it as serving noble ends or selfish ambition. As early as 1723, he complained that journalism was failing to enlighten. "Long has the Press groaned in bringing forth
an hateful, but numerous Brood of Party Pamphlets, malicious Scribbles, and
Billingsgate Ribaldry," the seventeen-year-old informed *New-England Courant*
readers. "The Rancour and bitterness it has unhappily infused into Mens
minds, and to what a Degree it has sowred and leaven'd the Tempers of Persons
formerly esteemed some of the most sweet and affable, is too well known
here, to need any further Proof or Representation of the Matter."[6] Nearly
two-thirds of a century later, he decried the "personal accusation, detraction,
and calumny" in the press, lamenting that it contains "party heat" and "violent personal abuse."[7] However, Franklin was adept at employing "malicious
Scribbles" when he felt it was necessary, such as to skewer rival printers like
Samuel Keimer and Andrew Bradford, who he felt had mistreated him, or to
seek revenge on the colonial authorities who had imprisoned his brother
James. These were exceptions, though, made when his passions overruled his
conscience.

Not only did Franklin deplore journalism's penchant for scurrility, he lamented that it crowded out much moral instruction for the masses. Since childhood, Franklin had benefited from just such instruction, which helped form his own character and contribute to his successes. At age four, he received a poem from his father, admonishing him that "In vertue, Learning, Wisdome progress make; Nere shrink at suffering for thy saviours sake; Fraud and all Falshood in thy Dealings Flee; Religious always in thy station be." Several years later, he read Cotton Mather's *Essays to Do Good,* which helped stimulate his desire to serve and enlighten others.[8]

Franklin decided he could best accomplish his mission by making moral instruction accessible to the multitudes, and thereby encouraging them to do good. Franklin expressed this view in an essay on the art of composition, suggesting that since "mutual Improvement seems to be the Duty of all Lovers of Writing," the best way to educate the lower classes was to keep writing simple. "The Fondness of some Writers for such Words as carry with them an Air of Learning, renders them unintelligible to more than half their Countrymen," he cautioned aspiring authors. "If a Man would that his Writings have an Effect on the Generality of Readers, he . . . would use no Word in his Works that was not well understood by his Cook-Maid."[9]

His own early writings sometimes did not emulate his advice about word choice, but they demonstrated Franklin's desire to impart virtuous teachings to a mass audience. Five weeks after his common-law marriage, Franklin instructed his readers on matrimonial felicity, cautioning them to be faithful, frugal, respectful, and cheerful, to endure amid ordeals, and to avoid any "Inclination to play the Tyrant." As "The Busy-Body," he penned a lofty essay advising, "*there was never yet a truly Great Man that was not at the same Time truly Virtuous.*" He opined that the virtuous person was likely "to be just in his Dealings, to be Temperate in his Pleasures, to support himself with Fortitude under his Misfortunes, to behave with Prudence in all Affairs and in every Circumstance of Life." As "Poor Richard," he exclaimed, "The excellency of hogs is fatness, of men virtue."[10]

Other journalistic efforts were subtler but nonetheless indicated his intent to promote virtue. After reporting in 1730 that "much Thieving" had occurred at a fire and chastising city fathers for the lack of "good Engines and other suitable Instruments" to combat it, Franklin extolled meritorious actions in order to tacitly encourage noble conduct. Thus, a 1735 fire was extinguished "by the extraordinary Diligence and Activity of the People," and a blaze the following year was "suppress'd beyond Expectation" by "the Diligence, Courage and Resolution of some active Men." In suppressing that fire, the

"Engines did great Service," Franklin conspicuously noted.[11] His "Pennsylvanus" observed that heroic actions such as the "saving of Goods surrounded with Fire, and rending off flaming Shingles" are not performed "for Sake of Reward or Money or Fame" but out of concern for others.[12]

These early efforts to foster virtue were merely harbingers for Franklin's more extensive exertions. Finally secure in his business, he warmed to the task of advancing his moral cause. The young and ambitious Franklin began to think on a larger scale, taking a more active role in promoting moral rectitude by spreading his ideology of virtue to other parts of colonial America. He chose to accomplish this through the press. Printing offered Franklin a pragmatic—and potentially lucrative—opportunity to communicate virtue to a wider audience than readers of his *Pennsylvania Gazette.*

Although Franklin was periodically vexed by journalism's potential to wound reputations, he always respected its power to persuade. Thus, he sought to harness that power for noble intentions. Franklin believed that if instructive writings could inspire moral rectitude on an individual level through the persuasive nature of journalism, then the wider their distribution and the more frequent their appearance, the more salutary an effect they would likely have on public virtue. As Franklin informed a reader in 1732, "the oftner you are told a good Thing, the more likely you will be to remember it."[13]

Therefore, when Franklin encountered a call from the South Carolina Assembly seeking the establishment of a printing press, he reasoned that he could promote virtue while simultaneously augmenting his wealth and aiding a faithful worker in his Philadelphia shop. His choice was Thomas Whitmarsh.

Franklin learned to trust and respect Whitmarsh while working with him in London. He sent for him to fill the void left after Franklin bought out erstwhile partner Hugh Meredith's interest in the printing business in 1730. Franklin admired Whitmarsh's work habits, which seemed so much like his own and so different from the many London pressmen with whom he had worked. He described his employee as "an excellent Workman" who labored "constantly & diligently," quickly enabling Franklin to repay much of the debt he had assumed to free himself from the lackadaisical Meredith. Whitmarsh was also a capable accountant, helping Franklin keep the ledgers of the printing business.[14]

Despite the obvious economic value of Whitmarsh remaining in Philadelphia, Franklin decided the following year to send his compositor to South Carolina. "I sent one of my Journeymen . . . where a Printer was wanting," he recalled offhandedly in his *Autobiography,* but his motivation was more complex than he allowed. Although recognizing the move as a gamble, Franklin envisioned the southernmost colonies, with Charles Town as their pith, as a new frontier for the spread of domestic journalism and moral education. Sending a trusted associate to the region would enable Franklin to register both altruistic and financial successes. Accordingly, he and Whitmarsh formed a partnership on September 13, 1731, requiring Whitmarsh to set up a shop in Charles Town, use equipment provided by Franklin, share the cost of materials with Franklin, and give him one-third of the profits. The arrangement was slated for six years.[15]

Franklin's decision to send Whitmarsh in answer to the South Carolina Assembly's solicitation for a printer offered no guarantee Whitmarsh would be the government's choice, but it was too intriguing a prospect to ignore. Besides, South Carolina seemed a fertile field in which to plant seeds of moral instruction.

The rich soil and hospitable climate that made the Carolinas one of the foremost agricultural regions in British America also caused the region to develop more slowly than northern seaports such as New York, Boston, Newport, and Philadelphia. The fact that it took years to grow and cultivate staple crops discouraged some settlers. Among those who endured, their propensity for large farms impeded the growth of populous communities. The development of a stable population base was further impeded because English settlement of the region did not occur until the late seventeenth century. The Carolinas also lagged behind the northern ports in receiving information, because it took between nine and eleven weeks to sail direct from London to Charles Town—several weeks longer than the voyage from London to Boston or New York. These disadvantages may have prompted printers to ignore the South Carolina legislature's earlier calls for the establishment of a regional press. In 1712 and again from 1722 to 1724, agents for the Assembly attempted to lure British printers to Charles Town, promising the financial boon of the government's printing contract. These efforts failed.[16]

However, the economic climate in South Carolina improved dramatically within the next decade. In September 1730 the British government removed a restriction forbidding the colony to export rice anywhere other than Great Britain. This opened up vast new markets for landholding Carolinians. Low-country planters hastily acquired more land and slaves, and the optimistic financial prospects for the region encouraged immigration. The population of Charles Town jumped from 3,500 in 1720 to 4,500 a decade later, and then to 6,800 by 1742.[17] "Carolina abounds with provisions," an anonymous writer claimed in 1732, and "men to instruct in the seasons & nature of cultivating the soil."[18]

Shipping to and from South Carolina had increased dramatically during the same period. At least one ship arrived per week in Charles Town from the northern colonies or the British West Indies, and about one per month from European ports. These vessels usually left laden with rice, particularly during the northern winter months. All that remained to make Charles Town a major social and economic center was mass communication. The products of a printing press would unify the populace and provide the business information that South Carolina's leading citizens needed to compete in the world marketplace. Thus, in 1730 the colony made another attempt to entice a printer, this time issuing the appeal to the printers themselves, particularly in the American colonies. The government promised the printing contract and a bounty of one thousand pounds provincial currency. This was ample inducement for Franklin and Whitmarsh.[19]

The Whitmarsh affiliation was the first in a series of partnerships Franklin formed during the eighteenth century. He solidified them with detailed contracts written in dense, precise legal language. Franklin recalled that his success in forming partnerships was "owing I think a good deal to the Precaution of having very explicitly settled in our Articles every thing to be done by or expected from each Partner, so that there was nothing to dispute." He recommended this method to others, suggesting that "whatever Esteem partners may have for & Confidence in each other at the time of the Contract, little Jealousies and Disgusts may arise, with Ideas of Inequality in the Care & Burthen of the Business, &c. which are attended often with Breach of Friendship & of the Connection, perhaps with Lawsuits and other disagreable Consequences."[20]

More subtly, the terms of the agreement also created a dependent relationship, because the fact that Whitmarsh was contractually bound to print only with Franklin's equipment effectively prevented his own expansion. Thus, Franklin had not only extended his influence to the South but also controlled Whitmarsh. Franklin had created the first strand in what was to become the web of his printing network.

Whitmarsh departed for South Carolina soon after signing the articles of agreement, arriving about two weeks later. According to Franklin's October 27 entry in his business journal, "By a letter from Tho's Whitemarsh it appears that he arrived in Charleston on the 29th of Sept. at night, so our partnership there begins October 1, 1731." Franklin made a particular note of this date because the contract stipulated that their affiliation would last for "the Term of Six Years next ensuing the Day of the Arrival of the said Thomas in the Port of Charlestown."[21]

Two other printers—Eleazer Phillips and George Webb—also responded to the colony's blandishments, arriving about the same time as Whitmarsh. The three men hastened to commence their own printing operations and appear firmly established as they vied for the government contract and bounty. Franklin was familiar with both of these competitors. Phillips was the son of a Boston bookbinder, and Franklin had likely known him during his tenure at the *New-England Courant.* Webb was a former nemesis of Franklin, whom Franklin first met while working for Samuel Keimer. Webb had been an Oxford student whose passage from England was paid by Keimer in exchange for four years of indentured servitude as a compositor. Shortly after Franklin and Meredith formed a partnership and left Keimer's employ, Webb bought out the balance of his own indenture and offered his services to the partners. They did not have sufficient work to employ him, but Franklin unwisely confided to Webb their plan to begin a newspaper to compete with Andrew Bradford's *American Weekly Mercury.* As discussed in Chapter 2, Webb revealed this plan to Keimer, who promptly preceded Franklin and Meredith by publicly announcing his plan to publish one, hiring Webb for the purpose. Keimer's newspaper failed within a year, and he immigrated to Barbados.[22]

Of the three printers to arrive in South Carolina, Phillips prevailed with the legislature, despite Governor Robert Johnson's opinion that "Whitmarsh is furnished with much better materials, and better qualified to perform the public business, besides that he was encouraged to come hither." Having failed to gain the bounty or government printing, Whitmarsh petitioned unsuccessfully in November 1731 and January 1732 for "the Consideration of both Houses for the Charge he had been at in coming here pursuant to a former Resolution for encouragement of a printer." He made a third plea for compensation on February 16, 1732, and this time received two hundred pounds.[23]

Disappointed in his efforts to secure the government work, Whitmarsh sold office supplies and books, most of which he received from Franklin, in his shop on Church Street, "at the Sign of the Table-Clock on the Bay." Franklin charged Whitmarsh for such literature as "100 book Almanacks," "1 doz Watts Psalms," "50 Gout Books," "2 doz. Aristotle," and "20 Bowman's Sermons." He also published legal forms, pamphlets, broadsides, and, beginning January 8, 1732, a newspaper, the *South-Carolina Gazette.*[24] At about the same time, Phillips launched his *South-Carolina Weekly Journal.*[25]

However, a yellow-fever epidemic in July 1732 slowed the fervent business activity fueling Charles Town's growth. The town's earliest decades were plagued by sporadic outbreaks of malaria, dysentery, tuberculosis, and yellow fever, which a Christian missionary in the 1730s blamed on the warmer and more humid weather in South Carolina. "Since ye beginning of last August I have been visited with a continued Fever, an intermitting Fever with several Relapses, a Dysentery, a Cough, & at Length, a Spitting of Blood: all of wch. I can discover no other Cause, beside ye disadvantages & sudden Changes of ye Climate," Stephen Roe wrote. The 1732 siege of yellow fever lasted for three months and claimed the lives of about seven percent of Charles Town's population. Phillips and Webb were among those who succumbed, leaving Whitmarsh to succeed Phillips as the colony's official printer and as the publisher of the only newspaper between Virginia and the West Indies.[26]

The precise date of Webb's death is unknown, but it is certain he died after November 8, 1731, when he, like Whitmarsh, petitioned for government compensation; but well before October 16, 1732, when an item in the *Barbadoes Mercury* noted that "of the three Printers that arrived" in Charles Town, "there is but one left; and he that received the *premium* is one that is lately dead," meaning Phillips. More likely, Webb died in the yellow-fever epidemic later that year. The *Barbadoes Mercury*'s account began, "We hear from South Carolina, that there has been such a sickness, that near twenty on a day have been buried there," and then notes that two of the town's printers were among the casualties. This fact would be of particular interest to a printer writing this item, and thus more likely to be mentioned. Indeed, the report mentions the death of printers, but not the demise of the wife and son of South Carolina Governor Robert Johnson.[27]

Having survived the demise of his competitors, Whitmarsh took advantage of the lack of competition and established his newspaper, the *South-Carolina Gazette,* as a southern version of Franklin's *Pennsylvania Gazette.* Both offered readers an assortment of news, poetry, and essays written locally and reprinted from other newspapers, and both sought to educate their audiences. From the first issue, Whitmarsh's editorial mission was apparent—to elevate public morality in the remote but growing colony. Whitmarsh conveyed this purpose to *South-Carolina Gazette* readers in doggerel, noting "Where Merit appears, tho' in Rags, I respect it, And plead Virtue's Cause, shou'd the whole World reject it."[28] In his second issue, Whitmarsh published a letter from sixteen-year-old "Martia" acting as moral censor, just as many of Franklin's characters had. Martia criticized the frivolous behavior of Charles Town's young men, who were damaging the reputations they would need for "making any considerable Figure or Advantage in Trade."[29]

To convey "some useful Hints," Whitmarsh exhibited Franklin's fondness for *The Spectator,* reprinting many of its discourses. He prominently featured many locally written essays, including ones dealing with such favorite Franklin themes as unity and idleness. "Philo-Carolinensis" argued that people must avoid factionalism "for the Advancement of our own Interests," while "Honestus" counseled that the best method "for filling up the empty Spaces of Life" is "the Exercise of Virtue, in the most general Acceptation of the Word." Whitmarsh earnestly conveyed the Franklinian view that a newspaper must be a public utility, informing readers, "the principal Thing in View, by publishing these Papers, is the general Service of the People residing in the Province."[30]

Whitmarsh also relied on Franklin's journalistic beliefs to help him cope with factionalism. In his inaugural statement, Whitmarsh cautioned prospective contributors to "avoid giving Offence, either publick, or private" and to "forbear all Controversies, both in Church and State." This was more a means of soothing governmental fears about the effects of his newspaper than a rigid requirement, though, for Whitmarsh became embroiled in several public disputes. A 1732 feud between Privy Council Chief Justice Robert Wright and the Commons House of the South Carolina Assembly involving the right of habeas corpus tested Whitmarsh's mettle, due to his financial reliance on the colonial government as its official printer. He adopted Franklin's posture of impartiality and allowed both sides to air their grievances. During a squabble over religious beliefs later that year, which involved his decision to publish an essay arguing "The Traditions of the Clergy" are "destructive of Religion," Whitmarsh defended his editorial judgment by reprinting most of Franklin's "Apology for Printers." This statement asserted, "Printers are educated in the Belief, that when Men differ in Opinion, both Sides ought equally to have the Advantage of being heard by the Publick."[31]

Functioning as an appendage of his senior partner, Whitmarsh reprinted other Franklin writings, particularly moralistic articles. Franklin's "Chatterbox on the Family of Boxes" appeared in the *South-Carolina Gazette* three months after publication in its sister newspaper. This essay exhorted readers to virtuous actions and honest labor. The character "Tinderbox" was described as a tradesman who "rises before day, and has by the single Force of Industry, got so much Money in a little time, that People think he has found a Treasure." Franklin also benefited from Whitmarsh's weekly, reprinting an assortment of news items about Charles Town shortly after Whitmarsh began publishing. Because of the partnership, *Pennsylvania Gazette* readers learned much about life in the southern colonies, including problems of currency, piracy and Indian relations, and the progress of early settlers in neighboring Georgia. Franklin told readers he would publish such items "as often as I imagine it may be in any way useful or entertaining." These reports broadened Americans' knowledge of and empathy for other colonies, gradually eroding perceptions of isolationism. Most colonists in the early eighteenth century identified more with England than other American colonies. This expanded awareness forged bonds of unity among Americans—a prerequisite to the subsequent American Revolution.[32]

The partnership between Franklin and Whitmarsh had proven successful for both men, but Whitmarsh was unable to fulfill the contract. He died of an unknown cause shortly after publishing the *Gazette*'s issue of September 8, 1733.[33] Whitmarsh's death meant ownership of the printing operation reverted to Franklin. Whitmarsh's executor was to "deliver up the Press, Tipes, and all the Materials of printing," plus the assets and debts, to Franklin within one year, according to the contract. Whitmarsh apparently died without heirs or a will, leaving court-appointed executors to settle the estate.[34]

Not wishing to lose the foothold he had established in South Carolina and the profitable government contract there, Franklin quickly replaced Whitmarsh. To avoid tipping off competitors with whom he exchanged newspapers that Charles Town was bereft of printers, Franklin never announced Whitmarsh's death in the *Pennsylvania Gazette*, hastily arranging a partnership with journeyman Louis Timothee on nearly identical terms in November 1733. Despite knowing that the three previous South Carolina printers had died within two years of arriving in the colony, Timothee, his wife, and four small children traveled to Charles Town that winter to re-establish one of only ten newspapers in North America.[35]

Timothee was born in Holland to French parents and became fluent in numerous languages. He met and married Elizabeth and learned the art of printing in Holland before emigrating to Philadelphia, which he reached in September 1731. Timothee advertised the following month in the *Pennsylvania Gazette* his intention to open "a Publick French School; he will also, if required, teach the said Language to any young Gentlemen or ladies, at their Lodgings." His linguistic abilities and knowledge of printing, coupled with the opening for a journeyman in Franklin's Philadelphia shop created by Whitmarsh's departure to South Carolina, prompted Franklin to hire Timothee. The new employee, who was also fluent in German, was probably in Franklin's shop by February 1732 when a lengthy German letter was translated to English for publication. Shortly afterward Franklin assigned Timothee responsibility for a short-lived German-language newspaper in Philadelphia and arranged for him to serve as a part-time librarian for the Philadelphia Library Company, one of Franklin's first philanthropic projects.[36]

Deciding Timothee "was a Man of Learning and honest," Franklin charged him with the same responsibility to propagate a utilitarian gospel of virtue. "I insert what I think may be useful to Mankind in general," Timothee informed South Carolina readers. Timothee promptly assumed the post of government printer and recommenced the *South-Carolina Gazette* on February 2, 1734, anglicizing his name to Lewis Timothy that April. In the first issue under his editorship, Timothy wrote an aggressive and terse statement that the "*Liberty of the Press,* is the most unlucky Scourge that can hang over the Heads of a *corrupt* and *wicked* Ministry." He argued that the press serves public morality by maintaining a sentinel function over official conduct. The "*Liberty of the Press* is absolutely necessary to the *Liberty of Great Britain,*" he insisted, predicting "*Slavery* and *Ruin*" if it is ever abridged.[37]

Timothy closely adhered to Franklin's journalistic style. Borrowing from Franklinesque characters like "The Busy-Body" and "Silence Dogood," Timothy introduced "The Meddlers Club." This supposed group of Charles Town denizens promised to promote virtue and "to let no Vice escape our censure."[38] Timothy also continued Whitmarsh's practice of reprinting essays encouraging people to be optimistic and virtuous. Meanwhile, Franklin continued to secure South Carolina news from Timothy, including statistics on trade in Charles Town's port (which Franklin compared with Philadelphia and other cities) and minister George Whitefield's success in raising contributions for a Georgia orphanage.[39]

However, Timothy died prematurely, like his predecessor Whitmarsh. Timothy informed readers that his publication of a pamphlet was delayed "by reason of Sickness, myself and Son having been visited with this Fever, that reigns at present, so that neither of us hath been capable for some time of working much at the Press." He died two months later, but whether he had contracted a fatal case of yellow fever is unknown. On January 4, 1739, the *South-Carolina Gazette* cryptically noted the cause was "an unhappy Accident."[40]

Aware that the three previous South Carolina printers had died soon after arriving in the colony, Timothy anticipated the likelihood of his own demise. According to a special clause inserted in the Franklin partnership contract, Timothy's eldest son Peter could succeed him if he died. Although already assisting his father, the thirteen-year-old Peter Timothy was not ready to assume the editorial and business responsibilities when his father died, so Franklin agreed to take on Elizabeth Timothy as a partner until her son was older.[41]

This was a risky decision, not only because it deviated from the explicit terms of the partnership contract, but also because few women had ever served as printers in the American colonies.[42] Franklin's willingness to forge a partnership with a woman may have been influenced by the nature of his own marriage. Franklin was bound by the cords of love, friendship, and, most significantly, respect, to Deborah Franklin, his common-law wife since 1731. Much of her appeal to him consisted of being a hard worker who helped in the shop and provided wise counsel in delicate interpersonal matters.[43] His respect for Deborah's business acumen prompted him to entrust her with the power of attorney in 1733, authorizing her to oversee his printing partnerships.[44]

Franklin gave Elizabeth Timothy the opportunity to show she possessed the same industriousness he admired in his wife. He was pleased with the result, for she proved to be a better business manager than her husband. Franklin respected Lewis Timothy, but found him to be "ignorant in Matters of Account; and tho' he sometimes made me Remittances, I could get no Account from him, nor any satisfactory State of our Partnership while he lived." However, unlike her husband, Elizabeth had been raised in Holland, "where as I have been inform'd the Knowledge of Accompts makes a Part of Female Education," Franklin recalled in his autobiography. He gleefully noted that upon succeeding her husband, Elizabeth "not only sent me as clear a State as she could find of the Transactions past, but continu'd to account with the greatest Regularity & Exactitude every Quarter, afterwards; and manag'd the Business with such Success that she not only brought up reputably a family of Children, but at the Expiration of the Term was able to purchase of me the Printing-House and establish her Son in it." As with so many of Franklin's writings, there was a moral: this one demonstrating the rewards of hard work. Franklin also took the opportunity to impart useful advice. "I mention this Affair chiefly for the Sake of recommending that Branch of Education [printing] for our young Females, as likely to be of more Use to them & their Children in Case of Widowhood than either Music or Dancing," he wrote. Such vocational training would work "to the lasting Advantage and enriching of the Family."[45]

Elizabeth Timothy had "six small Children and another hourly is expected," she informed readers upon succeeding her husband as printer, but she did not permit her husband's death to interrupt the newspaper's publication schedule. Five days after Lewis was buried, the weekly made its regular appearance, with Elizabeth's announcement that "Whereas the late Printer of this Gazette hath been deprived of his life . . . I take this Opportunity of informing the Publick, that I shall contain the said paper as Usual." She described herself as a "poor afflicted Widow," but promised to make the newspaper "as entertaining and correct as may be reasonable expected." When he turned twenty-one, Elizabeth yielded proprietorship to her son Peter, who maintained a close alliance with Franklin for three decades. Peter Timothy was "a very intelligent and good printer and editor, and was for several years clerk of the general assembly," his contemporary Isaiah Thomas wrote.[46]

Franklin began the 1730s a despairing and cynical young man. At one level he conveyed his disdain for human nature through his satiric literature, while at another level he painted his characters preposterously to caution readers about such vices as pride, intemperance, and greed. His message was simple—be virtuous or risk seeming as ridiculous as Franklin's fictitious characters. The youthful Franklin's journalism was a means of holding a mirror to his perception of colonial society. In his 1730 poem "The Rats and the Cheese," he struck a chord of contempt for avarice, commenting on the pretended civility that masked people's self-interested social and political behavior:

> Your Politicks are all a Farce;
> And your fine Virtues but mine A____
> All your Contentions are but these,
> Whose Art shall best secure the CHEESE.[47]

Later that decade, he inclined toward Thomas Hobbes's pessimistic view that man is naturally selfish, telling a colleague that Hobbes's "Notion, I imagine, is somewhat nearer the Truth than that which makes the State of Nature a State of Love." As a journalistic chronicler of human events, Franklin had seen people at their worst, committing murder, torture, rape, and theft. This doubtless augmented his pessimism.[48]

His voracious appetite for reading also enabled him to learn history's hard lesson—unchecked, greed and power create divisions, corrupt the heart, and crush benevolence. Rather than wring his hands in acquiescence, Franklin believed in doing something about the failings of human nature by using his press. He was sure that the essence of Christianity involved diligently teaching and ministering to others. However, he believed with almost equal certainty that his efforts to improve people's characters in spite of themselves would ultimately be in vain. In a philosophical dialogue titled "A Man of Sense," Franklin's character "Socrates" ruefully observed that despite easy access to virtuous examples and instruction, many people prefer to remain "ignorant and foolish." He concluded, "tho' it has been told him a thousand

Times from Parents, Press, and Pulpit, the Vicious Man however learned, cannot be *a Man of Sense,* but is a Fool, a Dunce, and a Blockhead."[49]

But for Franklin, making the effort to remedy mankind's failings—taking action rather than merely lamenting and complaining—was the more realistic challenge than actually succeeding on a grand scale. It was the process of doing good, coupled with the hope that a few seeds of virtue would fall on fertile soil and produce the desired effect, rather than the certainty of success, that he viewed as acceptably serving God. Franklin had envisioned himself teaching virtue in a more formal way, through his contemplated society that he dubbed the "Party for Virtue," which he felt sure "cannot fail of pleasing God."[50]

Franklin's proposed society to disseminate virtuous teachings never reached fruition due to "the Necessity I was under of sticking close to my Business," he lamented in 1788, but he managed to blend his moral imperative with his printing endeavors. Franklin was initially attracted by the substantial bounty the South Carolina Assembly offered, the absence of competition at the time, and his desire "to promote" a worker who had "behaved well," but he also envisioned a Charles Town printing operation as an extension of his own mission of using journalism to propagate moral instruction. This prompted him to charge four successive South Carolina partners to produce "useful" publications for the enlightenment of the masses. Whitmarsh and the three Timothys printed pamphlets, books, and government proceedings, but their most significant obligation was to publish a newspaper, which Franklin regarded as an effective "Means of communicating Instruction" to an audience of colonists who were morally adrift in a remote colony. This design proved lucrative rather than costly, as a philanthropic society would have, and did not take him away from his printing business.[51]

At the end of the 1730s Franklin was much less anxious and cynical than he had been at the decade's beginning. Through industriousness and good fortune, Franklin had become a family man, respected citizen, and successful entrepreneur. "My Business was now continually augmenting, and my Circumstances growing daily easier, my newspaper having become very profitable," he wrote. His partnership in South Carolina also contributed to his triumph over debt and his gratification of his own desire to elevate public morality.[52]

Thus, he began laying plans for more partnerships.

6

Network Expansion from New York to the Caribbean

One of Franklin's fond recollections of his early years in Philadelphia was having "form'd most of my ingenious Acquaintance into a Club, for mutual Improvement, which we call'd the Junto," in the autumn of 1727.[1] Like Franklin, its members were young tradesmen who possessed idealism and intellect, but only modest social status. His inspiration for the Junto had been the voluntary organizations proposed by Cotton Mather for propagating morality and Christianity, but Franklin secularized the idea and charged the association to promote virtue and be "serviceable to *mankind*." To fulfill that charge himself, Franklin launched such civic projects as fire insurance, a city watch, the Library Company, the American Philosophical Society, the University of Pennsylvania, and even a method to keep sidewalks navigable during inclement weather.[2]

These acts of public virtue supported Franklin's scientistic belief that evidence and actions, not promises and wishes, were the best measures of character. "I have always set a great value on the character of a *doer of good*," he told Mather's son. Part of doing good was maintaining a firm work ethic, one of the dominant themes of Franklin's professional life. He never forgot the lack of this trait in London printing houses, compelling him nearly fifty years later to criticize the indolence and drunkenness of pressmen with whom he worked. Franklin was therefore determined not to employ such workers once he became a master, and he resolved not to offer partnerships to the inept or lackadaisical. Excepting the Meredith partnership, which was formed mostly due to financial exigency, Franklin learned from the success of the South Carolina partnerships that he could select virtuous and conscientious colleagues to extend his mission and message.[3]

Despite some early accounting problems and the untimely deaths of partners Thomas Whitmarsh and Lewis Timothy, Franklin viewed the Charles Town experiment as a triumph for virtue, colonial journalism, and his own business acumen. Whitmarsh and the Timothys proved to be the dedicated and honest employees Franklin sought to help him instruct the public, make money, and extend the influence of domestic journalism. He saw the pragmatic and ideological possibilities in a system of these alliances. "The Partnership at Carolina having succeeded, I was encourag'd to engage in others, and to promote several of my Workmen who had behaved well, by establishing them with Printing-Houses in different Colonies, on the same Terms with that in Carolina," Franklin recalled proudly.[4]

Good conduct was the consistent theme of Franklin's partnerships and printing affiliations. By his own hard work, first to free himself from debt and raise a family, and later to augment his wealth and reputation, Franklin had become successful. He ascribed his achievements to his display of "Industry visible to our Neighbours," which brought him "Character and Credit" in a city and an era where such assets were essential for young tradesmen. His success led him to seek relationships with those who exhibited the virtues of industry, frugality, skill, and self-determination he admired in himself and advocated to others.[5]

This desire to unite with virtuous people and educate the masses was Franklin's underlying motivation for the Junto, the United Party for Virtue, the American Philosophical Society, and many other organizations he formed or proposed. As he noted, "to get the bad Customs of a Country chang'd, and new ones, though better, introduc'd, it is necessary first to remove the Prejudices of the People, enlighten their Ignorance, and convince them that their Interest will be promoted by the propos'd Changes." This desire also greatly influenced his decision to form his printing network. Printers' exhibition of the virtues Franklin esteemed, both in the workplace and in society, would be the determining factor in many of Franklin's partnership decisions, and it was what he meant when he expressed his desire to promote workers who behaved well.[6]

James Parker was foremost of these workers. He reminded Franklin of himself. Parker was a young, confident printing apprentice who had fled his master, just as Franklin had done a decade earlier. Born in Woodbridge, New Jersey, Parker had been apprenticed to New York printer William Bradford for eight years, beginning in 1727. However, he grew restless with the lengthy indenture, abandoning Bradford in 1733 because he believed his skills were superior to Bradford's.[7] Seeing in the nineteen-year-old Parker a reflection of his own earlier circumstances, Franklin hired the runaway apprentice for his

Philadelphia printing house. Soon after, Franklin reconsidered. Recalling that his own departure from his brother and master James Franklin was "one of the first great Errata of my Life," Franklin likely urged Parker to return to Bradford's shop to serve the remainder of his time, plus a penalty.[8]

Parker may have agreed to this because Franklin promised him a partnership once he had fulfilled his obligation to Bradford. After completing his apprenticeship, Parker then returned to Franklin to work for him as a journeyman and live in his home until they formed a partnership to open a New York printing office in 1742. Parker took advantage of this opportunity and became one of the most gifted and important printers of the era, as well as a close associate of Franklin. The partnership terms were nearly identical to those for the Charles Town printers, but to discourage Parker from being as dilatory in his bookkeeping as Lewis Timothy, Franklin required a quarterly rather than annual accounting. The new partners were motivated by the prospect of Parker succeeding the seventy-seven-year-old Bradford as New York's government printer, a lucrative position with guaranteed revenue. Parker assumed the official post the following year and began publication of *The New-York Weekly Post-Boy* on January 3, 1743.[9]

Inducing Parker to complete his apprenticeship appeased Franklin's conscience somewhat, but a more direct means to repay his elder brother James for running away presented itself in the autumn of 1733. Franklin visited James in Newport, Rhode Island, to make amends. "Our former Differences were forgotten, and our Meeting was very cordial and affectionate," Franklin remembered. The dying James asked Benjamin to take his ten-year-old son as an apprentice and teach him the printing trade. "This I accordingly perform'd, sending him a few Years to School before I took him into the Office," Franklin wrote. As a result, "I made my Brother ample Amends for the Service I had depriv'd him of by leaving him so early." James Sr. died sixteen months later. His wife Ann succeeded him at the press. The following year she was named printer to the Rhode Island General Assembly, becoming the first woman in the colonies whose imprint appeared on a book as publisher.[10]

James Franklin Jr.'s seven-year apprenticeship to his uncle began November 5, 1740, with the young Franklin pledging loyalty and promising to avoid fornication, matrimony, and gambling, and agreeing not to "haunt Ale-Houses, Taverns, or Play-houses; but in all Things behave himself as a faithful Apprentice ought to do." During the apprenticeship, Franklin recalled, James Jr., or "Jemmy," "was always dissatisfied and grumbling," which Franklin blithely attributed to "the nature of boys."[11]

This was the first nepotistic act by the printer who altered the family-based custom in the trades by using nonrelatives to form the foundation for his printing network. However, Franklin's experience with family members would differ from successful family networks like the Bradfords, Greens, and Kneelands. Ironically, Franklin would be more disappointed by the kin he drew into journalism than his nonfamily associates.

Perhaps inspired by James Jr.'s apprenticeship, Franklin's sister Jane and her husband, Edward Mecom, decided to apprentice their son to Franklin to learn the printing trade. Not needing another apprentice, though, Franklin suggested they send their son, Benjamin Mecom, to Parker's shop in New York, where, Franklin promised, "he will be kindly used."[12]

To supply his printing operations in Philadelphia, New York, and Charles Town, plus his family link with Ann in Newport, Franklin procured supplies and books from prominent London printer William Strahan. Their business correspondence blossomed into a friendship that lasted more than forty years, only minimally affected by ensuing divisions over American affairs.[13] Their relationship began when Strahan wrote to James Read, a relative of Deborah Franklin, asking if Read knew of an opening for one of his workers, David Hall. Strahan noted that he and Hall had served their apprenticeships together, and that Hall was then working in Strahan's shop and living in his home. Hall "understands his Business exceedingly well; is honest, sober, and Industrious to the last Degree," Strahan wrote. Read showed this letter to Franklin, who took particular note of Hall's virtues.[14] Franklin penned an encouraging reply to Strahan in July 1743, simultaneously indicating he had further expansion in mind. "I have already three Printing-Houses in three different Colonies, and purpose to set up a fourth if I can meet with a proper Person to manage it, having all Materials ready for that purpose," Franklin wrote. "If the young Man will venture over hither, that I may see and be acquainted with him, we can treat about the Affair, and I make no doubt but he will think my Proposals reasonable." If not, Franklin promised him a year's employment and partial payment for his return voyage to England. Hall agreed, and Franklin hired him in 1744 as a journeyman.[15]

Franklin's motives for assisting Parker, Hall, and other young printers were more complex than simply economic gain. Franklin sought to help others demonstrate Christian charity and follow the Golden Rule he learned in childhood. As Franklin told a correspondent, "when I am employed in serving others, I do not look upon my self as conferring Favours, but as paying Debts" for acts of "kindness from Men, to whom I shall never have any Opportunity of making the least direct Return. And numberless mercies from God, who is infinitely above being benefited by our Services. These

Kindnesses from Men I can therefore only return on their Fellow-Men; and I can only show my Gratitude for those Mercies from God, by a Readiness to help his other Children and my Brethren." Others had befriended and aided Franklin in times of need. By helping young printers who exhibited good character, Franklin was repaying debts and serving God. "The noblest question in the world is *What Good may I do in it?*" he wrote in the 1737 *Poor Richard's Almanack.*[16]

Franklin's repayment of his debt to those who had given him a chance was to do likewise for virtuous young tradesmen like Parker and Hall. Franklin believed that the cultivation of a virtue-based work ethic was the integral prerequisite to financial success. As "Poor Richard," he asserted, "Industry, Perseverance, and Frugality, make Fortune yield." Franklin observed these qualities in Hall, telling Strahan that Hall "is obliging, discreet, industrious but honest; and when these Qualities meet, things seldom go amiss. Nothing in my Power shall be wanting to serve him."[17]

However, Hall was less content with Franklin. He grew impatient that Franklin discussed the prospect of a partnership but cautiously declined to reveal its location. Hall complained to Strahan about Franklin's secrecy and repeatedly asked Strahan for his opinion of whether Franklin's proposal was sincere. "As to your Terms with Mr. F. I again tell you I think they are very fair," Strahan assured him, encouraging Hall to "trust to his Generosity; and I dare say he will deal honourably by you."[18]

Franklin's caution with Hall was due to earlier unhappy results of revealing his plans to others. In 1728, journeyman printer George Webb betrayed Franklin's confidence after "I foolishly let him know, as a Secret, that I soon intended to begin a Newspaper," Franklin recalled in his memoirs. A dozen years later, lawyer John Webbe ruined Franklin's plan to commence the first magazine in North America. After declining Franklin's invitation to edit the monthly, Webbe took the idea to Andrew Bradford. They published *The American Magazine* first, preceding Franklin's *The General Magazine* by several days.[19]

Because of such episodes, and fear that his latest partnership plan would be revealed to competitors, Franklin remained secretive until he developed more trust in Strahan and Hall. In early letters to Strahan, Franklin repeatedly mentioned his intention to establish Hall in a printing house, but continued to omit mention of where or when.[20]

Franklin finally revealed his plans to Strahan in November 1745. "I now have every Thing ready for Mr. Hall to go to the W. Indies," he wrote casually. Franklin delayed sending Hall, though, due to safety concerns involving

King George's War, the third in a sequence of four wars fought in North America between British and French colonists and their respective Native American Indian allies. Franklin confessed to Strahan "some Reluctance to part with him these hazardous Times."[21]

The longer Hall remained in Philadelphia, the more Franklin recognized his value. Hall's competence and stability enabled him to thrust himself into public affairs more directly than merely chronicling them. Finally free of debt, thanks to the success of his *Pennsylvania Gazette* and profits from his Charles Town and New York partnerships, and aided in his own shop by capable workmen Hall, Thomas Smith, and Samuel Holland, Franklin embraced opportunities to serve the public in philanthropy, politics, and science. Franklin, his Junto, and members of the Philadelphia clerisy established the Pennsylvania Hospital, the Academy of Pennsylvania, and the American Philosophical Society. Franklin's plan for the philosophical society involved uniting "Virtuosi or ingenious Men" throughout the colonies who would correspond with each other to "cultivate the finer Arts, and improve the common Stock of Knowledge."[22] To benefit society in the 1740s, Franklin invented an improved fireplace, devised a plan for a volunteer militia, and planned to enlarge the subscription library he started. He later credited the development of such libraries throughout colonial America with rendering "common Tradesmen & Farmers as intelligent as most gentlemen from other Countries."[23]

However, Franklin performed these acts of public virtue at the expense of his thriving print shop. He chided his friend Cadwallader Colden in June 1747 for contemplating retirement from the New York governor's council to engage in "Philosophical Meditation."[24] Perhaps inspired by Colden's plan, though, Franklin seven months later turned over the daily affairs of the shop to Hall, allowing him time for intellectual pursuits. "To obtain some Leisure, I have taken a Partner into the Printing House, but tho' I am thereby a good deal disengag'd from private Business, I [find] myself still fully occupy'd," he told Colden. Those duties included various government appointments. Franklin did not believe in declining appointive posts, but avoided seeking elective ones, following his credo that "I shall never *ask,* never *refuse,* nor ever *resign* an Office." In 1748 he discouraged friends from capitalizing on his "little present Run of Popularity" by nominating him to be a candidate for the Pennsylvania Assembly. Three years later, though, he consented to be elected, rationalizing that he could expand his influence for the public good. In an effort not to appear hypocritical, he noted in his autobiography, "My Election to this Trust was repeated every Year for Ten years, without my ever asking any Elector for his Vote, or signifying either directly or indirectly any Desire of being chosen."[25]

Franklin's increasing public responsibilities had compelled him to change the venue and circumstances of his partnership plans with Hall. Rather than send Hall to a Caribbean island, Franklin yielded the daily operation of the Philadelphia printing house to him in 1747. Franklin notified Strahan, "Mr. Hall will acquaint you of the Footing we are about to go upon," and advised him, "after the next Parcel of Books are paid for you will chiefly have to deal with Mr. Hall, into whose Hands I have agreed to put the Shop."[26] Franklin and Hall sealed the pact January 1, 1748, for a term of eighteen years. Hall was to manage the printing, bookselling, and finances, dividing the profits and costs equally with Franklin. This relationship benefited both, but especially Franklin, whose civic involvements had become time-consuming. Describing his work on one of these projects, the construction of the Philadelphia Academy in 1749, Franklin wrote, "I went thro' it the more chearfully, as it did not then interfere with my private Business, having the Year before taken a very able, industrious & honest Partner, Mr. David Hall, with whose Character I was well acquainted, as he had work'd for me four Years. He took off my Hands all Care of the Printing-Office, paying me punctually my Share of the Profits. This Partnership continued Eighteen Years, successfully for us both."[27]

Neither relinquishing daily management of the printing office nor his growing interest in public affairs dampened Franklin's enthusiasm for establishing a press in the West Indies, though. Instead, Hall's superintendence enabled Franklin to devote more time to expanding his printing network, his revenue, and his sphere of influence.

The Caribbean islands had long borne the reputation among British subjects as the place to make a fresh start. Just as time, distance, and ocean separated the North American colonies from England, rendering them semi-autonomous, so was the West Indies separated from colonial America and the rest of the British Empire. The early history of the West Indies was characterized by substantial political disorder, stemming from the protracted public debate over whether the proprietors had the right to govern, or whether an assembly should be formed for the purpose. The conflict led to minimal British governmental presence in the Caribbean. Limited government and geographic isolation weakened the rigidity of social and commercial classes, making the island chain an ideal place to which distressed British subjects could abscond and start over, in a less structured society.[28]

Some of Franklin's acquaintances took advantage. Childhood friend John

Collins journeyed to the West Indies to escape debt and failure. Soon after, Deborah Read's first husband, John Rogers, fled there to avoid prosecution for debt and bigamy. Franklin's erstwhile printing rivals Samuel Keimer and David Harry also immigrated to the Caribbean, envisioning Barbados as a tropical balm for their Philadelphia failures. The region had also nearly become a new frontier for Franklin. After floundering as a journeyman printer in England, he was hired by Quaker businessman Thomas Denham. Denham proposed to send Franklin to the West Indies and set him up as a merchant, but he died before executing that plan. His heirs dismissed Franklin, compelling the young man to return to the printing trade.[29]

The region's geographic isolation, rugged terrain, and oppressive heat, plus the preponderance of settlers who had been failures in Britain or North America, created a social, intellectual, and moral climate of laxity. During military maneuvers in Jamaica, British Army Colonel John Stewart described the island disparagingly. He attributed his soldiers' high mortality rate there to malaria and the effects of drink, which were exacerbated by stifling humidity. He wrote, "this Island instead of being a place of refreshment must always prove their grave without they could be incamped in some clear'd part of the mountains where they might be cool & at a distance from Rumm."[30] Liquor proved a means of escape from the weather for many islanders, as did roisterous conduct. Calling the West Indies "a most infernal place for worrying a poor Devil," a friend advised Franklin's grandson Benjamin Franklin Bache not to hold his wedding ceremony and honeymoon there. "I am told they will not suffer a fellow to get to Bed till morning" with his bride, Richard Smith wrote, for "if he goes before, they will be sure to haul them both out & toss them in a sheet or pelt them with oranges—this is not a Custom among the Vulger but a Fashion seized on all the Islands."[31]

Caribbean residents possessed a materialistic, self-gratifying attitude, which one historian called the "'live fast and die young' ethos of the region," concluding that "the cheapness of life in the tropics . . . suggests a stunted and deficient society."[32] Anna Maria Shirley, daughter of the provincial governor, compared West Indian society unfavorably with that of England. "The amusement[s] are not quite so Numerous as London boasts of," she wrote from the Bahamas. "Danceing is their most Favorite one, which I wonder at in so [dismal] a Climate." She told her correspondent that she preferred not to associate with West Indian residents, noting, "as to our society I cannot say a great deal for it. West India & English Educations are very different. Its a small place commonly in those the people do not agree so well as in large ones. It is nitheir proper nor agreable in our Situation to have any thing to do with their little annimossitys."[33] An Antigua minister also noted the educational deficiencies of the islanders. Acknowledging receipt of six copies of a Franklin leaflet on astronomy, the Rev. William Shervington responded dryly, "One would have sufficed for our island, as we are not overburthen'd with men, who have a taste that way."[34] Morality was equally at a premium in the Caribbean, where "swearing, Lying, Drunkenness & Whoredom" were commonplace, according to one writer of the era. She decried the "Extravagancy, voluptuousness and riotous living" that abounded in the islands.[35]

This lifestyle was considerably influenced by the lucrative but risky production of sugar, which led planters to exploit both land and slaves for short-term financial gain. One eighteenth-century diarist cited an Antigua planter who "was not thought to feed, and treat his Negroes properly, tho' on their labour, depended the advancement of his fortune."[36] Compounding the region's economic woes, the monarchy required island colonists to import goods from England, rather than the more proximate North American colonies.[37] An American traveling in the Caribbean called this arrangement "odious tyranny," and "from which tyranny results the escorbitant price of the most necessary articles of life in the West Indies, and the consequent high price paid for the produce of the soil."[38] With a volatile economy, an inhospitable climate, and a pervasive culture of moral abandon, West Indies residents—especially men—had short lifespans. A historian called the islands a "demographic disaster area."[39]

In this arduous setting, Franklin's erstwhile printing competitors Harry and Keimer experienced difficulties in both personal and vocational matters. Harry settled in Barbados in 1730 and hired Keimer as his assistant, prompting Franklin to wryly observe, "this Apprentice employ'd his former Master as a Journeyman." Succumbing to the region's wanton lifestyle, Harry "became more dissipated, and his profits from printing were not equal to his expenditures," according to Isaiah Thomas, who printed in the West Indies just a few decades later. Franklin reported that during Harry's brief career, he "dress'd like a Gentleman, liv'd expensively, took much Diversion & Pleasure abroad, ran in debt, & neglected his Business." These were all cardinal sins to Franklin, who regarded thrift and hard work as two of the foremost virtues. Harry returned to Pennsylvania in 1731, yielding the shop to Keimer, who commenced the *Barbadoes Gazette,* the first known newspaper in Barbados. Keimer lasted longer than Harry, remaining on the island until his death in 1738, but his livelihood was threatened at one point by a grand-jury presentment for libeling a member of the king's council.[40]

Despite the dismal demography and climate, and despite the island chain's history of journalistic indifference, Franklin resolved to establish a printing house in the West Indies. His motives were multifaceted. Several of his reasons were routine and could be said of any of his journalism partnerships: making money, promoting a trusted worker, extending his network, and disseminating intellectual enlightenment. However, Franklin also had three special reasons to extend his reach to the Caribbean.

The first was moralistic. Since his days as a London journeyman, Franklin had loathed the effects of alcohol on others' character and work habits. He decried the London pressmen's incessant consumption of beer, which he called "a detestable custom." Drunkenness left many of the workers in perpetual debt. Franklin's character sketches of others in the autobiography, including his first printing partner, Hugh Meredith, blamed their failures on alcohol.[41] He made the same point about Native American Indians.

Appointed to a committee to make a treaty with Indians in central Pennsylvania, Franklin was appalled at the tribe's rum-induced conduct. He suggested alcohol would lead to the collapse and ruin of these Indians, just as it "has already annihilated all the Tribes who formerly inhabited the Seacoast."[42] In his newspaper, Franklin advocated temperance by repeatedly printing news accounts and essays emphasizing the evils of drink, and he counseled readers that there is "Nothing more like a Fool, than a drunken Man."[43] Franklin attributed his "greater Clearness of Head & quicker Apprehension," his "long-continu'd Health," and his "good Constitution" to his own moderation. He regarded temperance as one of the chief human virtues, and envisioned a West Indies partnership as a means to impart moral instruction to an area needful of it.[44]

Franklin's second motive for extending his reach to the West Indies was pragmatic and provincial. To support his journalistic operation and lower his operating costs, Franklin became Philadelphia's postmaster in 1737.[45] This office allowed him to send and receive mail for free for any purpose. Thus, Franklin could distribute his newspapers without charge and receive newspapers from other regions, from which news could be reprinted in his *Pennsylvania Gazette*. For obvious financial reasons, Franklin found postal employment "very suitable to me," as he told a correspondent.[46] Also, being postmaster enabled Franklin to acquire information first, because the colonial post office served as a clearinghouse for information about other nations and other parts of the British empire. These perquisites of the position "facilitated the Correspondence that improv'd my Newspaper" and "encreas'd the Number demanded, as well as the Advertisements to be inserted, so that it came to afford me a very considerable Income," he wrote.[47] Although there were several small printing houses in the West Indies, little information from the islands reached the North American colonies. Franklin saw the benefit of establishing a printing shop, and especially a newspaper, in the region to serve as a news source for his *Pennsylvania Gazette*—news he could receive free of charge, before any other printer. This benefit not only enhanced news-gathering, but also rendered his newspaper more attractive to readers and advertisers. Franklin made extensive use of this advantage, reprinting two dozen news items from his network newspaper there between 1748 and 1751.[48]

Third and finally, a West Indies partnership would provide Franklin the satisfaction of succeeding where his former nemeses Harry and Keimer had failed. By selecting a partner who was competent (Keimer's weakness, in Franklin's opinion) and dependable (Harry's deficiency), Franklin confidently anticipated triumph. His choice for this alliance was Thomas Smith, who had spent several years as a journeyman printer for Parker in New York. Afterward, Smith was transferred to Philadelphia to work for Franklin and Hall, serving as an official witness to their partnership document.[49]

Like Hall, Smith had demonstrated the work ethic and good character Franklin sought in network members. With Hall remaining in Philadelphia instead of setting up in the West Indies as originally planned, Smith was the next worker in line for promotion "who had behaved well," in Franklin's estimation. Echoing a familiar theme in his partnership decisions, Franklin lauded Smith's character in a letter to Strahan. "I have lately sent a Printing-house to Antigua, by a very sober, honest and diligent young Man, who has already (as I am inform'd by divers Hands) gain'd the Friendship of the principal People, and is like to get into good Business," Franklin wrote several months after Smith arrived. Franklin recommended Strahan supply Smith with books and stationery, with the assurance that Smith "will make you good and punctual Returns."[50]

Franklin valued diligence, honesty, and sobriety. Almost as much, though, Franklin respected the interpersonal skills to win favor with influential persons, as Smith had demonstrated. A recurring theme in Franklin's autobiography is his ability to meet, impress, and gain from prominent benefactors. He wrote without embarrassment about these episodes, some of which bordered on sycophancy, as "exemplifying strongly the Effects of prudent . . . Conduct in the Commencement of a Life of Business," he told a friend.[51] Others, however, saw it differently. John Adams called Franklin "a base flatterer," and printer John Holt observed that Franklin's allegiances and public actions "seemed calculated to secure himself an Interest with the prevailing Party."[52]

Smith's partnership with Franklin contained the same terms as the others, with Franklin receiving one-third of the profit. Franklin opened accounts with Smith on April 16, 1748, when he charged Smith for limes, meat, and printing supplies. Their arrangement began harmoniously, with Franklin pleased to add a new partner who "always behav'd extreamly well." Smith began industriously, publishing a newspaper and books of poetry, agriculture, and medicine at the Antigua printing house.[53]

However, within three years Smith was awash in financial troubles. Upon setting up at Kerby's Wharf in the town of St. John's, Smith discovered West Indies residents were accustomed to acquiring goods on liberal credit terms. This created a cash-flow problem for the printer and caused him to fall behind in paying his own debts, especially to his partner Franklin and his supplier Strahan.[54] Strahan complained to Hall in February 1751 and also griped to Franklin the following month. Embarrassed at having promised Strahan that Smith would pay for supplies punctually, Franklin informed Strahan, "I have wrote to Smith at Antigua to quicken him in discharging his Debt to you." He added, "I am concern'd at your laying so long out of your Money, and must think of some Way of making you Amends."[55]

Smith continued the *Antigua Gazette* until at least September 1751, but afterward he became ill and died the following summer. In dour fashion, Franklin blamed the death on alcohol, in his view the cause of many unfortunate occurrences. "My late Partner there enjoy'd perfect health for four Years, till he grew careless and got to sitting up late in Taverns," Franklin wrote. Another possibility is that Smith contracted yellow fever in the intemperate climate. Whatever the cause, Smith died without heirs, half of his revenue on credit and uncollected. To recoup some of the money, Franklin engaged the Antigua merchant firm of Birkett and Booth, but nearly three years later he was still awaiting a remittance.[56]

While trying to settle Smith's affairs from overseas and understand how the sober and industrious worker he and Parker had groomed for success could have bungled the finances and possibly drunk himself to death, Franklin acted quickly to find a replacement printer for his Antigua operation. He knew the island's vacancy would not remain unfilled for long, because a printer there would have no competition for the governmental printing contract. He made a curious choice.

Perhaps because he had no other promising journeymen worthy of promotion at that time, or because he was so disappointed by Smith's failure that he felt it safer to choose a family member, Franklin sent his nephew Benjamin Mecom to St. John's. The nineteen-year-old Mecom was the son of Franklin's favorite sister Jane, and a nephew Franklin particularly liked. "I have a very good opinion of Benny in the main, and have great hopes of his becoming a worthy man," Franklin told Jane, adding that the nephew named after him "has many good qualities, for which I love him." Two weeks after Mecom sailed for Antigua in 1752, Franklin wrote reassuringly to Edward and Jane Mecom in Boston. "Antigua is the Seat of Government for all the Leeward Islands, to wit, St. Christophers, Nevis, and Montserrat. Benny will have the Business of all those Islands, there being no other printer." He noted that Mecom "will find the Business settled to his Hand, a Newspaper establish'd, no other Printing-house to interfere with him or beat down his Prices." Seeking to assuage parental fears that Mecom would meet the same fate as Smith, Franklin praised the island's salubrious climate, adding that the only danger to his health was alcohol, "which I have caution'd Benny to avoid, and have given him all other necessary Advice I could think of relating both to his health and Conduct, and hope for the best."[57]

With a strategically important printing location at stake, Franklin believed he could rely on a relative to avoid the temptations and mistakes that overwhelmed Smith, and to succeed where Smith had failed. However, Mecom had been showing signs of instability since childhood. Wanting their son to follow in his prosperous uncle's footsteps, Mecom's parents chose to engage him in the printing trade. Through Franklin, they arranged for Mecom to be apprenticed in Parker's New York shop. "I am confident he will be kindly used there, and I shall hear from him every week," Franklin wrote to Edward and Jane Mecom. Knowing of his nephew's recalcitrant demeanor, Franklin urged that he use the same ingratiating style that had benefited Franklin throughout his life. "You will advise him to be very cheerful, and ready to do every thing he is bid, and endeavour to oblige every body, for that is the true way to get friends," he cautioned the parents.[58]

It soon became evident that Mecom did not heed his uncle's advice. Mecom wrote a letter to his parents indicating a major rift with Parker. He complained of beatings, insufficient clothing, and poor treatment during a bout with smallpox. Franklin defended Parker as having "in every respect done his Duty" and called Mecom's allegations "groundless stories" and "little Misunderstandings." Franklin explained that Mecom stayed out all night, devised excuses to avoid attending church, and once tried to run away to sea aboard a privateer. Franklin dismissed these actions, as well as Mecom's complaints about Parker, as being "commonly incident to boys of his years."[59]

The roilings continued until Mecom, Parker, and Franklin jointly agreed to end the apprenticeship prematurely as a concession to Mecom's craving for independence and his satisfactory printing skills. Mecom promised to repay Parker for the balance of his time and accepted Franklin's invitation to succeed Smith in Antigua. Franklin was concerned about Mecom's maturity, however, and admonished him to govern his conduct. Franklin was unconvinced this instruction would suffice, telling Mecom's parents, "After all, having taken care to do what *appears to us to be for the best,* we must submit to God's Providence, which orders all things *really for the best*."[60]

Although anxious about the young man's unsettled character, Franklin sent Mecom to Antigua as a partner in August 1752, under the same terms as Smith. In recommending him to Strahan's attention, though, Franklin chose his words carefully, reluctant to give Mecom his unqualified endorsement. "I have settled a Nephew of mine in Antigua, in the Place of Mr. Smith, decea'd," he wrote to Strahan. "I take him to be a very honest industrious Lad, and hope he will do well there, and in time be of some Use to you as a Correspondent." Mecom revived the *Antigua Gazette* in October or November 1752, enabling Franklin and Hall to resume reprinting West Indies news, and published a book of poems and a schoolbook.[61] However, Mecom quickly began complaining that the terms of the partnership were too confining, especially the requirement that he remit one-third of the profits to Franklin. "I fear I have been too forward in cracking the shell, and producing the chick to the air before its time," Franklin ruefully informed Jane Mecom just three months after Benny arrived in Antigua.[62]

Under Mecom's direction, the Antigua printing house continued to lose money. Mecom blamed this on the partnership terms, but both Franklin and Strahan had come to realize that Mecom was an inept manager of money and supplies. When Mecom ordered an enormous stock of books, Strahan decided to warn Franklin before filling the order. "Pray keep him within Bounds, let him have good saleable Sortments, but small, and do not suffer him to be more than Fifty Pounds in your Debt, if so much," Franklin requested. From Smith's experience, Franklin had learned that West Indies residents were dilatory about paying for printed matter, an inclination Mecom did not seem to understand. "He is a young Lad, quite unacquainted with the World," Franklin proffered to rationalize Mecom's imprudence. Strahan did not impose these restraints to the necessary degree, for Mecom fell deeper into the London supplier's debt the next year. "I do not approve at all of B. Mecom's being so much in your Debt, and shall write to him about it," Franklin commented to Strahan. Franklin urged Strahan to demand the money, thereby compelling the young printer to be fiscally responsible.[63]

Partly to pacify the querulous Mecom regarding the partnership terms, and partly to reward his "diligent and careful" work, Franklin allowed Mecom to keep all the profits, provided he contribute toward his mother's rent payments and send Franklin some sugar and rum. His ultimate plan, as he told Jane Mecom, was to give the printing house to Benny, "but as he was very young and unexperienc'd in the World, I thought it best not to do it immediately but to keep him a little dependent for a Time, to check the flighty Unsettledness of Temper" he sometimes exhibited. Franklin did not tell his nephew of this planned beneficence, though. Mecom, chafing under Franklin's control, asked to purchase the printing house outright. Franklin ignored his query. This angered Mecom, who indignantly announced he was abandoning Antigua. Franklin ascribed the disintegration of the partnership to the fact that Mecom "lov'd Freedom, and his Spirit could not bear Dependance on any Man, tho' he were the best Man living."[64]

Following his 1756 departure from Antigua, Mecom failed at publishing ventures in Boston, New York, New Haven, and Philadelphia. He cascaded deeper into debt to Strahan, Franklin, and Parker—and began losing his sanity. His financial bungling prompted Parker to revoke the power of attorney he had granted Mecom, and a Connecticut grand jury presented Mecom for violating a colonial statute by "willingly and obstinately without any reasonabel excuse" refusing to attend church services for a month.[65] During the 1760s, as his career floundered, Mecom occasionally visited Zechariah Fowle's printing house in Boston, where Isaiah Thomas was an apprentice. Mecom "was handsomely dressed, wore a powdered bob wig, ruffles and gloves; gentlemanlike appendages which the printers of that day did not assume, and thus apparelled, would often assist, for an hour, at the press," Thomas recalled. Mecom's penchant for wearing his coat, wig, hat, and gloves while doing the sometimes grimy work of a printer, and his personality quirks, inspired other pressmen to nickname him "Queer Notions" behind his back, Thomas wrote.[66]

Franklin had viewed Mecom's behavior problems as mere "Fickleness" and an inability to "get fix'd to any purpose," excusing these qualities as foibles of youth. However, as Mecom grew older and his peculiarities became more pronounced, Franklin was finally forced to admit a serious problem existed. "I begin to fear things are going wrong with him," he confessed to Strahan in 1763.[67]

Mecom's inability to manage money, compounded by the need to support his wife Elizabeth and their children, pushed him into bankruptcy. Franklin helped manage Mecom's debts, paying off some and interceding with creditors, but he was powerless to halt his nephew's mental deterioration.[68] Later

Franklin network member William Goddard hired Mecom as a journeyman, but Mecom proved unreliable and left. He failed to hold a job at several other Philadelphia printing houses, and ultimately applied for a liquor license, planning to convert part of his home into a tavern. "We are not fond of the Prospect it affords," he candidly told city officials in his petition, "further than as it may contribute to support a Number of young growing Children, whose Welfare we would earnestly and honestly endeavour to secure."[69] This effort failed, too, and Mecom grew dependent on Franklin's wife, Deborah, and son William for succor. Trying to intercede for her son, Jane Mecom asked Franklin to dismiss the Boston postmaster and appoint her son to the post. He declined, explaining, "it is a rule with me, not to remove any officer that behaves well, keeps regular accounts, and pays duly; and I think the rule is founded on reason and justice." Franklin added, "I have not shown any backwardness to assist Benny, where it could be done without injuring another."[70]

Mecom's irresponsibility exasperated Franklin's son William. "His Pride and Laziness are beyond any Thing I ever knew, and he seems determin'd rather to sink than to strike a Stroke to keep his Head above Water," William disgustedly wrote to his father. "I look upon him to have a Tincture of Madness."[71]

The "Tincture" spread until it enveloped Benjamin Mecom, and he became one more woeful member of a tragic family. By 1775, only three of Jane Mecom's twelve children were alive. Depression and disease plagued her daughter Jane Collas, who had married a man Franklin distrusted enough to refuse him a letter of recommendation.[72] Both Benjamin Mecom and his brother Peter had become deranged. Their conditions prompted their mother to lament that they had brought her "nothing but miserey" due to their "Distracted" state.[73] Peter Mecom learned the trade of soap-making, but had been exhibiting signs of his affliction by age eighteen. Viewing Peter's conduct through his own lens of virtue, Franklin misunderstood the symptoms. The uncle ascribed Peter's behavior to laziness and suggested the boy needed to acquire "a habit of industry."[74] He later realized his inaccurate assessment and contributed toward the cost of boarding Peter at a private home, euphemistically referring to him as Jane's "unhappy Son." Jane herself referred to Peter's condition as "a dredfull Affair" and commented on the high costs of his maintenance, "God only knows what I shall do with him in the future."[75] Peter died in early 1779, bringing to an end Jane's "Perpetual anxiety." Peter, she explained, "has been no comfort to any won nor capeble of Injoying any Himself for many years."[76]

Jane accepted the many slow, lingering deaths of her children as God's will, informing Franklin after her daughter Polly's death of tuberculosis at age nineteen, "Sorrows roll upon me like the waves of the sea. I am hardly allowed time to fetch my breath. I am broken with breach upon breach, and I have now, in the first flow of my grief, been almost ready to say, 'What have I more?" But God forbid that I should indulge that thought, though I have lost another child. God is sovereign, and I submit." In her notebook, she wrote after Polly's death, "The Lord Giveth & the Lord taketh away oh may I never be so Rebelious as to Refuse Acquesing & & saying from my hart Blessed be the Name of the Lord."[77]

Like his brother Peter, Benjamin Mecom went insane. After New Jersey government officials judged Mecom to be violent, "very Dangerous," and "Depriv'd of his Reason," Franklin arranged for him to be confined in a New Jersey asylum, with Franklin assuming most of the expenses. Mecom remained there "in His deplorable state," as Jane described it, until he wandered away just after the Battle of Trenton on Christmas 1776 and was never heard from again.[78]

Before Mecom left Antigua in 1756, he recommended another printer as a successor to the Antigua printing house. Disappointed by his two failed partnerships there and not knowing this worker's character (for whom a recommendation from the inept Mecom would have been detrimental, in Franklin's eyes), Franklin refused, offering only to sell him the shop.[79]

Although Franklin declined to devise a third partnership in Antigua, he maintained journalistic ties to the West Indies for years after Mecom's departure. In 1754 Jamaica printer William Daniell solicited the firm of Franklin and Hall, inquiring about their charges for paper, potash, and other items and saying he was "Realy much in Want, and Do Not Intend to apply anywhere Else." The duo supplied Daniell for two years, until his death in 1756, at the same time exchanging news items with him.[80] Some historians have identified Daniell as a Franklin partner, but that is unlikely.[81] Daniell was printing by 1749, but it was not until five years later that he introduced himself to Franklin and Hall and asked about supplies. Also, the terms under which Franklin's partners operated makes it clear that Daniell was merely a business associate. According to the terms of his standard contract, Franklin was the sole supplier of printing materials and split the costs with his partners. Thus, there would have been no need for Daniell to write to Franklin making "a Proposal for Dealing with you for paper."[82]

In the 1760s, Franklin also had a business relationship with William Smith, who published *The Freeport Gazette; or, the Dominica Advertiser* in

Dominica from 1765 to 1767.[83] Like the Daniell affiliation, this link led some historians to assume a Franklin partnership, although there is no evidence to support this.[84]

Another Franklin tie to the Caribbean was William Dunlap, who owned a printing press from 1762 to 1772 in Bridgetown, Barbados. A cousin of Deborah Franklin, Dunlap printed in Lancaster and Philadelphia, served as Philadelphia postmaster, and later became an Episcopal clergyman. He formed a partnership with George Esmand to publish the *Barbados Mercury*.[85]

The West Indies had represented a geographic and entrepreneurial challenge to Franklin. Journalistic predecessors such as Harry, whom Franklin once regarded as "a powerful Rival," had tried and failed to establish a foothold in the islands.[86] However, with his printing partners and affiliates thriving in Charles Town, Philadelphia, Newport, and New York, Franklin decided to send a printer to the Caribbean to supplement the growth of Franklinesque journalism.

The West Indies project was subordinate to his desire for new challenges after thirty years of printing. Upon retiring and relinquishing the shop to Hall, "I flatter'd myself that, by the sufficient tho' moderate Fortune I had acquir'd, I had secur'd Leisure during the rest of my Life, for Philosophical Studies and Amusements," Franklin wrote.[87]

The Antigua animus was clearly still a high priority, though, for Franklin did not abandon it once he decided against sending Hall. Part of the project's allure was that it was a speculative but promising printing market. Franklin was encouraged by the fact that there was minimal competition in the West Indies, and none on the island Franklin selected. More significantly, it offered great promise for the dissemination of moral instruction. However, several printers of Franklin's acquaintance had previously failed there, leaving doubts whether this link in his journalistic chain would prove sufficiently sturdy. Nonetheless, Franklin was still intrigued by the prospect of extending his reach to the Caribbean, and therefore he sent Smith. Smith seemed to be cut from the same industrious cloth as Hall, Parker, and Timothy, but this partnership failed due to alcoholism and illness, just as burgeoning insanity contributed to the demise of Franklin's arrangement with Mecom several years later.

During their brief stints publishing in Antigua, Franklin's partners discharged their responsibility for disseminating knowledge and guidance. Smith printed instructive essays and books on medicine and agriculture. Mecom published a grammar book and a broadside promoting lectures on electricity by Franklin's friend Ebenezer Kinnersley. In his newspaper, Mecom followed

Franklin's practice of printing lengthy essays on the freedoms and responsibilities of the press. "Of the Use, Abuse, and Liberty of the Press, with a little Salutary Advice," from the pseudonymous "Reflector," appeared in his *Antigua Gazette.*[88]

However, both Smith and Mecom had proved unable to operate a profitable business. Where Smith was complaisant, Mecom was recalcitrant. Mecom had demonstrated this character quirk since his stormy apprenticeship with the forbearing Parker, and it became exacerbated as he grew older. Franklin sent Mecom to the West Indies for profit, but also for Mecom's own benefit. Franklin wanted to give him a fresh start after his unsettling apprenticeship, in a land that had been used by many others for the same purpose. Unfortunately, under Mecom's direction the West Indies shop continued to be a financial failure for Franklin, and he closed it after Mecom's return to the mainland.

The existence of the Franklin network was largely due to Franklin's ability to judge personal character and business acumen. He repeatedly conveyed his belief that a resolute work ethic is "the natural means of acquiring *wealth*," for "he that gets all he can honestly, and saves all he gets (necessary Expences excepted) will certainly become RICH."[89] Franklin also believed that hard work yielded other blessings than wealth, asserting, "God gives all Things to Industry."[90] For pragmatic and moral reasons, Franklin sought the virtue of honest labor in his workmen. When he found it, he considered those employees for partnerships. Franklin shepherded two of the eighteenth century's best printers, James Parker and David Hall, into successful partnerships because of his ability to gauge their character, as well as their talent. However, the West Indies experiment ranks as a notable exception. What stung Franklin most was that his laudatory assessments of his partners—one of his best journeymen and one of his nephews—proved wrong. Both had disappointed him by displaying a lack of the work ethic and stable character Franklin sought. As "Poor Richard" observed, "Men and Melons are hard to know."[91]

Franklin's pride in his ability to estimate virtue, a crucial component of his selection of workmen "who had behaved well," was reinforced by the partnerships in Charles Town, New York, and Philadelphia. However, it received a jarring blow in the West Indies. This may explain why little information has survived about his partnerships there, and why neither the printing house nor partners Smith and Mecom are mentioned in his *Autobiography*. There was little room for failure in Franklin's self-constructed image of the prudent businessman, and he did not wish to advertise his own failures on matters of importance to him, particularly his business, because they would detract from his credibility as a moral instructor. This was the underlying goal of his *Autobiography,* as he revealed to Benjamin Vaughn in 1788. "I omit all facts and transactions, that may not have a tendency to benefit the young reader, by showing him from my example, and my success in emerging from poverty, and acquiring some degree of wealth, power, and reputation, the advantages of certain modes of conduct which I observed," he wrote.[92]

Franklin evidently did not regard his West Indies foray as a suitable example for young readers.

7

The Political Imperative of the Pennsylvania German Partnerships

When Benjamin Franklin devised the contract making David Hall the managing partner of the Philadelphia printing house on January 1, 1748, he promised not to be involved in any other publishing ventures for the eighteen-year duration of the contract. However, he violated that covenant repeatedly, setting up other printing partnerships in the same colony and even the same city.[1] Franklin's reasons for doing so emanated from his political involvements, his moral convictions, his civic loyalties, and his desire to leave his ideological stamp on German immigrants, whom Franklin thought morally deficient.

Franklin's choice to take "the proper Measures for obtaining Leisure to enjoy Life and my Friends more than heretofore" by turning over the press to Hall and retiring from its daily labors at just forty-one years old opened him to new avenues for public service.[2] Indeed, he was probably not as surprised at the public response to his decision as he suggests in his autobiography. He wrote, "the Publick now considering me as a man of Leisure, laid hold of me for their Purposes; every Part of our Civil Government, and almost at the same time, imposing some Duty upon me." Franklin actually developed political aspirations early in life, less as a way to wealth than as a means of influencing public affairs. He began serving as clerk to the Pennsylvania Assembly in 1736. The Hall partnership allowed him to join the Philadelphia Common Council in 1748, become Grand Master of Pennsylvania in the Freemasons in 1749, and gain a seat in the Pennsylvania Assembly in 1751. As a public servant, he promoted such parochial concerns as clean streets, fire companies, a charity hospital, and a college, and such continental concerns as the abolition of slavery, the spread of Christianity, the establishment of a philosophical society, and the unification of the colonies for civil defense.[3] Throughout his life Franklin displayed a willingness to hold public office if there was sufficient public and political support. "I must own, that it is no small pleasure to me" to be re-elected to a third term as president of Pennsylvania, he admitted to his sister. He marveled that "I should be elected a third time by my fellow citizens, without a dissenting vote but my own, to fill the most honourable post in their power to bestow. This universal and un-bounded confidence of a whole people flatters my vanity much more than a peerage could do."[4]

Franklin's interest in governing was fueled by his early opinion that "few in Public Affairs act from a meer View of the Good of their Country" and "fewer still in public Affairs act with a View to the Good of Mankind." From the safety of his *Poor Richard's Almanack*, Franklin ridiculed political parti-sanship. "*Ignorance* leads Men into a Party, and *Shame* keeps them from get-ting out again."[5] Franklin pessimistically viewed politics as a haven for those who thrive amid "factions, cabals, dissensions, and violent divisions." This does not serve the public, for "as soon as a Party has gain'd its general Point, each Member becomes intent upon his particular Interest, which thwarting others, breaks that Party into Divisions, and occasions more Confusion." Franklin regarded most government officials as greedy and selfish, a view he held throughout his life, despite his long tenure in government. In politics, he informed a correspondent, "Avarice is infinite."[6]

Despite his misgivings, Franklin earnestly plunged into politics to influ-ence public virtue by working within the system. Years of service as clerk of the Pennsylvania Assembly had impressed upon him the power possessed by a colonial legislator—perhaps not as capable of shaping public opinion as a printer, but able to exert a more direct influence for the public weal. "I con-ceiv'd my becoming a Member would enlarge my Power of doing Good," Franklin recalled of his election to the legislature. He noted proudly that his "Promotions" to political posts stimulated his ambitions to manipulate gov-ernment affairs for the general good, and conceived of himself as having a mandate from the people, his elections "being so many Testimonies of the public's good Opinion, and by me entirely unsolicited."[7]

After being elected unopposed to the Assembly, Franklin quickly sought to ingratiate himself with all by maintaining an outwardly nonpartisan stance. He recognized that much of his support came from liberal factions among the Quakers, and it was with them Franklin most closely shared po-litical principles. However, he also acknowledged that cordial relations with the Proprietary party were essential to fulfilling his ambition. As he explained to Quaker correspondent Peter Collinson, "An Appearance of Impartiality in general, gives a Man sometimes much more Weight when he would serve in particular Instances."[8]

One of Franklin's foremost political challenges came from German immigrants, who flocked to Pennsylvania during the first half of the 1700s. Driven from their homeland by military conscription and economic woes, the Germans by midcentury were populous and powerful. They had the votes to dominate Pennsylvania politics, and both the population and fortitude to resist cultural mainstreaming into English-speaking society. Eighteen ships transported Germans to Philadelphia in 1732 and 1733, and from 1737 to 1754 ship arrivals from Germany averaged eleven annually. The Proprietary colony was the clear preference of Germans who migrated to the New World, most of whom (about fifty-five thousand) came between 1730 and 1756 due to the lure of a prosperous life in a free country. More than half came as indentured servants, having secured passage by binding themselves to ship captains, who auctioned them off to the highest Pennsylvania bidders.[9]

Pennsylvania was the preferred destination of German immigrants for three reasons: a solid reputation for opportunity, crafted by promoters and settlers who sent back favorable reports to their homeland; the willingness of Germans already settled in Pennsylvania to assist newcomers in relocating and starting a new life; and the readiness of Rotterdam merchants to adapt and implement the English system of transporting indentured servants to America to facilitate immigration and turn a profit.[10]

After arriving, most Germans received naturalization upon pledging "Allegiance to the King of Great Britain, and fidelity to the Proprietors of this Province." Informed that Germans comprised about 100,000 of Pennsylvania's 190,000 residents in 1753, proprietor Thomas Penn expressed surprise at the German majority. "The Number I imagined larger and a greater proportion of English and others, to the Germans," he wrote.[11]

According to a naturalization petition from more than one hundred Germans, they came because of "the great Blessings of Peace and Liberty enjoy'd by the People of Pennsylvania under a good and Pious Proprietor," but a more plausible motive for many German immigrants was the opportunity to re-create and reshape their culture in a new land with few societal traditions. Consequently, the frontier was attractive to many Germans. They could live relatively independent of Eastern laws and values. Residing in their own enclaves, both on the frontier and in seaboard communities such as Germantown, Germans were reluctant to assimilate into the English-speaking mainstream. Responding to a plan to make Germans adopt English culture and language, Franklin wrote, "Their fondness for their own Language and Manners is natural: It is not a Crime."[12]

It was, however, a serious threat to the balance of power. At first, working-class Germans declined to become politically active, preferring to concentrate on making a living. They later became involved, though, upon perceiving attacks on their cultural self-determination. The Germans' political clout, resulting from their sheer numbers, well-organized society, and reluctance to assimilate, made the British middle and upper classes fearful that French settlers in the West might entice the Germans into a military confederation.[13]

The Proprietarians thus decided to court the Germans. They had two motives: to gain their votes in order to break the Quaker stranglehold on the Assembly; and to assimilate them into British society, thereby steering them away from the Quaker influence. The Quakers had enjoyed success luring immigrant Germans to their political camp, promising that the pacifist principles of the religion—and its legislators—would protect Germans from the conscription and oppressive taxes that had impelled their trans-Atlantic voyage. According to a Maryland doctor visiting Philadelphia in 1744, the Quakers maintained political control by "making sure [of] the interest of the Palatines in this province, who of late have turned so numerous that they can sway the votes which way they please."[14]

To achieve their aim, the Proprietary party used vituperative pamphleteering. However, German-language printer Christopher Sauer responded with publications of his own, which convinced German immigrants the Proprietary party had hatched a plot to "enslave them; to force their young Men to be Soldiers, make them serve as Pioneers, and go down to work upon our Fortifications."[15] Most Germans who were eligible to vote supported pacifist Quaker candidates, prompting one observer to complain to Penn that the Germans were incapable "of using their own Judgment in matters of Government."[16] Franklin likewise grumbled, "I remember when they modestly declined intermeddling in our Elections, but now they come in droves, and carry all before them, except in one or two Counties."[17]

As tensions escalated between Proprietarians and Quakers shortly before election day in 1742, allegations that scheming Quakers would induce unnaturalized Germans to vote were countered by accusations that the Proprietary party would use violence to scare Germans away from the polls. Both proved true, and a bloody riot broke out. The violence was symptomatic of the ethnic and religious prejudice that fragmented Pennsylvania's politics and society.[18]

Although Pennsylvania Germans in the mid-eighteenth century were separated by culture and language from their British neighbors, one issue continually aroused interest in both cultural groups: military defense, especially against Native American Indians on the frontier. The German pietist sects were usually pacifist, preferring peaceful co-existence with the Indians. Their pacifism was based partly on morals, but also on their opposition to the expense of a militia and their fear of becoming serfs in a military state. As Conrad Weiser warned in a circular letter to his fellow Pennsylvania Germans, "the Governor & his Party, actually intended to deprive us of our Libertys, & and to obtrude upon us a Militia Act," requiring the establishment of frontier defense. Opposition to it aligned Weiser and other pacifist Germans with the Quakers, who opposed violence on religious principles.[19]

The matter came to a head in the summer of 1747. While England was fighting King George's War against France, attacks by privateers in Delaware Bay alarmed Philadelphia merchants. However, deadlocked by pacifist Quakers and Germans, the Assembly could take no action to protect the city. Franklin cut the Gordian knot with his pamphlet *Plain Truth,* in which he argued persuasively that an effective compromise would be to establish a voluntary provincial militia to protect the city against foreign incursion, particularly from the French and Spanish raiders. "The Way to secure Peace is to be prepared for War," he wrote. "All we want is Order, Discipline and a few Cannon." To marshal public support, Franklin appealed to Philadelphians' darkest fears, cautioning that without military defense of the city, "your Persons, Fortunes, Wives and Daughters, shall be subject to the wanton and unbridled Rage, Rapine and Lust, of *Negroes, Molattoes,* and others, the vilest and most abandoned of Mankind." Franklin carefully balanced his argument to avoid partisanship. He contended it was the people's responsibility to obey government, and government's reciprocal responsibility to safeguard the people. Franklin's pamphlet had the intended effect, for Pennsylvanians approved the plan within days, formed themselves into militia companies, and sent Franklin and other leaders to borrow cannons from New York governor George Clinton.[20]

Franklin's ability to unify the laboring classes and devise a politically expedient defense plan catapulted him to greater prominence throughout the province. Even Quakers, who had opposed military defense because of religious pacifism, grudgingly accepted. "Indeed I had some Cause to believe, that the Defence of the Country was not disagreeable to any of them, provided they were not requir'd to assist in it," Franklin wrote in his memoirs. "And I found that a much greater Number of them than I could have imagined, tho' against offensive War, were clearly for the defensive."[21] In addition to pamphleteering, Franklin used his newspaper to call for an end to factionalism. "O my Friends, let us on this Occasion cast from us all these little Party Views, and consider ourselves as Englishmen and Pennsylvanians," he wrote in the *Pennsylvania Gazette.*[22]

Franklin's facility to unite disparate ethnic, political, and religious groups to work for a common goal also made him a leader of the artisans and a tribune of the people. However, he rankled party leaders with his refusal to publicly commit to either the Proprietary or Quaker side. As provincial secretary Richard Peters wrote to Penn, "considering the popularity of his character and the reputation gained by his Electrical Discoveries . . . he may prove a Dangerous Enemy." Franklin's strength lay in his ability to appeal to what he called the "middling People, the Farmers, Shopkeepers and Tradesmen," whom he regarded as the most vital voting bloc in the province.[23]

Despite his popularity and burgeoning political success, Franklin was dismayed by the Germans' lack of support for the defense plan, even after flattering them in the pamphlet *Plain Truth* by calling them "*brave* and *steady*" and possessing "the most *obstinate Courage.*"[24] The immigrants were more influenced by the views of Sauer, the first successful German-language printer in the American colonies, who was as much a public-opinion leader among the Germans as Franklin was among the English. Sauer responded harshly from his press in Germantown, attacking *Plain Truth* in one pamphlet and publishing another anonymous one against it.[25] Sauer opposed the plan because of his pacifism, religious convictions, concern about cost, and fear that service in Franklin's militia would switch from voluntary to mandatory. He ridiculed Franklin's challenge to German pacifism, asserting that "Goods and blood, body, soul and life are not mine but only God's," and that God would protect the colony.[26]

Sauer's character attacks, plus Franklin's frustration with the Germans' reluctance to defend Philadelphia, augmented Franklin's dismal view of the ethnic group. He resented their unwillingness to assimilate, loathed their unquestioning belief in Sauer, and decided they lacked virtue. Although praising the German immigrants' husbandry and conceding "their industry and frugality is exemplary," Franklin faulted their tendency to "swarm into our Settlements, and by herding together establish their Language and Manners to the Exclusion of ours," and he complained the Germans "will never adopt our Language or Customs, any more than they can acquire our Complexion."[27]

London scientist Peter Collinson, who shared Franklin's fear of a political threat to Pennsylvania from the populous Germans, suggested that cultural assimilation could be best accomplished by shutting down German-language presses and prohibiting importation of German books. These actions would force the Germans to accustom themselves only to the English language.[28] However, the idea of fettering the press conflicted with Franklin's Enlightenment ideals. Instead, he believed that Germans simply needed greater access to anglicized information. He saw two ways to achieve this goal: provide free English schools and publish a competing German-language newspaper. Both projects were eventually implemented, but both failed due to the powerful Sauer's editorial disapprobation. In his *Pensylvanische Berichte* newspaper, Sauer attacked the plan to provide free English education for Germans as an imperial scheme to anglicize Germans. His criticism contributed to the project's collapse several years later.[29]

Sauer also contributed to the failure of Franklin's other effort to provide the immigrants access to anglicized information: a newspaper enabling him to instill his ideology of virtue (which by midcentury included political, as well as moral, virtue) into the German audience. Franklin had first attempted to publish a German-language newspaper in 1732. Recognizing that German immigrants were becoming a populous segment of Pennsylvania society, the opportunistic young Franklin had arranged for Louis Timothee to publish the *Philadelphische Zeitung* on alternate Saturdays. This was the first German-language newspaper in America. In the sample issue, Timothee told German readers, "My promise will be that through good Correspondence with Holland and England I will always have the most distinguished and noteworthy news from Europe as well as here." He also promised to publish ship schedules, market prices, a history of Pennsylvania, and a digest of provincial laws and rights. "To cover the overhead," Timothee wrote, he and Franklin required three hundred subscribers, and he asked readers to voluntarily distribute the *Zeitung* and collect revenues.[30]

Timothee and Franklin received only about fifty subscriptions. Puzzled, they suspected that German readers needed to see another issue of the *Zeitung* before committing their money and support. Seven weeks after the prospectus, the partners published the *Zeitung* again. "I thought that among the German Population of this Country I would be able to find more interest and support, especially among the young Persons, for a Newspaper," Timothee chided his readers in the June 24 issue. "Nevertheless I didn't want to fail in the beginning and hope that we will find some more supporters, otherwise I will be forced to cease." That is exactly what occurred. Few German immigrants supported the newspaper, and no known subsequent issues were published.[31]

Soon after the paper's demise, Timothee was named the librarian of the fledgling Library Company of Philadelphia, one of Franklin's philanthropic projects. Timothee subsequently relocated to South Carolina to replace the deceased Thomas Whitmarsh as Franklin's Charles Town printing partner.[32] In 1739 Sauer succeeded where Timothee and Franklin failed, with the inception of his *Hoch-Deutsch Pensylvanische Geschicht-Schreiber* newspaper in Germantown. By 1751 his subscription list was four thousand names, the largest paid circulation in the colonies, with pass-on circulation pushing his readership over twenty thousand.[33]

Sauer quickly became a persuasive and vigorous leader of the burgeoning Pennsylvania-German populace. A contemporary recalled him as "A religious man of a quick sharp understanding in Natural & Spiritual things" who was "not eloquent in speech but a ready writer."[34] Sauer's religious beliefs required him to devote his life to guiding his German brethren in ways he thought best. His principles dictated that his press issue only instructive reading material, clearly designed to impart moral and Christian teachings. "My small printing shop, now started, is dedicated to God, and I hope . . . that nothing shall be printed except that which is to the glory of God and for the physical or eternal good of my neighbors," he informed a correspondent. "What ever does not meet this standard, I will not print. I have already rejected several, and would rather have the press standing idle. I am happier when I can distribute something of value among the people for a small price, than if I had a large profit without a good conscience."[35]

Having fled Germany for personal freedom and religious toleration, the immigrant readers made the idealistic Sauer their de facto intellectual leader, rewarding him with their patronage. His prominence among the German community gave him a virtual monopoly on German-language printing, and competitors' efforts to make inroads into his revenue or influence consistently failed.

Sauer's ascendancy among the Germans irritated Franklin, who viewed his German counterpart as an isolationist, a foolhardy pacifist, and a vexatious impediment to cultural assimilation. In the wake of the Sauer-influenced German resistance to supporting the voluntary militia, Franklin felt compelled to again attempt to persuade the immigrants. He shared the Proprietary party's desire to lure the Germans away from the Quakers, teach them better politics, and secure their support for such provincial concerns as military defense. The problem, as Franklin saw it, was that the Germans were "of the most ignorant Stupid Sort of their own Nation."[36] He claimed that Pennsylvania's German immigrants consisted of "all the Refuse Wretches poor and helpless who are burthensome," and that many had been released from prison to emigrate.[37] He regarded them as dullards who routinely succumbed to lies but were habitually suspicious of truth. The difficulty of persuading the Germans was compounded by the fact that "as few of the English understand the German Language, and so cannot address them from either the Press or Pulpit, 'tis almost impossible to remove any prejudices they once entertain."[38]

Franklin could do little to influence the Germans from the pulpit, but it was within his means to influence them from the press. Undaunted by his 1732 failure with Louis Timothee, Franklin formed a partnership with immigrant copperplate printer Johann Bohm in 1749 to publish a German-language newspaper to compete with Sauer's *Pensylvanische Berichte* and an almanac to rival his *Hoch-Deutsche Americanische Calender*. The prospects for success were dubious. Since the establishment of Sauer's newspaper a decade before, two short-lived competitors had failed in their bids to secure a segment of his audience. In 1743 Joseph Crellius, a German acquaintance of Franklin, printed the *Hoch-Deutsche Pennsylvanische Journal* and tended an evening school. His paper, the first German weekly in the colonies, folded within the year. Former Sauer apprentice Gotthard Armbruster then began publication of his Philadelphia *Die Zeitung* in 1748.[39] Sauer magnanimously promoted his former worker's new venture in his own newspaper, adding, "please, may the dishonest who have never yet paid Sauer not do the same to him." Even with Sauer's endorsement, Armbruster also failed among German readers, and his newspaper ceased the following year.[40]

With no competitors to challenge Sauer's dominance of German public opinion, Franklin bought Armbruster's equipment and placed Bohm at the helm, referring to him as "the Man that takes Care of my Dutch Printing Office."[41] The partners' *Philadelphier Teutsche Fama* was published from 1749 until Bohm's death in July 1751. Undaunted, Franklin resumed the newspaper several weeks later with a new name and a new format. The *Hoch Teutsche und Englishe Zeitung* debuted August 10, 1751, and was published every two weeks. It contained news, opinion, and advertisements in both English and German, with the two languages usually printed in adjoining columns. Franklin's transparent attempt at cultural assimilation is evident in the newspaper's stated purpose: to publish "entertaining and useful Matters in *both Languages*, adapted to the Convenience of such as incline to learn *either*." Franklin hoped German readers would become anglicized through exposure to the English language, and that concomitantly some English patrons would learn German and thus be able to influence the immigrants in their own language.[42]

His half-German and half-English *Zeitung* sputtering along in Philadelphia, Franklin decided to geographically extend his journalistic mission
of influencing Germans. He formed a partnership with two of his former
journeymen, Samuel Holland and Henry Miller, for a printing shop in
Lancaster, a burgeoning town on Pennsylvania's western frontier that featured a large German population. The partners commenced publication of
the first newspaper there, the biweekly *Lancastersche Zeitung,* on January 15,
1752. Like Franklin's Philadelphia version, Holland and Miller's *Zeitung* was
printed in both German and English in an effort to break down cultural and
linguistic barriers. The Lancaster shop also sold German translations of *Poor
Richard's Almanack,* which counseled Germans, "When Reason preaches, if
you won't hear her she'll box your Ears." Pointedly indicting the pacifism of
Sauer and the Quakers, "Poor Richard" observed in 1753, "Serving God is
Doing Good to Man, but Praying is thought an easier Service, and therefore
more generally chosen." Franklin created his "Poor Richard" character to
provide tutelage. As Franklin explained, "I consider'd it as a proper Vehicle
for conveying Instruction among the common People," including German
immigrants.[43]

To sway German views, Franklin returned to the formula that had succeeded previously in constructing his printing network—he sent partners to
a town that had no local printer. This move, he reasoned, would erode Sauer's
influence on the frontier.

However, he was making no progress countering Sauer in Philadelphia.
Less than two weeks after Holland and Miller commenced their Lancaster
newspaper, Franklin stopped publication of the *Hoch Teutsche und Englishe
Zeitung* on January 25, 1752, following the thirteenth issue. In a valedictory
notice to readers, Franklin deftly avoided admitting defeat by noting, "This
English and Dutch Paper, No. 13 ending the half Year, will be no longer
printed in Philadelphia; one of the same kind being now done in Lancaster,
by good Hands." Using his privilege as Philadelphia postmaster, he offered a
subscription to it "without Charge of Postage." The real reason for the newspaper's demise was obvious, though—Sauer's proudly ethnic press had the
moral and economic support of German readers.[44]

Sauer had outlasted Franklin's competition in Philadelphia, and he did the
same in Lancaster. Although Franklin made Holland the town's postmaster
to provide him additional revenue and free access to the mail, the Lancaster
venture fared no better in siphoning off Sauer's audience. Within the first
few months Miller left the partnership. Holland published the *Lancastersche
Zeitung* for more than a year afterward, but discontinued it June 5, 1753.[45]
Nine days later, he and Franklin mutually voided their partnership contract,

replacing it with a lease. According to its terms, Franklin rented his printing press and assortment of types to Holland for twenty pounds per year.[46]

That Franklin let the discouraged Holland out of the partnership indicates Franklin's belief in Lancaster's strategic importance. Franklin wanted a printing house mirroring his views to remain in Lancaster, offering the hope of influencing and anglicizing frontier Germans. By abrogating the contract, Franklin recognized that Holland's low circulation and minimal advertising revenue would not allow him to pay Franklin the requisite one-third of the profits and remain in business. Thus, Franklin encouraged Holland to stay in Lancaster, relinquishing newspaper publication but continuing to print books, pamphlets, and sermons in German. Holland was unsuccessful, though, and ceased printing several months later. "I heard that S. Holland was broke up," Franklin wrote to Lancaster merchant Edward Shippen in February 1754. Holland's failure in Lancaster surprised Franklin, who believed that "a Printing-House would be thought a publick Convenience in such a Place."[47]

Franklin was frustrated by Holland's failure, but also by his discourteous departure from Lancaster without notifying Franklin what had become of the printing press and type case. However, he still desired to have a printer under his aegis communicating with the Germans on the Pennsylvania frontier. Franklin therefore formed a partnership with William Dunlap, who had married Deborah Franklin's niece. Franklin recommended him to Shippen as "a sober young Man" who "desires to make a little Tryal of Lancaster." Vexed by his own repeated failures to establish a foothold among German readers, Franklin seemed dubious about Dunlap's chances for success. He initially agreed to let Dunlap print in Lancaster only for several months, rather than drafting the standard six-year contract. "If he meets with Encouragement he will settle among you: Otherwise, he will bring away the Press and Letters," Franklin informed Shippen.[48] To help his relative and partner drum up business, Franklin named him postmaster of Lancaster and announced in the *Pennsylvania Gazette*, "All Sorts of Printing Work, Dutch and English, done by WILLIAM DUNLAP, Printer at Lancaster."[49]

Dunlap had been apprenticed to William Bradford in Philadelphia, where he helped publish the *Pennsylvania Journal*, and he arrived in Lancaster in 1754 intending to commence a newspaper there. He told a local merchant, "As I have got all Materials ready for the carrying on a Weekly Newspaper, and a pretty large Number of Subscribers engaged, intend to publish one in a short Time."[50] Whether he intended to resurrect Holland and Miller's half-English, half-German paper is unknown, but Dunlap never succeeded in his intention to publish a newspaper. He did engage in job-printing, though, producing a school primer, religious tracts, sermons, and a description of harsh treatment suffered by a colonist captive of the Indians. Dunlap left Lancaster for Philadelphia in early 1757.[51]

Franklin's propaganda efforts had failed, but he nonetheless remained worried about the German immigrants' growing political might. Furthermore, the threat of war between Britain and France for control of the Great Lakes and the Ohio Valley renewed his fears the Germans might not only refuse to fight with the British, but actually side with the French. "Unless the stream of their importation could be turned from this to other Colonies," Franklin wrote to Collinson in 1753, "they will soon so out number us, that all the advantages we have will not (in my Opinion) be able to preserve our language, and even our Government will become precarious." Franklin added that French soldiers and settlers in the Ohio Valley, "who watch all advantages," may "come to an understanding with" the Pennsylvania Germans. "[I]ndeed in the last war our Germans shewed a general disposition that seems to bode us no good," Franklin wrote, still angered by German rejection of his voluntary-militia idea during King George's War.[52]

When European religious leaders began soliciting funds for the classical education and spiritual formation of rural Germans in the province, Franklin and other prominent Pennsylvanians saw an opportunity to anglicize Germans through classroom training. The concept of free English schooling for Germans ostensibly began as a social and religious movement. An ardent supporter, the Rev. William Smith, claimed it was designed "to qualify the Germans for all the advantages of native English Subjects." However, the plan's true purpose was political. Free English education for the Germans would achieve two purposes: anglicize their thinking and behavior, thereby inducing them to share British concerns; and make them independent in thought and deed, and therefore less susceptible to the blandishments of Sauer and the Quakers. This was implicit in Smith's assertion that the project would enable the Germans, "in a Word, to judge and act entirely for themselves without being obliged to take Things upon the Word of others, whose Interest it may be to deceive and mislead them."[53]

In Franklin's mind, the remedy to the German problem was "to distribute them more equally, mix them with the English [and] establish English Schools where they are now too thick settled." As he informed Collinson, "The Dutch Wou'd fain save all the Money that they Touch; If they can have English Schooling gratis, as much as they love their own Language they will not pay for German schooling." The assimilation plan was executed soon after, with the establishment of the Society for the Relief and Instruction of

Poor Germans. The Society collected funds on both sides of the Atlantic and opened schools in several German-dominated Pennsylvania towns.[54] Asked to serve as a trustee of the Society, Franklin dutifully accepted, adhering to his credo "never to ask for an Office, and never to refuse one when offer'd."[55]

At their first meeting, in August 1754, the trustees read a letter from the Rev. Henry Melchior Muhlenberg, a German-born minister to Lutheran congregations in Pennsylvania. Muhlenberg praised the Society's "Scheme for promoting the Knowlege of God among the Germans in Pennsylvania &c. and for making them loyal Subjects to the sacred Protestant Throne of Great Britain." However, he expressed concern that "some ill-minded Persons would strive to defeat" the plan "to the Offence of many thousand ignorant, but well-meaning Souls, unless proper Measures were taken to prevent it." Muhlenberg named Sauer as the cause of the troubles, noting that he "persuades ignorant People to Quakerism and even Heathenism; For he often tells the People that Clergy of all kinds are Rogues and Tools of tyrannical Government to awe the Mob."[56]

Sauer recognized the charity-school plan for what it was—an attempt at cultural indoctrination of Germans—and vigorously attacked it in his *Pensylvanische Berichte*. Sauer editorialized that the Society's project was part of a plan to forcibly impose the English language and culture on immigrants, even in church. This would compel them "to hear English ministers preach and, being ignorant in that language, they would be obliged to sit in their meetings like geese, and hold their tongues like sheep, for which reason they would rather avoid such charitable gifts."[57]

Muhlenberg found darker motives in Sauer's editorial stance, though. Conceding Sauer's newspaper is "universally read by the Germans all over Pennsylvania and the neighbouring Colonies," Muhlenberg alleged that Sauer "is a professed Adversary to all regularly ordain'd Clergy." Muhlenberg lamented "that such a Man has it much in his Power, and too evidently in his Disposition, greatly to retard this good work and stir up the People" against both the Proprietary government and non-Quaker religious denominations.[58]

Muhlenberg lauded Franklin's journalistic efforts "to rescue the Germans out of Sauer's hands," attributing his repeated failures to the "Want of a German Printer with sufficient Skill and Correspondence, and a proper Interest made to support Mr. Franklin's Undertaking." Despite the setbacks, Muhlenberg stressed the importance of opposing Sauer's influence over the Germans. The "proper Measures" Muhlenberg envisioned to undermine Sauer's clout and "to cure this growing Evil" required the trustees to purchase a printing press "and make a proper Interest to support a News Paper." The

Society adopted his suggestion. It bought a press and types from Franklin at below market value, secured German immigrant Anton Armbruster to run the half-English and half-German newspaper, and made Franklin and Smith the editorial directors. Franklin and Armbruster formed a printing partnership, and the *Philadelphische Zeitung* commenced publication as the official organ of the first Americanization society for immigrants on July 12, 1755.[59]

By supporting the Society's plan and overseeing its printing press, Franklin had one final opportunity to redeem himself and accomplish what had been beyond his grasp—the cultural assimilation of German immigrants. He had long distrusted their isolation and stubborn preservation of their native tongue and customs, but as war with the French loomed on the horizon, Franklin felt a moral imperative to bring the Germans solidly under the English flag. For Franklin, it was a time "when unanimity is became more than ever necessary to Frustrate the Designs of the French," he wrote. This opportunity to establish a German-language press was slightly different, though. For the first time, he had the financial and political backing of a trans-Atlantic group of powerful men who would be sure the press received support. Franklin was further encouraged to make his fifth attempt to counteract Sauer's hold on German minds because he believed in the Society's mission. "I cannot but applaud most sincerely, so judicious, so generous, and so pious an Undertaking; and the Society may depend on everything in my Power that may contribute to its Success," he wrote to Collinson, one of the English architects of the plan.[60]

The Society began auspiciously. By April 1755 Smith was able to report to proprietor Thomas Penn that four schools were operating in the province, six more would soon be open, and fifteen more were being contemplated.[61] In addition to their biweekly newspaper, Armbruster and Franklin published education tracts, religious exegeses, and, to blunt criticism from Sauer, a German translation of the Society's history and aims, written by Smith. The profile emphasized that the charity schools would offer religious instruction to promote "Industry and true Godliness." The partners developed a cordial relationship, with Armbruster naming a son after Franklin.[62]

Just as the charity's inception was fostered by mass communication, so was its demise. Derogatory characterizations of Germans—the very group the Society was trying to aid and persuade—written for print by the two trustees serving as editorial directors contributed to the organization's disbandment several years later. In pamphlets published in 1755 and 1756, Smith called Germans "an uncultivated Race . . . liable to be seduced by every enterprizing Jesuit," and he described them as "insolent, sullen, and turbulent."[63] Franklin contributed to the insult when his "Observations Concerning the Increase of Mankind" pamphlet appeared in America in 1755. In it he described Germans as "Palatine Boors" who were turning Pennsylvania into "a Colony of *Aliens*, who will shortly be so numerous as to Germanize us instead of our Anglifying them."[64] Such slurs augmented German distrust of Franklin and the Society.

These views, coupled with Sauer's claims that the charity schools were ploys to subordinate German identity and interests to British will, spelled the beginning of the end. The *Zeitung*, which had fewer than five hundred subscribers, folded after the issue of December 31, 1757, with Armbruster

Portrait of Franklin J. S. Duplessis (1783)

This is an engraving of a portrait of Franklin that Duplessis painted during Franklin's stint as an American ambassador in France. The Duplessis painting now hangs in the National Portrait Gallery of the Smithsonian Institution.

deeply in debt and Franklin trying to distance himself from the group, the newspaper, and his partner. From London, Franklin instructed his wife "to speak to Armbruster not to make Use of my Name any more in his News Paper, as I have no particular Concern in it, but as one of the Trustees only."[65]

Glad to be free of the political tempest involving German immigrants, Franklin journeyed to London in 1757 as an agent for the Pennsylvania Assembly, trying to persuade the monarchy to rescind the Proprietors' provincial control. Upon returning in 1762, he resumed his role in Pennsylvania politics and the postal system. However, his popularity was waning. In 1756 he had gleefully written, "The People happen to love me," but by 1764 he was forced to concede, "I have many Enemies."[66] The political climate had changed, and Franklin was routed in his 1764 bid for re-election to the Assembly. His fierce opposition to the Paxton Boys' slaughter of peaceful Native American Indians alienated Scots-Irish frontiersmen; his polemic *Cool Thoughts on the Present Situation of Our Public Affairs* angered proponents of Proprietary government; and his character was assaulted by scurrilous pamphleteers, who accused him of greed, wickedness, and immorality. "I bore the personal Abuse of five scurrilous Pamphlets, and three Copperplate Prints, from the Proprietary Party, before I made the smallest Return; and they begin to think they might continue to affront me with Impunity," Franklin complained.[67]

A major factor in his abasement was German opposition, which had been fueled by widespread republication of his decade-old "Observations Concerning the Increase of Mankind" pamphlet insulting Germans. Although Franklin had by this time discarded the guise of political impartiality and made clear his opposition to the Proprietarians, the Quaker-aligned Germans voted against him. Franklin's enemies "carried (would you think it!) above 1000 Dutch from me, by printing part of my Paper," he recalled, "where I speak of the Palatine *Boors herding* together, which they explain'd that I call'd them a *Herd of Hogs*. This is quite a laughing Matter."[68]

During his stint as colonial agent, Franklin waged a pamphlet war in an effort to secure a royal charter for Pennsylvania. Such techniques of persuasion were "necessary to prepare the Minds of the Publick; in which the Proprietors will be gibbeted up as they deserve, to rot and stink in the Nostrils of Posterity."[69]

This propaganda campaign followed Franklin's efforts to prepare the minds of the Pennsylvania Germans. Franklin's involvement with them had been a source of continual frustration to him for nearly two decades, beginning with military defense of the province and ending with a disheartening defeat of his political plans. He had endeavored to use his German-language printing partnerships partly for political gain; but to Franklin, his personal ambitions were harmonious with his desire to exhort Germans to public virtue. His repeated attempts at mass persuasion were calculated to expand his network in a new direction—political influence and cultural assimilation. Like his efforts to extend his moral ideology to the West Indies, though, Franklin's bid to anglicize the Germans he distrusted were replete with failure.

Failure also haunted most of the men whom Franklin enlisted in his attempts to elevate German virtue. Holland faded from sight after he quit the Lancaster printing house. Dunlap's life was filled with tribulations, including bankruptcy, health woes, threats of scandal, lawsuits regarding his mismanagement of the Philadelphia post office, and a turbulent tenure as an Anglican rector. Armbruster was reduced to journeyman status after the charity's newspaper failed, serving under Isaac Collins and others while battling insolvency and insanity. "He imagined that he could, by a special charm, raise or lay the devil," printer Isaiah Thomas remembered, and "he apprehended that he had intercourse with invisible spirits."[70] When he and Franklin were both elderly, Armbruster wrote three pathetic letters seeking succor, "as there are Bonds between us." Franklin apparently never acquiesced.[71] Miller was the only colonial German-language printer to enjoy modest success against the Sauer dynasty—and that came years after he left Franklin's network.[72]

Ultimately, Franklin and his printing partners wielded little influence on the political and social conduct of immigrant Germans. None of his five attempts successfully countered the awesome influence of Christopher Sauer, who is credited with helping maintain the distinctly German character of Pennsylvania for several generations.[73] Fueled by political fervor and patriotic adherence to the emerging American national character, Franklin's ambition to educate and persuade the Germans had exceeded his capability.

8

Franklin Plants a Printer in His Native New England

After retiring from a successful printing career in 1748 and turning over the daily operation of his Philadelphia printing shop to partner David Hall, Franklin relished the opportunity to conduct scientific experiments. "I flatter'd myself that, by the sufficient tho' moderate Fortune I had acquir'd, I had secur'd Leisure during the rest of my Life, for Philosophical Studies and Amusements," Franklin recalled in his *Autobiography*. "I proceeded in my Electrical Experiments with great Alacrity."[1] Franklin's perceptive theories and successful tests resulted not only in international scientific fame and his first academic honors, but also in publication of Connecticut's first newspaper.

Franklin had long been interested in meteorology, partly to improve weather forecasts in his annual *Poor Richard's Almanack,* and partly to satisfy his scientific curiosity about lightning. He was not the first to identify that lightning consisted of electrical charges, but he was first to speculate that it could be demonstrated by experimentation. He theorized that lightning is attracted to certain substances (like iron) and not others (like wax). As a result, he postulated that people could control lightning's destructive power by use of lightning rods. He hoped this theory would "be of Use to Mankind." Franklin described his lightning-rod theories in a scientific pamphlet, and then explained the lightning rod for a general audience in his 1753 *Poor Richard's Almanack.*[2]

In recognition of his discoveries, Harvard College presented him with an honorary Master of Arts degree on July 25, 1753. Not to be outdone, Yale College conferred the same degree on him September 12.[3] "Thus without studying in any College I came to partake of their Honours," Franklin wrote.

"They were confer'd in Consideration of my Improvements & Discoveries in the electric Branch of Natural Philosophy."[4]

Franklin was unable to attend the latter ceremony, but he learned from Yale president Thomas Clap that the college and town needed a printer. Franklin furthermore noted that no newspapers had ever been published in the colony. He therefore became interested in establishing a printing partnership in New Haven, a community of about five thousand. It is "a considerable Town in which there is an University, and a Prospect that a Bookseller's Shop with a Printing House may do pretty well," he observed. He asked his London supplier, William Strahan, to secure a new set of type from famed English type founder William Caslon, and he ordered a new printing press built to his specifications.[5]

Franklin had already established printing houses in Philadelphia, Charles Town, New York, Antigua, and Lancaster, and he maintained a family connection with a press in Newport. However, the opportunity to plant a network printer in Connecticut was too good to pass up. Besides the economic prospect that thriving New Haven and Yale College presented, he also relished the chance to extend his expanding network to New England, which he had fled more than thirty years earlier as a runaway apprentice. He recognized that the printing field in his native Boston was crowded, but he saw opportunities for expansion elsewhere in New England. Other than Boston, and a short-lived attempt by his older brother James in Newport, Rhode Island, no newspapers had ever been printed north of New York. Situated between New York and Massachusetts, Connecticut seemed an excellent choice.[6]

Franklin held a strong personal affinity for Connecticut, which magnified as he became exasperated with acrimonious Pennsylvania politics. "I abhor these altercations," he wrote in 1755 amid the Proprietarian-Quaker struggles, "and if I did not love the Country and the People, would remove immediately into a more quiet Government, Connecticut, where I am also happy enough to have many Friends." Later that year, he noted he had "long entertain'd a Fondness for Connecticut. The Country and the People are both a good deal to my Taste."[7]

Envisioning New Haven as a valuable addition to his network, Franklin bought a small lot in November 1753 near the Yale College campus, on which he intended to erect a printing office. He made plans for the shop to be built, but then reconsidered. He wrote to local merchants, "reflecting on the Sum you suppose the Building will cost, and remembring from dear Experience that the final Amount is generally double the Computation, I

begin to think, that 'till we have made Trial how the Business is like to be encourag'd, it will be better to hire a Room or two, or accept of Mr. Clap's kind
Offer of a Room in the College for the first Year." The shop ultimately
opened in rented quarters.[8] Franklin later sold this lot to Parker in 1757 for
ninety dollars.[9]

Franklin intended to travel from Philadelphia to New Haven once the
press and types arrived from England and oversee the inauguration of the
printing office himself. "As soon as I hear of their Arrival, I purpose a Journey
into Connecticut," he wrote.[10] Franklin expected the materials to arrive in the
spring of 1754, but delays by both Caslon and the pressmaker postponed
their arrival until the fall.[11] Once the press and types arrived in New York,
printing partner James Parker sent them to New Haven under the care of
John Holt, a bankrupt Virginia merchant and former mayor of Williamsburg.
Because Holt was a brother-in-law of William Hunter, the *Virginia Gazette*
printer and (with Franklin) joint deputy postmaster-general of the colonies,
he had become acquainted with the Philadelphia printing magnate. Franklin
befriended Holt and persuaded Parker to teach him the printing trade at
Parker's printing house in Woodbridge, New Jersey, until the New Haven
supplies arrived.[12] This delay frustrated Franklin. "Not receiving the Printing
House as expected last Spring, has been a considerable Disappointment," he
admitted.[13]

Franklin faced even greater disappointment in the matter of who would
run the New Haven office. He initially planned to set up his nephew, James
Franklin Jr., in the shop. The young man's seven-year apprenticeship to
Franklin had expired in 1747, after which he joined his mother Ann in
Newport to carry on the printing business established by his deceased father.
Franklin decided it was time for his nephew, in his early twenties, to have his
own business. "I am now about to establish a small Printing Office in favour
of [a] Nephew, at Newhaven in the Colony of Connecticut in New England,"
Franklin announced in October 1753. A month later, this was still Franklin's
plan. He informed Strahan that the "small Printing House" that he desired
furnished with a new press and types was "intended for a Nephew of mine at
Newhaven in Connecticut." James later declined, though, preferring to remain in the family printing business in Newport that his father had left to
him and his mother.[14]

Franklin then offered the New Haven shop to another nephew, Benjamin
Mecom, who was running Franklin's Antigua printing shop. Although dissatisfied with the partnership terms in Antigua, Mecom declined to abandon
the shop in favor of New Haven. This left Franklin with a printing operation

in search of a printer. "My Nephews that are Printers having one after the other changed their Minds, and chusing to continue where they are, the one at Antigua, and the other at Newport," Franklin informed New Haven merchants who were eagerly awaiting the arrival of New Haven's first printer.[15]

Disappointed by his family connections, Franklin was forced to ask dependable network printer James Parker to take over temporarily in New Haven. "I must find another Hand for your Place," Franklin replied to the New Haven merchants in November 1754. "In the meantime, Mr. Parker of New York will come I believe and make trial this Winter."[16] Parker was a loyal associate, but hesitant to leave New York. He first tried to persuade one of his own workers, John Holt, to accept the New Haven post. "Before I began a News-paper at New-Haven, I offered him that Printing-House, on the same Terms I had it of you, but he declined it quite," Parker wrote to Franklin. Parker then reluctantly agreed to Franklin's request for him to leave his New Jersey and New York printing operations in the hands of his subordinates and relocate to New Haven. Parker decided "to beat the Way" to New Haven only because of his hope that the New Haven shop could be kept in his family by passing it on to his nephew Samuel Parker, whom he took to New Haven as an apprentice.[17]

To help Parker generate revenue and give him free access to the mail, Franklin appointed him postmaster of New Haven. Franklin also arranged for Parker to receive the printing contracts for the town and Yale College. Parker commenced publication of the *Connecticut Gazette,* the first newspaper in that colony, April 12, 1755.[18]

In the newspaper's inaugural issue, Parker asserted the importance of press freedom in Connecticut. In "a Land possess'd by the Offspring of a People, who bravely fought the howling Wilderness with all its savage Terrors, rather than become the servile Slaves of bigoted Tyrants," free expression must be respected, he wrote in a front-page editorial. "The press has always been an Enemy to Tyrants," he added, "and just so far as Tyranny prevails in any Part of the World, so far the Liberty of the Press is suppressed." Parker asserted his intention not to publish anything that might disturb the colony's tranquility, but added that the press performed an important surveillance function in society. He noted that it was "better to be alarmed falsely twice, than by one fatal Security suffer a real Harm."[19]

The following year, Parker returned to the theme of a newspaper's public utility. "The PRESS is not so much considered, as the Property of the Men who carry on the Trade of Printing, as of the Publick," he wrote. It provides citizens a means for "asserting all their just Rights, redressing Grievances, detecting Error, advancing useful Knowledge, and making an Appeal to the Reason and Justice of the whole Race of Mankind."[20] Religious enlightenment was one of the forms of knowledge the press could convey, a *Connecticut Gazette* contributor noted approvingly. Because of printing, "our Notions of Religion and the Deity, receive continual Improvements, and proceed in a Progressive State towards Perfection."[21] By publishing such religious matter, Parker adhered to Franklin's expectation that his partners extend his ministry of virtue to a wide audience.

Parker sought to fill his newspaper with items that would interest Connecticut residents. From the outset, he displayed a particular affinity for sensational news. His first issue contained a story of a man who killed his wife by beating her skull with a hammer. Afterward, he removed her clothing and placed her corpse in bed with the couple's two children, "one of whom was near four Years old, and to keep the Child from crying, he gave him a Piece of Bread to eat." Later, neighbors who entered the bedroom "found the poor Baby eating the Bread sopp'd in his Mother's Blood."[22] In an issue that summer, he reported that a British soldier stuck his rifle into his mouth to moisten it. The gun "accidentally went off, in his mouth, and tore his head asunder."[23] Other sensational news in the *Gazette* included reports of an earthquake in New Haven, a colony-wide drought that harmed crops, and how a New England slave took revenge for poor treatment by throwing his master's child down a well.[24]

Parker arranged to distribute the *Connecticut Gazette* throughout the New Haven area via street sales and the mail, and he hired a post rider to carry the newspaper to Hartford. Parker's print shop and newspaper were successful, but he was growing increasingly disconsolate. After six months, he wished to return to his wife and children in Woodbridge. At the same time, Holt—seeing Parker's success in New Haven—reconsidered Parker's earlier offer and asked to take over the New Haven operation. "As I had before offered it, I did not love to be worse than my Word," Parker wrote, although it was "after I had run the Risk and beat the Road." However, he also did not wish to abandon his plan to turn the shop over to his nephew Samuel once he completed his apprenticeship. Samuel had three years remaining on his apprenticeship, so Parker left Samuel in New Haven and turned over the operation to Holt in the fall of 1755. Holt and Samuel often quarreled, though, prompting Samuel to leave New Haven after slightly more than a year and return to New York. He completed his apprenticeship under Parker's New York partner, William Weyman.[25]

During Holt's tenure at the helm of the *Connecticut Gazette,* much of the news concerned the French and Indian War, in which Great Britain and France fought for control of North America. Holt was unabashedly partisan, reporting "daily Outrages on our Frontiers," particularly by Native American Indians allied with the French. One account Holt published described a British lieutenant from Connecticut who "was most cruelly massacred, having his Mouth cut open, and Tongue cut out, his Entrials taken out of his Body, and afterwards crammed into his Mouth." Not all the wartime news under Holt's editorial direction was gruesome, though. One story told of John Trumbull (later a renowned Connecticut writer), who took an entrance test for Yale College. Trumbull "passed a good Examination, although but little more than seven years of age; but on account of his Youth his father does not intend he shall at present continue at College."[26]

Holt remained in New Haven until February 1760, when Parker summoned him to run the New York office as a full partner. Holt asked for a delay until summer, so Parker superintended the New York office himself until Holt arrived. Holt then turned the New Haven shop over to an employee. He informed readers, "The business will be carried on as usual by Mr. Thomas Green."[27]

Following Holt's relocation to New York in 1760, Green superintended the New Haven shop and continued to publish the *Connecticut Gazette* under the name "James Parker & Company" until April 14, 1764, when Green decided to go into business for himself. He relocated to Hartford, published a specimen issue of the *Connecticut Courant* on October 29, and commenced weekly publication of the newspaper December 3. It continues to this day as the *Hartford Courant,* the oldest American newspaper in continuous existence.[28]

After Green departed New Haven in 1764, the *Connecticut Gazette* was suspended for more than a year, and New Haven was left without a printer until Franklin's nephew Benjamin Mecom arrived. Mecom had left the Antigua partnership in a huff in 1756, later failing at publishing ventures in Boston and New York. He sought the Boston postmastership, fully expecting his uncle would remove incumbent postmaster Tuthill Hubbart and install Mecom. In response to a letter from his sister Jane, seeking the post for her son, Franklin declined. He stated it would be wrong to dismiss a good worker, adding that he had already provided his nephew considerable assistance.[29]

Without the postmastership to give him the benefit of free mailing, Mecom decided not to print a newspaper in Boston. Instead, he briefly published a monthly magazine titled *The New England Magazine of Knowledge and Pleasure.* "Each number, when published, was sent about town for sale by

hawkers; but few copies were vended, and the work, of course, was discontinued," Boston printing apprentice Isaiah Thomas recalled. He described Mecom
wearing a powdered wig and clothes with ruffles, and noted that although he
was "a correct and good printer," he was "deficient in the art of managing
business to profit" and "singular in his manners." Thomas described Mecom's
behavior as "*queer.*"[30] Mecom tried to make his family believe he was succeeding in Boston. "I am glad to hear he is in so Prosperous a Way," Franklin
wrote to Mecom's mother Jane. Finally, though, Mecom had to admit failure
to his mother. "Ben has expearanced what is the common fate of all children
at some time or other but the Litle Rogues all want to be Pityed by them that
Loves them & I sopose to Recve that comfort he would be brought to you to
Kiss the Dear Lip after it was Hurt," his mother wrote to Deborah Franklin.[31]

As his mother predicted, Mecom did visit the Franklins in Philadelphia to
enlist financial support for a new publishing venture in New York. "Benja.
has been to see me as you supposed," Franklin reported to Jane in November
1762. Mecom commenced a newspaper called the *New-York Pacquet* in July
1763. It also failed, lasting less than two months and costing Franklin 200
pounds sterling. As Franklin wearily noted to Strahan that year, Mecom
"dropt his Paper, on which he built his last Hopes."[32]

Despite the continued failures, Franklin felt sorry for his nephew, whom
he described as "dejected and spiritless." He invited Mecom to revive the
Connecticut Gazette in New Haven and named him postmaster of the town.
The newspaper recommenced July 5, 1765, and continued until February
1768. During that time, Mecom mismanaged post-office funds. "I can't get
one Penny of Mecom and begin to fear, I never shall," Parker, in his capacity
as postal comptroller, complained to Franklin. "I have wrote pressingly, but
all won't do: I can't get the Post-Office Accounts of him."[33] Franklin interceded on Mecom's behalf with creditors, pleading for leniency and explaining
that he had endured a great deal of misfortune. One creditor in Scotland
wrote back sympathetically, "the young Gentleman is much to be pitied, as it
woud appear that his Circumstances in a good measure have gone wrong
thro an Act of Providence."[34] Mecom's financial bungling also prompted
Parker to revoke the power of attorney he had granted Mecom. Compounding
Mecom's self-inflicted difficulties, he also was prosecuted for violating Connecticut law by not attending church.[35]

Fittingly, the *Connecticut Gazette*'s final issue contained Mecom's plea for
delinquent subscribers to settle their accounts so Mecom could move his
family to Philadelphia.[36]

Connecticut's first newspaper came into existence as a result of Franklin's desire to expand the scope of his printing network to New Haven and establish a foothold for his network in New England. As a "famous first" in Connecticut history, the publication of the *Connecticut Gazette* by Benjamin Franklin's printing partner James Parker was successful. However, from a business standpoint, the New Haven printing shop was less so. Franklin was forced to place the new venture in the hands of the overworked but reliable Parker after two of his nephews declined. Far from his New Jersey home, Parker opened the shop at Franklin's behest with the intention of passing it on to his own ne'er-do-well nephew, but this plan also failed. Parker couldn't help but notice the irony, telling Franklin he started the New Haven shop only "for a Prospect of providing a Place for my Nephew," adding, "I believe you Sir, once designed a Favour for your Nephew but was disappointed as well as I."[37]

For Franklin, affairs concerning the New Haven printing office were frustrating. After Parker it passed through two other printers before ending up in the hands of Mecom, to whom it had originally been offered. All of Parker's successors proved unreliable in making payments, Franklin was forced to sue John Holt for his failure to make remittances as New Haven postmaster, and Parker spent years trying in vain to extract money Holt owed him from the New Haven press.[38]

In the end, Parker blamed the failures and the unreliability of their nephews on drink. He wrote to Franklin, "the present Race of young Printers seeming to me most of them, so abandoned to Liquor, as to deserve little Encouragement." Franklin, though, may have thought of his "Poor Richard" epigram written during the time of the New Haven partnership: "Neglect mending a small Fault, and 'twill soon be a great One."[39]

9

Renegade Second-Generation Printers

Thinking more of his successful early partnerships than of his disappointing mid-century forays, Franklin wrote of his associates, "Most of them did well, being enabled at the End of our Term, Six Years, to purchase the Types of me; and go on working for themselves, by which means several Families were raised."[1] Despite his inability to establish enduring printing houses in Connecticut, Antigua, or the Pennsylvania German culture, Franklin remained the head of the most influential journalism alliance in colonial America. As his associates struck out on their own, they collected employees, and some, partners, all the while remaining bound to Franklin by contract, indebtedness, or loyalty.

Franklin's most loyal and prominent printing partners were David Hall, Peter Timothy, and James Parker. After a cautious start, Hall and Franklin enjoyed a warm relationship until Hall's death in 1772. "Mr. F. writes in the handsomest Manner of you, and is perfectly pleased with your Conduct and Behaviour," Hall's mentor William Strahan told him. In a letter to Franklin, Hall offered an idea of why he had earned Franklin's admiration and respect—he remained faithful, stayed sober, worked diligently, and never challenged Franklin's authority. "I flatter myself that my Conduct, in general," he wrote, "is satisfactory to you, for I can, with great Truth, say, I have never done any thing, either with respect to public or private Business, but with a View to please all Parties; and if I have not altogether succeeded in it, I am sorry for it; it must be imputed to an Error of my Judgment, not of my Will."[2]

Timothy, more feisty than the placid and businesslike Hall, periodically involved himself and his newspaper, the *South-Carolina Gazette*, in controversy.

He was cited in a grand-jury presentment for printing protests against South Carolina governor James Glen's enforcement of Sunday laws and for attacking the governor's frontier policies.[3] He also was sanctioned for his attacks on Glen's handling of colonial relations with Choctaw Indians. "The wretched Management of Indian Affairs by that Gentleman has occasioned the imposing Silence on my Press, under various Pretences," Timothy informed Franklin. Despite his periodic brushes with royal authority, Timothy printed in the colony for forty years. "Timothy was a decided and active friend of his country," according to Isaiah Thomas, who spent two years working in Charles Town for one of Timothy's rival printers, Robert Wells. "He was a very intelligent and good printer and editor," and "As a citizen he was much respected."[4]

Parker was the most active of Franklin's associates, and he was the one on whom Franklin placed the greatest demands. Franklin asked him to serve the post office as comptroller and the printing network as accountant, attorney, and master printer in several locations. During his career, Parker operated presses in New York, New Haven, and both Woodbridge and Burlington, New Jersey. Parker began as a master printer in 1741, when Franklin set him up as a New York partner after his exemplary service as a journeyman in the Philadelphia shop. Two years later, Parker established the *New-York Post-Boy* newspaper, changing its name to the *New-York Gazette, or Weekly Post-Boy* in 1747. Parker was quick-tempered and melancholy, but his loyalty to Franklin was unquestionable. "I never in my Life, acted any Thing with Design to pain you, but am fully convinced I have often done what has pained me to try if I could give you any Satisfaction," he told Franklin.[5] Parker's tireless devotion to Franklin and the network prompted Franklin to call him "a very honest and punctual Man," and "my trusty and loving Friend."[6]

Just as Franklin was frustrated in his bid to place relatives in charge of the New Haven press, Parker was also disappointed when he tried to utilize family members to operate his various printing houses. Parker's son Samuel Franklin Parker and his nephew Samuel Parker learned the printing trade in Parker's New York shop, but both were too young to be of much help during Parker's expansion into Woodbridge and New Haven. Without family help for his printing operations—which by mid-century had grown dramatically due to increasing job printing, government printing, a successful book trade, and his thriving newspaper—Parker turned to others for assistance. It was a decision he would come to regret.[7]

Franklin's expanding network during the mid-eighteenth century paled in comparison to his emerging prominence as a statesman and key figure in the colonies. Thus, he was not able to spend as much time controlling his printing concerns, leaving that responsibility to be increasingly shouldered by Hall and Parker. Departing for England in 1764 to act as an agent for the Pennsylvania Assembly, Franklin yielded formal control of the network to Parker, giving him power of attorney to oversee "long Accounts of Partnership."[8]

As network members sensed Franklin's lessened influence and interest in his printing enterprises, rifts began to surface within the ranks, especially among the "second generation" printers. Left to the control of the embattled, gout-ridden Parker, Franklin's fragile web of printers began to twist and tear.

Several network members had difficulties with disloyal apprentices, about whom they informed Franklin. Timothy had a troublesome relationship with apprentice Charles Crouch, who gambled, drank excessively, and was often absent from the printing shop. Thus, Timothy published warnings about Crouch's character and penchant for swindling. In 1750 Timothy printed a notice that Crouch had run away and warned, "whoever harbors or entertains him will be prosecuted with the utmost severity." Crouch was returned, but the following year, the sixteen-year-old Crouch "absented himself" again, prompting Timothy to comment that the apprentice "hath since (as well as at many other times) been seen tipling and gaming in divers public houses in this town." Timothy described him as having "a mighty pleasant countenance," although "his knees incline inward to each other."[9] Crouch seems to have stayed put for two years before wanderlust struck again in February 1753. This time, he tried to collect Timothy's debts for his own use. Timothy warned "that no person whosoever, do pay any monies on my account to Charles Crouch, or have any dealings with him in my name." Timothy reported that Crouch was "at Port-Royal, where he pretended to be free and that he was sent to collect my debts in the country." Crouch was apprehended, but he ran away again in June, only to return again.[10] Timothy's patience was finally exhausted by the following year. "I discharged my villainous Apprentice, gave him two Years Time, quitted all Claims on him for Monies received and gamed away, for Loss of Time, and Charges," the printer wrote to Franklin. "A Lad very capable of the Business, and might have been of vast Service to me, but for 3 Years has always pulled the Contrary Way, owing to an unhappy Affection for Drink, Play, and scandalous Company."[11]

Parker also had difficulties with perfidious apprentices. Franklin arranged for his nephew Benjamin Mecom to learn the trade in Parker's New York shop, but Mecom proved dilatory and irresponsible, clashing with Parker's industrious character and attention to detail. Franklin sided with Parker, telling Mecom's parents, "I believe Mr. Parker has in every respect done his Duty by him; and in this Affair has really acted a generous Part." The relationship worsened, though, and Parker generously consented to release Mecom from the apprenticeship "on the first Mentioning of it," Franklin wrote.[12]

Franklin directed another vexatious apprentice to Parker after the boy's father, a London printer, asked Franklin to assign him to a print shop. The boy, Lewis Jones, was prone to "Irregularities and Extravagancies" in his social life, thus prompting the father to ask Franklin to "give Instructions to the Person whom you shall think proper to place him under, that he may [be] kept closely to work, and not suffer'd to ramble out after the Hours of Business." A family friend asked that Jones be placed with David Hall, but Franklin instead chose Parker as the master.[13] Parker reported to Franklin that Jones fled to join the British army in 1766. "He loves Drink rather too much, and he is now a Flogger and Drummer in the Army: so he is lost to Goodness and Virtue: and I have lost the Money and Service that was due to me," Parker noted. During Jones's service "he never was any Advantage to me," Parker recalled later, while informing Franklin that Jones had tried to frame Parker's son for counterfeiting.[14]

Parker's difficulties with partners dwarfed his ill fortune with apprentices, though. His efforts to emulate Franklin's practice of offering printing partnerships to nonfamily members were replete with failure, causing major rifts in the Franklin network. The first occurred in the 1750s. William Weyman, who had served his apprenticeship with William Bradford in Philadelphia, worked as a journeyman in Parker's New York printing house. Encouraged by several friends, Weyman left Parker in 1750 to set up his own shop and compete against Parker in New York. Weyman journeyed to London to purchase the needed equipment, but the financial backing on which he counted did not materialize. Weyman chronicled his woes in a letter to Parker, adding that he was too ashamed to return to Parker's employ.[15] Moved by sympathy and seeing the opportunity to create a second generation of the Franklin network by emulating Franklin's practice of partnerships, Parker purchased the press and printing materials of the Zenger family and offered them to Weyman "on reasonable Terms to save his Credit," Parker recalled.[16]

In 1751, another of Parker's journeymen, Hugh Gaine, notified Parker that a brother had just arrived from Ireland. Parker housed the brother for five weeks without charging rent and, being impressed with his character, offered to set him up as a bookseller in Parker's hometown of Woodbridge, New Jersey, where he owned a house and shop. Parker and Hugh Gaine were each to receive one-fourth of the profits, while the brother kept the other half

Drawing of Hugh Gaine

Hugh Gaine had a long and financially successful career as a New York printer. However, he is best remembered for his two betrayals: first of his printing mentor and partner James Parker, and later of the Patriot cause when he transferred his allegiance to the Royalist cause in 1776.

of the profits and had "the Use of my House, Shop, Bed and Negroes gratis," Parker wrote.[17]

While Parker was setting up one Gaine in business, the other was seething. Unbeknownst to Parker, Hugh Gaine had seen Parker's letter offering the Zenger press to Weyman. Although he never let Parker know he was angry, Gaine was upset that Weyman, the deserter, and not he, the faithful employee, had been offered the partnership. Smarting from rejection, and feeling as though he, Weyman, and Parker were re-enacting the Biblical story of the Prodigal Son, Gaine covertly planned to establish his own shop. He ordered a press from England and sent his own letter to Weyman asking if he was interested in a partnership. Adding fuel to Gaine's fire was the fact that Parker dismissed Gaine's brother in February 1752. According to Parker, the brother was losing money and mistreating the "two old Negroes, and two Negro Children belonging to me." His brother's dismissal was the last straw for Hugh Gaine. He left Parker days later and set up shop in New York.[18]

After selling books and stationery for several months, Hugh Gaine received his press in the summer of 1752. About the same time, both he and Parker received a letter from Weyman, informing them he would not decide which offer to accept until he arrived in New York several months later. Gaine was confident Weyman would accept his proposal, though, prompting him to advertise books and writing paper for sale "by WEYMAN and GAINE, at their House on Hunter's Key." In an effort to sweeten the offer to Weyman and lure him away from Gaine, Parker then decided that, instead of selling the Zenger press to Weyman and letting him establish himself independently, he would allow Weyman to take over the New York operation while Parker himself would take the Zenger press to the Woodbridge shop.[19]

Parker aspired to an arrangement like the one shared by Franklin and Hall in Philadelphia, in which Franklin gradually withdrew from daily printing operations and left matters in Hall's charge. Parker believed that this arrangement and the lessened responsibilities of publishing in the small Woodbridge shop would allow him to pursue other interests, just as Franklin did. For Parker, these included serving as a county judge, militia officer, and lay reader in the Episcopalian church, the latter of which was his favorite. "In that Employ, tho' a poor Workman, I think I labour for a good Master, who has often rewarded me far more largely than I deserve," he wrote. He also hoped the partnership with Weyman and concomitant relocation to Woodbridge would be easier on his health, which was plagued by fatigue and gout in his ankles, feet, and hands.[20]

Weyman ultimately chose Parker's offer, although he did not agree until the next year to take over the New York operation. "I resigned entirely to his management," Parker claimed, "and as it was inconsistent with Reason to have two Masters on the Spot, I left him to command." According to their partnership terms, Weyman was to provide monthly accounts to Parker, but he never did, nor did he give Parker a sufficient share of the profits. Weyman was also the defendant in several costly suits, and he mismanaged the business by failing to collect debts. By late 1758, even the patient Parker could no longer tolerate Weyman's incompetence and wrote, "some high Words have passed." Parker demanded Weyman either settle accounts or resign from the partnership. Weyman refused, as though daring Parker to take him to court. Jacob Goelet, a friend to both men, interceded. At length they arranged a deal whereby Parker bought out Weyman for two hundred pounds. In exchange, Weyman was to relinquish his printing materials February 1, 1759, collect all debts by May 1 of that year, and vacate the New York premises by the same date. Parker reluctantly planned to return to New York to resume the operation.[21]

Without fully compensating Parker, Weyman purchased a press and persuaded the New York Assembly to name him its printer in place of the incumbent Parker, who had been New York's public printer since 1743. Weyman remained in this capacity from 1759 until his death in 1768. Although he claimed to have been surprised by this charge, Parker must have known his loss of the government printing contract was imminent. At least three times between 1752 and 1759, his and Weyman's newspaper had aroused the ire of the DeLancey faction, which held the majority in the New York Assembly. On one of those instances, Parker and Weyman published a letter in the *New-York Post-Boy* that claimed the colony's legislature was not providing sufficient military defense during the French and Indian War. The two printers were found guilty of contempt and spent ten days in jail. In winning the government contract, Weyman convinced the Assembly that his earlier defamation was under Parker's order.[22]

Parker had often been troublesome to the New York provincial government. When it issued a stamp tax in 1756 on newspapers and legal documents, Parker complained bitterly in his newspaper, alleging the colony's tax was discriminatory and would put him out of business.[23] He continued his laments in a broadside, ridiculing the government's rationale of taxing newspapers because they were luxury items. "If News-Papers are tax'd, because they are a Luxury," Parker queried, "why might not all other Branches of Luxury in Tradesmen also? I could mention several; in particular, Silver-Smith's Work."[24] On another occasion, the governor's council indicted Parker for blasphemous libel after publishing a fictional tale about the religious beliefs of Native American Indians that ridiculed Christian doctrines of Heaven and Hell.[25]

Parker's freedom of expression angered New York colonial governor Charles Hardy. Hardy particularly objected to newspaper reports revealing the British army's troop movements during the French and Indian War. "Printers take a liberty of Communicating to all the Publick by means of their Papers, Every March the Forces take, when Convoys of Provisions are going, and to go to the Army," he complained. "Surely they may be said to be the Publick Intelligencers to the Enemy." As a result, Hardy sought the support of other governors to restrain the press from publishing the military information. "I am aware how Clamorous the World is in being deny'd the Liberty of the Press, that shall not discourage me, as I am certain such a Licentiousness is Incompatible with the Publick Service," he wrote to Pennsylvania governor William Denny. Hardy resolved to "crush the printers in New York" because of their "impudence and arrogance."[26]

By 1759, Parker was too incapacitated with gout to leave his New Jersey home and return to the New York printing shop as he had planned, so he sent his nephew Samuel Parker. The younger Parker, who had been his uncle's apprentice from about 1752 to 1758, had formerly served in the elder Parker's New Haven printing house. When Samuel Parker took over the New York printing house in 1759 in lieu of his infirm uncle, Weyman began to publish a newspaper with the same name as Parker's, the *New-York Gazette,* adding only his last name to the title. In response, Samuel Parker settled on *Parker's New-York Gazette: or, the Weekly Post-Boy.* The two gazetteers then waged journalistic warfare, with Weyman firing the first volley against both the Parkers in the pages of *Weyman's New-York Gazette.* Financially, the young Parker's newspaper was inferior to Weyman's, as Weyman had kept the subscriber list from his days of partnership with James Parker. Samuel Parker was also overmatched in writing skills, appearing more vituperative in print than the calm and witty Weyman. After numerous essays detailing Weyman's financial negligence and shady character, New York readers became annoyed by Samuel Parker's penchant for airing dirty laundry in public. Eventually, public outcry compelled the young Parker to promise silence on the matter.[27]

James Parker declined to be silent. He lambasted Weyman in a 1759 broadside and sued him later that year for violating the terms of their agreement. The case dragged on, with Parker planning to take it to trial for public vindication. Before it got that far, Weyman admitted his guilt on July 11, 1761. Through court referees, he agreed to pay Parker 250 pounds within one year. Meanwhile, Samuel Parker "took to drinking immoderately and I saw he would soon run to Wreck and Ruin," James Parker recalled. Samuel relinquished the newspaper early in 1760 and moved to the West Indies, where he died shortly thereafter. His nephew having deserted him, Parker turned to Holt in February 1760, asking him to leave New Haven and run the New York office as a full partner. When Holt asked for a delay until July, Parker superintended the office himself until Holt arrived.[28]

Once the crafty Holt took over, he initiated a series of shrewd business moves to counter the success of Weyman and Gaine. He changed the publication day from Monday to Thursday to secure timely news via the midweek mail from Albany and Philadelphia. In December 1761, Holt and Parker financed a mail run from New York to Boston via New Haven, Hartford and Springfield, forbidding the post riders to carry any other newspapers than their own. Holt also boosted the number of original and reprinted essays in the newspaper and slashed the advertisement price from five shillings for one ad—the same price Weyman charged—to five shillings for five ads. These measures adversely affected both Gaine and Weyman. The latter, however, was suffering even more from the same business blunder he had committed while working for Parker—failing to collect for his work. He was sued at least seven times by creditors from July 1762 through April 1764. He lost all of the suits, including another one to Parker for the 250 pounds Weyman already owed plus 300 pounds in damages and penalties. These suits wiped him out financially and forced him on two separate occasions to sell the contents of his printing shop. "Weyman continues yet, but I am credibly informed, he owes more than he is worth, and every Thing he has is under Execution, but they let him go on as they can't do any Thing better," Parker informed Franklin.[29]

Unable to induce his customers to pay, the financially destitute Weyman plummeted from his lofty position in New York printing. His fate was sealed with the passage of the Stamp Act of 1765, which taxed paper products, among other goods. His finances too depleted to print newspapers for which a tax had to be paid in advance, Weyman published his *Gazette* sporadically from June 1765 to December 1767 until permanently discontinuing it. He also yielded the government printing contract to Gaine in exchange for a year's pay. In his newspaper's valedictory issue, Weyman blamed Parker and Franklin for his woes, claiming that Parker in his capacity as postal comptroller and Franklin as deputy postmaster-general covertly misused the postal system to favor the distribution of some newspapers and inhibit others. Parker sarcastically notified Franklin in England of Weyman's "elegant Expressions," which he wrote "are a Mixture of Truth and Lies, jumbled in one vile Language." Weyman died a few months later, hopelessly insolvent. Thus Parker had lived to see the ruin of the former partner who had treated him shabbily.[30]

Gaine, on the other hand, enjoyed modest success after breaking away from Parker and founding *The New-York Mercury,* which commenced publication in 1752. Parker labeled him one of "my Antagonists," enviously noting that Gaine had acquired "new Types, but mine are bad." Parker was also jealous that Gaine, rather than Parker, received the Assembly's appointment as government printer when Weyman relinquished it.[31]

However, Gaine soon discovered the complexities of the editorial decision-making process. As the colony of New York made plans to open a public college under religious control, controversy surrounded the issue of which Protestant denomination should be chosen. When New York lawyer William Livingston and his allies editorialized against Anglican control, Gaine, an Irish Catholic-turned-Anglican, refused to print their essays. Livingston then attacked Gaine's judgment and character in a newspaper he and others paid Parker to publish, the *Independent Reflector*. Livingston wrote:

> I could name a Printer, so attached to his private Interest, that for the sake of advancing it, set up a Press, deserted his Religion, made himself the Tool of a Party he despised, privately contemned and vilified his own Correspondents, published the most infamous Falsehoods against others, slandered half the People of his Country, promised afterwards to desist, broke that Promise, continued the Publication of his Lies, Forgeries and Misrepresentations; and to compleat his Malignity, obstinately refused to print the Answers or Vindications of the Persons he had abused.[32]

Parker could not resist the opportunity to chide his former employee. He noted that a printer should publish "what is conducive of the general Utility." If he refuses, "Such Refusal is an immediate Abridgement of the Freedom of the Press." Gaine changed his mind and published their essays, but he complained that one of their writings "could have no other Tendency than to display the Author's *Plagiarism*, as the first two Paragraphs are taken from Vol. 4, No. 287, of Mr. Addison's *Spectator*."[33]

Gaine became notorious for his flip-flopping during the Revolutionary War. Initially espousing the Patriot cause, Gaine wanted to print New York governor Cadwallader Colden's Royalist view of the 1775 battles of Lexington and Concord. He later changed his mind, though. Colden attributed the reason to public pressure. "Hancock and Adams came to Town on Saturday, and were probably consulted by some of the Party here, and with them determined still to suppress every account but their own," he wrote to a British general.[34]

The following year, Gaine reversed himself and pledged allegiance to Great Britain, devoting his newspaper to the British cause. Late in 1776, he reported encouragingly "that the Quakers begin to speak openly of their Attachment to the British Constitution, in which they are joined by other loyal Subjects of the Province in great Numbers."[35] However, as the war drew to a close in 1781 with American independence virtually assured, Gaine began to fear persecution for his role as a Royalist mouthpiece, so he petitioned the New York Assembly to allow him to remain in the state. Gaine's request was granted, but knowing his newspaper would have minimal public support, he discontinued it. Writers lambasted Gaine's inconsistency. The most damaging literary broadside was fired by Philip Freneau, who penned "Hugh Gaine's Life" for the *Freeman's Journal*. Adopting Gaine's persona, Freneau wrote:

> As matters have gone, it was plainly a blunder,
> But then I expected the Whigs must knock under,
> And I always adhere to the sword that is longest,
> And stick to the party that's like to be strongest.[36]

Like Weyman and Gaine, Holt also broke away from the Franklin sphere of influence. While running Parker's New York and New Haven operations, Holt squabbled with Parker about the same topics that caused ill feelings between Weyman and Parker: money and accounting. Initially Parker and Holt enjoyed a harmonious relationship. Holt was a bankrupt Williamsburg merchant whom Parker taught the printing trade at Franklin's request. Holt learned the trade quickly, and served Parker's needs by overseeing the New Haven and New York printing houses. However, like Weyman, Holt took advantage of Parker by giving him neither accounts nor his share of the profits. Parker objected to Holt's mismanagement but allowed the contract between the two to continue until its expiration in December 1757. Parker then offered Holt the choice of selling his share of the partnership or buying him out. Holt declined both, asking for an extension to the partnership and promising Parker a complete accounting. Upon succeeding Samuel Parker in New York in July 1760, Holt instituted the reforms that helped topple Weyman, but he found myriad reasons to avoid providing Parker with the accounts. Without them, Parker had no idea of the company's financial solvency or the amount of profits due to each partner. After one such delay, Parker complained to attorney Jared Ingersoll, "Five Months ago he promis'd me a Copy of [the accounts], but there are so many Mountains in the Way, that no Progress has yet been made."[37]

Meanwhile, Holt amassed debts due to his failure to collect payment and keep adequate records, yet the patient Parker merely expostulated with his partner, who placated him with small sums of money. "I have tried every possible Means I know of to get him to a Settlement, but he eludes it continually,"

Parker lamented.[38] While parrying Parker's pleas, Holt hypocritically complained about his post rider, James Mookler, who had successfully sued him for payment of ninety pounds. "I have to do with persons who seem to have no sort of Regard to Justice, but make use of every Quirk of the Law or practice in order to take an unfair advantage," Holt complained.[39]

Alerted to Holt's misdeeds by Parker, Franklin intervened in 1765. He urged Parker to return to New York and recommence printing as soon as his contract extension with Holt expired. To underscore his advice, Franklin, in his capacity as deputy postmaster-general for North America, ordered Parker, the postal comptroller, to move his office to New York. Franklin also provided additional income to offset the higher cost of living in New York for Parker and his family by procuring for him an appointment as a customs officer.[40]

After his contract with Parker expired, Holt set up his own shop in New York, where he identified himself as a devoted patriot and vigorously attacked the Stamp Act. This earned him the financial support of the Sons of Liberty, a group of radical Whigs. "In the present unhappy Times, when the Sons of Liberty carry all before them, Mr. Holt has gained very great Popularity, and being back'd by them, seems to have a Run of Business," Parker informed Franklin. Making matters worse for Parker, mounting tensions between England and the colonies prompted many colonists to be suspicious of those who held Royal offices. This included Parker, the postal comptroller. He noted the Sons of Liberty and their adherents "look with bad Aspect upon every King's Officer." Aware of the inherent difficulty in suing the newly popular Holt, Parker nonetheless commenced legal actions against him. "I will leave no Stone unturned, to get it done—tho' we are both hastning to the Grave," he wrote.[41]

Holt gave Parker numerous excuses for not settling the accounts. "I am continually interrupted, & my Attention called off to other Matters" that "appear'd to me to be the most immediately necessary, and to demand my present Attention," Holt informed him, adding that the reckoning "is really complicated & difficult." Parker's apparent willingness to accept these excuses allowed Holt to forestall a trial until October 1769. Parker finally admitted Holt's chicanery. "I am aware he has the Subtlety of Lucifer himself, and will try every Means to delay," Parker wrote. "[S]uch a detestable Spirit of Litigation is more painful to me than my Losses. I think I have suffered by Holt about a Thousand pound Loss."[42]

Before the case came to trial Holt agreed to settle out of court, but then resumed his delaying tactics. This proved a severe financial blow to Parker.

Illness had curtailed Parker's ability to work, and his abortive partnerships with Weyman, Gaine, and Holt had drained his savings. "I always imagined I had my full Share of the Troubles of Life, but all my former Life, till about 18 months ago, has been but as Children's Play," Parker wrote to Franklin in 1766, while recounting a litany of personal and business woes.[43] Parker found himself, at the end of his life, with debts nearly equal to his assets. He told creditors his affairs with Holt had driven him "almost to my Ruin," adding, "If you knew all, I think you would not more blame me, than pity me." Holt's scheme worked, and Parker died in 1770 at age fifty-six "of a nervous fevor," which he contracted while traveling on behalf of the post office, his wife informed Franklin. Holt then refused to pay a shilling to the estate.[44]

Franklin became only minimally involved with these ordeals, despite Parker's repeated complaints to him. Although Franklin identified himself on a legal document as a printer in 1757, his interests drifted elsewhere after he turned over the Philadelphia printing house to Hall in 1748.[45] As Franklin withdrew from printing to pursue other challenges during the 1750s and 1760s, the next generation of master printers was emerging—but under Parker's aegis, not Franklin's. Franklin had turned over the reins to the overworked and morose Parker, who lacked Franklin's firm guidance and leadership. Franklin may have given Parker and the periodically beleaguered Timothy instructions and advice on how to handle their wayward workers and problematic partners, although most of Franklin's letters to them have been lost. Franklin might not even have made any recommendations, though, reasoning that because he was not profiting from printers such as Weyman, Gaine, and Holt, their transgressions were not his problem.

Whether he gave it, Franklin's partners did seek his advice and intercession. "Now let me conclude, with asking your Opinion, Shall I launch into Business; get Stock again buy and sell, push forwards, strive hard in my old Age, or be content with small Matters, and live as I do, without getting a-head[?]" Parker asked Franklin in 1766.[46] Writing to his lawyer about possible courses of action in a lawsuit against Holt, Parker took the opportunity to "wish heartily that Mr. Franklin may come home" and help rectify the problem. By this time, though, the rising politician Franklin understood that to maintain his public character and elevate his prominence, he would have to choose his battles judiciously. The pragmatic Franklin elected not to expend political capital to extricate Parker from his morass of partnership woes, preferring to adopt an air of resignation. "I begin, as I grow old, to be more willing than I us'd to be, that the World should take its own Course, without my officiously intermeddling with its Affairs," he noted in 1764.[47]

Ultimately, Parker was wounded as much by his failure to follow Franklin's business practices as by the betrayals of his larcenous partners. He failed to follow the guiding principle of Franklin's partnerships: "the Precaution of having very explicitly settled in our Articles every thing to be done by or expected from each Partner, so that there was nothing to dispute." His partnerships, including those with his own son and nephew, provided Parker more strife than profit. Parker brought on some of his own troubles because of his disinclination to punish wayward printing associates and to resist the problems Franklin kept handing him, such as the Mecom and Lewis Jones apprenticeships, Holt's employment, and the New Haven printing shop. Parker's acquiescent nature allowed his partners to abuse his trust, forgiveness, and generosity for their own financial gain. Holt was the most adept at exploiting Parker's tolerance. "We both of us profess to be Christians," he reminded his erstwhile master while cajoling him into postponing legal proceedings. "That Enmity that has apparently subsisted between us for some Time, seems quite inconsistent with the Characters we pretend to."[48]

Justice, both temporal and spiritual, was a recurring theme in Parker's life and printing partnerships. A former county-court magistrate, he believed the law would solve his financial problems and avenge the unjust treatment that vexed his later years. Although obvious to him that Holt and other debtors were procrastinating, Parker still clung to his faith in the courts. He wrote, "they are all, like Holt, for putting off every Tittle of Justice, till they cannot help it. Therefore I have no Hopes of any Thing from them, but the Law." Other times he despaired of earthly justice, though. "I told you all Holt's Treachery," he wrote to Franklin, "which I leave to Heaven to avenge." Parker wondered whether his worldly sufferings were due to his "ill Nature" and "fretful Temper," but professed his faith that "the good Providence of God" would ultimately balance the ledger.[49]

Of the three master printers who entered the Franklin network through Parker—Weyman, Gaine, and Holt—the first went bankrupt, the second suffered public humiliation, and the third probably lived in fear of retribution. Weyman died penniless, his credit obliterated, and Gaine went to his grave an object of scorn and derision, bearing the stigma of being one of the most notorious turncoats of the Revolution. Had these men remained in the good graces of Franklin and Parker, they might have avoided their dismal ends. Weyman could have benefited by remaining within the Franklin sphere of influence instead of striking out on his own, for his business skills probably would have been honed with more seasoning and a longer partnership. Gaine could have profited, too, for Franklin might have counseled him on the appropriate posture to take regarding the escalating British-colonial conflicts and the eventual war. Franklin provided just such counsel to David Hall.[50]

Although Holt gained prominence as an outspoken opponent of the Stamp Act and the Crown, he too could only have helped himself by adhering to his network allegiances, thus avoiding years of worry over what revenge Franklin or his allies might extract for the mistreatment of Parker. Holt's dread of retaliation is evident in a letter he wrote to disgruntled Franklin network member William Goddard, who was planning to publish an attack on Franklin. After questioning Franklin's loyalty to the United States and dismissing him as greedy and nepotistic, Holt expressly forbade Goddard from implicating him. "If it should be *supposed* that I have had the least Share or Concern in, or even been privy to your Attack upon the Doctor," Holt wrote, "such a Supposition would considerably hurt my Interest and be a great Disadvantage to me. You will therefore carefully guard against giving Reason for such a thought of my Agency or Concurrence."[51]

Like other Parker partners, Holt ultimately became a financial failure because of mismanagement. By the close of the Revolutionary War, Holt had discontinued his newspaper because of delinquent accounts, and relied almost entirely upon government printing work. Petitioning the New York Senate and Assembly for work in 1783, he wrote, "almost the Whole Support of my Business in this place, at present, is the Money I receive from the Legislature, for printing their Acts and Journals." He died early the following year.[52]

The Franklin network entered the Revolutionary Era in disarray, with few members and a dearth of strong leadership from its nucleus. Several loyal members remained, like Parker, Hall, and Timothy, but renegades like Gaine, Weyman, Holt, Mecom, and Goddard abounded. The 1760s was a decade of despair for Franklin, who suffered political defeat, organized character assassination, and the gradual disintegration of his printing network. His despondency, tempered by resignation, was evident in a 1764 letter to his sister. "Our only Comfort under such Afflictions is, that God knows what is best for us, and can bring Good out of what appears Evil," he wrote, adding that no one is happy "while in this Life."[53]

10

The Franklin Network and the Stamp Act

"Some Political Revolutions will probably mark the Beginning of the next Session; for the Struggle for Power is constant in this Country; nor can I see an End to it," William Strahan wrote to David Hall from London in 1764. Parliament, in the midst of a governmental shakeup, would in the next session be "endeavouring to extinguish, in some Degree at least, our enormous Debt, which, if it is suffered to increase, must sooner or later overwhelm us."[1]

These two forces, political reorganization and the enormous national debt, prompted Parliament to devise the Stamp Act. This measure, which taxed publications and legal papers, jeopardized the revenue of printers and lawyers—the two groups most capable of leading public opinion—and set the stage for the American Revolution.

Lord George Grenville advocated the tax as a means of collecting revenue, effectively forcing the colonies to pay a portion of the costs incurred during the French and Indian War. This military victory enabled Great Britain to become the predominant world power, albeit a nearly bankrupt one. By January 1763, the British national debt was 130 million pounds sterling. Saddled with a huge debt, Parliament decided that since the American colonists had benefited from the victory, they should shoulder part of the financial burden.[2]

At the beginning of that war, colonial assemblies had approved stamp taxes in Massachusetts in 1755 and New York in 1757 to raise revenue for military expenditures. These received a mixed response from printers in the Franklin network. Hugh Gaine raised the subscription price of his newspaper and defended the tax as a necessary expense to protect the colony from

French incursions. James Parker also raised the price of his newspaper, but publicly opposed the stamp duty, claiming luxury items should be taxed instead.[3] In a pamphlet purportedly responding to an advocate of the tax, Parker argued the duty was burdensome to printers and the public, restricted press freedom, and, taking a Franklinesque stance, instead proposed a tax on periwigs and other objects of "Luxury."[4]

Opposition to these taxes was limited, though, because they were imposed by the colonial legislatures themselves, with some public support, and also because they were not overly burdensome to colonists. The levies were modest and sporadically enforced, and the acts creating them expired during the war. Ever vigilant for opportunities to promote virtue, Franklin tried to find a moral in the levies. As "Chearful," Franklin wrote of the taxes in 1758, "when they are heavy, they oblige people to be more industrious and more frugal. And so the evil, if indeed it be an evil, contributes naturally to its own cure." His "Poor Richard" noted the same year, "We are taxed twice as much by our *Idleness*, three times as much by our *Pride*, and four times as much by our *Folly*."[5]

However, by the war's end, colonial contributions to defray the costs of the lengthy military campaign were nominal. This prompted such key figures in British government as the Earl of Halifax, Charles Townshend and the Earl of Bute to conclude the colonies would not voluntarily remit their share to reduce the debt. They determined that Parliament would have to force the colonists to pay for their defense.[6]

Grenville's plan, which had been suggested by merchant and land speculator Henry McCulloh, required that a stamp be placed on all legal documents, including loans, bills of sale, court briefs, college degrees, appointments to office, and indentures of apprenticeship, as well as on all dice, cards, almanacs, and newspapers. The tax would be almost impossible to violate because without the stamp colonists jeopardized their property, liberty, and economic prosperity. In short, British officials believed that self-interest would compel colonists to comply with the law. The tax also seemed meritorious because it would be easy to collect and would facilitate the enforcement of other laws, such as charging fees on bonds and bills of lading. These documents would have to bear the stamp or be regarded as evidence of attempted fraud or smuggling.[7]

However, Royal officials knew it would be difficult to convince Americans to accept an intercolonial tax their assemblies had not approved. One Connecticut legislator used Franklinesque rhetoric to justify it. "The Stamp Duty may in some respects be distressing to ye present Generation, tho they would certainly be a means of promoting industry," William Johnson wrote. Upon learning from a member of Parliament about the Stamp Act's imminent passage, lawyer Jared Ingersoll responded, "You say America can and ought to contribute to its own Defence. We, one and all, say the same on this Side of the Water, we only differ about the Means."[8]

Grenville's plan received the support it needed. Parliament approved it with little dissent on February 27, 1765. It was signed into law by King George III the following month and designated to take effect November 1, despite Franklin's arguments in London against the tax. Appearing before Parliament in his capacity as a colonial agent, Franklin contended colonists would bridle at an internal tax that neither they nor their legislatures had approved. According to Franklin, British officials countered by insisting "the Colonies were all virtually represented in Parliament." He offered an alternative to the tax, recommending the Crown raise revenue by establishing a general loan office in America that would issue paper currency, charge interest on it, and use the interest to pay the military debts. Since colonists needed a reliable medium of exchange, they would not object to paying the interest, Franklin argued.[9] However, Grenville opposed issuing paper money as legal tender and asserted the right of Parliament to tax the colonists. He was, Franklin observed, "besotted with his Stamp Scheme."[10]

Despite the suspicion among some colonists that Franklin had encouraged the passage of the Stamp Act (a view exacerbated by the fact that Franklin arranged for several of his friends to become stamp distributors), Franklin remonstrated against passage of the tax. London printer William Strahan told David Hall that Franklin "took all possible Pains to remove some of the Inconveniencies" of the Stamp Act, "tho' without Effect. But to think of his preventing the Tax being imposed altogether, he is as little able to stem the Tide at London Bridge with his little Finger."[11]

Franklin repeatedly asserted his opposition to the Stamp Act. "God knows I did all in my Power to prevent" the tax, he assured Hall, and told Pennsylvania politician Charles Thomson, "I took every Step in my Power, to prevent the passing of the Stamp Act."[12] Beaten by Grenville's resolve, though, Franklin counseled that submitting to the tax was the most prudent course. "We might as well have hinder'd the Suns setting," he wrote to Thomson. "But since 'tis down, my Friend, and it may be long before it rises again, Let us make as good a Night of it as we can. We may still Light Candles. Frugallity and Industry will go a great way towards indemnifying us." Thomson responded that such infringements on colonial liberties as trade curtailment, the creation of vice-admiralty courts to prosecute offenses against the Stamp

Act without juries, and a press "so restricted that we cannot complain" had stirred up vigorous public resentment. "I much fear instead of the candles you mention being lighted, you will hear of the works of darkness," he predicted, adding that if colonists do not obediently pay the tax, "what remains but by violence to compel them to obedience. Violence will beget resentment, and provoke to acts never dreamt of."[13]

Thomson's assessment was accurate. Colonists were incensed, contending that a political body to which they did not send representatives should not tax them. The colonists' reluctance to be governed by Englishmen, rather than Americans, was not new in 1765. In fact, it was evident in the character of their ancestors a century earlier. Responding to a British plan to send officials to America to compel colonists' obedience to British laws in 1664, Massachusetts governor John Endecott expressed his opposition to the chancellor of Great Britain, claiming British enforcement of colonial laws would be "altogither inconcistant with the charter & priviledges" that King Charles II promised "not in the least to violate or infringe."[14] A century later, Americans bristled again at heavy-handed external control.

Inspired by journalistic rhetoric, they retaliated with nonimportation of British goods and mob actions. Crowds gathered, riots erupted, and citizens threatened government officials in most of the colonial cities. Predicting "poor America is like to Bleed" under the Stamp Act, James Parker forecast "an End to all Government here," because "the People are all running Mad; and say it is as good to dye by the Sword as by the Famine."[15]

The day after the tax took effect, a New York mob attacked a British military officer's residence. As a participant recalled, "with one Consent [we] began upon the house and in Less than 10 Minutes had [it] down," then plundered and burned its contents.[16] The following day a larger group, numbering in the thousands, "resolv'd to have the Governor Ded or Alive" if he enforced the Stamp Act. He did not. As one New York observer noted, "the Tempers of the people are so alter'd by the frightfull Stamp Act, tis beyond Conception, so violent & so universal." He added, "Strange Scenes we have had, Madness & folly triumphant."[17]

Acerbic newspaper printers and their correspondents, recognizing the tax as a threat to their livelihoods and to free expression, mounted a fierce propaganda campaign to rally public support. The Stamp Act's arrival was heralded with ringing denunciations equating the tax with despotism and proclaiming that taxation without Parliamentary representation constituted tyranny. Throughout the colonies, essayists and orators argued that if the tax revenue were used to pay military expenses, colonial assemblies would lose the means

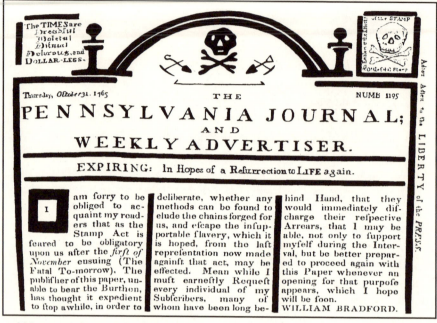

A Newspaper Protests the Stamp Act

"The TIMES are Dreadful Doleful Dismal Dolorous, and DOLLAR-LESS," Franklin's long-time printing adversary William Bradford lamented on the eve of the Stamp Act's inception. Fearing the economic harm the tax would represent for printers, Bradford bid adieu to press freedom in his October 31, 1765, Pennsylvania Journal and Weekly Advertiser.

to control royal officials, especially governors. The two groups most directly burdened by the Stamp Act—lawyers and printers—offered the most persuasive excoriations. Because the measure placed a duty on all legal documents, on the paper used to publish newspapers, and on newspaper advertisements (which James Parker called "the Life of a Paper"), these practitioners used their powers of persuasion to escalate the tax issue into an epic conflict between freedom and slavery.[18]

Colonial printers opposed the stamp tax in various ways. A few suspended publication rather than affix the stamp to their newspapers, some published without titles or other identifying references, and others openly defied the tax by printing without stamps. The *New-Hampshire Gazette* equated the tax with slavery and claimed the law to be "as fatal to almost all that is dear to us, as the *Ides of March* were, to the Life of *Caesar*." The *Connecticut Courant* opined of the stamps, "it is hoped that every Lover of his Country will spurn, with the highest Indignation, the base Thought of ever purchasing a single one; and despise, execrate and detest the wretch who shall presume to countenance the Use of them, in any way whatever."[19] In the pages of the press, "all the Colonys from Philadelphia to [New] Hampshire have Remonstrated Home against the Late Impositions," Rhode Island merchant Nicholas Brown wrote, adding "we hope for a Discontinuance of them."[20]

The press had much to do with whipping up public fervor against the stamp tax and its agents. As Joseph Galloway complained to Franklin, "The Printers on the Continent hav[e] combined together to print every thing inflamatory and nothing that is rational and Cool." Thus, "the people are Taught to believe the greatest Absurdities, and their Passions are excited to a Degree of Resentment against the Mother Country, beyond all Description."[21]

Many newspapers faithfully reported on colonial assemblies and town meetings that protested the tax, opening up their columns to writers condemning the measure. Newspapers also printed the names of stamp-tax collectors, calling them "mean mercenary Hirelings or Parricides among ourselves, who for a little filthy lucre would at any time betr[a]y every Right, Liberty, and Privilege of their fellow subjects."[22] The tax collectors were intimidated and hung in public effigy. Pennsylvania stamp agent John Hughes, repeatedly threatened by mobs, suspected he would be killed and vowed, "I will defend my House at the Risque of my Life." Connecticut stamp master Jared Ingersoll told a friend about mob violence, including house burnings of government officials, who "were threatened in the highest manner with political death, so strong are the peoples resentments against the Stamp Act." He added that he had suffered "the indignity of being burnt in Effigy & of having every ill natured thing published of me in News papers in the most unrestrained manner. I have been called Traitor, Parricide & the hardest of Names [and] am charged with having contributed to get the Stamp Act passed & all to Secure myself the office of Distributor."[23]

Franklin, serving in England as an agent for the Pennsylvania Assembly, was out of touch with the tenor of the times. He was genuinely surprised by the extent of public outcry against the Stamp Act in general, and against the collectors of the stamp tax in particular. Maryland stamp master Zachariah Hood reported to him that a mob stabbed a naval officer, "pull'd down my House, and obliged me to flie (with a single Suit) or expect the same Fate as the Officer." Pennsylvania stamp master John Hughes told Franklin that a "Frenzy or Madness has got such hold of the People of all Ranks" that his life was in danger. Franklin cautioned Hughes to remain in his post, noting hopefully, "Coolness and Steadiness . . . will by degrees reconcile" the people.

However, he was ultimately compelled to resign and was vilified for years afterward.[24]

An ocean away from the scenes of public and journalistic uprising, Franklin underestimated the colonial opposition occasioned by the economic restraint on the press, its advertisers, and its audience. Ever the pragmatist, Franklin accepted the tax as the law of the land. He therefore advised his network printers on how to minimize financial losses and on what editorial stance to take in the face of the growing public anger against the Stamp Act. "I think it will affect the Printers more than anybody," he predicted to Hall months before the tax took effect. Fully expecting the measure to be enforced, Franklin advocated placid neutrality and submission as being in America's best interest. "Loyalty to the Crown and faithful Adherence to the Government of this Nation," he wrote to Hughes, "will always be the wisest Course for you and I to take, whatever may be the Madness of the Populace or their blind Leaders, who can only bring themselves and Country into trouble and draw on greater Burthens by Acts of rebellious Tendency."[25] Franklin advised Hall to stop selling *Pennsylvania Gazette* subscriptions and advertising space on credit and to raise the newspaper's price. He also ordered oversized half-sheets of newsprint for the Philadelphia printing shop, in a misguided effort to pay only half the tax. Franklin guessed that about ten percent of the subscribers would drop the *Gazette* due to the higher costs, but Hall painted a gloomier picture. He told Franklin most of the readers "will drop the Paper, when the Act takes Place, being resolved, as they say, not to pay any thing towards that tax they can possibly avoid; and News Papers, they tell me, they can, and will, do without; so that there is the greatest Reason to fear that the Number of our Customers, from the First of November next, will be very trifling."[26] Two weeks before the tax took effect, Hall told Franklin that at least five hundred subscribers had canceled, with more expected. Hall doubted the diminished revenue justified continuing the newspaper, but Franklin urged him to continue publishing the *Gazette*.[27]

Heeding Franklin's admonition to do nothing that might injure the colonies' reputation in England, Hall refrained from vigorous editorial criticism of the Stamp Act. Although many Pennsylvanians disdained Hall's stance, Franklin approved of his partner's editorial judgment. When Hall declined to publish vitriolic essays against the Stamp Act, Franklin endorsed the decision. "I think you have acted very prudently in omitting the Pieces," he wrote to Hall from London. "Nothing has done America more Hurt here than those kind of Writings . . . I should have been equally averse to printing them." Hall had always managed his press with circumspection, much to

Franklin's delight. "Your prudent Conduct . . . gives me great Satisfaction," Franklin informed him.[28] Hall, whom Franklin described as "so faithful a Partner," won Franklin's admiration with diligent business practices and careful selection of material to print. When Franklin wrote a controversial essay condemning violence against American Indians, Hall cautiously avoided the dispute by arranging for Franklin's former German-language partner Anton Armbruster to print the pamphlet.[29]

Hall's mild position on the Stamp Act was further influenced by his desire to spare Franklin embarrassment while serving as the Pennsylvania Assembly's agent in England. Hall's former London employer Strahan also counseled patience and obedience, suggesting that the economic impact of the tax might drive off several of Hall's Philadelphia competitors. This thought might have comforted Hall, who had become concerned about the increasing number of printing houses in the city.[30]

With his two printing mentors advocating full compliance with the Stamp Act, the law-abiding Hall resolved to submit to its mandates. However, he was deeply troubled by the effect the levy would have on the economic fortunes of American printers. In private correspondence, Hall called the Stamp Act a "horrid Law" that "will ruin us all in this Part of the World." Because all the stamped paper had to come from England, the measure would "ruin all our Paper-Makers" in the colonies, Hall lamented.[31]

Although Franklin regarded Hall's cautious neutrality as a virtue, his conduct during the Stamp Act controversy angered many of his readers. Aroused colonists interpreted Hall's resistance to publishing anti-tax essays as timidity, and they responded with subscription cancellations and personal harangues. Besieged by "the Clamours of the People" less than two months before the tax commenced, the worried Hall informed Franklin of the widespread public view that because "our Gazette, spreads more generally than all the other Papers put together on the Continent, our not Publishing, as the Printers of the other Papers do, will be an infinite Hurt to the Liberties of the People." Chafing under the restrictions of British law and Franklin's instructions, Hall complained, "all the Papers on the Continent, ours excepted, were full of Spirited Papers against the Stamp Law, and that because, I did not publish those Papers likewise, I was much blamed, got a great Deal of Illwill, and that some of our Customers had dropt on that Account." He concluded he would have to appease the public and print some anti-tax essays, despite Franklin's instructions to calmly submit to the tax. "So that how to Behave, I am really at a loss, but believe it will be best to humour them in some Publications, as they seem to insist so much upon it."[32]

Hall suspended publication of the *Pennsylvania Gazette* the day before the tax took effect, blaming "the most *Unconstitutional Act* that ever these Colonies could have imagined," but resumed publication a week later, issuing the newspaper without a heading or imprint and proclaiming "No Stamped Paper to be had."[33]

The Stamp Act led to similar economic and political dilemmas for Franklin's other network members. Like Hall, Peter Timothy found himself entangled in the stricture of the law, the neutrality Franklin advocated, and the passion of the people. Although privately regarding the tax as a "hellish Idea," he received and followed the same pragmatic business advice Franklin had given Hall. Timothy told readers "the STAMP-ACT must necessarily occasion an advance in the price" of the *South-Carolina Gazette,* and he noted that "READY MONEY" must accompany all advertisements because of the tax, "which the printers are to pay weekly." He changed his mind the day before the tax took effect, though, and, like Hall, announced the suspension of his newspaper because it would be "impossible to continue without great loss to the printer." Charles Crouch, Timothy's dishonest former apprentice, quickly filled the journalistic void. Charles Town radicals set up Crouch with his own printing shop and newspaper and, as Timothy informed Franklin, supported this "worthless Fellow" with "their utmost Zeal and Interest." As a result of following Franklin's cautious counsel and "declining to direct, support and engage in the most violent Opposition," Timothy found himself "from the most *popular* reduced to the most *unpopular* Man in the Province."[34]

James Parker, who had opposed colonial efforts to impose stamp taxes the previous decade, railed privately against "the fatal *Black-Act,*" likening it to "a killing Frost" that "strikes a deadly Blow" at the printing trade. Parker had leased his New York newspaper to John Holt before the tax took effect, and thus he was not compelled to take an editorial stance on the subject. He regarded it as a blessing that "I am not a Master-Printer at New-York, or perhaps the Impetuosity of my Temper would have plunged me deep" into the controversy. Parker had planned to commence a newspaper in Burlington, New Jersey, but told Franklin "the News of the killing Stamp, has struck a deadly Blow to all my Hopes on that Head."[35]

Younger printers who had risen through the ranks in the Franklin network were more ardent in their opposition to the tax. "The press is the test of truth; the bulwark of public safety; the guardian of freedom, and the people ought not to sacrifice it," Benjamin Mecom wrote in the unstamped *Connecticut Gazette* the day the tax took effect.[36] Holt was indecisive until pressured into radicalism by the New York Sons of Liberty. The first issue of Holt's *New-*

York Gazette: or, the Weekly Post-Boy that appeared after the tax took effect announced it would ignore the tax, noting that the paper stood for "LIBERTY and PROSPERITY, and no STAMPS." Parker commented bitterly that Holt's defiant posture was a ploy to align himself with the radical factions. "Holt, who is grown so elate and popular, by his Appearance against the Act, had Nothing to lose: for had he suffered for it, I should have suffered the Loss of my Tools &c. whilst he got the Credit of it," Parker wrote. After his lease with Parker expired, Holt started his own newspaper, the *New-York Journal,* with financial backing from the Sons of Liberty. Indebted to Parker both financially and morally, Holt nonetheless appropriated the *Post-Boy's* subscription list and accused Parker in the *Journal's* inaugural issue of having "deserted the Cause of Liberty" during the Stamp Act crisis.[37]

Parker's other erstwhile partners were less bold. The nearly bankrupt William Weyman suspended publication of his newspaper several months before the Stamp Act took effect, resuming late in the year. Hugh Gaine opened the pages of his *New-York Gazette and Weekly Mercury* to both sides of the controversy, publishing essays denying Britain's right to tax America without direct representation, and ones delineating the British view that the colonies had effectual representation in Parliament because its members superintended the entire empire. Gaine told subscribers he maintained an open press because "to be well acquainted with those Arguments, in Support of Measures which so nearly concern us, is undoubtedly desired by every judicious Reader."[38]

Angered by the Stamp Act's discriminatory double tax on printed material in languages other than English, Franklin's former German-language printing partner Henry Miller adopted a vigorous anti-tax posture in his *Pennsylvanischer Staatsbote.* He printed synopses of protests and resolutions by the Sons of Liberty, often accompanied by sarcastic comments. Shortly before the tax took effect, Miller joined Hall and other Philadelphia printers in temporarily suspending newspaper publication after they jointly sought legal counsel. Miller's announcement closely paralleled Hall's, citing "the most unconstitutional law these colonies have ever seen . . . places too heavy a burden on the editor." He resumed it three weeks later without stamps, confident of public support.[39]

The most intriguing publication of the era was *The Constitutional Courant,* a single-issue screed printed in New Jersey to resemble a newspaper. Attacking the Stamp Act under the veil of pseudonymity, the paper was so reprobate that New York printers refused to publish it.[40] It was the product of Franklin network member William Goddard. Born in New London, Connecticut, Goddard served his apprenticeship under Parker and Holt at the

New Haven printing office. In 1758, he traveled to New York and Wood-bridge to help Parker at his presses in those towns. Rather than remaining within the network, Goddard worked for several months in 1762 as a jour-neyman printer for Samuel Farley's *New-York American Chronicle*. When a fire destroyed Farley's shop and ended the newspaper, Goddard started *The Providence Gazette* on October 20, 1762, competing for Rhode Island's busi-ness with the established Franklin press in Newport. James Franklin Jr. had died on August 22 of that year, and Ann took on a new partner, Samuel Hall. The nepotistic Franklin overlooked Goddard's challenge to his family con-nection in Newport, though, and probably on Parker's recommendation made Goddard the postmaster of Providence.[41]

Without the government printing contract, Goddard had to rely heavily on subscriptions. However, these were "inadequate to the inconceivable Ex-penses attending its publication," he informed *Providence Gazette* readers.[42] He abandoned the newspaper in May 1765, explaining to readers in its penultimate issue that it stood in the way of "some other Concerns in which he is about to be engaged in order to establish himself on a more advanta-geous Footing." Goddard was referring to Holt's invitation to join him as a partner in New York.[43] Despite his previous explanations for discontinuing the Providence newspaper, Goddard added a new one in the paper's last issue—the Stamp Act. He blamed the closure on "the oppressive and insupportable STAMP-DUTIES, with which the colonies are threatened." Leaving the shop in the care of his mother Sarah, Goddard departed for New York. Sarah thus became the first American woman printer who did not take over for a deceased or incapacitated husband.[44]

During his 1765 stint with Holt and Parker, Goddard published the *Constitutional Courant* on Parker's Woodbridge press. The publication con-sisted primarily of two essays that acrimoniously condemned the stamp tax, although they took different stances on how Americans should respond. One advocated violent resistance, while its more tempered counterpart suggested that force would discredit righteous opposition. Its imprint claimed it was published "by Andrew Marvel at the Sign of the Bribe refused, on Constitution Hill, North America" in September 1765.

The *Constitutional Courant* consisted of the printer's address "To the PUBLIC"; two essays on liberty, one written pseudonymously by "Philo-leutherus" and the other by "Philopatriae"; and a notice about changes in the British Ministry. Additionally, the *Constitutional Courant* bore the celebrated Benjamin Franklin illustration of the segmented serpent, with each part rep-resenting a colony, under the exhortation "JOIN OR DIE."[45]

Goddard's appropriation of Franklin's "JOIN, OR DIE" (minus the comma) was innovative in that it lent a new meaning to the emblem. Franklin had initially used it in his *Pennsylvania Gazette* of May 9, 1754, on the eve of the French and Indian War, to call for colonial unity against invaders. The emblem was soon widely reproduced in other newspapers. Goddard reprinted it eleven years later as a symbol of colonial opposition to the Stamp Act in particular and British authority in general.[46]

In the guise of Marvel, Goddard told readers he welcomed the chance to perform a public service by printing the polemical essays, which "are thought to be wrote with greater freedom than any thing that has yet appeared in the public prints." Indeed, the writings of Philoleutherus and Philopatriae supported Marvel's comment on the bold liberty of expression. The first essay, by Philoleutherus, was a rambling tirade not so much against the particulars of the Stamp Act as against the slavery the author contended the tax represented. After claiming no Englishman could be taxed without his consent or that of his representatives, Philoleutherus informed readers the tax represented "the yoke of slavery" being placed on colonists—not by King George III, but by "the vile minions of tyranny and arbitrary power" who misrepresented to the king both the status of the American colonies and the equity of the tax. Philoleutherus wrote, "We never can suppose that our sovereign, when our state is properly represented to him, will employ that power to execute a law so evidently iniquitous and unreasonable" as the Stamp Act. This was one of the many essays during the early years of the Revolution that laid the blame not on the virtuous king but on his wicked advisers.[47]

After claiming his "free thoughts" were not treasonous and that "the British Parliament should be treated with all possible respect" unless "they transgress the bounds prescribed them by the constitution," Philoleutherus turned his invective on colonists who would not speak up in opposition to the tax, calling them "mushroom patriots" and "dastards" who "are thinking of nothing but tamely yielding their necks to the yoke" of abject slavery. However, he saved his most vicious epithets for those who were holding posts as stamp distributors. Philoleutherus addressed them as hard-hearted miscreants who thought only of increasing their own wealth. He cautioned them, "Ye blots and stains of America! Ye vipers of human kind! Your names shall be blasted with infamy, the public execration shall pursue you while living, and your memories shall rot, when death has disabled you from propagating vassalage and misery any further." For good measure, he added, "Murder your fathers, rip up the bowels of your mothers, dash the infants you have begotten against the stones, and be blameless;—but enslave your country! This, this is guilt, this calls for heaven's fiercest vengeance."[48]

Philopatriae was more restrained, even apologizing for mob violence against the Stamp Act. Yet he too placed the blame on the British, contending, "the guilt of all these violences is most justly chargeable upon the authors and abettors of the Stamp Act. They who endeavour to destroy the foundations of the English constitution, and break thro' the fence of the laws, in order to let in a torrent of tyranny and oppression upon their fellow-subjects, ought not to be surprized if they are overwhelmed in it themselves."[49]

Philopatriae resorted to the standard arguments perpetuated throughout the Revolution—that fundamental human liberties were being denied and taxation without representation was unjust and illegal. While professing loyalty to King George III and his court and noting "we are ready to risk our lives and fortunes in his and their defence," Philopatriae warned, "at the same time, we cannot yield up to her [Great Britain], or to any power on earth, our inherent and most valuable rights and privileges. If she would strip us of all the advantages derived to us from the English constitution, why should we desire to continue our connection? We might as well belong to France, or any other power; none could offer a greater injury to our rights and liberties than is offered by the Stamp Act."[50]

Although printed in New Jersey, the *Constitutional Courant* first appeared in New York, where street hawkers sold it. Copies of the screed were also delivered to other colonies via post-riders. It was sold as far away as Charles Town, was reprinted in Boston and Philadelphia, and enjoyed sales in the thousands.[51]

The *Constitutional Courant* made a considerable sensation in England as well. The English *Annual Register for 1765* labeled it the most influential Stamp Act essay to appear in North America. It noted that the *Constitutional Courant* contained "things of the most serious nature, and such as the most despotic tyrant might expect to see remonstrated against by the most abject vassals."[52] In the London *Public Ledger*, "Rationalis" warned, "we must have reason to believe, that union is forming, which, according to the wisest opinions, it must ever be for our greatest interest and security to give no cause for being affected, and therefore the policy must have been erroneous which has contributed thereto."[53]

The *Constitutional Courant*'s rousing denunciation of the impending Stamp Act alarmed colonial officials. Boston governor Francis Bernard sent a copy to London, terming it "seditious" and "an infamous libell against the Government of Great Britain."[54] New York's acting governor Cadwallader

Colden, who had previously been involved in a libel indictment against Parker, assumed Parker was responsible.[55] He wrote to Franklin, claiming that one or more bundles of the *Constitutional Courant* "were deliver'd to the Post Rider at Woodbridge by James Parker." Afterward, the copies of the publication "were distributed by the Post Riders in several parts of this Colony & I beleive likewise in the Neighbouring Colonies: the doing of which was kept Secret from the Post Master in this Place." Colden's letter portrayed the *Constitutional Courant* as a presumptuous assault on British authority, designed to incite riots against the stamp tax. Colden sent Franklin a copy of the publication, asking for confirmation of his suspicion that Parker printed it by requesting that Franklin identify the printing types used. There is no evidence Colden received a response, although Franklin, in his capacity as deputy postmaster-general for the colonies, was likely embarrassed by the apparent involvement of Parker, the postal comptroller.[56]

Colden also informed Henry Seymour Conway, the British Secretary of State for the Southern Department, who was praised in the *Constitutional Courant* as "a great friend to America, and a strong opposer of the Stamp Act." Colden asserted that inflammatory newspapers designed to arouse the people posed a serious threat to civil order. He sent Conway a copy of the *Constitutional Courant,* noting, "The most remarkable of these Papers is inclosed." However, Colden had to confess his impotence to Conway, writing that members of the governor's council "think it prudent at this time to delay the makeing [of] more particular Enquiry least it should be the occasion of raising the Mob, which it is thought proper by all means to avoid."[57] Major General Thomas Gage also informed Conway that Colden and his council had "apprehensions about prosecuting the Printers at this juncture." According to Gage, the commander of British troops in North America, the Stamp Act could only be enforced by a large number of soldiers in each city—a luxury Great Britain could not afford. As a result, a perplexed and frustrated Gage could only watch as publications like the *Constitutional Courant* "raise people of all degrees against the Stamp Act" and cause them to be "transported with phrenzy," he wrote back to London.[58]

The *Constitutional Courant* and other American newspaper essays denouncing the tax were distributed to members of Parliament. Some, like Grenville, called the colonial response "downright Rebellion," and others proposed minor alterations to the tax.[59] However, several key speeches and witness testimonies in January and February of 1766 persuaded Parliament to repeal the Stamp Act. Franklin was one of those witnesses. Called to testify on February 13, he fueled Parliament's fear that Grenville's Stamp Act and the rigid policies of enforcement had unleashed a colonial movement for economic liberty. Franklin portrayed the colonists as loyal subjects who did not object to all taxes—merely ones levied without legislative representation and inimical to their interests.[60]

In his testimony, Franklin asserted that colonists objected to the "inexpediency" of the tax, which he explained as "the poverty and inability of those who were to pay the tax; the general discontent it has occasioned; and the impracticability of enforcing it." He cautioned Parliament that sending soldiers to America to enforce the Stamp Act would be dangerous. "They cannot force a man to take stamps who chooses to do without them. They will not find a rebellion; they may indeed make one." He also warned that if the tax was not repealed, it would cause "A total loss of the respect and affection the people of America bear to this country, and of all the commerce that depends on that respect and affection."[61]

The desire to quell the rebellion in the colonies compelled Parliament to repeal the despised Stamp Act in the early morning hours of February 22, 1766, with 275 members of Parliament favoring repeal and 167 opposing it. In a face-saving effort following the repeal, Conway—who had been praised in the *Constitutional Courant* as a friend to the colonies—told colonial governors that because of the "Moderation, the Forbearance, the unexampled Lenity and Tenderness of Parliament towards the Colonies" exemplified in the repeal, their citizens were expected to show "chearful obedience to the laws and legislative authority of Great Britain" and "respectful gratitude to the mother country."[62]

The repeal "will make thousands of hearts leap for joy," the Rev. George Whitefield predicted, while a Connecticut legislator wrote his wife that the news "is Joy and Gladness to all true sons of Liberty."[63] The chief catalysts were the British economy's woes caused by the nonimportation movement, coupled with the riotous behavior in the colonies that portended an emerging spirit of independence.

Following the repeal, some disgruntled members of Parliament discussed a plan to make the colonies pay for the stamped paper that had been refused and destroyed. Writing as "F.B.," Franklin responded in an essay in Goddard's next newspaper venture, the *Pennsylvania Chronicle, And Universal Advertiser*. He wrote that the proposal reminded him of a Frenchman who heated a poker and asked an Englishman to let him insert the poker into his backside. When the Englishman refused, the Frenchman requested payment for the trouble and expense of heating the iron.[64]

It is difficult to imagine a Parliamentary action more ill-conceived than the Stamp Act. By placing the heaviest tax burden on the two groups most capable of directing public opinion, the British government kindled flames of resentment and nationalism that it could never extinguish. Lawyers (through speeches and journalistic writings) and printers (by publishing their own writings and those of others) fanned these flames. In doing so, they manufactured a reality for their audience chiefly to serve their own purposes—generating public opposition to a tax that would most directly affect them. Because of their central role in the social construction of knowledge, the dissemination of "news," and the shaping of popular sentiment, printers succeeded in making their fight one for all colonists, catalyzing the American Revolution.

Aggressive young printers who received their vocational training within the Franklin network, such as Charles Crouch, William Goddard, and John Holt, used their presses to frame the most extreme and influential arguments for colonial solidarity. Their elder counterparts, such as David Hall and Peter Timothy, followed Franklin's counsel of deference, prudence, and equanimity, only to suffer public resentment until they united their presses with the radical cause.

Franklin based his advice and instructions to them on his beliefs about what was best for the people and nation. Just as with the subject of moral virtue, Franklin thought himself well qualified to judge how colonists should behave regarding the Stamp Act. Living in London, he believed in the wisdom of British officials, and was therefore confident that submission, coupled with peaceful and reasoned remonstration, was the surest way to secure change. This was the calm and compliant message he wanted his printing partners to convey to colonial readers, while he helped several of his friends secure stamp distributorships.

Instead of calming the populace, Franklin's posture of acceptance had the opposite effect. Mobs identified Franklin as one of the leading proponents of the Stamp Act, and his reputation suffered severe damage. "They industriously sounded the Alarm of Danger and pleased themselves with the Hope, That the Stamp Act might give Birth, to as much prejudice, among the Ignorant, against You As the harmless Word, Boor had done last year," Quaker politician Samuel Wharton wrote Franklin, referring to his 1764 pamphlet calling German immigrants "Palatine Boors." Wharton informed Franklin that besides his own, the houses of Franklin, stamp master John Hughes, and politician Joseph Galloway had been targeted for destruction by angry mobs who believed, Wharton wrote, "that you had obtained the Stamp Act and We were warm Advocates for the carrying it, into Execution." Deborah Franklin confirmed this, notifying her husband that relatives and friends armed themselves and joined her to defend their house in Philadelphia from an angry mob.[65]

Franklin was aware of this as he testified in Parliament. He spoke not only as an American political representative, but also as a man who urgently needed to repair his damaged reputation. Toward that end, he had his London printer friend William Strahan publish a copy of the transcript in pamphlet form, and he arranged for Hall and Parker to publish and distribute it in America. This strategy helped considerably. "Your Enemies at last began to be ashamed of their base insinuations and to acknowledge that the Colonies are under obligations to you," Thomson reported to Franklin in 1766. "I shall ever deem it a kind dispensation of Providence that brought you to London at this most critical conjunction."[66] Some were unconvinced, though. Nearly a year after Franklin's testimony before Parliament, Hugh Hughes, a vigorous opponent of the Stamp Act (and, ironically, the brother of Pennsylvania stamp distributor John Hughes) alleged it was a sham. "Hugh says your Examination is all a designed and premeditated Thing between you, and Mr. Grenville, &c. he being fully of the Mind you were a Friend to the Stamp," Parker reported to Franklin. The *Pennsylvania Journal* also published a supplement in the fall of 1766 that insisted Franklin had encouraged the Stamp Act.[67]

From London, Franklin had done all he could to restore his reputation with the help of his printing allies. "Your Consolation, my Friend, and mine, under these Abuses, must be, *that we do not deserve them*," he wrote to Galloway. Franklin hoped that with the passage of time, public tranquility—and his reputation—would be fully restored. In the meantime, he would have to rely on his public virtue. "Dirt thrown on a Mud-Wall may stick and incorporate," he added, "but it will not long adhere to polish'd Marble."[68]

11

Rebellion and Network Loyalties

During and immediately following the Stamp Act crisis, Benjamin Franklin's political opponents continued the attacks on his character that had led to defeat in his 1764 Pennsylvania Assembly re-election bid. They claimed that while he was in England serving as a colonial agent for the Assembly, Franklin promoted passage of the detested Stamp Act for the personal gain of himself and his friends. Philadelphia merchant James Pemberton notified Franklin of "the charge industriously propagated of thy being a promoter of the Stamp Act," and David Hall warned Franklin that he had "many Enemies" who believed he took an active role in devising the tax.[1]

The press and the Assembly repeated the accusation. *Pennsylvania Journal* publishers William and Thomas Bradford printed "An ESSAY, Towards discovering the Authors and Promoters of the memorable STAMP ACT," branding Franklin as the act's chief architect. After Parliament repealed the tax, Joseph Galloway informed Franklin that Pennsylvania Chief Justice William Allen "publickly Asserted in the House that you were the greatest Enemy to the Repeal of the Stamp Act, of all the Men in England." Trying to seem unruffled, Franklin wrote to Hall, "It shall be my Endeavour, with God's Help, to act uprightly; and if I have the Approbation of the Good and Wise, which I shall certainly have sooner or later, the Enmity of Fools and Knaves will give me very little Concern."[2] He was concerned, though.

Maintaining his good name was essential to Franklin's success as a statesman and purveyor of virtuous teachings to a mass audience, just as it had been for his success as a printer. An emerging political leader and moral bellwether in colonial America, Franklin had a vested interest in carefully guarding the sanctity of his reputation. He believed, as "Poor Richard" noted, "Glass, China, and Reputation, are easily crack'd, and never well mended."[3] Concomitantly, though, he disdained the appearance of descending from his moral high ground—and thus undermining his credibility as a proponent of public virtue—if he reacted to all attacks on his character. From his earliest years in journalism, Franklin advocated repaying evil with good and not responding in kind to vicious actions. He claimed there was no need for him to defend himself against "base Calumnies" because his friends were acquainted with his character, "and Time will open the Eyes of others."[4] As his political reputation grew, he found himself the subject of increasing anonymous attacks. "A Number of Falshoods are now privately propagated to blast my Character, of which I shall take no Notice 'till they grow bold enough to show their Faces in publick," he wrote to a friend in 1755. "Those who caress'd me a few Months since, are now endeavouring to defame me every where by every base Art." During the hotly contested Assembly elections of 1764, Franklin told a correspondent, "I bore the personal Abuse of five scurrilous Pamphlets, and three Copperplate Prints, from the Proprietary party, before I made the smallest Return."[5]

Franklin's solution to the problem of protecting his reputation without getting his hands dirty in the process was to have others defend his character from attacks. "I seem to have some Right to ask the Care of my Friends, to watch 'em and guard my Reputation and Interest," he asserted. They did. When two of his London friends were asked about Franklin's complicity in the Stamp Act, they replied, "Benjamin Franklin was so far from proposing the stamp act or joining with it in any manner, that he at all times opposed it, both in word & writing, tho' in vain, as neither his nor any other endeavour cou'd influence the then ministry to relinquish the design."[6] Another ally, immigrant German merchant Daniel Wister, defended Franklin's reputation among the Pennsylvania German population. "I am exceedingly oblig'd to my Friends for the constant Care they take of my Good Name in my Absence in defending it from the Slanders of my Enemies," Franklin wrote to Wister. "Among the rest, I beg you would accept my thankful Acknowledgements for the generous Part you have always taken in that kind Work, and that you will be assured I shall never forget your Kindness."[7]

Franklin's network printers also assisted him by publishing essays that both rehabilitated Franklin's reputation in the wake of his suspected Stamp Act collusion with Parliament and lionized him as a cornerstone of American political leadership.[8] Led by Hall, printing associates throughout the colonies republished Franklin's House of Commons testimony advocating repeal of the tax. Hall noted this document was "of great Use to his Character with many, in regard to his being alledged a Friend to the Stamp Act." Hall also published a signed letter from Galloway calling the Bradfords' journalism partisan and "designed to defame the publick reputations of Doctor Franklin and myself" by suggesting they supported the Stamp Act.[9]

Indeed, Franklin expected this support based on moral imperative. He perceived his social and diplomatic role in London as so vital to Pennsylvania that maintaining a good image was in the public's best interest. Before commencing his service as a colonial agent in London, Franklin instructed Galloway to protect his reputation from "Enemies . . . of the Publick" who "will take every Opportunity of injuring me in my Absence."[10]

During his diplomatic errand to England, Franklin adopted a deferential posture toward England and its "virtuous young King," George III, for whom no one would exceed Franklin in "thinking my own King and Queen the very best in the World and the most amiable."[11] It was not until shortly before the Revolutionary War began that Franklin even entertained thoughts of American independence. He had long before dismissed the specter of independence as disagreeable to wealthy colonists and impossible to arrange. He had tried in vain to unite the colonies in 1754 "For Their Mutual Defence and Security, and for Extending the British Settlements in North America," but he found their governments, societies, and interests too disparate.[12] Viewing people as innately immoral and selfish, he also feared what might happen if the civilizing force of English government should be expelled.

For Franklin, conciliation and compromise were the only viable means of redressing colonial grievances. Accordingly, he desired to play the role of intermediary, whose ratiocination, goodwill, and virtue would bring other virtuous men to agreement. He enjoyed the political process of moderation and negotiation, and detested confrontation and rebellion. Believing Parliament's intentions good and the king honorable, Franklin criticized mob actions during the early years of the Revolution. He cautioned, "some Punishment seems preparing for a People who are ungratefully abusing the best Constitution and the best King any Nation was ever blest with." Franklin particularly disdained inciters of civil disorder as devoid of public virtue and beyond the influence of calm leaders like himself. To Franklin, they were motivated merely by the desire for "Luxury, Licentiousness, Power, Places, Pensions and Plunder."[13]

However, the Stamp Act and its 1767 successor, the Townshend Acts—taxes Parliament placed on glass, lead, paint, paper, and tea—forced Franklin to become an exponent rather than intercessor, and to side with the rabble-rousers he detested. Franklin had been deferential toward England, but the rising tide of American opposition to the Empire's taxes and restraints on colonial self-determination threatened to wash away his burgeoning status as a wily American spokesman, unless he sided with the Patriot cause. Thus, despite being suspected "in England of being too much an American, and in America of being too much an Englishman," Franklin turned to the press to plead the American case to British readers.[14]

Between 1765 and 1775, he wrote at least 126 newspaper articles supporting America's character and explaining its plight. These essays ranged from informative to comical. Franklin jovially defended the quality of American breakfasts, sarcastically responded to a British writer who advocated that martial law be imposed in the colonies, and lampooned British ignorance about America. "The very Tails of the American Sheep are so laden with Wool, that each has a Car or Waggon on four little Wheels to support and keep it from trailing on the Ground," he claimed, and marveled that "the grand Leap of the Whale . . . up the Fall of Niagara is esteemed by all who have seen it, as one of the finest Spectacles in Nature!"[15] In his caustic "Rules by Which a Great Empire May Be Reduced to a Small One," Franklin advised, "suppose them always inclined to revolt, and treat them accordingly" and "harrass them with novel Taxes." The following year, he proposed "A Method of Humbling Rebellious American Vassals," which called for the castration of American males to stem the rapid population growth in the colonies.[16]

Franklin's intent, as he told his son William, was to reveal England's abuse of the colonies "in a short, comprehensive, and striking view, and stated therefore in out-of-the-way forms, as most likely to take the general attention."[17] Franklin used his pseudonymous essays more to ridicule intemperate governmental measures and chastise anti-American sentiment than to offer direct refutation. Responding to a British newspaper essay denouncing the colonists and asserting Parliament's right to tax them, Franklin replied, "the gentle terms of *republican race, mixed rabble of Scotch, Irish and foreign vagabonds, descendants of convicts, ungrateful rebels* &c. are some of the sweet flowers of English rhetorick, with which our colonists have of late been regaled. Surely, if we are so much their superiors, we should shew the superiority of our breeding by our better manners!"[18] Franklin even skewered the British press. He condemned British writers for advocating war on the colonies, and also compared British newspapers to ambassadors, noting that both "are sent abroad to lie, not only for the Benefit of the Publick, but also for that of particular Persons."[19]

On the other side of the Atlantic, Franklin's network printers ventured into the Revolution emulating their mentor's characteristic circumspection. Philadelphia partner David Hall, an immigrant from Scotland, was an American adherent in conflicts between the colonies and England, but he refrained from conveying that bias in the *Pennsylvania Gazette.* This was partly due to his chary nature, but also due to his fidelity to Franklin's views. In 1765, Franklin applauded Hall's decision not to publish harsh essays against the Stamp Act, and he praised his editorial neutrality. Franklin instructed him not to offend the Pennsylvania Assembly, "whose good Will I would have you by all Means cultivate and preserve."[20] Hall's resolve was waning, though, because "the Clamours of the People increase against me, for my Silence in the Paper."[21]

Facing the threat of physical and financial harm, Hall acquiesced to the rebellion. Upon repeal of the Stamp Act, he censured England by congratulating Patriot writers, through whose efforts "The Instruments and Abettors of cruel Tyranny and Oppression [have been] branded with just contempt!" After passage of the Townshend Acts, Hall vigorously advocated nonimportation pacts, labeling colonists who ignored the agreements enemies of the public.[22] However, his press remained open to pro-British views. His refusal to exclude either Loyalist or Patriot views from his newspaper prompted Franklin's son William to dismiss him as "a meer Snake in the Grass."[23]

Peter Timothy also tried initially to steer a moderate course in his *South-Carolina Gazette,* but met with the same public disapprobation as Hall. Having become unpopular when his former apprentice Charles Crouch became the favorite printer of Charles Town radicals, Timothy made the same pragmatic decision as Hall and aggressively supported nonimportation agreements in his colony as an "absolutely necessary, part of the American plan of defence." He printed a pamphlet discouraging the exportation of rice and indigo to Great Britain because "Union ought to be a grand object in all our proceedings," and nonimportation pacts are useless unless they are unanimous.[24]

In March 1772 Timothy fell ill and decided to retire, yielding his printing shop to Edward Hughes and Thomas Powell. However, later that year he informed Franklin he did not have enough savings for retirement and asked if Franklin could arrange for him to be appointed as an officer in the Royal Navy. Franklin replied that he could not secure such a position, and chastised Timothy for his decision, asserting, "to leave a good Trade in hopes of an Office, is quitting a Certainty for an Uncertainty, and losing Substance for Shadow." Franklin advised Timothy to return to printing. After Hughes died and Powell relinquished the newspaper, Timothy returned to the *South-Carolina Gazette* by November 8, 1773. He continued it until 1780, when British forces occupied Charles Town late in the Revolutionary War and forced him to shut it down.[25]

During the war, Timothy became an American spy, watching British troop ships in Charles Town harbor and filing confidential reports with an American general. He reveled in this role, lauding the infant United States as a "new Empire" borne of "glorious Events." Timothy later boasted to Franklin that he alone raised "the Opposition to Tyranny" against "strenuous and indefatigable open and secret Enemies."[26]

Although the feisty James Parker feared his temper "would have plunged me deep one way or the other" into the escalating political tensions on both sides of the ocean, he exercised caution in managing his press, just as Franklin advised. Accordingly, he told readers of his *New-York Post-Boy* that he would not print an account of a skirmish between British soldiers and New Yorkers, dubbed the "Battle of Golden Hill," until an unbiased one was submitted to him. Parker printed a similarly sanitized account of the Boston Massacre two weeks after it took place, which never used the inflammatory term "massacre."[27]

Younger printing associates, less influenced by Franklin's prudential admonitions, took less cautious paths into the American Revolution. After leaving Parker, Hugh Gaine proved moderately successful publishing the *New-York Mercury* until he made a catastrophic error in editorial judgment. During the turbulent early years of the American Revolution, Gaine professed tepid allegiance to the Patriot cause in his newspaper. When the British occupied New York in 1776, Gaine acted like a rebel and fled the city, crossing the Hudson River to Newark, New Jersey. Gaine later decided the Revolutionary cause was hopeless, returned to British-occupied New York in November 1776, and converted his newspaper to a British mouthpiece. "The shattered Remains of the Rebel Army, 'tis said, are got over into the Jersies," the turncoat editor wrote in an effort to convince patriot sympathizers of the hopelessness of their cause. "Humanity cannot but pity a Set of poor misguided Men who are thus led on to Destruction, by despicable and desperate Leaders, against every idea of Reason and Duty, and without the least Prospect of Success." Gaine's editorial views and his personal inconstancy were reviled and lambasted in newspapers throughout the colonies.[28]

Within several years, it became clear that Gaine had sided with the wrong army. During the waning days of the war, after New York was reclaimed by American troops, Gaine was indicted for "adhering to the Enemies of this State," although he was allowed to remain in New York. "Gaine's political creed, it seems, was to join the strongest party," Revolution printer Isaiah Thomas mused.[29]

John Holt adhered to American aims, though, chiefly because he enjoyed the support of the powerful New York Sons of Liberty. When he published a pamphlet in 1767 attacking Royal government in the colony, a grand jury concluded Holt's chief purpose "is to mortify Governor Colden." The grand jury ruled the pamphlet to be "a Scandalous Libel against the Judges, Assembly & Government" and ordered all copies "to be burnt by the Hand of the Common Hangman." Holt feared no personal punishment, though, writing, "I am not apprehensive of an Indictment, or any Ill Consequence. The presentment it self will be very unpopular."[30] After the British occupied New York City in 1776, Holt fled upstate to the village of Esopus, where he served as the official printer for the fledgling state of New York. Holt dismissed editorial impartiality in his *New-York Journal,* stating he only desired to publish essays that were "on the right side" of the American struggle. New York printer Thomas Greenleaf admiringly observed that Holt "zealously asserted the Cause of Freedom" throughout the Revolution.[31]

After publishing the *Constitutional Courant* and ending his partnership with Holt in New York, William Goddard mistakenly assumed the conclusion of the eighteen-year Franklin-Hall partnership contract meant they were quitting the business. Sensing an opportunity, Goddard traveled to Philadelphia to open a printing shop in November 1766. Upon arriving to find Hall still in business but with a new partner, William Sellers, Goddard was recruited by rising young politician Joseph Galloway, wealthy Quaker merchant Thomas Wharton, and Franklin's illegitimate son William, the royal governor of New Jersey. The three men were integral members of Franklin's antiproprietary faction, which opposed the Penn family's proprietorship in the province and objected to the unique, tax-exempt status of Penn family lands. With the exemption removed, Pennsylvanians might pay lower taxes, which is what the antiproprietarians wanted. It would also mean a closer affiliation with the king, which the Penns and proprietary allies preferred to avoid.[32]

Disgusted by Hall's editorial balance, Galloway, Wharton, and William Franklin sought to finance a newspaper to disseminate their political beliefs. With Galloway and Wharton as silent partners, Goddard's *Pennsylvania Chronicle* became the standard-bearer of the antiproprietarians. Galloway and Wharton needed "a Press henceforth as open and safe to them, as Hall's and Bradford's are to the other Party," William Franklin informed his father. Galloway and Wharton promised to put up half the capital in exchange for half the profits. Galloway, using his position as speaker of the Pennsylvania Assembly, assured Goddard the legislative printing contract. An article of the agreement required Goddard to consult with his partners "in every material step, or transaction, relating to said business." In this manner, Galloway and Wharton planned to exercise editorial control of the newspaper. They also planned to make Franklin a partner when he returned from England.[33] Word that Franklin provided financial support to Goddard's print shop reached Hall, who objected to his erstwhile partner aiding a competitor. Franklin denied financing the *Pennsylvania Chronicle*, although he did allow Goddard to use an office he owned and use the printing press Franklin had previously leased to Benjamin Mecom and James Parker.[34]

The partnership began calmly, with Goddard publishing Galloway's pro-Crown essays and rehabilitating Franklin's reputation, bruised due to the Stamp Act. He also declined an anti-Galloway essay because it was unnecessary to print "all the Trash which every rancorous, illiberal, anonymous Scribbler" submitted, and he later refused space to a letter criticizing his own editorial conduct. Proprietarians thus accused Goddard of being a Galloway puppet. Stung by the accusations, but beginning to see truth in them, Goddard asserted his press freedom following passage of the Townshend Acts, a thinly disguised successor to the Stamp Act. Goddard was the first American to publish proprietarian John Dickinson's "Letters from a Farmer in Pennsylvania," which proposed limiting Parliament's power. These essays "deserved the serious attention of all North-America," Goddard wrote. This view diametrically opposed the sentiments of his Loyalist partners. The enraged Galloway "ridiculed my notions about liberty and the rights of mankind," Goddard recalled. Goddard also used his newspaper to attack Franklin, whom he closely identified with the now-despised Galloway. Goddard reprinted portions of an earlier Dickinson pamphlet that accused Franklin and others of using the Stamp Act to place the "fatal fetters" of slavery on the colonies and secure "part of the horrid plunder in oppressive offices for THEMSELVES and THEIR CREATURES."[35] As a further snub, Goddard refused to print a Franklin essay on smuggling, after promising he would.[36]

Goddard severed the partnership with Galloway and Wharton in May 1769 and commenced a fierce campaign to discredit Galloway in his 1770 bid for re-election to the Assembly. He published *The Partnership*, a pamphlet exposing Wharton and Galloway's manipulation of the newspaper, calling them "enemies to their country." Galloway narrowly retained his seat. Goddard later blasted the two Loyalists repeatedly in the *Pennsylvania Chronicle*.[37] From London, Franklin congratulated Galloway on his victory and consoled him on the defamations. "We must not in the Course of Publick Life expect immediate Approbation, and immediate grateful Acknowledgement of our Services," Franklin wrote. "But let us persevere, thro' Abuse and even Injury. The internal Satisfaction of a good Conscience is always present, and Time will do us Justice in the Minds of the People, even of those at present the most prejudic'd against us." Although Galloway won the battle and retained his seat in the Assembly, he and his faction lost the war. Other key antiproprietarians lost their Assembly seats in 1770 and 1772, and Galloway never regained his former popularity, especially among merchants and mechanics who were influenced by Goddard's diatribes. By 1772, Galloway's party was virtually extinct.[38]

Although Goddard upheld the right to criticize public officials, his pamphlet *The Partnership* earned Franklin's disdain. Goddard had not merely rebelled against the conventions of the Franklin network, as Holt, Mecom, and others had done; he had gone farther. By attacking Galloway, Franklin's friend and closest political ally in Pennsylvania, and by playing an integral role in crippling Franklin's political party, Goddard had invited the printing patriarch's wrath. Upon receiving a copy of *A True and Faithful NARRATIVE,* Goddard's 1771 sequel to *The Partnership* that continued the attack on Galloway, Franklin responded, "I cast my eye over Goddard's Piece against our Friend Mr. Galloway and then lit my Fire with it. I think such feeble malicious attacks cannot hurt him."[39] However, they did, and Franklin knew it.

The cessation of his partnership with Galloway and Wharton and the loss of government printing proved too great a financial hardship for Goddard. He left Philadelphia in 1773 to commence the first newspaper in Baltimore, the *Maryland Journal,* leaving his sister, Mary Katherine Goddard, to superintend the *Pennsylvania Chronicle.* Postal problems with both newspapers made Goddard increasingly concerned. Newspaper publishers were particularly sensitive to flaws in the British postal system, because they relied on it to deliver mail for newsgathering purposes and to carry their newspapers to other towns. Goddard suspected Franklin, in his capacity as deputy postmaster-general, was deliberately impeding mail service for Goddard's newspapers. Announcing he was forced to pay for a private postal rider, Goddard informed Pennsylvania readers that his newspaper "will, by the Establishment of a new Northern Post, be able to visit its old Friends in this Province, from whom it hath, for some Time, been cut off by . . . one of the D. Postmasters Gene[ral]." The reference to Franklin was clear.[40]

Goddard resolved to remedy the postal system's flaws and circumvent Franklin's power to exact revenge. In February 1774 he closed his Philadelphia newspaper, sent for his sister to succeed him at the helm of the *Maryland Journal*, and traveled throughout the colonies establishing a voluntary network of local offices paid for by subscribers. These would be supervised by a postmaster-general in New York who would be elected by provincial postal committees and operate the entire system at cost. After securing the support of Committees of Correspondence throughout the colonies, Goddard's spectacular "Constitutional Post" was implemented. It was immediately successful, and drove the British post out of business in 1775, ending Royal control of colonial correspondence.[41]

Printers throughout the colonies aided Goddard's cause. Isaiah Thomas of the *Massachusetts Spy* praised the plan and Goddard, who "has long been noted as the Proprietor and Employer of a very FREE PRESS." Thomas explained Goddard's mission by informing readers that the British Post was "obstructing intelligence from colony to colony, by subjecting the newspapers to an ENORMOUS POSTAGE," which "nothing can prevent but establishing posts of our own."[42]

Goddard presented his "Constitutional Post" to the Second Continental Congress during the summer of 1775. This system became the model for the United States Postal Service. It was readily accepted by the Continental Congress, which was pleased to take over a system already in operation from Maine to Virginia. When Franklin returned from London, he immediately became a candidate for postmaster-general by virtue of his experience as head of the British post. The Congress unanimously chose the renowned and personable Franklin, sweeping aside Goddard. Goddard then sought the second-ranking position of comptroller, for which he, as founder of the system, would have been a logical choice.[43] However, Franklin—motivated by revenge and nepotism—selected son-in-law Richard Bache for the job, even though Franklin had told him the previous year he had no power to secure a postal position. Goddard was instead offered the job of surveying postal roads.[44]

Goddard felt cheated by politicians who had forgotten his postal contribution. Seeking salve for his wounded pride, he applied to the Congress for a political appointment as a lieutenant colonel in George Washington's Continental Army during the summer of 1776. Washington rejected the petition, claiming that Goddard's appointment would cause jealousy among the ranks and "would be attended with endless confusion."[45] Goddard was further confounded when Franklin left for France on a diplomatic mission and appointed Bache as the new postmaster-general on November 7, 1776. However, Goddard was not promoted to the vacated comptroller post. By

Drawing of William Goddard

William Goddard entered the Franklin network under the auspices of James Parker. The fiery printer later angered several Patriot groups and helped configure the prototype for the United States postal service. Goddard was furious when Franklin was named the first U.S. Postmaster-General and remained embittered toward Franklin until his death.

this time Goddard was sure of a Franklin vendetta, so he resigned as surveyor in January 1777.[46]

Embittered and angry with Franklin for his snubs, Goddard returned to Baltimore and joined his sister in publishing the *Maryland Journal*. Still seething in 1778, he wrote to Holt for advice on attacking Franklin in print. This was rare for the times, as Franklin had become regarded as a vital founder of the infant nation. Holt responded that such an attack was justified due to Franklin's involvement with the Stamp Act and the fact that he arranged for several of his friends to be named stamp masters. Holt claimed that Franklin was motivated chiefly by gain for himself and his family.

Assailing Franklin's character, Holt called him "a dangerous person, primarily attentive to his own Interest, and always acting in Subserviency to it upon all Occasions, even when it clashed with that of the Publick."[47]

There is no evidence Goddard launched this proposed attack. However, still bitter more than three decades later, Goddard flagellated Franklin's memory in a letter to Isaiah Thomas, who was collecting reminiscences about early American journalism for a revised edition of his book on the history of printing. Goddard alleged that Franklin had entered into a "conspiracy" with Galloway and Wharton to overthrow Pennsylvania's proprietary government so that the three could have "Wealth & Power for themselves & Connexions." When this plan failed, "from a Royalist he insidiously turned into a dark Republican," Goddard wrote. When Franklin returned to America in 1775, "he was considered a suspicious doubtful character—and Mr. S. Adams, & other Patriots, asked me my opinion of him, at Philadelphia being very suspicious of him. I told them if they could convince him that it would redound to his INTEREST to support the American Cause, he would soon declare himself in its Favour, and not otherwise. This they did, & Franklin became, as they advised me, an unsuspected confidential PATRIOT."[48]

Goddard had good reason to be angry with Franklin, or at least jealous of him. Franklin went on to become the American icon of freedom, patriotism, and ingenuity, while Goddard plunged into obscurity. Likewise, Franklin, not Goddard, is commonly credited with the establishment of the postal system. In his book on printing history, Thomas wrote of Goddard, "When the loaves and fishes were to be divided, aspiring, interested, nominal patriots crowded him into the background, and his services were in a great measure forgotten."[49]

Franklin's transition to the status of patriot was long and difficult. Shortly before the Revolution commenced, Franklin expressed unshakable faith in the merit of King George III and the future felicity of colonial relations with Great Britain. "I am of Opinion, that his Virtue, and the Consciousness of his sincere Intentions to make his People happy, will give him Firmness and Steadiness," Franklin forecasted, "and when that Firmness is fully perceiv'd, Faction will dissolve and be dissipated like a Morning Fog before the rising Sun, leaving the rest of the Day clear, with a Sky serene and cloudless. Such, after a few of the first Years, will be the future Course of his Majesty's Reign, which I predict will be happy and truly glorious." However, the course of events throughout the Revolutionary era, plus the pressure of public opinion, compelled Franklin to revise his views. By the eve of the Revolutionary War, he observed to Galloway that English virtue had rotted, while Americans could be proud of "the glorious publick Virtue so predominant in our rising Country."[50]

Printer-turned-statesman Franklin was a late and somewhat reluctant participant in the American Revolution. He preferred to wait for passions to cool and then strengthen colonial ties with Great Britain, but the rising tide of American opposition to Great Britain's taxes prompted him to be less conciliatory. Franklin realized his public commitment to the Patriot cause was essential if he was to retain the position of moral teacher he had carefully cultivated since his days as "Silence Dogood" and "The Busy-Body" a half-century earlier, and which he extended through the creation of his printing network.[51] However, he advised his printing partners and associates to remain impartial, fearing financial losses and a curtailment of press freedom would otherwise result. Most network printers initially obeyed, but they soon became ardent revolutionaries to swim with the tide of public opinion.

Franklin was ultimately forced to abandon the very impartiality he advocated for the press. He revealed his sentiment about the widening breach between Americans and British in a pamphlet published in 1768 and reissued in 1774. He was apologetic for "the wild ravings of the at present half distracted Americans," which resulted in mob actions and property damage, and stated, "I do not pretend to support or justify them." But he added his desire "that these people had never been thus needlessly driven out of their senses" by British obstinacy. Foreshadowing American independence, Franklin wrote in a British newspaper that "this unhappy system of politics tends to dissolve those bands of union, and to sever us for ever." The Declaration of Independence completed the dissolution and shattered "that fine and noble China Vase," the British Empire.[52]

12

The Moral Reform of a Scurrilous Press

"He that best understands the World, least likes it," a cynical Benjamin Franklin wrote in 1753 under the guise of "Poor Richard."[1] Franklin had grown pessimistic during the middle decades of the eighteenth century due in part to stories about crime, greed, and immorality that he read, wrote, and published in the colonial press. His misanthropy was augmented by failed printing partnerships, particularly in the West Indies and the Pennsylvania German community.

However, he was most resentful of public attacks on his character. During Franklin's 1764 bid for re-election to the Pennsylvania Assembly, his opponents appeared "sworn to load him with all the Filth, and Virulence that the basest Heads and basest Hearts can suggest," a Franklin supporter commented. After his defeat and subsequent appointment as colonial agent to Parliament, critics denounced him as unacceptable. He is "very unfavorably thought of by several of his Majesty's Ministers," and his character "is so extremely disagreeable to a very great Number of the most serious and reputable Inhabitants of this Province of all Denominations and Societies," according to a newspaper editorial signed by many prominent Pennsylvanians.[2]

Franklin was keenly aware of the animosities awakened by his political prominence and ability to influence public opinion. "I have many enemies (all indeed on the Public Account, for I cannot recollect that I have in a private Capacity given just cause of offence to any one whatever) yet they are Enemies and very bitter ones," he informed his daughter a month after the 1764 election. The longer he was in public life, the more the press assailed him. Exhibiting bitterness after two decades of vilification, Franklin warned a new political officeholder, "the Publick is often niggardly even of its Thanks, while you are sure of being censured by malevolent Criticks and Bug Writers, who will abuse you while you are serving them, and wound your Character in nameless Pamphlets, thereby resembling those little dirty stinking Insects, that attack us only in the dark, disturb our Repose, molesting & wounding us while our Sweat & Blood is contributing to their Subsistence."[3]

However, the conclusion of the American Revolution rejuvenated Franklin and restored a flicker of his faith in humanity. "Thank God, the world is growing wiser and wiser; and as by degrees men are convinced of the folly of wars for religion, for dominion, or for commerce, they will be happier and happier," he wrote in 1788.[4] The attacks on his reputation by adversaries in Pennsylvania politics, the Stamp Act crisis, and the quest for independence were burnished with the creation of a new country—and a new national identity—for Americans. As his fears of an American mobocracy subsided in the 1780s, Franklin hoped his new countrymen could be coaxed to lead more virtuous lives as citizens of an infant nation than they had as British colonists. Writing to British scientist Joseph Priestley during the war, he lauded scientific advances but lamented, "O that moral Science were in as fair a Way of Improvement, that Men would cease to be Wolves to one another, and that human Beings would at length learn what they now improperly call Humanity!" Conveying his desire to see "the Discovery of a Plan" for improving moral philosophy, an exasperated Franklin wrote to another friend the same week, "When will human Reason be sufficiently improv'd to see the Advantage of this!"[5]

Once the Treaty of Paris furnished diplomatic assurance of the new nation's viability, the aged Franklin saw for himself an enormous opportunity to implement just such a plan. Although still skeptical about human rectitude, Franklin was willing to resume his efforts to trumpet virtue. He had been frustrated in his efforts to lead American *colonists* to uprightness, but *United States citizens*, developing their own identity after nearly two decades of rebellion, might prove more malleable. He optimistically informed Europeans that the infant United States was a land of "Industry, Frugality, Ability, Prudence and Virtue," and he wrote that the American lifestyle and economic system "are great preservatives of the Morals and Virtue of a nation." However, Franklin privately viewed Americans as rougher, simpler, more incitable, and less refined than their trans-Atlantic counterparts. They needed an instructor in morality to guide them to the virtuous conduct necessary for a successful republic.[6]

Although well past seventy years old, his fame and fortune secure,

Franklin embraced the resumption of his lifelong ambition to disseminate a moral ideology. As a result, while serving as a wartime American ambassador in France, he wrote and published numerous essays extolling virtue. In a "Dialogue Between Franklin and the Gout," Franklin inserted himself into a moralistic essay to show that illness is the result of indolence and gluttony.[7] The game of chess is a microcosm of life, Franklin explained to readers of his bagatelle "The Morals of Chess," because success in both requires foresight, circumspection, and perseverance. "The game is so full of events," Franklin wrote, "that one is encouraged to continue the contest to the last, in hopes of victory by our own skill, or, at least, of giving a *stale mate,* by the negligence of our adversary." In a pamphlet designed to laud virtue and persuade Europeans of the integrity of United States citizens, Franklin advised prospective immigrants seeking "to live upon the Public, by some Office or Salary" due to prominent lineage against journeying to the new nation, for they "will be despis'd and disregarded." Noble birth "is a Commodity that cannot be carried to a worse Market than that of America," he noted, adding that the United States would welcome people with vocational skills who are laborious, frugal, and well-behaved.[8]

Franklin's *Autobiography* was the capstone of his didactic writings. Begun in 1771, its first part contained what he called "several little family Anecdotes of no Importance to others."[9] He discontinued it that summer. However, after friends urged him to "think of bettering the whole race of men" by leading "the Youth to equal the Industry & Temperance of thy early Youth," Franklin resumed in 1784, his tales now "accordingly intended for the Publick."[10] Galvanized by his admirers, Franklin embraced the project as a means of providing moral instruction to the masses. His own assessment of the memoirs was that it "will be of more general use to young readers, exemplifying strongly the effects of *prudent* and *imprudent conduct* in the commencement of a life of business," he informed a French duke.[11]

Franklin had long regarded it essential to teach morality to the young. He wrote to American theologian and educator Samuel Johnson, "I think with you, that nothing is of more importance for the public weal, than to form and train up youth in wisdom and virtue." Teaching morals to the young was vital, Franklin noted, for "virtue is more probably to be expected and obtained from the *education* of youth, than from the *exhortation* of adult persons; bad habits and vices of the mind, being, like diseases of the body, more easily prevented than cured."[12]

While Franklin was trying to prevent moral cankers from infecting youthful souls, he also endeavored to cure them in adults—especially printers.

Franklin perceived that most of his printing brethren, especially younger members who had entered the vocation during the Revolution, had no scruples about publishing defamation. While in France, Franklin sometimes refused to lend American newspapers because "the Pieces of Personal Abuse, so scandalously common in our newspapers . . . would disgrace us."[13] Besides their tendency to embarrass, Franklin believed that scurrilous newspapers jeopardized press freedom. He wrote in a newspaper editorial, "nothing is more likely to endanger the liberty of the press, than the abuse of that liberty, by employing it in personal accusation, detraction, and calumny." He found this particularly true in Philadelphia, where "the Spirit of Rancour, Malice, and *Hatred* that breathes in its NewsPapers" fueled the fires of party factionalism. Reading the city's newspapers would lead outsiders "to conclude, that Pennsylvania is peopled by a Set of the most unprincipled, wicked, rascally, and quarrelsome Scoundrels upon the Face of the Globe," he complained.[14]

To Franklin, the character and credit of the new nation was on trial in the court of international public opinion, and a fractious domestic press injured its case. "The Conductor of a Newspaper should, methinks, consider himself as in some degree the Guardian of his Country's Reputation, and refuse to insert such Writings as may hurt it," Franklin exhorted in 1782.[15] American journalism's penchant for obloquy made his job as ambassador to France more difficult and presented a stark contrast to Franklin's emerging European identity as the quintessential American—simple, honest, peaceful, and virtuous. "The British Newswriters are very assiduous in their endeavours to blacken America," Franklin warned a printer. He cautioned the proprietors of his old newspaper, the *Pennsylvania Gazette,* that European newspapers delighted in reprinting calumnies from the United States press to portray America as divisive and chaotic.[16]

Early in his journalism career Franklin adopted a posture of placid neutrality and suggested that printers were mere laborers who were obliged to publish virulent essays provided they were accompanied by money. He informed readers that "Printers naturally acquire a vast Unconcernedness as to the right or wrong Opinions contain'd in what they print" and thus "print things full of Spleen and Animosity, with the utmost Calmness and Indifference." Vituperative writings are continually submitted to printers, he claimed, "because the People are so viciously and corruptly educated that good things are not encouraged."[17]

However, as he matured and realized printing's unique ability to influence public beliefs and conduct, his editorial policy became more selective. Franklin adopted the editorial posture that his newspaper was not like a stagecoach, providing space to everyone who paid. He excoriated people who communicated malicious gossip, comparing them to flies for whom "a *sore Place* is a Feast."[18]

Franklin's solution to the problem of scurrilous submissions was to print them privately, rather than include them in his *Pennsylvania Gazette*. Pamphlets were attractive not only because essays of greater length could be presented in a unified form, but also because they allowed printers to distance themselves from defamatory or polemical writings. However, their newspapers were more closely linked to their identity in the community and more integral to their ideology of public service. "If People will print their Abuses of one another, let them do it in little Pamphlets, and distribute them where they think proper. It is absurd to trouble all the World with them; and unjust to Subscribers in distant Places, to stuff their Paper with Matters so unprofitable and so disagreable."[19]

Franklin viewed his newspaper as a means to instruct the masses about the blessings of virtuous conduct, but he feared its noble purpose would be nullified by the hypocrisy of printing calumny. "In the Conduct of my Newspaper I carefully excluded all Libelling and Personal Abuse, which is of late Years become so disgraceful to our Country," Franklin wrote in his *Autobiography* in 1788:

> Whenever I was solicited to insert any thing of that kind, and the Writers pleaded as they generally did, the Liberty of the Press, and that a Newspaper was like a Stage Coach in which any one who would pay had a Right to a Place, my Answer was, that I would print the Piece separately if desired, and the Author might have as many Copies as he pleased to distribute himself, but that I would not take upon me to spread his Detraction, and that having contracted with my Subscribers to furnish them with what might be either useful or entertaining, I could not fill their Papers with private Altercation in which they had no Concern without doing them manifest Injustice.[20]

However, most printers in the new nation seemed to be under no such moral stricture, as scurrility and virulent writings filled the pages of the nation's newspapers in the 1780s. This type of press freedom was merely an absence of restraint, rather than a service to society, Franklin lamented. Editor Benjamin Russell concurred, asserting that "the liberty of the press" in the early republic had become "very little short of the liberty of burning our houses." Published defamation only detracted from the press's role of conveying republican enlightenment, useful education, and moral teachings. Franklin believed printers had an obligation to refuse space to rancorous writings. "Now many of our Printers make no scruple of gratifying the Malice of Individuals by false Accusations of the fairest Characters among ourselves, augmenting Animosity even to the producing of Duels, and are moreover so indiscreet as to print scurrilous Reflections on the government of neighbouring States, and even on the Conduct of our best national Allies, which may be attended with the most pernicious Consequences," Franklin warned in his *Autobiography*. "These Things I mention as a Caution to young Printers."[21]

Franklin's challenge in the new country was formidable—impart moral instruction to a mass audience and overcome the deleterious effects of scurrilous journalism, which eroded the edifice of public virtue Franklin had spent a lifetime trying to erect.

To enlist assistance in this mission, Franklin decided to rejuvenate his moribund printing network. Franklin had only minimal direct involvement with his printing associates after his formal link to journalism, the Hall partnership, expired in 1766. Although its termination meant "a great Source of our Income is cut off," Franklin wrote to his wife, it freed him to be a full-time diplomat. It also relieved him from the burden of managing the disputes that were tearing apart the network, as Peter Timothy contended with radicals and his former apprentice Charles Crouch in Charles Town, Hall was at odds with Proprietary pacifists in Philadelphia, and James Parker was waging financial and editorial battles against all his former partners. Franklin's desire to distance himself from the worries of publishing prompted him to decline a printing partnership in 1767 "because I did not care to be again concerned in Business," he wrote.[22]

As time passed, Franklin's connections to members of his printing network faded. Franklin outlived most of his old partners, including Parker, Hall, and Timothy, all of whom died during the Revolution. After succumbing to a fever while traveling on postal business, Parker died July 2, 1770.[23] Hall died two years later, on Christmas eve at age fifty-eight, after a long illness.[24] Timothy died in a shipwreck off the Delaware capes in 1782, shortly after being released by the British following a year's captivity as a political prisoner.[25]

Their sons had succeeded the three stalwart partners, with William Hall and David Hall Jr. printing in Philadelphia, Samuel Franklin Parker in New York, and Benjamin Franklin Timothy (along with his mother Ann Timothy) in Charles Town. Franklin enjoyed seeing the next generation thrive. Upon learning of the elder David Hall's death, Franklin wrote, "I lament the death of my good old Friend Mr. Hall, but am glad to understand he has left a Son fit to carry on the Business, which [I] wish he may do with as good a Character and as good Success as his Father." However, there was no contractual relationship between Franklin and the sons. They respected him, but their businesses required neither his formal partnership nor his moral guidance.[26]

Franklin's family connections to the printing trade had likewise dissipated. His nephew James Franklin Jr. and sister-in-law Ann Franklin died in 1762 and 1763, respectively, and their *Newport Mercury* passed to Ann Franklin's son-in-law Samuel Hall.[27] In 1776, nephew Benjamin Mecom wandered away from the New Jersey insane asylum where he was confined and vanished.[28] Franklin's cousin by marriage, William Dunlap, left the business in 1766 to become an Episcopal clergyman.[29]

Of those few network members remaining, their bodies had been weakened by age and their finances depleted by business setbacks. Anton Armbruster, once Franklin's partner in publishing German-language newspapers, wrote him pathetic letters pleading for alms after his press and printing materials had been confiscated in partial satisfaction of his long-standing debt to Franklin. "And as there are Bonds between us I think it Reasonable, in Your Honor's own candid Consideration, they are to be given up, as I lost all," Armbruster wrote in 1785 to Franklin, who had just been chosen president of the Supreme Executive Council of Pennsylvania. The following year Armbruster suggested "some Assistance could perhaps, set me in a way, to make out a living." However, by 1788 Armbruster, writing in a tremulous hand, was more desperate. "I humbly obediently intreat your Excellencys kind and generous Heart" for "a little Assistance and Alms," he implored, as "I am almost incapable of working" due to being "ailing and old."[30] Franklin appears never to have responded, probably because Armbruster still owed him money and because Franklin's son-in-law Richard Bache gave Franklin an unflattering report of Armbruster's character. Armbruster "is an idle, drunken good for nothing Fellow," Bache wrote.[31]

With the veteran network members gone and no extant partnerships, Franklin decided to resuscitate his printing network. His objectives were to convey moral virtue to the new nation and plant worthy young printers into influential positions within the firmament of American journalism. Franklin's intention was that these new partners not only educate their readers, but also set an example for contemporary printers, as Franklin had done during his publishing career.

Relying upon familiar and comfortable methods, Franklin re-established his network with two young printers whose character, conduct, and skill impressed him. Benjamin Franklin Bache and Francis Childs both enjoyed success as printers in the early years of the new nation. Childs became the official printer for New York State and commenced the second daily newspaper there. Bache became the standard-bearer for the Jeffersonian Republicans in the 1790s and the foremost journalistic foe of presidents Washington and Adams.

The two printers attained their prosperity by very different paths. Bache was Franklin's grandson. He came from a prosperous family, grew up in Europe amid wealth and the highest social circles, and received an elite education in France and Switzerland. Childs, by contrast, was a stranger to Franklin. He was raised in a large and impoverished family, warranting Franklin's attention only because he had been recommended by one of Franklin's trusted political allies. They were a study in contrasts in other ways, as well. Bache learned printing from his grandfather and typefounding from the most prominent typographer in France; Childs served a humble apprenticeship to a Philadelphia printer. Bache was a prolific and vituperative writer; Childs wrote little. Bache was aggressive and prominent; Childs was sedate and inconspicuous. Despite their dissimilar backgrounds and characters, Franklin saw in both men the qualities he sought in partners from years past. This impelled him to set up both in partnerships. The results were not what Franklin expected.[32]

When Franklin was dispatched to France in 1776 to serve as the United States ambassador, he brought his two grandsons with him. William Temple Franklin, age sixteen, served as his personal secretary, and seven-year-old Bache entered a French boarding school. The younger boy having impressed Franklin as "a good honest lad" who will become "a valuable man," Franklin sought to train him in the arts of printing and typefounding. He established a typefoundry in Passy and had a printing press operating by 1779.[33]

The notion of establishing a letter-casting business had intrigued Franklin for decades. "I am much oblig'd to you for your Care and Pains in procuring me the Founding-Tools; tho' I think, with you, that the Workmen have not been at all bashful in making their Bills," Franklin wrote to his English colleague and supplier William Strahan in 1744. There is no other evidence Franklin succeeded in forming a type foundry, but the quality of printing type was still a concern to him thirty-five years later. "I thank you for the Boston Newspapers," he wrote from France to a family member in Boston, "tho' I see nothing so clearly in them as that your Printers do indeed want new Letters. They perfectly blind me in endeavouring to read them. If you should ever have any Secrets that you wish to be well kept, get them printed in those Papers."[34]

Franklin recognized a need for proficient typography in the United States. While creating and defining a national character, Americans were developing a credo of self-sufficiency; it became a source of national pride to fill nearly all their needs with domestic products. This sentiment extended to the printing trade. Printers had been obligated to import their presses and types from England until 1769, when Connecticut craftsmen cast the first type and constructed the first printing press made in America. Silversmith Abel Buell produced the type, and New Haven clockmaker Isaac Doolittle erected the press for William Goddard. A Boston newspaper reported that Doolittle "has lately compleated a Mahogany Printing-Press on the most approved Construction, which, by some good Judges in the Printing Way, is allowed to be . . . equal, if not superior, to any imported from Great-Britain."[35] Paper-making was a related industry that commenced during the Revolution and flourished afterward. As one entrepreneur wrote in 1785, "the art of Manu-factureing of Paper" is "of Great Public Utility."[36]

These domestic industries grew following the completion of the Revolutionary War, as printing became a vital means of unifying the new republic. Believing that typefounding was essential to a strong and self-sufficient domestic press, Franklin arranged for his grandson to study under the tutelage of French expert Francois-Ambroise Didot. Franklin acknowledged Didot "has a Passion for the Art" of printing, and his "Zeal & indefatigable Application, bids fair to carry the Art to a high Pitch of Perfection." His grandson agreed. "I am now learning to print at Mr. Didot's, the best Printer that now exists & maybe that has ever existed," Bache informed his parents, adding that he was also receiving lessons in engraving type.[37]

Franklin vowed to provide Bache with "a Trade that he may have something to depend on, and not be oblig'd to ask Favours or Offices of anybody." As Bache grew to manhood, though, Franklin became increasingly convinced that printing was the appropriate profession for him. By 1788, he was able to inform a French friend that Bache "is preparing to enter into Business as a Printer, the original Occupation of his Grandfather."[38] Franklin still desired that Bache ply the typefounding trade in America, prompting the patriarch to purchase the requisite supplies from Didot, but Franklin's plans for the boy's future had changed.

Franklin esteemed his grandson's character so highly that he believed Bache could better serve the nation by propagating information, education, and opinion among a large audience, rather than working as a craftsman in a foundry. "He is docile and of gentle Manners, ready to receive and follow good Advice, and will set no bad Example," Franklin wrote. "He gains every day upon my Affections." Bache's formidable intellect, philosophical demeanor, and virtuous character prompted Franklin to see Bache as his ideological successor, imparting ethical instruction and serving as a moral bellwether amid the turmoil of a scurrilous press. "I am too old to follow printing again myself, but loving the business, I have brought up my grandson Benjamin to it, and have built and furnished a printing-house for him,

Portrait of John Jay by Albert Rosenthal

John Jay, American diplomat and first Chief Justice of the Supreme Court of the United States, was the patron of Franklin's printing partner Francis Childs. Childs later allowed disappointed office-seeker Lewis Littlepage to attack Jay in a pamphlet Childs published.

which he now manages under my eye," Franklin wrote with pride in 1789. His dedication to the art—and the mission he sought to accomplish by its means—was rekindled by the hope that Bache represented.[39]

Francis Childs was another symbol of Franklin's hope for the future of American journalism. He was born in Philadelphia in 1763 and raised in what John Jay described as "a large and helpless family" in New York.[40] Childs was apprenticed to Philadelphia printer John Dunlap through the patronage of Jay, who would later author some of the Federalist Papers, negotiate the infamous Jay Treaty with Great Britain, and become the first Chief Justice of the United States.[41] Jay paid for Childs's education and encouraged his interest in printing, counseling him that "Professional Knowledge, added to Diligence and Prudence, must sooner or later be successful; especially in a Country like ours."[42]

On January 1, 1783, Childs informed Jay that he aspired to re-establish a New York print shop that had been evacuated by British troops as the Revolutionary War drew to a close. Then in Paris serving as secretary of foreign affairs, Jay encouraged Childs's enterprise. "You do well to look forward to the means of exercising your profession to advantage," he wrote, adding, "You shall continue to have my aid and protection in such measure and season as circumstances may render proper and expedient." This was an important promise, as many early American printers relied on powerful backers for economic support, often in the form of government publishing contracts. This method of official subsidy could be used to encourage certain printers at the expense of others.[43]

Having learned about Franklin's printing network from Dunlap, whose uncle William had been a member, Childs asked Jay to solicit Franklin's advice on printing prospects. Jay told Childs of a press belonging to Franklin that the British army had commandeered, but which would soon be retrieved. Jay added that Franklin told him, "when the enemy left Philadelphia they carried from thence to New York a printing-press of his, and that it is now in the possession of one Robinson, a printer, at New York. As by the provisional treaty the British forces are not to carry away any effects of the inhabitants, this press may perhaps be recovered."[44]

To help his nineteen-year-old charge, Jay recruited Franklin's benefaction. Franklin wrote to Childs, acquainting him with the names of other members of the printing network. Franklin expressed "a willingness to assist you in setting up your business, on the same terms as I had formerly done with other young printers of good character, viz., Whitemarsh and Timothy in Carolina, Smith and afterwards Mecon in Antigua, Parker at New York, Franklin at

Rhode Island, Holland [and] Miller at Lancaster, and afterwards Dunlap, and Hall at Philadelphia." Franklin was persuaded to assist Childs because of "The good character given of you by Mr. Jay," which, he noted, "is my inducement to serve you if I can."[45]

The importance of Franklin's phrase "good character," which he used twice in the same letter, cannot be underestimated. Since young adulthood, when he had been deceived and disappointed by callous and self-indulgent people, Franklin had been a vigorous exponent of virtue. "He is ill-cloth'd, who is bare of Virtue," he counseled in his inaugural *Poor Richard's Almanack*. He returned to the theme many times in the almanac. "You may be more happy than Princes, if you will be more virtuous," he instructed readers in 1738, adding, "Sell not virtue to purchase wealth, nor Liberty to purchase power."[46] He saw—and encouraged readers to see—a clear connection between virtue and eternal rewards. "Learning to the Studious; Riches to the Careful; Power to the Bold; Heaven to the Virtuous," he noted in 1754. He believed that maintaining such virtues as industry, frugality, logic, and self-discipline represented the best service to God and man and was essential to prudent government and social tranquility. These beliefs remained intact throughout his life.[47]

Three other factors aided Childs in securing Franklin's patronage. That Childs successfully served an apprenticeship under the tutelage of Dunlap, publisher of the *Pennsylvania Packet* and a relative of Franklin's wife, enhanced Franklin's estimation of Childs's character. The second factor was Franklin's lifelong affinity for assisting neophyte tradesmen. Motivated by gratitude for kindnesses extended to him when he was a struggling young printer in the 1720s, but recalling some of his failed partnerships, Franklin wrote in his memoirs that he was "often more ready than perhaps I should otherwise have been to assist young Beginners." The third—and perhaps most important—reason Franklin sponsored Childs was his dedication to countervailing the abundance of journalistic invective in the early republic. From his vantage point in France, he had observed that American newspapers influenced European opinions about the United States. "The excesses some of our papers have been guilty of in this particular, have set this State in a bad light abroad," Franklin asserted.[48]

To help his young protégé get started, Franklin informed Childs he would carry "a very large quantity of types" on his return trip to America in the summer of 1785, "when we may carry this proposal into execution, if it shall suit you." In the interim, Franklin encouraged Childs to seek other opportunities, "for I am old and infirm, and accidents may prevent us," and suggested he visit Parker's widow in New Jersey to see a sample Franklin partnership contract. He noted, "she can show you the agreement between her husband and me, and you may consider the terms of it before my arrival."[49]

Once he became Franklin's partner, Childs took possession of the printing press and opened his shop in New York, then the nation's capital and a thriving city of thirty thousand. Childs described the municipality as the "peaceful seat of the happiest empire in the universe." Situated at "17 Duke-Street, the first Door from the Corner of the Old-Slip and Smith-Street," Childs unveiled the *New-York Daily Advertiser* on March 1, 1785. It was the first newspaper in American history to commence as a daily, and only the fourth daily ever on the continent.[50]

The twenty-one-year-old Childs had set up shop in a city governed by commercial interests, and he fashioned his newspaper accordingly. Finally free of the British occupation forces and the Revolution's hardships, New York warmly embraced economic development. "The history of the City of New York," early republic diarist Elihu Hubbard Smith complained, "is the history of the eager cultivation & rapid increase of the arts of gain." This history was unflaggingly recorded by newspapers such as the *Daily Advertiser,* which, by their focus on "the history of public contests & private intrigues," contribute to "the fatal progress of the demon of Speculation," Smith wrote.[51]

Childs endeavored to fashion the *Daily Advertiser* as New York's chief source of business information. He chose the title to reflect his newspaper's primary function, proclaiming in its nameplate, "ADVERTISEMENTS INSERTED ON THE LOWEST TERMS." True to its name, the *Daily Advertiser* relied heavily on commercial interests for revenue, usually filling about two-and-a-half of its four pages with advertisements, including the entire front page. The use of illustrations and aggressive persuasion techniques in advertising was rare in early America, with little more attention-grabbing than a "headline" in slightly larger type than the standard text. Other commercial information Childs published for the benefit of his readers included ship and stagecoach travel schedules and commodities prices. In a regular feature called "Price Current," Childs listed London prices for such goods as turpentine, mahogany, flax, beeswax, "Pot ashes," and "Rackoon."[52]

Childs's idea to establish a newspaper with an economic focus, designed for a major port city during an era of rapid domestic growth, proved to be an excellent one. Childs enjoyed immediate success, enabling him to proudly inform Franklin, "I am convinced you will with pleasure receive the information that my Paper is one of the best established in N. Yk." Franklin replied that he was glad to hear Childs's newspaper "is well established, and likely to be profitable."[53]

Within one year, Childs's advertising revenue had increased to justify creation of a second publication. He opted to divert much of the financial news
and some of the advertisements to a new venture, the *American Price-
Current.* Launched May 1, 1786, it was one of the first business publications
in American journalism. In it, Childs told readers they could find the market
prices of every commodity, as well as stock prices, insurance premiums, auc-
tion sales, and "a variety of other useful information." Childs later yielded
daily management of this publication to Aeneas Lamont (who was likely one
of his journeymen), preferring to devote all his time to the *Daily Advertiser.*
In August 1786, the *American Price-Current* was restructured into a new
publication, the *New-York Price-Current,* which functioned as a supplement,
"given free (gratis) every Monday, to the Subscribers for this Paper," according to a *Daily Advertiser* notice.[54]

Business fare was the *Daily Advertiser's* chief content, but it also contained
social and political news, most of which had been reprinted from Philadelphia,
Boston, and London newspapers. Childs seldom wrote for his own newspaper,
preferring to solicit reader contributions, especially those promoting moral
improvement. To underscore the point, Child included the phrase "The Noblest
Motive is the Public Good" on the nameplate.

Following his partner Franklin's advice, Childs often printed essays cham-
pioning public virtue. One of these, by "Bartholemew Plaintruth," offered "to
cultivate the minds, [and] regulate the manners" of his fellow New Yorkers to
the extent that it "will be honourable to themselves and promotive of the
happiness of society."[55] In another, "Monitor" warned what steps the fledgling United States must take to retain its freedom, writing, "it behoves every
citizen of our infant empire, to contribute his mite towards the public weal;
to check in their progress the vices of the age [and] to encourage virtue."
Otherwise, "liberty will degenerate into licentiousness, commerce deviate
from national interest to selfish mercenary views, freedom become a curse."[56]

Others were even more strikingly Franklinesque. "An Admirer of the Fine
Arts" observed that "Those efforts of genius are the most laudable which,
while they please the fancy . . . communicate to the mind the most useful instruction. Virtue is taught most successfully by being recommended under
the appearance of amusement; and those lessons make the deepest and most
lasting impression, which, at the same time, convince and interest." Betraying
some of Franklin's pessimism, "A Curious Fellow" wrote of how regrettably
rare it was "to see merchants oeconomical, mechanicks industrious, politicians sensible and unbiased, magistrates conforming strictly to the laws, and
honest men receive encouragement."[57]

Secure in its niche, the *Daily Advertiser* endeavored to broaden its appeal. Childs added the subtitle "Political, Commercial, and Historical" to the nameplate and added poetry and history to its content. To capitalize on the fame of his partner, Childs published some of Franklin's writings, laudatory accounts of Franklin's diplomatic accomplishments, and news about celebrations and testimonials given in Franklin's honor upon his return from France.[58]

Although not yet formally guaranteed in the First Amendment, Childs relied on early American journalism's tradition of freedom as he steered his newspaper's editorial course. He opened the *Daily Advertiser*'s pages to harsh criticism of the New York legislature, which "A Litchfield-County Farmer" suggested "is made up principally by a set of selfish knaves and ninnyhammers." Underscoring the emerging conflict between state and federal authority, an unnamed correspondent wrote, "that we have a wise CONGRESS, is not doubted, but they cannot guide the helm for want of a necessary power, which is withheld by a certain *small number of designing men,* who are pursuing *selfish plans,* to the ruin of national prosperity." The writer laid the blame on the state legislature, asserting, "New-York is the political curse of the nation."[59] Childs also published criticism of other governments. When the Massachusetts legislature instituted a stamp tax on newspaper advertisements, just two decades after the British Stamp Act had inspired overwhelming resentment and helped incite the American Revolution, "Your Friend and Humble Servant" labeled it "a tax, of extraction truly British, of name ever odious, and of operation mischievous in the extreme, not only to the printers, but the readers of news-papers." Childs himself decried the "ill-judged" and "infamous" levy's economic impact on printers. Echoing James Parker's complaints of three decades earlier, Childs claimed the tax "shackles the Press, by robbing it of its subsistence."[60]

Childs occasionally allowed individuals to express their grievances in print. Irishman "Paddy Whack" railed against ethnic prejudice suffered by his countrymen in the United States. Childs also published personal quarrels. Patrick Dunn accused auctioneer Robert Hunter of cheating him in the consignment sale of soap, branding him a "knave" and a "highwayman." Two days later, Hunter branded the charge "A MALICIOUS and defamatory libel" filled with "abusive epithets."[61]

Childs even published lengthy and vitriolic attacks on his benefactor Jay. He filled nine full columns, or more than half of an entire issue, with a bitter anti-Jay diatribe from Lewis Littlepage, a social climber whom Jay had once befriended but who had later fallen into the statesman's disfavor. Littlepage cursed and mocked Jay, describing him as scheming and greedy. Having printed this polemic, Childs then published Jay's response to "this Young Man's Ebullitions" in pamphlet form, and he also published Littlepage's retort.[62] Their virulent exchange prompted one New Yorker to observe that Childs's publications "have given Rise to a most violent Quarrel between them and occasioned considerable Parties in this City."[63]

Such rancorous essays were not in Childs's newspaper because they served the public interest. Rather, Childs was utilizing a long-standing tradition in the early American press, of which Franklin disapproved: publishing personal attacks in newspapers if their authors paid for them. For example, Franklin partner Peter Timothy requested that letters from political factions intended for print "be paid for proportionably as advertisements." The payment would thus signify the writings as "properly recommended." During a controversy involving fees charged by a medical clinic, Timothy claimed he would not publish opinions on the subject unless they were "properly and sufficiently recommended."[64] Network member John Holt announced his decision "to prefer those Pieces that come attended with Money." Bache also notified readers that he would "shut his paper against" additional submissions regarding a protracted quarrel "except on the footing of advertisements."[65] No surviving evidence confirms that Littlepage paid to attack Jay in print, but on January 30, 1786, Jay paid Childs fifty-six pounds sterling to print two hundred copies of his pamphlet response.[66]

To Franklin's chagrin, Childs adopted an editorial posture of placid neutrality to promote financial success. Childs was influenced by Franklin's early advocacy for journalistic detachment, which was well known in the early republic through publication and distribution of many of Franklin's writings. As a young printer in 1732, Franklin asserted that "Being thus continually employ'd in serving all Parties," printers become ideologically insouciant about the essays they publish, satisfied to "chearfully serve all contending Writers that pay them well." However, as his moral code developed, and as printers became more influential in the middle decades of the eighteenth century, Franklin recognized that such editorial apathy could cause unjust and severe damage to reputations. Franklin's financial stability also played a role in his evolving editorial philosophy: in 1732, he was deeply in debt and thus rationalized the publication of scurrility accompanied by payment. In later years, free of debt, he revised his professional values to abhor defamatory writings.[67]

Having spent his youth in poverty, the ambitious Childs was eager to adopt the remunerative posture of neutrality, just as Franklin had as a young printer. However, after a long career in journalism and government service, the older and wiser Franklin had seen the ill effects of libel, and he sternly advised young printers like Childs to avoid it. By resisting the temptation to defame for pay, printers will be more likely to gain many important friends, Franklin counseled in his *Autobiography*. Directly addressing the concern for money, he assured them, "such a Course of Conduct will not on the whole be injurious to their Interests."[68]

As Franklin wrote these words in August 1788, he may well have been thinking of Childs. Franklin surely thought Childs went too far by allowing a minor figure like Littlepage to repeatedly skewer Jay, whom Franklin respected as "so able a Minister" and whose service "gave me the Pleasure of seeing the Affairs of our Country in such good Hands." Franklin was also appalled that Childs would publish an attack on Jay, who had fostered Childs's rise from poverty to prominence, and then make Jay pay to reply.[69]

Relations between Franklin and Childs were further strained by Childs's repeated complaints about supplies that Franklin sent from France, and particularly the type that Bache had cast. Upon receiving a shipment from Franklin, Childs wrote, "I have the misfortune to find that the types are in very bad order—all the paper and Cords being rotten." After several such letters, Franklin sharply reproached his young partner, prompting Childs to respond, "There is nothing Sir, I prize more than your good opinion, and believe me that your last has given me very severe sensations. I hope Sir you will never occasion again to be disple[ased]."[70] However, Childs persisted in his complaints. "It has been a great misfortune that the Letter has been so imperfect," he wrote, adding, "I find still a considerable deficiency of some sorts." An exasperated Franklin vigorously defended his grandson's craftsmanship, replying, "You are always complaining of Imperfections in the Founts, which I suppose to proceed from your not having right Ideas of that Matter. They were all cast after the best Rules of the Founderies in England, and in the same Proportions." As a further expression of annoyance, Franklin pressed his demands for his share of the partnership's profits, with which Childs had been delinquent.[71]

Franklin acceded to Childs's request for more time to pay, but after several broken promises, the elder statesman's patience had worn thin. He sternly reminded Childs of the debt, cautioned him to "remember that Punctuality is the Life of Credit," and informed him that the expense of building five houses in Philadelphia had left him "in *real & great* Want of Money." He concluded, "I hope and entreat that as I have shown my self willing and ready to serve you, you will now in return exert yourself to me by paying off the Debt, at a time when I so much want it."[72] However, Childs never paid during Franklin's lifetime. Franklin bequeathed to his son-in-law Richard Bache the responsibility of collecting from Childs.[73]

The matters of editorial philosophy, supplies, and money had created a rift between Childs and Franklin, so Childs took journeyman John Swaine into partnership on July 2, 1789. The two men had served their apprenticeships together in Dunlap's shop, and had remained friends since. It is open to conjecture whether the pact with Swaine signaled the cessation of Franklin's partnership with Childs, or whether Swaine joined Childs in partnering with Franklin. The fact that only one letter apparently passed between Franklin and Childs after July 2, 1789—offering no indication the partnership was extant—suggests they may have ended their affiliation in 1789, with the understanding that Childs would eventually buy out Franklin's interest.[74]

Childs later formed an alliance with Philip Freneau to publish the *National Gazette,* a Republican newspaper in Philadelphia. This was another example of Childs's paradoxical proclivities in an era of growing partisan sentiment. By setting up Freneau as a junior partner, who under Thomas Jefferson's protection would spearhead the opposition to the Federalist policies of George Washington, John Adams, Alexander Hamilton, and Jay, Childs displayed the same surprising catholicity of politics as in the Jay-Littlepage dispute several years earlier. Seemingly, neither loyalty to person nor party could deter Childs from his Janus-faced journalism.[75]

Assessing Childs's political sentiments, the shrewd Hamilton dubbed him "a very cunning fellow." Hamilton wrote to New York Senator Rufus King that "In Philadelphia in the person of his proxy Freneau, he is a good Antifederalist Clintonian; in New York he is a good Federalist and Jayite—Beckley & Jefferson pay him for the first & the Federal Citizens of New York for the last."[76] New Jersey Congressman Jonathan Dayton underscored the paradoxical nature of Childs's political loyalties, informing Hamilton about Childs's involvement with Freneau's *National Gazette,* "He, you know, is one of the printers, and interested in the paper, and altho' I am well assured that he entirely disapproves the manner in which it is conducted, yet it is natural to suppose that he would not willingly be instrumental in the establishing of any fact which might operate to it's disrepute or prejudice." Dayton's assertion about Childs's true political sentiments may have been more a reflection of what the Federalist congressman wanted to believe, or what Childs wanted him to believe, than reality.[77]

Franklin's involvement with Bache was more satisfying than his partnership with Childs. Bache had been molded in his grandfather's image and imbued with his ideals and work ethic. After nine years in France, the sixteen-year-old Bache returned with Franklin to Philadelphia, receiving a gradual introduction to American printing. His grandfather established a printing house for him to do typefounding and book publishing while he learned about American society and politics. Bache also attended the University of Pennsylvania. "Ben is at College to compleat his Studies," Franklin noted. Moral philosophy was one of his courses. After his graduation, Bache and Franklin worked in their Philadelphia typefoundry and print shop.[78]

Bache's moral education was furthered by close exposure to the precepts in his grandfather's memoirs. Franklin, saddled with three "incurable" ills, "the gout, the stone, and old age," felt his life slipping away. "I am on the whole much weaker," he reported to one correspondent in the fall of 1788. "But possibly that may be the effect of age, for I am now near eighty-three, the age of commencing decrepitude." He finally had to enlist Bache's help in 1789 as an amanuensis in copying the *Autobiography*. He admitted wishing he had enlisted Bache's help earlier; if he had, "I think I might by this time have finished my Memoirs, in which I have made no progress for these six months past," he reported to a friend late in 1789.[79]

He never finished it, though, spending his final year taking opium to ease his suffering from the kidney stones. "For my own personal Ease, I should have died two Years ago," he wrote to George Washington in the fall of 1789, adding, "those Years have been spent in excruciating Pain."[80]

After considering Franklin's thirteen-point "Project of arriving at moral Perfection" in the memoirs, Bache found himself intrigued by the question of mankind's inherent disposition to virtue. He concluded, just as his grandfather had a half-century earlier, that people's inclination to be virtuous is contrary to their nature. Like his grandfather, he concluded people needed to be taught virtuous conduct, as it was not inherent in them. And like his grandfather, he concluded that his desire to be useful to his new country required that he take on the role of moral educator. Finally, his method for serving the public good required a newspaper, just as it had for his grandfather.[81]

Bache issued a prospectus for a newspaper he intended to publish in Philadelphia. He invited submissions from writers who "deliver their sentiments with temper & decency, and whose motive appears to be, *the public good*," Bache announced. "The strictest impartiality will be observed in the publication of pieces offered with this view."[82]

Bache's plan to publish a newspaper concerned some of his friends, who feared he might not be able to maintain the impartiality he promised in the prospectus. After reading the prospectus, Pennsylvania Senator Robert Morris cautioned him, "it is difficult for a Press of such Reputation as you would choose yours to be, to maintain the Character of Freedom & impartiality, connected with Purity." Rather than publishing a newspaper, Morris advised, "you might be more honorably & more lucratively employed by the Printing of Books."[83]

Bache was not dissuaded, and by age twenty-one announced he was ready to fill the role of moral instructor his grandfather had intended for him. He thus commenced his *General Advertiser* as a Philadelphia daily newspaper on October 1, 1790, promising "that no consideration whatever shall induce him blindly to submit to the influence of any man or set of men: His PRESS SHALL BE FREE." Its editorial focus on useful knowledge and instruction was inspired by "the advice which the Publisher had received from his late Grand Father," he informed readers.[84] Bache's interest in printing was partly inspired by the fact that "it is lucrative," as he informed the father of one of his apprentices, but also by his sincere belief that "it is first in respectability on the score of usefulness in a free state." Bache regarded the press as the protector of civic prosperity because "it leads legislators to be cautious in enacting laws, lest they infringe on the rights of man" and enables the people to discern "errors or designs of an administration which have an unfavorable aspect on the public interest and happiness."[85]

In the early years of his journalism career, Bache furnished didactic instruction as his grandfather had. Cautioning readers, "It is a sign of great prudence to be willing to receive instruction," he noted that "the felicity of life . . . arises only from virtue." A month after he began publishing his newspaper, Bache informed young readers that "The ORNAMENTS of YOUTH" consist of such virtues as modesty, cheerfulness, serenity, reverence, "a pleasing benevolence and readiness to do good to mankind."[86]

Emulating his grandfather, Bache intended his newspaper as a purveyor of moral teachings. "Many people read newspapers who read little else," he acknowledged. "To a retired man, a newspaper is always company—sometimes instruction." Bache's exhortative early issues prompted his great-aunt Jane Mecom to comment that his newspaper "Apears to me very Respectable." If he continues to steer this editorial course, she wrote to Bache's wife Margaret, "it may soon create for him an Estate in the clouds as his Venerable Grandfather used to say of His Newspaper."[87]

Franklin viewed his journalism as service to God and humanity, and hoped it would merit him a heavenly estate. However, Bache's journalism gradually strayed from this course. Despite promising that "Impartiality and independence shall still be the characteristic" of his newspaper when he changed its name to *The Aurora and General Advertiser* in 1794, Bache had by this time succeeded Philip Freneau as the most aggressive and partisan of the nation's Republican editors.[88] Inspired by Federalist affronts to his father and grandfather, Bache became a virulent critic of the Washington and Adams administrations.[89] Bache claimed that "If ever a nation was debauched by a man, the American nation has been debauched by Washington," who had held himself up as "an idol" during his Presidency, and he branded Adams an inept, warmongering monarchist. One of his correspondents, "Codrus," warned readers, "You are on the verge of tyranny" and "Your Constitution is in danger" because of Washington's malfeasance.[90] When Washington left office, Bache delighted in his departure. "If ever there was period for rejoicing, this is the moment," he wrote, "that the name of WASHINGTON from this day ceases to give a currency to political iniquity; and to legalize corruption."[91]

Federalists reacted with alarm at Bache's lack of restraint. "Mr. Bache has thrown off every appearance of Modesty" and has been "profuse in his abuse of the President," Director of the U.S. Mint Elias Boudinot wrote. He lamented that Bache's writers regularly vilify Washington and "will scarcely admit that he possesses even the semblance of any one Virtue." Bache took obvious pleasure in his task of excoriating the first two Federalist presidents. "The art of Printing is that which men in office dread exceedingly," Bache noted gleefully.[92]

John Adams saw Bache's scurrilous journalism as a perpetuation of his grandfather's animosity toward Adams. Franklin "had conceived an irreconcilable hatred to me" and "had propagated and would continue to propagate prejudices, if nothing worse, against me in America from one end of it to the other," Adams wrote Philadelphia physician Benjamin Rush. "Look into Bache's *Aurora* . . . and see whether my expectations have not been verified."[93]

In donning the mantle of Republican standard-bearer, Bache abandoned his own early advice to readers—to demonstrate a "hatred of calumny and slander"—and ignored his own recommendation that they form "a habit of speaking well of others."[94] More significantly, he abandoned the ethical teachings of his grandfather, who made dissuading printers from scurrility one of his foremost ambitions in his final years. Franklin's most satirical and pointed attack on journalistic defamation was "An Account of the Supremest Court of Judicature in Pennsylvania, viz., The Court of the Press," published seven months before his death. In it he decried that the press can "promulgate accusations of all kinds, against all persons and characters" and "condemn to infamy, not only private individuals, but public bodies" with impunity. The sole guardians and beneficiaries of this power are the "one citizen in five hundred, who, by education or practice in scribbling," can write or publish. "This five hundredth part of the citizens have the privilege of accusing and abusing the other four hundred and ninety-nine parts at their pleasure; or they may hire out their pens and press to others for that purpose," Franklin mused.[95]

Franklin claimed that the concept of press freedom is highly regarded but misunderstood by the public. To Franklin, it meant the free flow of political discourse in the public interest. "If by the *liberty of the press* were understood merely the Liberty of discussing the Propriety of Public Measures and political opinions, let us have as much of it as you please: But if it means the Liberty of affronting, calumniating, and defaming one another, I, for my part . . . shall cheerfully consent to exchange my *Liberty* of Abusing others for the *Privilege* of not being abus'd myself." To avoid infringing on the liberty of the press, Franklin sarcastically posited that people should be granted "the *liberty of the cudgel*."[96]

This alternative liberty was taken several times with Bache. His harsh writings prompted Clement Humphreys, the son of a ship architect, and Federalist editor John Ward Fenno to publicly assault Bache in separate incidents.[97] The former occurred on board a U.S. Navy ship being built in a Philadelphia harbor. "I was thus standing, alone as I thought, still looking at the bell, when I felt a violent blow on my head," Bache informed readers. He recalled that Humphreys was angered because Bache "abused the President on the day of his resignation." In the latter incident, Bache reported that Fenno "scratched the nose of his antagonist and his teeth took off the skin of the editor's knuckles; for which he got in return a sound rap or two across the head and face."[98]

Bache's rabid anti-Federalist partisanship crippled his newspaper. Fellow Philadelphia printer Mathew Carey observed, "the attacks on Gen. Washington blasted Bache's popularity, and almost ruined the paper. Subscribers withdrew in crowds—and the advertising custom sank to insignificance."[99]

The Franklin printing network finally expired with the dissolution of the Childs partnership and Bache's death in the 1798 yellow-fever epidemic. The disease killed more than 3,600 of the 15,000 people who remained in Philadelphia. Five of every six people who contracted the fever died from it.[100] The twenty-nine-year-old Bache opted to stay in the city, which had also been ravaged by the disease five years earlier, rather than escape to the countryside. Although acknowledging "The disorder still increases, & Kills more than it did in '93," he never expected it to claim his life. As the fever spread throughout Philadelphia, Bache reassured his parents that "our danger now is nothing to what it then was." Bache remained in the city to publish the *Aurora*, choosing to risk disease "rather than sacrifice my interest so materially as an abandonment of my paper at this time would," he wrote. "I cant fly and ask others to stay & mind my business; besides it would not be done to my mind." Eight days later, he was dead.[101]

Childs enjoyed a much longer life, turning the *Daily Advertiser* over to John Morton in 1796 before entering politics. In his valedictory, Childs acknowledged public support for the newspaper and noted, "Duty and interest, combined to render the *Daily Advertiser* an impartial, and free depository of speculative and political opinions."[102] He later served as a United States governmental agent in France and Germany and ambassador to Great Britain. Upon returning to the United States, he settled in Vermont, where he was elected to that state's legislature. He died in 1830.[103]

Of all Franklin's network printers, Francis Childs was one of the most remarkable. In addition to producing a pioneering daily newspaper and contributing to the fledgling American business press, his was among the last and least satisfying of the partnerships Franklin established to aid the development of early American journalism. Childs used the partnership to great advantage, as other network members had, but he alienated Franklin with his willingness to peddle defamation for profit and with his repeated complaints about the printing supplies Franklin furnished. Also, in an era of intense ideological inclinations, Childs allowed monetary concerns and his conception of editorial neutrality to override his loyalty to his benefactor Jay, thus allowing him to be attacked in print by a disappointed office-seeker.

Childs was unusual for his curiously apolitical stance in an era of intense partisanship, particularly among printers. While conducting a Federalist newspaper in New York, he also helped establish the opposition Republican press in Philadelphia. In doing so, he exhibited the same impartiality and "vast Unconcernedness" about defamatory writings that Franklin advocated early in his printing career but later repudiated.[104] Although not possessing Franklin's creative genius and apparently reluctant to contribute his own commentary to his newspapers' columns, Childs tailored Franklin's strategy of editorial neutrality to his own use, enabling him to outlast many more controversial and partisan printers.

Bache was an equally intriguing study in contrast. Resolute in his convictions, he launched one of the most effective challenges to the Federalists' creation of central government in the United States. His newspaper criticism of executive policies contributed to American political thought and provided an early test of the new nation's support for press freedom. Although he adhered to Franklin's republican principles and fostered press scrutiny of public officials during his career, Bache descended into obloquy and became the very sort of journalist about whom Franklin expressed dismay in his public writings.

Despite showing early promise, both Bache and Childs ultimately disappointed Franklin's aspiration to set up young printers who would teach moral virtue while eschewing calumny. Childs's querulous business practices and pecuniary neutrality, and Bache's character assassinations and indifference to his grandfather's concern for the nation's image diverged from Franklin's reasons for reviving the network.

Franklin's ambition to reform the United States press from within, as a legacy to his beloved profession, had been foiled. In the last months of his life, he was forced to conclude that printers, editors, and writers enjoy "tearing your private character to flitters" and thereby inviting "the odium of the public." This was an abuse of the understanding of press freedom Franklin had long supported. Since, as he told one writer, "Such personal public Attacks are never forgiven," the only remaining remedy to scurrility and defamation was an expression of private resentment. "Thus, my fellow-citizens, if an impudent writer attacks your reputation, dearer to you perhaps than your life, and puts his name to the charge, you may go to him as openly and break his head."[105]

Conclusion

God, Humanity, and Franklin's Legacy

"If you wou'd not be forgotten As soon as you are dead and rotten, Either write things worth reading, Or do things worth the writing," "Poor Richard" advised.[1] Franklin did both. Concerned with the moral legacy he would leave to the new nation, he vigorously pursued public projects in his final years. Upon returning from France in 1785, he became Pennsylvania's governor, a delegate to the Constitutional Convention, and president of the Pennsylvania Society for Promoting the Abolition of Slavery. In his later years, Franklin had become an ardent slavery opponent, calling it "the abominable African Trade" and "the diabolical commerce."[2] Anxious to retire and spend his remaining years among his extended family in Philadelphia, Franklin nonetheless accepted these offices to help chart a moral course for the United States.

Upon gaining the freedom to govern itself, the country also appeared to embrace freedom from virtue and self-restraint, Franklin noted ruefully. This was especially true in the more remote areas, removed from the civilizing influences of education and religion. "In our Way of sparse and remote Settlements, the People are without these Advantages, and we are in danger of bringing up a Sett of Savages of our own Colour," Franklin complained in 1787. He had held this opinion about rural settlers for many years. "The people that inhabit the frontiers, are generally the refuse of both nations, often of the worst morals and the least discretion, remote from the eye, the prudence, and the restraint of government," he wrote in his "Canada Pamphlet."[3]

In his estimation, the increased liberty accompanying the successful outcome of the Revolution caused many Americans to descend more deeply into sloth, avarice, and immorality. "A virtuous Action it would be, and a vicious one the killing of them, if the Species were really worth producing or preserving; but of this I begin to doubt," Franklin wrote cynically of human reproduction.[4]

The absence of self-restraint was especially manifest in the press, which simultaneously mirrored and magnified the social disorder, Franklin concluded disapprovingly. He lamented the scurrility and invective that accompanied journalistic consideration of the Constitution, once it was submitted for ratification. "Many objections were made to it in the public papers, and answers to these objections," he wrote. "Much party heat there was, and some violent personal abuse."[5] For this reason he composed several public essays at the end of his life to admonish printers to use their presses responsibly and teach probity, not peddle wanton scurrility for the sake of profit or prominence.[6]

Franklin sought to augment his moral writings by resuming work on his *Autobiography* in 1788. "Being now free from public business, as my term in the presidentship is expired, and resolving to engage in no other public employment, I expect to have it finished in about two months," he predicted in October.[7] Although wracked by pain from gout and kidney stones, he returned to the project as a moral mission, sensing the end was near. "I do not expect to continue much longer a Sojourner in this World, and begin to promise myself much Gratification of my Curiosity in soon visiting some other," he wrote in April 1788. Six months later, he informed another correspondent, "I have been harassed with Illness this last Summer, am grown old, near 83, and find myself very infirm, so that I expect to be soon call'd for."[8]

Franklin had decided a decade earlier that he wanted the *Autobiography* to receive public distribution because of its moral teachings. The memoirs "should prove of Use to the Publick," he noted in 1779, and will "benefit the young reader" by using his life story to show the blessings of noble deeds and the consequences of ignoble ones. "I fancy, on reading over what is already done, that the book will be found entertaining, interesting, and useful, more so than I expected when I began it," he informed a friend. In the section written in 1788, Franklin included a lengthy passage of advice to printers so that "they may see by my Example" that publishing instruction, rather than defamation, would benefit their businesses by gaining the respect and patronage of readers.[9]

As his strength and health slipped away from him, Franklin realized, once again, his ambitions had exceeded his ability to overcome obstacles. He was forced to conclude he would not complete his *Autobiography*. In September 1789 Franklin lamented being "afflicted with almost constant and grievous

Pain, to combat which I have been obliged to have recourse to Opium, which indeed has afforded me some Ease from time to time, but then it has taken away my Appetite and so impeded my Digestion that I am become totally emaciated, and little remains of me but a Skeleton covered with a Skin." As a result, he informed his friend Louis Le Veillard, "I have not been able to continue my Memoirs, and now I suppose I shall never finish them."[10]

His outline shows he intended to write about his service as a colonial agent in England, his travels to various European nations, and his opposition to the Stamp Act and Townshend Acts. He also planned to elaborate on his observation that it "Costs me nothing to be civil to inferiors, a good deal to be submissive to superiors." However, Franklin ran out of time. In April 1790 his lungs formed an abscess that he became too weak to expel. "Whenever I approached his Bed, he held out his Hand & having given him mine he would take it & hold it for some time," his grandson Benjamin Franklin Bache recalled. Franklin stopped taking nourishment the morning of April 17, and died about 11 P.M. "I think there is something remarkable in his end," Bache wrote. "His mental Faculties unimpaired or but little impaired, at his Age. His Resolution unshaken. His Principles fixed even in Death, shew a Man of a superior Cast."[11]

News of Franklin's death elicited many encomiums extolling his virtues. Boston legislator Ezekiel Price lamented the loss of "the late Venerable Dr. Franklin." Quaker minister John Pemberton labeled him "a Zealous Friend to the Cause of the Injured Africans." Thomas Jefferson called his longtime political colleague "the greatest man & ornament of the age and country in which he lived."[12] Newspapers and magazines of the era were profuse in their plaudits for Franklin. One predicted that he "will shine with distinguished lustre in the page of history as a philosopher, a politician and a legislator."[13] His former journeyman Mathew Carey celebrated him in his magazine as one of a "glorious band of patriots" who secured American independence, and a Boston newspaper noted that Franklin served, along with the "godlike unparalleled, great Washington," to infuse the new nation with a distinctive character.[14]

Franklin's influence was felt, and his memory honored, throughout the next century. Newspapers such as Utica, New York's *Columbian Gazette* and Danville, Pennsylvania's *The Watchman* commenced publication in the early nineteenth century at shops bearing large signs depicting Franklin as the patron of journalism.[15] Reflecting on Franklin's character, Massachusetts senator Charles Sumner noted in 1856, "He was so great a man, one sighs that he was not a little greater. With a little of Charming he would have been a divinity."[16] A journalist writing in the same year linked Franklin with the essence of republicanism. "FRANKLIN was the true type of the pure, noble, *republican* feeling of America," a *New York Daily Times* reporter wrote after witnessing thirty thousand people in Boston attend the unveiling of a statue honoring Franklin. "GEORGE WASHINGTON was but a noble British officer, made a Republican by circumstances. FRANKLIN was a Republican by birth, by labor, by instinct, and by thought." A magazine writer echoed this notion at the centennial of Franklin's death, noting, "now that he has been at rest these hundred years he stands forth on the page of history as the first American—not even second to Washington himself."[17]

Rhapsodizing about Franklin's accomplishments, a nineteenth-century poet found the source of Franklin's avocation to dispense moral instruction in his father Josiah, a soap maker and tallow chandler:

> Those candles prefigured the mind
> To break through the darkness o'ershading;
> Those soaps the wisdom refined
> To cleanse men of errors pervading.[18]

The adulation of Franklin was not merely posthumous. In his own lifetime, David Hume praised him as "the first Philosopher, and indeed the first Great Man of Letters" in America. John Adams enviously asserted that the history of the Revolution will record only *that Dr. Franklins electrical Rod, smote the Earth and out sprung General Washington. That Franklin electrified him with his rod—and thence forward these two conducted all the Policy, Negotiations, Legislatures and War.* These underscored lines contain the whole Fable Plot and Catastrophy."[19] By 1779, Franklin had become a cultural icon in France, where "the pictures, busts, and prints, (of which copies upon copies ere spread every where) have made your father's face as well known as that of the moon," Franklin explained to his daughter, "so that he durst not do any thing that would oblige him to run away, as his phiz would discover him wherever he should venture to show it." Despite his endeavors to practice humility as part of his thirteen-point plan for attaining moral perfection, Franklin finally had to acknowledge, "I have the happiness of being universally respected and beloved."[20]

Franklin's life was a monument to virtue tempered by pragmatism and ambition tempered by prudence. He conducted his journalistic affairs accordingly. To the end of his life, Franklin regarded himself as a printer. When he drafted his will in 1788, he identified himself as "BENJAMIN FRANKLIN, of Philadelphia, printer, late Minister Plenipotentiary from the United States of America to the Court of France, now President of the State of Pennsylvania."[21] His printing network was one of the lengthiest endeavors of his life. His first partnership was forged in 1729 when he was an obscure young printer, and his final one came more than half a century later, when he was among the foremost men in the world.

The network was both one of the most successful and least successful ventures of his life. Through its manipulation and expansion, Franklin succeeded in making his fortune, setting up some of the principal printers in early America, preserving and magnifying his own reputation, and helping journalism spread throughout the settled regions of America. At the time of his first partnership, in 1729, there were seven colonial newspapers. When he died in 1790, the number had risen to about ninety.

The network was at its apex in the 1740s and 1750s. As the year 1755 came to a close, eight of the fifteen newspapers in the North American and West Indian colonies were published by printers who were partners with Franklin or had entered the trade through his auspices.[22] Of the seven non-network newspapers in colonial America, one had extensive interactions with Franklin. North Carolina printer James Davis purchased printing supplies and books from Franklin.[23] Three others were in Boston. Perhaps harboring old grudges against the printers there for refusing him employment after he fled his apprenticeship to his brother James, Franklin conspicuously refrained from establishing partnerships in that city.[24]

By the eighteenth century's midpoint, the Franklin influence had extended far and wide. Peter Timothy and his mother Elizabeth were printing in Charles Town; James Parker was in New York; Thomas Smith was in Antigua; James Franklin Jr. and his mother Ann were in Newport; and both Johann Bohm and David Hall were in Philadelphia. The human resources underlying the development of the network often came from the apprentices and journeymen in his shop. Franklin selected for partnerships those who, in his estimation, epitomized his sense of virtue. Parker, Smith, Hall, Whitmarsh, and Lewis Timothy were initially hired as journeyman printers in Franklin's Philadelphia shop and rose to partnership with him, while former apprentice James Franklin Jr. became a partner with his mother. Of this group, all but Hall moved on, establishing themselves elsewhere with Franklin's backing. These six men received some or all of their training from Franklin and were elevated to master status by him, forming the backbone of his printing network. They also hired employees who were exposed in one form or another to Franklin's ethos of virtue.

Thus, Franklin's impact upon the moral ideology of American printers expanded geometrically as he built a bridge between a system of vocational training and a system of business and political alliances. Franklin's formation of a printer network contributed to the growth of the vocation and was one of the earliest trade organizations in the colonies not motivated by biological ties.

However, the network could equally be viewed as a failure. Most of the partnerships folded within a few years, including Franklin's proselytizing efforts to establish enduring presses for the West Indian and Pennsylvania German audiences. This atrophy resulted from Franklin's waning involvement in printing as his involvement with public affairs waxed. After retiring from active management of his Philadelphia print shop in 1748, Franklin permitted himself to be recruited for various organizations and causes, while "every part of our Civil Government, and almost at the same time, impos[ed] some Duty upon me," he wrote.[25] Saddled with myriad public concerns, Franklin relinquished the cares of the largest and most influential network of printers in the eighteenth century. Franklin's lessened grip on the reins of early American printing was only one reason for the network's shortcomings, but it was a vital one, because it set off a chain of events that led to the disintegration of his alliance. Franklin might have heeded "Poor Richard's" advice: "For want of a Nail the Shoe is lost; for want of a Shoe, the Horse is lost; for want of a Horse the Rider is lost." Six years later, he found another way to convey the same message: "A little Neglect may breed great Mischief."[26]

Franklin sought to turn over the business affairs to Hall and especially Parker. Parker was a singularly devoted partner and ally. "I have not served my God so faithfully as I have you," he admitted to Franklin. However, Parker lacked Franklin's equanimity and management skills. He introduced printers into the network who were not trained by Franklin and who lacked the character and ideologies Franklin sought. The printers comprising the network's "second generation," schooled in Parker's printing houses, were to have carried on the journalistic traditions Franklin espoused. However, they proved to be grave disappointments. Protégés Weyman, Holt, Gaine, and Jones, plus Parker's own son and nephew, filled Parker's latter years with quarrels, debts, and lawsuits.[27]

Even the normally unflappable Franklin had difficulties with young printers. William Goddard, who had been apprenticed to Parker, plotted a vicious public attack on the venerable Franklin's reputation. Former Franklin journeyman Jonas Green's financial negligence prompted his erstwhile employer to conclude, "he uses me extreamly ill" and "has not an honest Principle, I fear."[28] Ann Franklin's partner in Newport—and husband of Franklin's niece Sarah—Samuel Hall owed Franklin a considerable amount of money for years without paying principle or interest, forcing Franklin to sue him. Hall only paid part of the money, which Franklin turned over to his sister Jane Mecom for her subsistence.[29]

Meanwhile, Franklin's own family disappointed him. His grandson Benjamin Franklin Bache practiced the scurrilous journalism that Franklin felt was so poisonous to the interests of the new nation, nephew James Franklin Jr. declined a partnership that would have helped his uncle further his moral ambitions in the West Indies, and vexatious nephew Benjamin Mecom proved to be a quarrelsome and irresponsible partner. Mecom's mother Jane conceded in 1779 that she and her children, particularly her deranged sons Benjamin and Peter, had always been a burden to Franklin.[30]

Less tangibly, but more importantly for Franklin, his own writings and the work of his printing associates were largely unsuccessful in leading the American public to mass-mediated virtue. One newspaper essayist judged the new country to be "in a very advanced state of depravity and corruption." Another, "The Observer," suggested that moral turpitude caused the United States to be "on the brink of inevitable ruin." A third even suggested the new republic had failed. "Now, a republican is among the last kinds of government I would choose," he wrote. "I would infinitely prefer a limited monarchy, for I would sooner be subject to the caprice of one man, than to the ignorance and passions of a multitude."[31]

Franklin tried to be publicly optimistic during the turbulent years of the early republic. He informed an acquaintance that he was impressed with "the growing felicity of mankind, from the improvements in philosophy, morals, politics, and even the conveniences of common living."[32] Despite this outward show, Franklin privately conceded to his close friends that Americans during the early republic were naturally "lazy and indolent." He ruefully observed that people are "more easily provok'd than reconcil'd, more dispos'd to do Mischief to each other than to make Reparation, much more easily deceiv'd than undeceiv'd, and [had] more Pride & even Pleasure in killing than begetting one another."[33]

Franklin's network was the epitome of potential. Had he fully succeeded in implementing his design, it might have charted an entirely different course for American journalism. Ultimately, though, it was not the structure, but rather the aberrations and conflicting personalities of the people in it, that caused the network's demise. The quirks and rivalries of Franklin's printing partners and associates confounded his plans for an informal American press confederacy imparting moral instruction and useful information. By the end of his life, his network nearly extinct, Franklin could only watch in dismay as the new nation's press drifted from enlightenment and instruction toward scurrility and political partisanship. Printer Isaiah Thomas noted that Franklin had a "pointed dislike of prostituting the press to purposes of defamation and scurrility."[34]

Despite its failures, the network contributed substantially to Franklin's emergence as an integral figure in American history, and to the establishment of a new nation and free press. The Franklin network was important to the form and function of the early American press. Understanding the inner workings of eighteenth-century journalism is essential, because this was the era during which the free-expression guarantees of the First Amendment were devised. Those guarantees were built on the foundation that had been laid for them prior to 1787—the legacy of press freedom and press constraints. Throughout the nation's history, Americans have looked to the original intention of the founders to understand the Constitution and Bill of Rights. Thomas Jefferson insisted that to understand the Constitution, Americans must go "back to the time when the Constitution was adopted, recollect the spirit manifested in the debates, and instead of trying what meaning may be squeezed out of the text, or invented against it, conform to the probable one in which it was passed."[35]

The Founding Fathers' original intention for the First Amendment, ensuring that Congress would not perpetuate Britain's abridgment of colonial free expression, was based on press practices of the era. Thus, it is vitally important to understand the various factors that contributed to the establishment and growth of the early American press and to examine such integral mechanisms of control and development as partnerships and networks.

Many of journalism's practices and liberties in early America were controlled less by exterior forces such as formal law, than by extralegal entities, such as trade associations and networks. These "private governments," as they have been called, can circumvent formal law to gain greater freedom, or they can curtail freedom by dictating conduct, with the implicit understanding that sanctions will be imposed on violators.[36]

Examples of the Franklin network acting as a private government abound. In 1752 Parker printed in his newspaper a deistical essay attacking Christian beliefs on damnation, revelation, and salvation. The essay, probably authored by apothecary Patrick Carryl, was written as an American Indian chief's response to a Swedish missionary's sermon. It offended some readers, who objected to the publication of anti-Christian literature. Parker responded to one such aggrieved reader that Christianity was too stable a force to be injured by criticism, and that its opponents should have the same access to the press as its proponents. As a result of printing the essay, Parker was indicted for blasphemous libel. Franklin quickly interceded by writing to his friend Cadwallader Colden, an influential member of the governor's council in New York. Calling Parker "a thorough Believer" who is "now much in his Penitentials," Franklin promised that his partner will "be very circumspect and careful for the future, not to give Offence either in Religion or Politicks." Franklin persuaded Colden to obtain a "nolle prosequi" for Parker, effectively ending the libel case.[37] Just as Franklin circumvented the law of blasphemous libel to extricate Parker from legal sanction, Parker intervened to rescue one of his wayward apprentices from the sentence of hanging for producing counterfeit New Jersey currency.[38]

Franklin also offered advice and instructions to network printers on journalistic practices when he believed prudential interests were at stake. In 1765 Franklin instructed Hall on the appropriate editorial stance to take in the face of growing rebellion in the colonies attending passage of the Stamp Act. Hall thanked Franklin for the advice.[39] That same year, he intervened in a dispute between Parker and Holt by using his capacity as deputy postmaster-general to relocate Parker, his postal comptroller. Franklin ordered Parker to move his office to New York from Burlington, New Jersey. Parker later turned to Franklin for important business advice.[40] Franklin also gave Peter Timothy advice that prompted him to relinquish his retirement and return to printing.[41]

Franklin exerted the power to suppress editorial content when press freedom would undermine political or military objectives. In 1759 Franklin became concerned about a report in a Boston newspaper that the Susquehannah Company planned to buy Indian land along the Susquehanna River, within Connecticut's chartered boundaries. Fearing that the French might take "some preventive Measures" on the frontier, Franklin expressed his belief to Yale College president Thomas Clap that such reports "should not be made publick till they are ripe for Execution, lest Obstacles are thrown in the Way," and he vowed to use his influence to suppress further reports of the plan. "I shall endeavour to prevent the reprinting of that Paragraph in the Papers here and to the Southward," Franklin wrote from New York. Several years later he ordered a news delay on reports of General Braddock's defeat during the French and Indian War.[42]

A network's tendency to circumvent some controls but impose others demonstrates how an informal social institution shapes the contours and content of knowledge the press produces and the public uses. Since networks were important social forces that influenced the early American press at a time when press practices and liberties were being forged, it is important to understand their structure and function. However, delineating them is difficult. Few sources acknowledge the existence of early American printing networks or convey that their printers avowed they were part of a larger structural and economic entity. In Franklin's case, the most explicit acknowledgment is found in a 1785 letter to Francis Childs. Responding to Childs's solicitation of aid, Franklin agreed to the proposal and listed ten "young printers of good character" who had been his partners. Franklin's reference to their good character suggests his approval of their behavior and subtly conveys his expectation that Childs will follow suit. This is important to the concept of Franklin's controlling influence over a substantial segment of American journalism.[43]

Franklin's relationships with his partners and other network members underscore the interconnectedness and mutual dependence of the early American press. Printers relied on each other for moral and economic support, as well as for news of other communities, colonies, and nations, which they reprinted. The practice of exchanging newspapers and reprinting selected items represented the first collective newsgathering effort and was the primary method by which early American readers learned of developments in distant locales.

The newspaper exchange was regarded as sufficiently important to the American colonies that when deputy postmasters-general Franklin and William Hunter devised the first official policy on newspaper circulation through the postal system, they levied a fee on newspaper recipients to cover delivery expenses of the post-riders but permitted printers to continue exchanging their papers free of charge. They announced in 1758 that the "Spreading of News-Papers . . . are on many Occasions useful to Government, and advantageous to Commerce, and to the Publick."[44]

The importance of this newspaper exchange is reflected in the inaugural issues of newspapers. In his *Pennsylvania Gazette,* Franklin promised to "procure the best and earliest Intelligence from all Parts" by reprinting information from "all the noted Publick Prints from Great Britain, New-England, New-York, Maryland and Jamaica." He also reproduced "Extracts from the Spectator and other moral Writers." Franklin's partner Louis Timothee informed readers of his German-language newspaper, "My promise will be that through good Correspondence with Holland and England I will always have the most distinguished and noteworthy news from Europe as well as here." In the revolutionary era, Ann Franklin's erstwhile partner Samuel Hall boasted that his Newburyport newspaper would regularly publish "the most material pieces contained in the Portsmouth, Salem, Boston, Connecticut, Rhode-Island, New-York, Philadelphia, Maryland, South Carolina, and Quebec news-papers, which we are regularly supplied with."[45]

However, after the Declaration of Independence, printers shifted the emphasis from international to domestic news. One wrote in his debut issue, "I must beg of the Printers thro'out the United States (particularly in the capitals) to be as punctual and generous as they can, in sending their papers; for without their assistance the best of country papers can wear but a barren and unprofitable appearance." The *Hartford Gazette*'s proprietors apologized that "THE want of established correspondance with other parts of the United States . . . have hindered the EDITORS from giving so good a summary of intelligence, in this day's paper, as they could wish." In the first number of *The American Journal,* its conductors hoped "the indulgent Public will suspend their Judgment of the Merits of this Paper, for a few Weeks, till their Correspondence with the other Printers, &c. on the Continent, becomes fully established and regular."[46]

Reliance on other "brethren of the type," as one Connecticut printer labeled his colleagues, was also important to those who sought to market certain materials. Franklin sold his "Poor Richard's Almanack" through his network members. His former journeyman Mathew Carey arranged a distribution network for his own *American Museum* magazine. Isaiah Thomas, who later emulated Franklin's alliances, used his affiliations with other printers to distribute his *Royal American Magazine* from New Hampshire to South Carolina.[47] Franklin's supply network was still functioning in the new nation. In addition to providing materials for his partners Bache and Childs, Franklin sold printing supplies to Connecticut publishers and the Virginia House of Burgesses.[48]

There are many instances of printers relying on their associations to succeed financially and journalistically, while circumventing laws designed to inhibit editorial content. As such, the early American press in general, and Franklin's network in particular, is a microcosm of society, in which people are interdependent and inevitably associate in groups for mutual support and protection.

Franklin network members exchanged such commodities as workers, finances, advice, sanctions, publications, and supplies. Many of their interactions occurred in person, and thus are hidden forever from historical view. Of their written communications, only a comparative few have survived. Even though many Franklin letters exist, he noted that many others have been lost. "By one of the Accidents which War occasions, all my Books containing

Copies of my Letters were lost," he informed a niece in 1788. "There were Eight Volumes of them, and I have been able to recover only two."[49] From the letters that have survived, though, it is possible to infer patterns of association; and from these, in turn, to construct the reality of Franklin's printing network. For Franklin's associates, the most important commodities flowing through the network were information and opinion. These goods influenced how printers conducted their presses, and in turn influenced the substance and purpose of their mass communication that reached the larger network of eighteenth-century society.

As the printing network's center, Franklin wielded power, not merely over his partners but over the early American press, and thus over public perceptions of reality during the colonial era and the crucial first years of the new republic. Through his numerous relationships in printing, he influenced the transmission of commodities and information. Beyond the scope of Franklin's formal partnerships, many of his linkages with other printers were tenuous. However, this seeming weakness also represents a strength in social-network theory. Macroscopically, social systems lacking weak ties are fragmented because information tends to be homogenous and new ideas spread more slowly. Printers with weak linkages, or ties, to one network were freer to have ties to other printers or even other networks.[50] This allowed a printer to serve as an important communication bridge between a network and members outside its boundaries. For example, printer James Adams worked for Franklin and Hall in Philadelphia, where he presumably imbibed some of Franklin's moral ideology. Adams then became a master printer in Delaware, where he trained Shepard Kollock and Isaac Collins, both of whom later worked for William Goddard (a second-generation Franklin network member) before setting up their own shops in New Jersey.[51]

The printing activities of Franklin and his cohorts indicate the significance of associations among printers. These associations, when interconnected, formed loosely structured but nonetheless influential networks that aided printers by providing the capital to set up shop and the materials to remain in business. The Franklin network also served as a means by which information, assistance and sanctions could be disseminated along associational lines. Printers also used the network to share their writings, and those of their correspondents, with other audiences, particularly to promote Franklinesque understandings of moral virtue. The network enlarged the scope of the early American printing trade, aided in the dissemination of information and opinion, and impressed the significance of journalism upon the collective consciousness of early America.

The foundation of the Franklin network was the existence of formal partnerships that legally bound a printer to work with Franklin under certain conditions for many years. Guided by the prudence and circumspection that became hallmarks of his character, Franklin devised elaborate contracts with explicit terms. "Partnerships often finish in Quarrels," Franklin wrote in his autobiography, "but I was happy in this, that mine were all carry'd on and ended amicably; owing I think a good deal to the Precaution of having very explicitly settled in our Articles every thing to be done by or expected from each Partner, so that there was nothing to dispute." Although Franklin's 1788 retrospection that all his partnerships ended amicably was filtered through rose-colored bifocals, these copious contracts were essential to the stability of the partnerships and the network.[52]

Augmenting his success was his novel use of apprentices and journeymen. Apprentices were often indentured to relatives who were printers, so that once the apprentices became journeymen or masters, they would forge business alliances with their kin. Unlike the common practice of cultivating casual printing associations through familial relationships, Franklin's network was the first in America to consist chiefly of nonfamily members. Franklin aided these printers "by establishing them with Printing-Houses in different Colonies," he recalled.[53]

During its halcyon days, the apprenticeship system made a major contribution to American journalism. The arrangement, in which youths offered themselves as cheap labor in exchange for the promise of vocational education, fostered the structural growth of the early American press. Apprentices, typically adolescent males, came from various social classes, because printing was less class-based than many other trades of the era. Once they had mastered the trade, many apprentices sought to become journeyman printers and earn a living via their printing skills. Commonly, these journeymen aspired to save enough money to buy a shop and supplies of their own, thereby achieving master-printer status. This custom of vocational training and advancement not only filled the ranks in the printing trade, but also encouraged its expansion by providing more skilled craftsmen.

The encouragement of the printing trade's growth represented a considerable departure from European customs, which used apprenticeships to limit the craft because it was overrun with aspiring printers. Apprenticeships therefore became available only for those whose families could provide sufficient financial inducements to a master. "The Artisans, who fear creating future Rivals in Business, refuse to take Apprentices, but upon Conditions of Money, Maintenance, or the like, which the Parents are unable to comply with," Franklin wrote of the European apprenticeship system. "Hence the

Youth are dragg'd up in Ignorance of every gainful Art, and oblig'd to become Soldiers, or Servants, or Thieves, for a Subsistence."[54]

Franklin not only altered the European practice, but the American printing custom as well, by recruiting some of his apprentices and journeymen for partnerships in which he provided a press and types and established them with printing houses in communities that either had no printer or offered room for competition. As these partners formed their own associations, and as Franklin formed others on his own, the Franklin printing network took shape. To construct the network, Franklin recruited workers whose character most impressed him (and probably reminded him of his own pursuit of frugality, sobriety, and industry) and placed them in situations of mutual gain by promoting them to partnerships. Some of Franklin's partners emulated this practice. The apprenticeship system supplied a pool of talent that aided the network's success.[55]

With Franklin supplying the capital and materials for his workers to set up shop—and thus eliminating the financial obstacle that prevented many early American journeymen from becoming master printers—his partners formed associations through which materials and information flowed. These commodities helped make their businesses economically viable. Such trade alliances signaled a movement away from reliance on governmental and social elites, who had provided financial support for the press in order to control a means of articulating and advancing their views. The fact that a segment of the laboring class assumed control of American mass communication presaged an increase in political activity among the lower classes, as newspapers, mostly of the anti-administration ilk, appealed to laborers.[56]

Although they had their own views and aspirations, Franklin and his partners adhered to a similar political and moral ideology. This harmony of belief appears to have been a prerequisite for a Franklin partnership. Franklin suggested as much in his memoirs, when he mentioned offering partnerships to well-behaved workers who were "of good character."[57] It is equally likely that Franklin, recalling the laxity and customary antipathy toward masters he found in European printing houses, as well as the problem of runaway apprentices on both sides of the Atlantic, sought to avoid these labor difficulties by extending the prospect of partnership to his workers as an incentive for good work and correct beliefs.

Others subsequently borrowed Franklin's idea. The most notable eighteenth-century successor was Isaiah Thomas, who formed partnerships in New England—a region in which Franklin's printing activities were nominal.[58]

Franklin had numerous reasons for creating the network: nepotism, political persuasion, creation of his fame, augmentation of his wealth, an aspiration to assist the spread of domestic journalism throughout North America, and the reason he offered to the public: "to promote several of my Workmen who had behaved well."[59]

The chief reason, though, was Franklin's altruistic desire to help Americans to be virtuous. This instruction was, in Franklin's mind, the foremost way he could serve God. Shortly before death, Franklin informed Yale College president Ezra Stiles that God "ought to be worshipped" and that "the most acceptable Service we render to him is doing good to his other Children." Years before, Franklin had written to a minister that God "prefer'd the Doers of the Word to the meer Hearers."[60]

To Franklin, his calling to do good, and thereby to serve God, was to urge and educate the populace to moral rectitude. This was the purpose behind Franklin's newspaper, almanac, partnerships, and many of his public writings. Notable among them is the *Autobiography*, which contains parts of a book Franklin never finished, tentatively titled "The Art of Virtue." In it, Franklin "would have shown the *Means & Manner* of obtaining Virtue, which would have distinguish'd it from the mere Exhortation to be good, that does not instruct & indicate the Means."[61]

The exhortation to moral rectitude Franklin intended to impart in "The Art of Virtue" was manifest throughout his journalism career, as he conveyed virtue through his art. He hoped his teachings of virtue would be a legacy to the citizens whom he strove to serve but whose collective unwillingness to yield to his admonitions frustrated him. Franklin viewed virtue as a guide to personal happiness and social utility, and he intended his network of printers to teach it and encourage its adoption. He believed that people became enlightened and righteous not only by exercising wisdom and seeking knowledge, but also by acknowledging God's periodic intervention in human affairs. Franklin publicly expressed his belief that God "sometimes interferes by his particular providence," and he urged readers of his almanac to "Seek Virtue, and of that possest, To Providence, resign the rest."[62] Privately, he informed Stiles, "I believe in one God, Creator of the Universe," who "governs it by his Providence." Franklin attributed the successful outcome of the American Revolution to God's intercession, and he proposed that the Constitutional Convention offer prayers for divine guidance.[63]

Despite a youthful flirtation with deism, Franklin believed in God—not an abstract deistic creator, but the active God of the Israelites, the prophets, and the apostles. Franklin sprinkled his correspondence with Biblical references and quotes from both Old and New Testaments; he exhorted himself to "imitate Jesus"; and he noted of his earthly successes and sources of happiness, "These are the blessings of God, and depend on his continued goodness."[64] In his 1750 and 1757 wills, Franklin wrote an extensive expression of divine praise. "Thanks to GOD," he began. "I bless that BEING of BEINGS who does not disdain to care for the meanest of his Creatures."[65]

He trusted God's active involvement in the world's affairs, informing newspaper readers, "I have so much Faith in the general Government of the world by *Providence*." He was less attracted to Christianity's mysteries of Heaven, the Trinity, and the divinity of Christ, and more concerned with how its values and virtues could help humanity. "The things of this World take up too much of my Time, of which indeed I have too little left," he replied in 1787 when a correspondent asked for his theological opinions.[66]

Franklin had little patience for doctrinal squabbles, but when God's existence was attacked, he rose to the defense. When Thomas Paine submitted his controversial treatise "The Age of Reason" to Franklin in manuscript form, Franklin objected to Paine's effort to "strike at the Foundation of all Religion," advising him "to burn this Piece before it is seen by any other Person." Franklin couched his objections to Paine's denigration of organized religion in pragmatic terms, focusing on its effect. "But think how great a Proportion of Mankind consists of weak and ignorant Men and Women, and of inexperienc'd, and inconsiderate Youth of both Sexes, who have need of the Motive of Religion to restrain them from Vice, to support their Virtue, and retain them in the Practice of it till it becomes *habitual*." Advising Paine "not to attempt unchaining the Tyger," Franklin urged the social benefits of religion from his customarily cynical view. "If men are so wicked as we now see them *with religion*, what would they be *if without it*," he queried.[67]

To Franklin, religion, education, and communication were the foremost boons to moral conduct. He wrote to Georgia governor Samuel Elbert that enlightened citizens in the new nation should have "the Advantage of giving Schooling to their Children, securing their Morals by the Influence of Religion, and improving each other by civil Society & Conversation." Religion offered a wealth of noble precepts to guide its followers, and education unlocked the door to knowledge and wisdom using the key of literacy. As Franklin noted, ancient moralistic writings "had little Effect because the Bulk of the People could not read."[68] Franklin believed that printed materials might point the way to virtue, but he grew concerned that scurrilous journalism would have a countervailing effect. "When they produce public Altercation," Franklin wrote of published abuse, "the Ignorant are diverted at the Expense of the Learned."[69] Defamatory printers derive their support from "the depravity of such minds, as have not been mended by religion, nor improved by good education."[70]

Franklin's journalism career, like many facets of his life, was devoted to serving God and benefiting mankind by teaching virtue. "Now by the Press we can speak to Nations," Franklin wrote to a friend. "The Facility with which the same Truths may be repeatedly enforc'd by placing them daily in different Lights, in Newspapers, which are every where read, gives a great Chance of establishing them. And we now find that it is not only right to strike while the Iron is hot, but that it is very practicable to heat it by continual Striking."[71]

Franklin's printing network was designed to disseminate Franklin's moral truths to a mass audience by "continual Striking," from New England to the West Indies. It was a logical and ambitious extension of his call to serve God and humanity.

Abbreviations

Archives

AAS	American Antiquarian Society
APS	American Philosophical Society
CHS	Connecticut Historical Society
CSL	Connecticut State Library
HSP	Historical Society of Pennsylvania
JCB	John Carter Brown Library
LC	Library of Congress
LCP	Library Company of Philadelphia
MDHS	Maryland Historical Society
MHS	Massachusetts Historical Society
NHC	New Haven Colony Historical Society
NJHS	New Jersey Historical Society
N-YHS	New-York Historical Society
NYSL	New York State Library
RIHS	Rhode Island Historical Society
YB	Beinecke Library, Yale University

Names

BF	Benjamin Franklin
DH	David Hall
JP	James Parker

Primary Sources

Autobiography	Lemay, J. A. Leo and P. M. Zall, eds. *The Autobiography of Benjamin Franklin: A Genetic Text.* Knoxville: University of Tennessee Press, 1981.
PBF	Labaree, Leonard W., et al., eds. *The Papers of Benjamin Franklin.* 37 vols. to date. New Haven: Yale University Press, 1959–.
PG	[Philadelphia] *Pennsylvania Gazette*
WoBF	Bigelow, John, ed. *The Works of Benjamin Franklin.* 12 vols. New York: Knickerbocker, 1904.
WrBF	Smyth, Albert Henry, ed. *The Writings of Benjamin Franklin.* 10 vols. New York: Macmillan, 1905–7. Reprint, New York: Haskell House, 1970.

Secondary Sources

PMHB	*Pennsylvania Magazine of History and Biography*
WMQ	*William and Mary Quarterly,* third series

Notes

Preface

1. *Poor Richard*, 1739, in *PBF*, 2:220.
2. Samuel Davies to John Holt, January 23, 1761, Rush Papers, HSP.
3. BF to Noah Webster, December 26, 1789, in *WrBF*, 10:79–80.
4. *Poor Richard*, 1738, in *PBF*, 2:194.

Introduction: The Challenge of Franklin's Printing Network

1. Ralph Frasca, "Benjamin Franklin's Printing Network," 145–58.
2. Reprinted in James Alexander, *A Brief Narrative of the Case and Trial of John Peter Zenger*, 81. See also Alison Olsen, "The Zenger Case Revisited: Satire, Sedition, and Political Debate in Eighteenth-Century America," 223–45. On the press's function as a check on government, see Vincent Blasi, "The Checking Value in First Amendment Theory," 521–649.
3. H. W. Brands, *The First American: The Life and Times of Benjamin Franklin;* Walter Isaacson, *Benjamin Franklin: An American Life,* 2.
4. Peter Coclanis, "The Lightning-Rod Man: Franklin of Philadelphia," 616.
5. The Franklin network's existence has been acknowledged by early historians Elizabeth Christine Cook, *Literary Influence in Colonial Newspapers, 1704–1750,* 230; John Clyde Oswald, *Benjamin Franklin, Printer,* 138–50; Marion R. King, "One Link in the First Newspaper Chain: The *South Carolina Gazette*," 257–68; and Carl Van Doren, *Benjamin Franklin,* 115–23. It has also been noted by more recent historians Stephen Botein, "'Meer Mechanics' and an Open Press: The Business and Political Strategies of Colonial Printers," 154–55; Charles W. Wetherell, "Brokers of the Word: An Essay in the Social History of the Early American Press, 1639–1783,"

1–19; and Jeffery A. Smith, *Printers and Press Freedom: The Ideology of Early American Journalism,* 124–41. The most detailed explorations of the Franklin network to date have been Frasca, "Benjamin Franklin's Printing Network," 145–58, and idem, "From Apprentice to Journeyman to Partner: Benjamin Franklin's Workers and the Growth of the Early American Printing Trade," 230–31.

6. BF to Francis Childs, February 8, 1785, in *WoBF,* 11:8–9.

7. *Autobiography,* 51, 57. For other examples in Franklin's memoirs, see ibid., 28–29, 54.

8. John Donne, *Devotions Upon Emergent Occasions,* 98; Cotton Mather, *A Christian at His Calling . . . ,* 42–43.

9. For a related theory, see the "ABX Model" in Theodore Newcomb, "An Approach to the Study of Communication Acts," 393–404.

10. Emil W. Menzel Jr., "General Discussion of the Methodological Problems Involved in the Study of Social Interaction," 306; Florence L. Goodenough, *Anger in Young Children,* 3.

11. There are various references in Franklin's papers to the *Poor Richard* almanac and its distribution. For example, see "Ledger D, 1739–47," in *PBF,* 2:233–34; *Poor Richard,* 1748, ibid., 3:262n.

12. BF to Edward Newenham, October 2, 1783, in *WrBF,* 9:102.

13. In the former category is Leonard W. Levy, *Freedom of Speech and Press in Early American History: A Legacy of Suppression,* and idem, *Emergence of a Free Press.* In the latter category are Larry Eldridge, *A Distant Heritage: The Growth of Free Speech in Early America;* Robert W. T. Martin, *The Free and Open Press: The Founding of American Democratic Press Liberty, 1640–1800;* David A. Rabban, "The Ahistorical Historian: Leonard W. Levy on Freedom of Expression in Early American History," 795–856; and Smith, *Printers and Press Freedom.*

14. Stewart Macaulay, "Private Government," 445, 502. See also idem, "Law and the Behavioral Sciences: Is There any 'There' There?" 149–87.

15. "The Busy-Body, No. 1," *American Weekly Mercury,* February 4, 1729.

1. The Art of Virtue and the Virtue of the Art

1. William Cocke to BF, June 15, 1786, in Jared Sparks, ed., *The Works of Benjamin Franklin,* 10:260–6; BF to William Cocke, August 12, 1786, in *WrBF,* 9:534. The State of Franklin was formed in 1784 when settlers in sparsely populated western North Carolina declared themselves a separate state, initially with North Carolina's blessing. The latter state soon recanted, though, and the State of Franklin had a brief, tempestuous, and contested existence until it disbanded in 1788. It was located in what is now eastern Tennessee and portions of southwestern Virginia and northwestern North Carolina. See Samuel Cole Williams, *History of the Lost State of Franklin.*

2. Richard C. Wade, *The Urban Frontier: The Rise of Western Cities, 1790–1830,* 319. One such interior land is Iowa. "The proprietor of the county seat site . . . first

had named the town Benjamin, assuming it would be appropriate, as the noted statesman's and philosopher's family name had been given to the county" (I. L. Stuart, ed., *History of Franklin County, Iowa*, 121). One town named in Franklin's honor during his lifetime is Franklin, Connecticut, christened in 1786. See Samuel Nott, "Sketch of Franklin," 1800, Woodward Papers, CHS.

3. Bernard Mayo, *Henry Clay, Spokesman of the New West*, 121; [Philadelphia] *Pennsylvania Packet*, June 3, 1780.

4. Lyman H. Butterfield, ed., *Letters of Benjamin Rush*, 1:85; BF to Jane Mecom, November 26, 1788, in *WrBF*, 9:685; Eric Foner, *Tom Paine and Revolutionary America*, 34–36. For assorted tributes to Franklin's memory, see Nian-Sheng Huang, *Benjamin Franklin in American Thought and Culture, 1790–1990*.

5. For Cobbett's attacks on Franklin, see e.g. William Cobbett, *Porcupine's Works*, 7:81; [Philadelphia] *Porcupine's Gazette*, December 4, 1797. For Adams, see e.g. *The Boston Patriot*, May 15, 1811, reprinted in Charles Francis Adams, ed., *The Works of John Adams*, 1:649. For Franklin's status as an American popular-culture hero, see Richard D. Miles, "The American Image of Benjamin Franklin," 117–43.

6. "The Life of Dr. Franklin," [Rutland] *The Herald of Vermont*, June 25, 1792; Nathanael Emmons, *The Dignity of Man*, 3. One historian noted sardonically that Franklin was perceived to be adept at "traversing with almost supernatural ease the disciplinary boundaries of science, politics, philosophy, religion and commerce" (Ronald A. Bosco, "'He that best understands the World, least likes it': The Dark Side of Benjamin Franklin," 525).

7. The Benjamin Franklin Tercentenary Commission, *www.benfranklin300.com*; U.S. Congress, Senate, *Benjamin Franklin Memorial Fire Service Bill of Rights Act*, 101st Cong., 1st sess., 1989, S. 16375; Thomas Jefferson to Benjamin Rush, October 4, 1803, in Paul Leicester Ford, ed., *The Writings of Thomas Jefferson*, 8:265.

8. John Adams to Benjamin Rush, April 4, 1790, in Alexander Biddle, ed., *Old Family Letters*, 55; May 10, 1778, in Lyman H. Butterfield, ed., *Diary and Autobiography of John Adams*, 2:367.

9. March 14, 1756, in Butterfield, ed., *Diary and Autobiography of John Adams*, 1:13; John Adams to Thomas McKean, September 20, 1779, in Gregg L. Lint, et al., eds., *Papers of John Adams*, 8:162. For more on their frosty relationship, see William B. Evans, "John Adams' Opinion of Benjamin Franklin," 220–38.

10. BF to Jane Mecom, November 26, 1788, in *WrBF*, 9:685.

11. See e.g. Jennifer Jordan Baker, "Franklin's Autobiography and the Credibility of Personality," 274–93; Ormond Seavey, *Becoming Benjamin Franklin: The Autobiography and the Life*; Esmond Wright, ed., *Benjamin Franklin: His Life as He Wrote It*, 1–10.

12. BF to Abbe Morellet, December 10, 1788, in *WrBF*, 9:691; BF to William Vaughn, December 9, 1788, ibid., 688; BF to Benjamin Vaughn, October 24, 1788, ibid., 676.

13. *Autobiography*, 1.

14. Isaacson, *Benjamin Franklin*, 100; David M. Larson, "Franklin on the Nature of Man and the Possibility of Virtue," 118.

15. James Campbell, *Recovering Benjamin Franklin*, 25; Seavey, *Becoming Benjamin Franklin*, 43; Esmond Wright, "'The fine and noble china vase, the British Empire': Benjamin Franklin's 'Love-Hate' View of England," 435.

16. BF to Benjamin Vaughan, October 24, 1788, in *WrBF*, 9:676.

17. Abel James to BF, ca. June 1782, in Julian P. Boyd, et al., eds., *The Papers of Thomas Jefferson*, 9:485; Benjamin Vaughan to BF, January 31, 1783, in Sparks, *Works of Benjamin Franklin*, 9:478–86.

18. *Autobiography*, 78–82.

19. Ibid., 52, 82.

20. Ibid., 78, 87.

21. BF, "Observations on the Proceedings Against Mr. Hemphill," 1735, in *PBF*, 2:53; Aristotle, *The Nichomachean Ethics*, 85, Book II, iv. For Franklin's conception of virtue in general terms, see Myra Jehlen, "'Imitate Jesus and Socrates': The Making of a Good American," 501–24; Norman S. Fiering, "Benjamin Franklin and the Way to Virtue," 199–223.

22. *Autobiography*, 76; BF to Joseph Huey, June 6, 1753, in *PBF*, 4:505–6. Pennsylvania Royal Governor William Keith was one person who made such a promise to Franklin. See *Autobiography*, 28–29, 34, 39, 41–42. For a more extensive discussion of Keith's promise, see Chapter 2.

23. Matt. 5:20, 5:28, in *The New Jerusalem Bible* (Garden City, N.Y.: Doubleday, 1985), 1616.

24. BF to —, December 13, 1757, in *PBF*, 7:294; *Poor Richard*, 1744, ibid., 2:397.

25. "Father Abraham's Speech," in *Poor Richard*, 1758, ibid., 7:350. This essay is now better known as "The Way to Wealth."

26. "The Busy-Body, No. 3," ibid., 1:119–21.

27. *Autobiography*, 88–89.

28. BF to Benjamin Vaughan, July 26, 1784, in *WrBF*, 9:243. Franklin made a similar point about luxury in a public writing at about the same time. See "The Internal State of America; Being a True Description of the Interest and Policy of that Vast Continent," 1784, in *WoBF*, 10:400. On Bostonian perceptions of virtue, see Myron F. Wehtje, "The Ideal of Virtue in Post-Revolutionary Boston," 67–83.

29. *Autobiography*, 48–49.

30. Ibid., 94; BF to William Strahan, June 2, 1750, in *PBF*, 3:479; BF to Peter Collinson, November 5, 1756, ibid., 7:14; BF to Thomas Cushing, June 10, 1771, ibid., 18:124.

31. *Autobiography*, 68, 90.

32. Ibid., 88–89; BF to Lord Henry Kames, October 21, 1761, in *PBF*, 9:375.

33. *Autobiography*, 88–89; BF to Lord Henry Kames, May 3, 1760, in *PBF*, 9:104.

34. *Autobiography*, 59, 94; "Aristides," *Boston Gazette*, April 5, 1784; Benjamin Rush to Anthony Wayne, August 6, 1779, in Butterfield, ed., *Letters of Benjamin Rush*, 1:238; February 9, 1779, in Butterfield, ed., *Diary and Autobiography of John Adams*, 2:347; William Smith, "An Introduction to the Study of Rhetoric," 111–60. For more on Adams and morality, see John D. Burton, "John Adams and the Problem of Virtue," 393–412.

35. *Autobiography*, 45, 70. On Benjamin Franklin's sexual proclivities, see Claude-

Anne Lopez, *Mon Cher Papa: Franklin and the Ladies of Paris;* Claude-Anne Lopez and Eugenia Herbert, *The Private Franklin: The Man and His Family,* esp. 16–29, 120.

36. [Hugh Williamson], *What Is Sauce for a Goose Is Also Sauce for a Gander* (Philadelphia, 1764), reprinted in *PBF,* 11:381–84; George Roberts to Robert Crafton, October 9, 1763, in *PBF,* 11:370–71n. For more information on the Williamson pamphlet, see Paul Leicester Ford, *Who Was the Mother of Franklin's Son?*

37. BF, *Observations Concerning the Increase of Mankind,* 1755, in *PBF,* 4:234; BF to Abiah Franklin, April 12, 1750, ibid., 3:475; *Autobiography,* 69–70, 79.

38. BF, *A Dissertation on Liberty and Necessity, Pleasure and Pain,* 1725, in *PBF,* 1:57–71. Later, Franklin "began to suspect that this Doctrine tho' it might be true, was not very useful." He came to regard the pamphlet as "another Erratum" of his life (*Autobiography,* 43, 58–59).

39. "The Busy-Body, No. 1," *American Weekly Mercury,* February 4, 1729. Franklin acknowledged the influence of *The Spectator* on his writing style in *Autobiography,* 13–14.

40. See James T. Kloppenburg, "The Virtues of Liberalism: Christianity, Republicanism, and Ethics in Early American Political Discourse," 9–33; Robert E. Shalhope, "Toward a Republican Synthesis: The Emergence of an Understanding of Republicanism in American Historiography," 49–80; idem, "Republicanism and Early American Historiography," 334–56.

41. BF to Lord Henry Kames, May 3, 1760, in *PBF,* 9:105.

42. Jonathan Bayard Smith to John Dunlap, February 7, 1811, Isaiah Thomas Papers, AAS; *Providence Gazette,* January 12, 1765; *New-York Evening Post,* November 17, 1794.

43. *Autobiography,* 94; *Poor Richard,* 1749, in *PBF,* 3:340.

44. *Autobiography,* 93; "The Busy-Body, No. 4," *American Weekly Mercury,* February 25, 1729.

45. *Autobiography,* 94; BF to Josiah and Abiah Franklin, April 13, 1738, in *PBF,* 2:202–4; *Poor Richard,* 1747, ibid., 3:105.

46. Thomas Jefferson to John Garland Jefferson, February 5, 1791, in Boyd, ed., *Papers of Thomas Jefferson,* 19:252–53.

47. *PG,* October 2, 1729; [Philadelphia] *Independent Gazetteer,* April 13, 1782; *Mott and Hurtin's New-York Weekly Chronicle,* January 1, 1795; *Providence Gazette,* January 12, 1765. On literacy, see Kenneth A. Lockridge, *Literacy in Colonial New England: An Enquiry into the Social Context of Literacy in the Early Modern West;* Sanford Winston, *Illiteracy in the United States.*

48. Frasca, "Benjamin Franklin's Printing Network," 145–58.

49. Because postage was a considerable expense for colonists, Franklin regarded the job as "very suitable to me." Not only would it eliminate the cost of correspondence between network members and himself, but it would also enable him to "execute a Scheme long since form'd," the establishment of the American Philosophical Society, which, he told a correspondent, "would soon produce something agreable to you and to all Lovers of Useful Knowledge, for I have now a large Acquaintance among ingenious Men in America" (BF to Peter Collinson, May 21, 1751, in *PBF,* 4:135).

50. *Autobiography,* 108. For contracts, see e.g. "Articles of Agreement with Thomas Whitmarsh," September 13, 1731, in *PBF,* 1:205–8; "Articles of Agreement with Louis Timothee," November 26, 1733, ibid., 339–42.

51. W. J. Rorabaugh, *The Craft Apprentice: From Franklin to the Machine Age in America,* 8–9; Lucien Febvre and Henri-Jean Martin, *The Coming of the Book,* 129, 134–35; David T. Pottinger, *The French Book Trade In the Ancien Regime,* 265–68, 279–80. For a contrasting view, see John U. Nef, *Industry and Government in France and England, 1540–1640,* 22.

52. Frasca, "From Apprentice to Journeyman to Partner," 229–48; Wetherell, "Brokers of the Word," 122–26.

2. From Apprentice to Journeyman to Master Printer

1. David Chambers to Joseph Chambers, April 23, 1796, in David Chambers Papers, AAS. Chambers's assertion that Franklin believed butter harmed printers is unsupported in other documents. In fact, Franklin recalled that as a journeyman printer in London, he persuaded some of his fellow pressmen to relinquish "their muddling Breakfast of Beer & Bread & Cheese" in favor of "a large Porringer of hot Water-gruel, sprinkled with Pepper, crumb'd with Bread, & a Bit of Butter in it." This, he wrote, "was a more comfortable as well as cheaper Breakfast, & kept their Heads clearer" (*Autobiography,* 47).

2. Joseph Chambers to David Chambers, April 28, 1796, in David Chambers Papers, AAS.

3. In 1810, Chambers moved to Zanesville, Ohio, where he established a newspaper and was elected state printer. He died in Zanesville in 1864. See *Biographical Dictionary of the American Congress, 1774–1971,* 722.

4. For the apprentice's obligations, see Samuel Richardson, *The Apprentice's Vade Mecum,* 2–20. On the menial nature of some tasks, see O. Jocelyn Dunlop and Richard D. Denman, *English Apprenticeship and Child Labour: A History,* 19–20; Sharon V. Salinger, *"To Serve Well and Faithfully": Labor and Indentured Servants in Pennsylvania, 1682–1800,* 7. On beatings of printing apprentices, see W. J. Rorabaugh, *The Craft Apprentice: From Franklin to the Machine Age in America,* 11, 43, 93, 103, 193.

5. An Order of the Councell for Trade, December 12, 1661, Great Britain Collection, LC; Carl Bridenbaugh, *Cities in the Wilderness: The First Century of Urban Life in America, 1625–1742,* 45, 199–200.

6. Indenture of Gardhill Darling, November 27, 1792, Miscellaneous Manuscripts, NYSL; Indenture of James Franklin, November 5, 1740, in *PBF,* 2:261–63. See also Indenture of Thomas C. Porter, September 18, 1794, Book Trades Collection, AAS.

7. Richard B. Morris, *Government and Labor in Early America,* 363–89. Demonstrating Enlightenment thinking, seventeenth-century London printer Joseph Moxon claimed typography, comprising punch-cutting, founding, and printing, is a mathematical science. See Joseph Moxon, *Mechanick Exercises on the Whole Art of Printing,* 10–12.

8. Rorabaugh, *Craft Apprentice,* 6–7; Mary Ann Yodelis, "Who Paid the Piper? Publishing Economics in Boston, 1763–1775," 1–2.

9. BF to Jane Mecom, ca. June 1748, in *PBF,* 3:301–4. Rorabaugh, *Craft Apprentice,* also cites many examples of poor behavior by both masters and apprentices.

10. Ebenezer Hazard to Jeremy Belknap, December 19, 1783, Belknap Papers, MHS; Robert Aitken to Jeremy Belknap, December 22, 1783, ibid.

11. Jeremy Belknap to Ebenezer Hazard, May 18, 1787, ibid.

12. *Autobiography,* 10–11. For more on Franklin's father and the life of a colonial tradesman, see Nian-Sheng Huang, *Franklin's Father Josiah: Life of a Colonial Boston Tallow Chandler, 1657–1745.* For a comparison of European and American apprenticeships, see "Information to Those Who Would Remove to America," 1782, in *WrBF,* 8:603–14. See also "Some Observations on North America, and the Colonies of Great Britain There," July 1766, in *PBF,* 13:356. On the correlation between apprenticeships and social class hierarchy, see John Clapham, *A Concise Economic History of Britain,* 133. Shoemaker's apprentice George Robert Twelves Hewes was an example of an apprentice plying a low-status trade because he could not afford the expected fee. See Alfred F. Young, "George Robert Twelves Hewes (1742–1840): A Boston Shoemaker and the Memory of the American Revolution," 561–623.

13. *South-Carolina Gazette,* April 6, 1752; August 19, 1756. There are enough examples of Timothy using the term "well-recommended" to mean payment that his intent regarding apprentices is clear. Timothy requested that letters from political factions "be paid for proportionably as advertisements." The payment would thus signify the writings as "properly recommended" (*South-Carolina Gazette,* November 21, 1754). The next year, during a controversy surrounding fees charged by a Charleston medical clinic, Timothy insisted on remaining impartial and refused to print solicitations on the subject unless they were "properly and sufficiently recommended" (*South-Carolina Gazette,* July 3, 1755).

14. Journeymen have been referred to as "nothing else than vagabond persons, bound to no master" (I. F. Grant, quoted in Clapham, *Concise Economic History of Britain,* 133–34). In Europe journeymen were theoretically men who had completed their apprenticeships but had not been received as masters in the guild. This lack of acceptance was usually due to one of two factors—insufficient capital with which to set up a shop or legal restrictions on the number of masters, in which case journeymen would wait for a vacancy to occur. See David T. Pottinger, *The French Book Trade in the Ancien Regime,* 241.

15. London printers William Bowyer Sr. and William Bowyer Jr. kept a ledger of their employees' work performed and wages earned from March 1730 to August 1739. See K. I. D. Maslen and J. Lancaster, *The Bowyer Ledgers: The Printing Accounts of William Bowyer, Father and Son, Reproduced on Microfiche, with a Checklist of Bowyer Printing, 1699–1777.*

16. Rorabaugh, *Craft Apprentice,* 8, 94; Lawrence C. Wroth, *The Colonial Printer,* 158–59; Henry Rosemont, "Benjamin Franklin and the Philadelphia Typographical Strikers of 1786." Few reliable sources exist suggesting the average duration of an American apprenticeship during the early eighteenth century. However, one scholar found 189 of 198 apprenticeships in New York from 1718 to 1727 were for seven

years or more, with 120 of those requiring exactly seven years. See Paul H. Douglas, *American Apprenticeship and Industrial Education*, 40. Interestingly, Douglas claims that trades in colonial America could be mastered in less than five years. An apprenticeship that required more time than this "was an exploitation of the boy" (51).

17. This document was so named because of its indented edges, which served as a legal precaution. Articles of indenture were printed in duplicate on one sheet of paper, with each part signed and witnessed before the document was torn in half. The master kept one part and the apprentice's parents or guardian retained the other. In the event of a legal dispute between the parties, the authenticity of the document could be verified by matching the indentations on the two documents, protecting against fraud. See Rorabaugh, *Craft Apprentice*, 7.

18. Indenture of James Parker, January 1, 1726, APS; *New-York Gazette: or, Weekly Post-Boy*, May 25, 1752; James Parker, "An Humble Address to the PUBLICK," May 30, 1766, in Beverly McAnear, "James Parker versus John Holt," part 1, 95; Alan Dyer, *A Biography of James Parker, Colonial Printer*, 3–4. Parker's estimation of his printing skill is supported by Isaiah Thomas, a contemporary, who noted that Parker "was a correct and eminent printer. . . . He possessed a sound judgment, and a good heart; was industrious in business, and upright in his dealings" (Isaiah Thomas, *The History of Printing in America*, 520).

19. *New-York Gazette*, May 17, 1733; *American Weekly Mercury*, June 21, 1733; BF to Jane Mecom, ca. June 1748, in *PBF*, 3:301. Although settlements between masters and runaway apprentices were often reached via a cash payment to the master, it is likely Parker served a penalty for running away, because he said he worked eight years as an apprentice and worked in Bradford's print shop in 1741. Had Parker never completed his apprenticeship, it is doubtful Bradford would have hired him eight years later. See Dyer, *Biography of James Parker*, 4–5.

20. Franklin's indentures have disappeared. This account is based on *Autobiography*, 11, and on items typically found in apprenticeship agreements (including those Franklin formed with his apprentices).

21. *Autobiography*, 18–20.

22. Ibid., 20–27.

23. Margaret Gay Davies, *The Enforcement of English Apprenticeship, 1563–1642*, 82; Dunlop and Denman, *English Apprenticeship and Child Labour*, 85; Rorabaugh, *Craft Apprentice*, 5, 7. While skilled workers in printing and several prestigious crafts were in demand, less of a market existed for workers in low-level crafts. See Billy G. Smith, "The Material Lives of Laboring Philadelphians, 1750 to 1800," 163–202; Gary B. Nash, *The Urban Crucible*, chaps. 3, 5, 9, passim.

24. *Autobiography*, 98–99.

25. *American Weekly Mercury*, June 13, 1728; [Williamsburg] *Virginia Gazette*, December 12, 1745; [Annapolis] *Maryland Gazette*, May 2 1765; [Boston] *New-England Courant*, September 30, 1723.

26. *Autobiography*, 28–29, 34. On Keith, see Nash, *Urban Crucible*, 148–54; Thomas Wendel, "The Keith-Lloyd Alliance: Factional and Coalition Politics in Colonial Pennsylvania," 289–305.

27. *Autobiography*, 39–42.

28. Ibid., 42–43, 45.

29. Ibid., 45–47. On the English tradition of "St. Monday," see E. P. Thompson, "Time, Work-Discipline, and Industrial Capitalism," 56–97.

30. *Autobiography*, 32–33, 46, 120–21.

31. Ibid., 46. Franklin may have had the incident of the scattered types in mind when—and if—he composed the following poem on the need for caution when handling printing materials. It has been attributed to him without evidence in the Isaiah Thomas Papers, Box 1, folder 2, AAS:

> All you that come this Curious Art to see,
>
> To handle any thing must cautious be,
>
> Lest, by a slight touch, ere you are aware,
>
> That mischief may be done you can't repair:
>
> Lo! this advice we give to every stranger,
>
> Look on, and welcome; but to touch there's danger.

32. *Autobiography*, 50–51. On Denham, see Frederick B. Tolles, "Benjamin Franklin's Business Mentors: The Philadelphia Quaker Merchants," 60–69.

33. *Autobiography*, 39–40, 42–45. On Ralph, including his subsequent literary efforts, see Robert W. Kenny, "James Ralph: An Eighteenth-Century Philadelphian in Grub Street," 218–42.

34. *Autobiography*, 33–34, 43, 45.

35. "Plan of Conduct," 1726, in *PBF*, 1:99–100; *Autobiography*, 43, 51–52, 78. For the argument Franklin exhibited a disputatious and contemptuous "dark side" throughout life, see Bosco, "The Dark Side of Benjamin Franklin," 525–54.

36. *Autobiography*, 52, 70, 79–80.

37. Ibid., 43, 58; BF, *A Dissertation on Liberty and Necessity, Pleasure and Pain*, 1725, in *PBF*, 1:57–71.

38. *Autobiography*, 48–50.

39. Ibid., 52–53.

40. Ibid., 53–54, 64; "A Letter to a Gentleman in the City of New-York," November 2, 1759, quoted in Beverly McAnear, "James Parker versus New York Province," 323.

41. *Autobiography*, 36, 57. Keimer's poor management plunged him into bankruptcy and imprisonment in England in 1715. While in debtors' prison, he authored seditious screeds against King George I. This may have resulted in an additional prison sentence. After his release, he abandoned his wife and family and emigrated to America in 1721. See Stephen Bloore, "Samuel Keimer: A Footnote to the Life of Franklin," 255–87; C. Lennart Carlson, "Samuel Keimer: A Study in the Transit of English Culture to Colonial Pennsylvania," 357–86.

42. *Autobiography*, 53–56, 59–60.

43. Ibid., 63; *Universal Instructor*, January 21, 1729; *American Weekly Mercury*, January 28, 1729. For the ponderous contents of Keimer's newspaper, see Chester E. Jorgenson, "A Brand Flung at Colonial Orthodoxy: Samuel Keimer's *Universal*

Instructor in All Arts and Sciences," 272–77. For science news in the colonial press generally, see David L. Ferro, "Selling Science in the Colonial American Newspaper: How the Middle Colonial American General Periodical Represented Nature, Philosophy, Medicine, and Technology, 1728–1765."

44. *American Weekly Mercury,* February 4, 18, 1729; *Universal Instructor,* February 25, March 13, September 25, 1729.

45. *Autobiography,* 64. For analysis of the "Busy-Body" essays, see Elizabeth Christine Cook, *Literary Influences in Colonial Newspapers, 1704–1750,* 57–92.

46. *PG,* October 2, 23, 1729; *Autobiography,* 64.

3. The Moral Foundations of Franklin's Journalism

1. Charles F. Adams, ed., *The Works of John Adams,* 1:661.

2. June 23, 1779, entry in Butterfield, ed., *Diary and Autobiography of John Adams,* 2:391.

3. William Robertson to William Strahan, February 18, 1765, in *PBF,* 12:70.

4. *Autobiography,* 58–59; *A Dissertation on Liberty and Necessity,* 1725, in *PBF,* 1:55–71.

5. BF to Ezra Stiles, March 9, 1790, in *WrBF,* 10:84.

6. Kerry S. Walters, *Benjamin Franklin and His Gods,* 3. See also James Campbell, *Recovering Benjamin Franklin;* David T. Morgan, "Benjamin Franklin: Champion of Generic Religion," 723–29.

7. *Poor Richard,* 1753, in *PBF,* 4:406; 1737, ibid., 2:171. The Bible verses are Prov. 22:6 and James 2:18.

8. *A Dissertation on Liberty and Necessity,* 1725, in *PBF,* 1:55–71; *Autobiography,* 59.

9. *Boston News-Letter,* February 12, 1722; *American Weekly Mercury,* October 22, 1730. See also Karl J. Weintraub, "The Puritan Ethic and Benjamin Franklin," 223–37.

10. *New-England Courant,* July 3, 1725; *Boston Gazette,* November 24, 1755.

11. David Paul Nord, *Communities of Journalism: A History of American Newspapers and Their Readers,* 47; *Autobiography,* 6.

12. BF to Joseph Huey, June 6, 1753, in *PBF,* 4:505. Franklin used this idea in his *Poor Richard* almanac the same year, observing, "Serving God is doing good to man, but praying is thought an easier service and therefore is more generally chosen" (*PBF,* 4:406).

13. On the inoculation episode, see John B. Blake, "The Inoculation Controversy in Boston: 1721–22," 489–506. For Massachusetts epidemics, see John D. Burton, "'The Awful Judgements of God Upon the Land': Smallpox in Colonial Cambridge, Massachusetts"; Maxine de Wetering, "A Reconsideration of the Inoculation Controversy," 46–67; C. Edward Wilson, "The Boston Inoculation Controversy: A Revisionist Interpretation," 16–19, 40. For a favorable account of Mather's role in the inoculation furor, see Otho T. Beall Jr. and Richard H. Shryock, *Cotton Mather: First Significant Figure in American Medicine.*

14. "Diary of Cotton Mather, 1709–1724," 639, 663; *Boston Gazette,* January 29, 1722; *New-England Courant,* February 12, 1722.

15. Despite ministerial support for vaccinations as early as the 1720s, public fears of inoculation persisted throughout the eighteenth century. During a smallpox epidemic in 1793, some community leaders tried in vain to establish a hospital in Rhode Island to vaccinate the populace. "We are well aware that the Prejudices, which at present prevail against Inoculation here, prevent its advocates from giving it the necessary Support," they conceded (Caleb Fiske and Pardon Bowen to Welcome Arnold, May 1, 1793, Collection, JCB).

16. *Autobiography,* 11; BF to Samuel Mather, May 12, 1784, in *WrBF,* 9:208–10.

17. BF to Samuel Mather, May 12, 1784, in *WrBF,* 9:208. For more on the relationship between Franklin and Mather, see Mitchell Robert Breitweiser, *Cotton Mather and Benjamin Franklin: The Price of Representative Personality.*

18. *Autobiography,* 58, 77.

19. Ibid., 76, 78, 80; BF to Joseph Huey, June 6, 1753, in *PBF,* 4:505; Gerald R. Cragg, "What We Moderns Owe to Puritanism," Sixth Hooker Lecture, First Church of Christ, Hartford, Connecticut, May 1, 1968, Collections, CHS, 3. In 1728, Franklin devised a private liturgy of religious beliefs and devotional prayers to help him worship God without denominational doctrine. See his "Articles of Belief and Acts of Religion," November 20, 1728, in *PBF,* 1:101–9.

20. BF to Joseph Huey, June 6, 1753, in *PBF,* 4:505; *Poor Richard,* 1754, ibid., 5:185.

21. BF to Elizabeth Hubbart, February 22, 1756, in *PBF,* 6:407.

22. *Autobiography,* 77, 96; Merton A. Christensen, "Franklin on the Hemphill Trial: Deism versus Presbyterian Orthodoxy"; Walters, *Benjamin Franklin and His Gods,* 136–40.

23. *Autobiography,* 77; BF to Joseph Huey, June 6, 1753, in *PBF,* 4:505–6; Luke 13:6–9, James 1:22–25, in *New Jerusalem Bible,* 1712, 1997.

24. *Autobiography,* 13, 90.

25. *Autobiography,* 2; *New-England Courant,* February 11, 1723; "On Literary Style," *PG,* August 2, 1783, in *PBF,* 1:331.

26. Jonathan Edwards, "Sinners in the Hands of an Angry God," 1741, in Harold P. Simonson, ed., *Selected Writings of Jonathan Edwards,* 96–113. See also Kenneth P. Minkema, "Old Age and Religion in the Writings and Life of Jonathan Edwards," 674–704.

27. *A Dissertation on Liberty and Necessity,* 1725, in *PBF,* 1:55–71.

28. BF to Benjamin Vaughn, July 26, 1784, in *WrBF,* 9:243.

29. "Apology for Printers," *PG,* June 10, 1731, in *PBF,* 1:194–99; "Speech in the Convention on the Subject of Salaries," 1787, in *WrBF,* 9:591–92.

30. BF to John Fothergill, March 14, 1764, in *PBF,* 11:101.

31. Ibid. Years later, Franklin continued to regard physical maladies as punishment for immoderate behavior, and he found virtue in suffering. He informed a correspondent that he would "content myself in submitting to the Will and Disposal of that God who made me . . . that he will never make me miserable, and that even Afflictions I may at any time suffer shall tend to my Benefit" (BF to Joseph Huey,

June 6, 1753, in *PBF,* 4:503). Franklin even esteemed his painful and chronic gout as a "real friend" who motived him to diet and exercise through the deceptively simple method of pain ("Dialogue Between Franklin and the Gout," October 22, 1780, in *WrBF,* 8:154–62).

32. BF to Joseph Huey, June 6, 1753, in *PBF,* 4:502–3.

33. "Apology for Printers," *PG,* June 10, 1731. The advertisement was not printed in the *Pennsylvania Gazette;* it was a handbill that his apprentices "stuck up round the Town as usual," Franklin noted in the "Apology."

34. "On the Abuse of the Press," 1788, in *WrBF,* 9:639; "Apology for Printers," *PG,* June 10, 1731.

35. *PG,* July 24, 1740. On Franklin's relationship with Kinnersley, see J. A. Leo Lemay, *Ebenezer Kinnersley: Franklin's Friend.*

36. *PG,* June 10, 1731; August 2, 1733; April 11, 1734. *Autobiography,* 94–95.

37. "Plan of Conduct," in *PBF,* 1:100; BF to ?, November 25, 1786, in *WrBF,* 9:549.

38. *PG,* April 11, 1734.

39. Stephen Botein argued early American printers had to be impartial so as not to offend their customers, upon whom printers depended for economic survival. Printers were also disinterested in press liberty and "would disclaim all interest whatsoever in the political or intellectual functions of their craft, and explain their preference for impartiality merely as a business instinct to serve all customers" (Stephen Botein, "'Meer Mechanics' and an Open Press," 179–80).

40. *Autobiography,* 19; *New England Courant,* July 9, December 4, 1721.

41. BF to Edward Newenham, October 2, 1783, in *WrBF,* 9:102–3.

42. "An Account of the Supremest Court of Judicature in Pennsylvania, viz., The Court of the Press," September 12, 1789, in *WrBF,* 10:36–40.

43. *Autobiography,* 94–95.

44. *Poor Richard,* 1733, in *PBF,* 1:313.

45. *PG,* June 10, 1731, October 18, 1733.

46. Ibid., March 13, 1730.

47. "Observations on My Reading History in Library," May 9, 1731, in *PBF,* 1:192–93; *Autobiography,* 91–93; Benjamin Franklin's Commonplace Book, ca. 1732, Dreer Collection, HSP. After years of government service, Franklin took a more charitable view of public officials, blaming their malfeasance not on ill will but on the burdens of their offices. "Those who govern, having much Business on their hands, do not generally like to take the Trouble of considering and carrying into Execution new Projects," Franklin wrote in his memoirs. "The best public Measures are therefore seldom *adopted* from *previous Wisdom,* but *forc'd by the Occasion*" (*Autobiography,* 132).

48. *Autobiography,* 28, 57, 61–62; BF to Joseph Huey, June 6, 1753, in *PBF,* 4:504–5. For examples of discussion topics the Junto considered, see "Standing Queries for the Junto," ca. 1732, in *PBF,* 1:255–59; "Proposals and Queries to be Asked the Junto," ca. 1732, in *PBF,* 1:259–64.

49. *Autobiography,* 93.

4. Communicating Instruction in Philadelphia

1. *PG*, October 2, 1729.

2. Ibid.; *Autobiography*, 7, 56.

3. On Andrew Bradford, see Anna Janney DeArmond, *Andrew Bradford, Colonial Journalist.*

4. *Autobiography*, 17. Franklin's recollection here was amiss. The second American newspaper was William Brooker's *Boston Gazette*, begun December 21, 1719, with James Franklin in charge of the shop. James initiated the *New-England Courant* on August 7, 1721. See Edward Connery Lathem, *Chronological Tables of American Newspapers, 1690–1820*, 2.

5. Kenneth A. Lockridge, *Literacy in Colonial New England: An Enquiry into the Social Context of Literacy in the Early Modern West*, 13–27; Worthington C. Ford, *Broadsides, Ballads &c. Printed in Massachusetts, 1639–1800*, 5. On ballads bridging oral and literary cultures, see David C. Fowler, *A Literary History of the Popular Ballad;* G. Malcolm Laws Jr., *The British Literary Ballad.*

6. *Autobiography*, 12. Neither of Franklin's printed broadsides has been found. However, one historian argued that an anonymous eighteenth-century ballad on piracy is actually Franklin's. See Thomas Leonard, "Recovering 'Wretched Stuff' and the Franklins' Synergy," 444–55.

7. Jeremy Black, *The English Press in the Eighteenth Century*, 2. On press freedom in England generally, see Frederick S. Siebert, *Freedom of the Press in England, 1476–1776.*

8. King Charles II, "Instruccons to Our Trusty & Welbeloved . . . Commissioners," 1664, Original Letters Relating to the American Colonies, JCB; King Charles II to John Endecott, April 23, 1664, ibid.

9. John Endecott to Edward Hyde, Earl of Clarendon, November 8, 1664, ibid; Edward Hyde, Earl of Clarendon to John Endecott, March 15, 1665, ibid.

10. William Cobbett, ed., *Cobbett's Parliamentary History of England . . .*, 1:1495.

11. Other official fetters on the press were easing by the late seventeenth century. For example, printing in Massachusetts was permitted only in the inland village of Cambridge, where it had been conducted for Harvard College under ecclesiastical authority until the General Court of Massachusetts rescinded the edict in 1674. Thus, because of its importance as a business and transportation nexus, Boston became the seat of American colonial printing. See Clyde Augustus Duniway, *The Development of Freedom of the Press in Massachusetts*, 41–82; Wroth, *Colonial Printer*, 16–18.

12. *Rex v. Twyn*, in Thomas Bayly Howell, comp., *A Complete Collection of State Trials to 1783*, 6:513 (1663); *Rex v. Sidney*, ibid., 9:818 (1683). For the view that seditious-libel prosecutions stifled free expression until the American Revolution, see Leonard W. Levy, *Emergence of a Free Press.* For a contrary view, see Smith, *Printers and Press Freedom.*

13. *Publick Occurrences, Both Forreign and Domestick*, September 25, 1690.

14. September 25, 1690, in M. Halsey Thomas, ed., *The Diary of Samuel Sewall, 1674–1729*, 267.

15. Leonard W. Labaree, ed., *Royal Instructions to British Colonial Governors, 1670–1776,* 2:495–96.

16. Magistrate of Boston to Samuel Sewall, October 21, 1681, Massachusetts Archives Collections 58.114, MHS. Sewall was a judge of the Massachusetts Supreme Court of Judicature, but he dabbled in business ventures, including printing. For four years he served as publisher while Samuel Green, of the prominent Green printing family, operated the printing shop at the "Sign of the Dove," between Washington and Tremont streets. See Thomas, ed., *The Diary of Samuel Sewall, 1674–1729,* 1:50–51, 56; Ola Elizabeth Winslow, *Samuel Sewall of Boston,* 60–61.

17. William Berkeley to the Lords of the Committee of Colonies, June 20, 1671, in George Chalmers, ed., *Political Annals of the Present United Colonies, From Their Settlement to the Peace of 1763,* 328.

18. *Boston News-Letter,* August 14, 1721.

19. Ibid., August 10, 1719.

20. The increased availability of type was mostly due to William Caslon's establishment of his very productive type foundry in England in 1720. The quantity of type made literature more available and thus occasioned the growth of both journalism and the novel. See Deborah D. Rogers, "The Commercialization of Eighteenth-Century Literature," 171–78.

21. Levy, *Emergence of a Free Press,* passim; Botein, "'Meer Mechanics' and an Open Press," 127–225.

22. Daniel Boorstin, *The Americans: The Colonial Experience,* 324–40.

23. Timothy Green to Isaiah Thomas, August 8, 1792, Isaiah Thomas Papers, AAS. On the Green clan, see Sidney E. Berger, "Innovation and Diversity Among the Green Family of Printers," 2–20; William C. Kiessel, "The Green Family: A Dynasty of Printers," 81–93; Douglas C. McMurtrie, "The Green Family Printers," 364–75.

24. For other prominent printing families in eighteenth-century America, see Stephen L. Longenecker, *The Christopher Sauers: Courageous Printers Who Defended Religious Freedom in Early America;* John William Wallace, *An Old Philadelphian: Colonel William Bradford, the Patriot Printer of 1776;* Wetherell, "Brokers of the Word," 86–87, 100–101, 110–13.

25. Although conceding Keimer "was something of a Scholar," Franklin regarded him as "an odd Fish, ignorant of common Life," who displayed "a good deal of the Knave in his Composition" (*Autobiography,* 27, 57).

26. *Boston News-Letter,* March 7, 1723; *PG,* October 2, 1729.

27. Ian K. Steele, "Time, Communications, and Society: The English Atlantic, 1702," 1–21. In *The English Atlantic, 1675–1740: An Exploration of Communication and Community,* 158–59, Steele noted the average age of London news by the time it was printed in the *Boston News-Letter* in 1717 was slightly more than four months; by 1739, the elapsed time had diminished to just under three months in the *News-Letter* and two other early American newspapers. In their content analysis of Franklin's newspaper, Charles E. Clark and Charles Wetherell, "The Measure of Maturity: The *Pennsylvania Gazette,* 1728–1765," 279–303, found that more than

two-thirds of all news items 1728–65 were at least three months old by the time they were printed.

28. For the argument that the *Pennsylvania Gazette* and other early American newspapers were emulating the *London Gazette,* see Clark and Wetherell, "Measure of Maturity," 283, 289, 295.

29. *PG,* August 2, 1733; *Autobiography,* 13–14.

30. *PG,* November 19, 1730; March 18, 25, 1731; *Autobiography,* 62–63; "Advice to a Young Tradesman, Written by an Old One," in *PBF,* 3:307.

31. *PG,* October 22, 1730.

32. Ibid., November 20, 27, 1735.

33. "The Busy-Body, No. 4," *American Weekly Mercury,* February 25, 1729; *PG,* September 12, 1732.

34. Samuel Miller, *A Brief Retrospect of the Eighteenth Century,* 2:172–74; Thomas Jefferson to Nathaniel Burwell, March 14, 1818, in Ford, ed., *Writings of Thomas Jefferson,* 10:103–4.

35. BF to Joseph Priestley, June 7, 1782, in *PBF,* 37:444.

36. "The Speech of Miss Polly Baker," in *PBF,* 3:120–25. Lemay finds that Polly's qualities "all characterize human nature, as Franklin saw it. It is precisely because Polly Baker is, finally, a laughing-stock that she is Franklin's representative man" (J. A. Leo Lemay, "The Text, Rhetorical Strategies, and Themes of 'The Speech of Miss Polly Baker,'" 112). On Franklin's hoaxes and his influence on the genre, see Max Hall, *Benjamin Franklin and Polly Baker: The History of a Literary Deception.*

37. Bernard Capp, *English Almanacs, 1500–1800: Astrology and the Popular Press; Poor Richard,* 1739, in *PBF,* 2:217–18.

38. *Poor Richard,* 1739, in *PBF,* 2:218.

39. *Autobiography,* 93–94. On Franklin's almanac journalism, see Paul W. Conner, *Poor Richard's Politicks: Benjamin Franklin and His New American Order;* Cameron C. Nickels, "Franklin's Poor Richard's Almanacs: 'The Humblest of his Labors,'" 77–89.

40. *Poor Richard,* 1733, in *PBF,* 1:314; 1737, ibid., 2:169; 1740, ibid., 2:252.

41. *Autobiography,* 93; *PG,* February 11, 1735.

42. *PG,* October 2, 1729; August 2, 1733.

43. David Paul Nord, *Communities of Journalism: A History of American Newspapers and Their Readers,* 31–64; Capp, *English Almanacs, 1500–1800,* 144–50; Joseph Frank, *The Beginnings of the English Newspaper, 1620–1660,* 272; Mitchell Stephens, "Sensationalism and Moralizing in 16th and 17th Century Newsbooks and News Ballads," 92–95.

44. *Autobiography,* 68.

45. Ibid., 64–66.

46. Ibid., 66; "From Hugh Meredith: Dissolution of Partnership," July 14, 1730, in *PBF,* 1:175; *PG,* May 6, 15, 1731; George Simpson Eddy, *Account Books Kept by Benjamin Franklin: Ledger "D,"* 1739–1747.

47. *Autobiography,* 68–69. HSP has Harry's shopping list of supplies for the Philadelphia shop he established, including a "Printing-Press, with utensils belonging to it, as Friskets, Sheep's-Foot" and "50 Weight of French Canon" ("David

Harry's List of Printing-House Needs," ca. 1729, Logan Papers, HSP). Harry did not stay in Barbados long before returning to Pennsylvania. Keimer remained and published the *Barbados Gazette* from 1731 to 1742. See Howard S. Pactor, comp., *Colonial British Caribbean Newspapers: A Bibliography and Directory,* 18.

48. *Poor Richard,* 1735, in *PBF,* 2:7.

49. Franklin later encouraged Joseph to collect and publish his father's poems. See *Autobiography,* 26; *PG,* June 28, 1739.

50. *Autobiography,* 71.

51. Ibid., 76.

52. BF to Madame Brillon, November 23, 1780, in *PBF,* 34:47. On Deborah, see Jennifer Reed Fry, "'Extraordinary Freedom and Great Humility': A Reinterpretation of Deborah Franklin," 167–96.

53. BF to Deborah Franklin, June 27, 1760, in *PBF,* 9:175.

54. *PG,* March 4, 1735; BF to Bethia Alexander, June 24, 1782, in *PBF,* 37:520.

55. BF to John Sargent, January 27, 1783, in *WrBF,* 9:14; BF to Thomas Jordan, May 18, 1787, ibid., 583.

56. *Autobiography,* 61, 64.

57. Richard B. Morris, *John Jay: The Winning of the Peace—Unpublished Papers, 1780–1784,* 713; J. A. Leo Lemay, *The Canon of Benjamin Franklin, 1722–1776,* 96.

58. *A Modest Enquiry into the Nature and Necessity of a Paper-Currency* (Philadelphia: Benjamin Franklin, 1729), Collections, LCP; *Autobiography,* 67. On colonial currency, see Wyman Parker, "'Off With Their Ears': Colonial & Continental Paper Currency," ca. 1975, Collections, CHS. Franklin's brother James, in desperate financial straits, tried but failed to secure a similar printing contract in Rhode Island the previous year. See *Records of the Colony of Rhode Island and Providence Plantations, in New England,* 4:401; *Acts and Laws of Rhode Island,* 156.

59. *Autobiography,* 64; J. A. Leo Lemay, "Franklin's Suppressed 'Busy-Body,'" 307–11; Smith, *Printers and Press Freedom,* 120.

60. *Autobiography,* 25–27, 69, 101; *American Weekly Mercury,* April 4, 1728; *PG,* December 11, 1740; DeArmond, *Andrew Bradford, Colonial Journalist,* 223–32. For a sample of the accusations, see *American Weekly Mercury,* December 4, 18, 1740; *PG,* December 11, 1740.

61. Frank L. Mott, *A History of American Magazines, 1741–1850,* 24, 71–77; *PG,* February 26, 1741; *Autobiography,* 27. For Bradford's reply to Franklin's mockery, see *American Weekly Mercury,* March 5, 1741.

62. For Franklin's opinion of himself as a poor speaker, see *Autobiography,* 90.

5. Spreading Virtue to South Carolina

1. Social-responsibility theorists have dubbed the two strains "positive liberty" and "negative liberty," to distinguish between freedom for beneficial conduct and freedom from restraint. See Commission on Freedom of the Press, *A Free and Responsible Press;* Frederick S. Siebert, Theodore Peterson, and Wilbur Schramm, *Four Theories of the Press.*

2. *PG,* September 5, 1732.

3. *New-England Courant,* June 11, 1722; *Autobiography,* 19.

4. *PG,* September 12, 1732.

5. BF to Jane Mecom, November 26, 1788, in *WrBF,* 9:685.

6. *New-England Courant,* February 11, 1723. Franklin's father Josiah cautioned him to avoid lampooning and defaming. Other Bostonians regarded the young man unfavorably for his satirical skill. Their censures did not seem to trouble Franklin, who noted his "being esteemed a pretty good Riggite, that is a jocular verbal Satyrist," helped make him popular among the London pressmen with whom he worked (*Autobiography,* 19, 31, 47). For examples of Franklin's early malicious satire, see "Juba to 'Your Honour,'" *New-England Courant,* February 4, 1723; "Martha Careful" and "Caelia Shortface," *American Weekly Mercury,* January 28, 1729; "The Busy-Body, No. 3," *American Weekly Mercury,* February 18, 1729.

7. BF to the Editors of the *Pennsylvania Gazette,* ca. 1788, in *WrBF,* 9:639; BF to Louis Le Veillard, October 24, 1788, ibid., 673.

8. Acrostic from Benjamin Franklin (the Elder), July 15, 1710, in *PBF,* 1:5; *Autobiography,* 11. For Mather's influence on Franklin, see Breitweiser, *Cotton Mather and Benjamin Franklin.*

9. *PG,* Aug. 2, 1733.

10. *PG,* October 8, 1730; "The Busy-Body, No. 3," *American Weekly Mercury,* February 18, 1729; *Poor Richard,* 1736, in *PBF,* 2:141. Franklin described the circumstances of his marriage in *Autobiography,* 70–71.

11. *PG,* April 30, 1730; April 10, 1735; May 20, 1736.

12. Ibid., December 20, 1733.

13. Ibid., November 9, 1732.

14. *Autobiography,* 68.

15. Ibid., 95; "Articles of Agreement with Thomas Whitmarsh," September 13, 1731, in *PBF,* 1:205–8.

16. Converse D. Clowse, *Economic Beginnings in Colonial South Carolina, 1670–1730,* 42–94; Edward McCrady, *The History of South Carolina Under the Royal Government, 1719–1776,* 144–46. For a gloomy view of the region's economy, see Peter A. Coclanis, *The Shadow of a Dream: Economic Life and Death in the South Carolina Low Country, 1670–1920.*

17. Charles Joseph Gayle, "The Nature and Volume of Exports from Charleston, 1724–1774," 25–33; Peter C. Mancall, et al., "Conjectural Estimates of Economic Growth in the Lower South, 1720–1800"; M. Eugene Sirmans, *Colonial South Carolina: A Political History, 1663–1763,* 164–67.

18. *South-Carolina Gazette,* December 2, 1732.

19. Jack P. Greene, et al., eds., *Money, Trade, and Power: The Evolution of Colonial South Carolina's Plantation Society;* Steele, *English Atlantic,* 34. For the role of print culture in the southern colonies, see Richard Beale Davis, *Intellectual Life in the Colonial South, 1585–1763;* Cynthia A. and Gregory A. Stiverson, "The Colonial Retail Book Trade: Availability and Affordability of Reading Material in Mid-Eighteenth Century Virginia"; Calhoun Winton, "The Colonial South Carolina Book Trade."

20. *Autobiography*, 108.

21. October 28, 1731, entry in "Journal, 1730–1737," Eddy, ed., *Account Books*, 15; "Articles of Agreement with Thomas Whitmarsh," in *PBF*, 1:205.

22. Thomas, *History of Printing in America*, 566–67; *Autobiography*, 53, 63.

23. A. S. Salley, "The First Presses of South Carolina," 32; Douglas C. McMurtrie, *A History of Printing in the United States*, 2:314.

24. Eddy, *Account Books*, 15, 97. On Whitmarsh and his newspaper, see Hennig Cohen, *The South Carolina Gazette;* Elizabeth Christine Cook, *Literary Influences in Colonial Newspapers*, 230–65; King, "One Link in the First Newspaper Chain," 257–68; Jeffery A. Smith, "Impartiality and Revolutionary Ideology: Editorial Policies of the *South-Carolina Gazette*, 1732–1775," 511–26.

25. Edward Connery Lathem's *Chronological Tables of American Newspapers, 1690–1820*, does not acknowledge that Phillips's newspaper existed. Clarence S. Brigham's *History and Bibliography of American Newspapers, 1690–1820*, 2:1042, reveals that no copy of Phillips's *Weekly Journal* has been located. Its existence is inferred from a notice in the *South-Carolina Gazette* of January 13, 1733, in which Eleazer Phillips Sr. asked payment of persons indebted to his son for "six months subscriptions to the South Carolina Weekly Journal."

26. Stephen Roe to the Secretary of the Society for Propagation of the Gospel, December 1738, Society for the Propagation of the Gospel Manuscripts, LC; John Duffy, "Yellow Fever in Colonial Charleston," 189–97; idem, "Eighteenth Century Carolina Health Conditions." Phillips's death on July 11, noted under the heading "Printer in this Town," is in the *South-Carolina Gazette*, July 15, 1732.

27. *Barbadoes Mercury*, October 16, 1732, reprinted in the [Boston] *Weekly Rehearsal*, December 25, 1732. Cohen, *South Carolina Gazette*, 231, follows Salley's conclusion in "The First Presses in South Carolina," 31, that the absence of surviving samples of Webb's printing during this time indicates he died early in 1732. This is dubious reasoning, considering that no copies of Phillips's newspaper have been found, even though it was apparently printed weekly for six months.

28. *South-Carolina Gazette*, January 8, 1732.

29. Ibid., January 15, 1732.

30. Ibid., February 5, March 11, 1732.

31. Ibid., January 8, October 14, 1732; Sirmans, *Colonial South Carolina*, 180–82; *PG*, June 10, 1731.

32. *PG*, March 7, 1732; January 11, May 17, May 24, July 5, 1733. *South-Carolina Gazette*, January 29, 1732; March 24, March 31, April 14, 1733. For factors (including the press) that encouraged colonial unity, see Thomas C. Leonard, *The Power of the Press: The Birth of American Political Reporting*, 33–53; Harry M. Ward, *"Unite or Die:" Intercolony Relations, 1690–1763;* Michael Warner, *The Letters of the Republic: Publication and the Public Sphere in Eighteenth-Century America*, 1–72; Steele, *English Atlantic*, 251–71.

33. McCrady, *History of South Carolina*, 147, asserts without attribution that Whitmarsh died of yellow fever.

34. "Articles of Agreement with Thomas Whitmarsh," September 13, *PBF* 1:207; Cohen, *South Carolina Gazette*, 233.

35. "Articles of Agreement with Louis Timothee," November 26, 1733, in *PBF,* 1:339–42.

36. Thomas, *History of Printing in America,* 567; *PG,* February 15, October 14, 1731; "Agreement between Louis Timothee and Directors of the Library Company," November 14, 1732, in *PBF,* 1:250–52. For the German-language newspaper, the *Philadelphische Zeitung,* see Chapter 6.

37. *Autobiography,* 95; *South-Carolina Gazette,* February 2, 1734; March 20, 1735. Timothy may have changed the spelling because of ethnic prejudice toward those of French Huguenot ancestry. See *South-Carolina Gazette,* April 6, 1734.

38. *South-Carolina Gazette,* August 30, 1735.

39. *PG,* August 8, 1734; March 27, 1735; April 8, 1736; April 23, 1747; *South-Carolina Gazette,* June 1, 1734; January 25, 1735.

40. *South-Carolina Gazette,* October 12, 1738; January 4, 1739.

41. "Articles of Agreement with Louis Timothee," November 26, 1733, in *PBF,* 1:341. The provision for Timothee's son was the only substantive difference between his partnership contract and Whitmarsh's. The contract stated, "But if the said P shall relinquish this Agreement and shall be unwilling to continue the Copartnership hereby made, Then he shall not work at the Business of printing at all in the province of Carolina aforesaid until the Term of Copartnership aforesaid be compleatly expired." This "escape clause" for his son may have been a condition requested by Timothee, to which Franklin had agreed in order to expedite the arrangement.

42. On the few women printers in colonial America, see Leona M. Hudak, *Early American Women Printers and Publishers, 1639–1820.*

43. *Autobiography,* 71, 76. On Franklin's relationship with Deborah, see Sheila Skemp, "Family Partnerships: The Working Wife, Honoring Deborah Franklin," 19–36; Carole Chandler Waldrup, *More Colonial Women: 25 Pioneers of Early America,* 44–53; Lopez and Herbert, *Private Franklin,* 42–58.

44. "Power of Attorney to Deborah Franklin," in *PBF,* 1:331–32. This was not an uncommon practice in colonial America. For example, Maryland men often bequeathed considerable authority to their widows, both to manage existing businesses and property and also to dispose of property for income. See Lois Green Carr and Lorena S. Walsh, "The Planter's Wife: The Experience of White Women in Seventeenth-Century Maryland," *WMQ* 34 (October 1977): 542–71.

45. *Autobiography,* 95–96. On Elizabeth Timothy, see Ira L. Baker, "Elizabeth Timothy: America's First Woman Editor," 280–85; Cohen, *South Carolina Gazette,* 238–41; Hudak, *Early American Women Printers and Publishers;* Ellen M. Oldham, "Early Women Printers of America," 16–21.

46. *South-Carolina Gazette,* January 4, 1739; Thomas, *History of Printing in America,* 569.

47. *PG,* September 24, 1730.

48. BF to James Logan, ca. 1737, in *PBF,* 2:185. For Franklin's reporting—and commentary—on acts of human cruelty, see the story of a murdered daughter, *PG,* October 24, 1734.

49. "Observations on my Reading History in Library," in *PBF,* 1:192–93; *PG,* February 11, 1735.

50. "Observations on my Reading History in Library," in *PBF,* 1:192–93.

51. *Autobiography,* 93–94, 108. On Peter Timothy, see J. Ralph Randolph, "The End of Impartiality: *South-Carolina Gazette, 1763–75,*" 702–9, 720.

52. *Autobiography,* 108.

6. Network Expansion from New York to the Caribbean

1. *Autobiography,* 61.

2. Cotton Mather, *Bonifacius: An Essay Upon the Good . . . ,* 171–73; "Standing Queries for the Junto," [1732], in *PBF,* 1:257. For examples of Franklin's civic proj-ects, see *Autobiography,* 71–72, 101–3, 117–19; "Articles of the Union Fire Company," [1736], in *PBF,* 2:150–53; "A Proposal for Promoting Useful Knowledge," May 14, 1743, ibid., 378–83; "An Account of the New Invented Pennsylvania Fire-Places," [1744], ibid., 419–46; "Petition for the Pennsylvania Hospital," January 23, 1751, ibid., 4:408–11; *PG,* January 11, 1733; February 4, 1735.

3. BF to Samuel Mather, May 12, 1784, in *WrBF,* 9:208; *Autobiography,* 46–47.

4. *Autobiography,* 108.

5. Ibid., 62–63, 68, 75.

6. BF to Alexander Small, September 28, 1787, in *WrBF,* 9:614–15; *Autobiography,* 93, 108.

7. James Parker Apprenticeship Indenture, January 1, 1726/27, Miscellaneous Manuscripts Collection, APS; *New-York Gazette: or, Weekly Post-Boy,* May 25, 1752; James Parker, "An Humble Address to the PUBLICK," May 30, 1766, in McAnear, "James Parker versus John Holt," part 1, 95. Parker's estimation of his own talent is supported by printing contemporary Isaiah Thomas, who noted that Parker "was a correct and eminent printer" who "possessed a sound judgment, and a good heart; was industrious in business, and upright in his dealings" (Thomas, *History of Printing in America,* 520).

8. *PG,* May 17, 1733; *Autobiography,* 20; Alan Dyer, *Biography of James Parker,* 4–5.

9. BF to Jane Mecom, ca. 1748, in *PBF,* 3:301; "Articles of Agreement with James Parker," February 20, 1742, ibid., 2:341–45; Dyer, *Biography of James Parker,* 5. According to Daniel Boorstin, "it was the needs of the colonial governments that supported printers." He added, "In the earliest years the bulk of what issued from the presses was government work: statutes and the votes and proceedings of colonial assemblies." Thus, "Printing began under government sponsorship in all the colonies" (Boorstin, *The Americans,* 324–25, 332).

10. *Autobiography,* 98–99; Franklin sent James Jr. and his own son William, who were about the same age, to a school run by Dr. Alexander Annand in Philadelphia. See Bill from Alexander Annand, ca. 1738, in *PBF,* 2:388. For Ann Franklin, see Margaret Lane Ford, "A Widow's Work: Ann Franklin of Newport, Rhode Island"; Oldham, "Early Women Printers of America," 10–14.

11. "James Franklin: Indenture of Apprenticeship," November 5, 1740, in *PBF,* 2:262; BF to Jane Mecom, ca. June 1748, ibid., 3:304.

12. BF to Edward and Jane Mecom, ca. 1744–45, in *PBF,* 2:448.

13. The Franklin papers are rife with examples of Franklin ordering supplies from Strahan. See e.g. BF to Strahan, April 14, 1745, in *PBF,* 3:21–22.

14. William Strahan to James Read, January 17, 1743, Miscellaneous Manuscripts Collection, APS. For Hall, see Robert Hurd Kany, "David Hall: Printing Partner of Benjamin Franklin."

15. BF to William Strahan, July 10, 1743, in *PBF,* 2:383–84.

16. BF to Joseph Huey, June 6, 1753, ibid., 4:504–5; *Poor Richard,* 1737, ibid., 2:171.

17. *Poor Richard,* 1744, ibid., 2:397; BF to William Strahan, February 2, 1745, ibid., 3:14.

18. Strahan to DH, March 9, 1745, David Hall Papers, APS.

19. *Autobiography,* 63; "Advertisement of the General Magazine," *PG,* November 13, 1740; "The Detection," *American Weekly Mercury,* November 17, 1740.

20. BF to William Strahan, September 18, 1744, in *PBF,* 2:416–17; BF to Strahan, November 2, 1744, ibid., 2:418.

21. BF to Strahan, November 16, 1745, ibid., 3:46. For King George's War, see Philip J. Haythornthwaite, *The Colonial Wars Source Book;* Bruce P. Lenman, *Britain's Colonial Wars, 1688–1783.*

22. *Autobiography,* 108; "A Proposal for Promoting Useful Knowledge among the British Plantations in America," May 14, 1743, in *PBF,* 2:380–81. The American Philosophical Society, which Franklin and botanist John Bartram devised, began promisingly in 1744. Cadwallader Colden viewed it as a means of "promoting usefull Arts and Sciences in America." It soon lapsed into an elite social club, though, prompting Franklin to complain, "the Members of our Society here are very idle Gentlemen; they will take no Pains" to conduct research (Cadwallader Colden to BF, ca. October 1743, in *PBF,* 2:387; BF to Cadwallader Colden, August 15, 1745, ibid., 3:36). Undaunted, Franklin, Bartram, and Thomas Bond laid plans for "carrying it on with more dilligence then ever which we may very easily do if we could but exchange the time that is spent in the Club, Chess & Coffee House for the Curious amusements of natural observations." Despite early setbacks, which Colden attributed to the "difficulties that allwise attend the forming of Societies in their Beginning," the American Philosophical Society survived and continues to the present day in Philadelphia (John Bartram to Colden, October 4, 1745, in *Letters and Papers of Cadwallader Colden,* 3:160; Colden to BF, December 1744, in *PBF,* 2:447).

23. "An Account of the New-Invented Fire-Places," 1744, in *PBF,* 2:419–46; "Plain Truth," November 17, 1747, ibid., 3:180–218; *Autobiography,* 72. Franklin chronicled his midcentury public activities in *Autobiography,* 108–29. For the library, see Edwin Wolf II, *"At the Instance of Benjamin Franklin": A Brief History of the Library Company of Philadelphia, 1731–1976.*

24. BF to Cadwallader Colden, June 5, 1747, in *PBF,* 3:141.

25. BF to Cadwallader Colden, January 27, 1748, ibid., 272–73; BF to Cadwallader Colden, September 29, 1748, ibid., 317–18; *Autobiography,* 111, 120.

26. BF to William Strahan, June 1, 1747, in *PBF,* 3:140; BF to William Strahan, July 29, 1747, ibid., 165.

27. "Articles of Agreement with David Hall," January 1, 1748, ibid., 263–67; *Autobiography*, 119. Strahan also noted Hall's prompt payments, warning him when he ordered ink powder, "I am only afraid your great Anxiety to be, I think, *overpunctual* in remitting, may be an Inconvenience to you, which . . . would give me great Pain if I thought it was the case" (William Strahan to DH, May 4, 1750, Society Collection, HSP). Strahan repeated his worry later. See William Strahan to DH, June 26, 1756, Conarroe Collection, HSP.

28. Richard S. Dunn and Gary B. Nash, *Sugar and Slaves: The Rise of the Planter Class in the English West Indies, 1624–1713;* Keith A. Sandiford, *The Cultural Politics of Sugar: Caribbean Slavery and Narratives of Colonialism.* For West Indies cultural and business affairs, see Jack P. Greene, "Society and Economy in the British Caribbean during the Seventeenth and Eighteenth Centuries." For one island's ethnohistory, see David B. Gaspar, *Bondsmen and Rebels: A Study of Master-Slave Relations in Antigua.*

29. *Autobiography*, 33–34, 50–53, 68–69. For the obscure Denham, see Frederick B. Tolles, "Benjamin Franklin's Business Mentors: The Philadelphia Quaker Merchants," 60–69. For the eclectic nature of Denham's wares, from Madeira wine to German indentured servants, see his advertisements in the *American Weekly Mercury,* e.g. July 12, December 18, 1722.

30. John Stewart to Lord Stair, September 10, 1741, Osborn Collection, YB.

31. Richard Smith to Benjamin Franklin Bache, June 12, 1790, Society Collection, APS.

32. Trevor Burnard, "Inheritance and Independence: Women's Status in Early Colonial Jamaica," 99.

33. Anna Maria Shirley to Miss Norris, June 13, 1769, September 13, 1775, Osborn Collection, YB.

34. William Shervington to BF, June 20, 1753, in *PBF,* 4:509.

35. Hannah Cooper, "A Faithful Warning to the Inhabitants of Barbadoes," ca. 1740, Pemberton Papers, HSP.

36. Thomas Hulton, "Account of Travels," n.d., Miscellaneous Collections, JCB. For how planters, profits, and sugar production influenced West Indian society, see Hilary Beckles and Verene Shepherd, eds., *Caribbean Slave Society and Economy;* Kenneth Morgan and Maurice Kirby, eds., *Slavery, Atlantic Trade and the British Economy, 1660–1800.*

37. Great Britain Board of Trade Report, ca. 1752, Miscellaneous Collections, LC.

38. "Letter of an American Traveller to His Friend in Connecticut," July 1794, Osborn Collection, YB.

39. For the claim "Life expectancy was abysmally low, families were characteristically broken, deaths usually exceeded births, and the number of young adults was extremely high," see Burnard, "Inheritance and Independence," 99.

40. *Autobiography*, 68–69; Thomas, *History of Printing in America,* 604. For early newspapers of the West Indies, see Pactor, comp., *Colonial British Caribbean Newspapers.*

41. *Autobiography*, 46, 65.

42. Ibid., 121.

43. *Poor Richard*, 1733, in *PBF*, 1:317. For Franklin's newspaper writings on alcohol, see *PG*, February 1, 1733, October 24, 1734. Franklin began writing about the topic in the newspaper press at age sixteen. See "Silence Dogood, No. 12," *New-England Courant*, September 10, 1722.

44. *Autobiography*, 15, 79, 88.

45. Alexander Spotswood to BF, October 12, 1739, in *PBF*, 2:235–36. For Franklin's postmastership, see Ruth L. Butler, *Doctor Franklin, Postmaster General;* Arthur Hecht, "Pennsylvania Postal History of the Eighteenth Century."

46. "Philadelphia Post Office Record Books, 1737–53," in *PBF*, 2:178–83; BF to Peter Collinson, May 21, 1751, ibid., 4:135. For the relationship between the press and the post office and the commercial advantages of postmasterships, see Jerald E. Brown, "'It Facilitated the Correspondence:' The Post, Postmasters and Newspaper Publishing in Colonial America"; Richard B. Kielbowicz, *News in the Mail: The Press, Post Office, and Public Information, 1700–1860s;* Wesley E. Rich, *The History of the United States Post Office to the Year 1829.*

47. *PG*, January 28, 1735; *Autobiography*, 101.

48. Wilberforce Eames, "The Antigua Press and Benjamin Mecom, 1748–1765."

49. "Articles of Agreement with David Hall," January 1, 1740, in *PBF*, 3:267. For Franklin's assessment of Keimer and Harry, see *Autobiography*, 27, 57, 68–70.

50. *Autobiography*, 108; BF to William Strahan, October 19, 1748, in *PBF*, 3:322.

51. BF to Louis-Alexandre, duc de La Rochfoucauld, October 22, 1788, in *WrBF*, 9:665. For Franklin's talent for associating "with many principal People," see *Autobiography*, 28, 57, 62.

52. John Adams to Francis Adrian Van der Kamp, March 19, 1793, John Adams Letters, HSP; John Holt to William Goddard, February 26, 1778, Book Trades Collection, AAS.

53. BF to Jane Mecom, June 28, 1756, in *PBF*, 6:464; Eddy, *Account Books,* 116. For the products of Smith's press, see Bradford F. Swan, "A Checklist of Early Printing on the Island of Antigua," 285–92.

54. BF to William Strahan, November 27, 1755, in *PBF*, 6:277.

55. BF to William Strahan, June 28, 1751, ibid., 4:142; William Strahan to DH, February 13, 1751, David Hall Papers, APS.

56. BF to William Strahan, November 27, 1755, in *PBF*, 6:277; BF to James Birkett, March 1, 1755, ibid., 5:500.

57. BF to Jane Mecom, ca. June 1748, ibid., 3:304; BF to Edward and Jane Mecom, September 14, 1752, ibid., 4:356–57.

58. BF to Edward and Jane Mecom, ca. 1744–45, ibid., 2:448.

59. BF to Jane Mecom, ca. June 1748, ibid., 3:301–4; BF to Edward and Jane Mecom, September 14, 1752, ibid., 4:356–57. Mecom's flight from his apprenticeship to become a sailor may have been inspired by his uncle Josiah Franklin and cousin William Franklin, both of whom boarded privateers as young men after having witnessed the "prizes brought in, and quantities of money shared among the

men, and their gay living." Franklin confessed that he too was tempted to do the same as a youth, which may explain why he dismissed Mecom's action as inconsequential (*Autobiography,* 10–11; BF to Jane Mecom, ca. June 1748, in *PBF,* 3:302–3).

60. BF to Edward and Jane Mecom, September 14, 1752, in *PBF,* 4:356–57.

61. BF to William Strahan, May 9, 1753, ibid., 4:487; Eames, "The Antigua Press and Benjamin Mecom," 325; Douglas C. McMurtrie, *Early Printing on the Island of Antigua,* 5–6. For instances of the *PG* reprinting Antigua news during Mecom's tenure, see December 7, 1752, and succeeding issues.

62. BF to Jane Mecom, November 30, 1752, in *PBF,* 4:385.

63. BF to William Strahan, April 18, 1754, ibid., 5:264; BF to William Strahan, November 27, 1755, ibid., 6:277.

64. BF to Jane Mecom, June 28, 1756, ibid., 6:464–65.

65. Declaration of James Parker, September 18, 1766, James Parker Papers, YB; New Haven Grand Jury to Jared Ingersoll, Justice of the Peace, April 14, 1766, James Parker Papers, YB.

66. Thomas, *History of Printing in America,* 141–42.

67. BF to Jane Mecom, June 28, 1756, in *PBF,* 6:465; BF to William Strahan, June 2, 1763, ibid., 10:271.

68. Mecom married Elizabeth Ross in 1757. She was the daughter of the mayor of Elizabeth Town, New Jersey. BF to Jane Mecom, May 21, 1757, ibid., 7:215–16. For Mecom's debts and creditors, see e.g. BF to William Strahan, June 25, 1764, ibid., 11:240; JP to BF, November 6, 1765, ibid., 12:355; John Balfour to BF, November 21, 1765, ibid., 12:383.

69. Benjamin Mecom to the Mayor, Recorder and Aldermen of Philadelphia, September 11, 1770, Wallace Collection, HSP.

70. BF to Jane Mecom, May 30, 1757, in *PBF,* 7:223.

71. William Franklin to BF, ca. January 2, 1769, ibid., 16:5–6. Mecom's final printing employment was in 1774, as a journeyman in the New Jersey shop of Isaac Collins. See Thomas, *History of Printing in America,* 394.

72. BF to Jane Mecom, December 11, 1787, in *WrBF,* 9:623.

73. Jane Mecom to Catharine Greene, November 25, 1775, in *PBF,* 22:272.

74. BF to Jane Mecom, May 21, 1757, ibid., 7:215; BF to Jane Mecom, May 30, 1757, ibid., 221–22.

75. BF to Jonathan Williams, November 28, 1763, ibid., 10:384; Jane Mecom to BF, August 15, 1778, ibid., 27:257–58.

76. Jane Mecom to BF, February 14, 1779, ibid., 28:541–42.

77. Jane Mecom to BF, December 1, 1767, ibid., 14:334; "Book of Ages," ca. 1767, in Carl Van Doren, ed., *The Letters of Benjamin Franklin & Jane Mecom,* 101. For more on the tragic Mecom family, see Lopez and Herbert, *Private Franklin,* 108–15, 221–22.

78. John Lawrence and William Smith to BF, July 19, 1776, in *PBF,* 22:517–18; Jane Mecom to BF, August 15, 1778, ibid., 27:257; Jane Mecom to BF, February 14, 1779, ibid., 28:541.

79. BF to Jane Mecom, June 28, 1756, ibid., 6:464–65.

80. William Daniell to BF, November 16, 1754, ibid., 5:440; William Daniell to

BF and DH, June 29, 1754, ibid., 364. For other correspondence regarding this business arrangement, see William Daniell to BF, June 23, 1754, ibid., 355; BF to Deborah Franklin, ca. 1754, ibid., 463; Daniell to BF, July 21, 1755, ibid., 6:111. See also Eddy, *Account Books*, 51–52, 72. For Daniell's service as government printer and his death, see Frank Cundall, "The Press and Printers of Jamaica Prior to 1820;" idem, *A History of Printing in Jamaica from 1717 to 1834*, 10, 33.

81. See e.g. Bernard Fay, *Franklin: The Apostle of Modern Times*, 233; Carl Van Doren, *Benjamin Franklin*, 122.

82. William Daniell to BF, June 23, 1754, in *PBF*, 5:355. For the clauses that "all Charges for Paper . . . and other Things necessary to printing . . . shall be divided into three equal Parts," with Franklin paying one of those parts and the partner paying the other two parts, and that the partner "shall not during the Term of the Copartnership aforesaid work with any other printing Materials than those belonging to the said Benjamin Franklin," see e.g. "Articles of Agreement with Thomas Whitmarsh," September 13, 1731, ibid., 1:206–7.

83. For the scant evidence on William Smith, see Douglas C. McMurtrie, *The First Printing in Dominica;* Pactor, *Colonial British Caribbean Newspapers*, 40; Thomas, *History of Printing in America*, 608–9.

84. Scholars assuming a partnership between Franklin and William Smith include Fay, *Franklin*, 233, Alfred M. Lee, *The Daily Newspaper in America*, 31; John Clyde Oswald, *Benjamin Franklin, Printer*, 141; Van Doren, *Benjamin Franklin*, 122. All four make the assertion cursorily, with neither details nor attribution. It is likely they simply relied on each other without independent verification.

85. Eustace M. Shilstone, "Some Notes on Early Printing Presses and Newspapers in Barbados," 27–29; Mary D. Turnbull, "William Dunlap, Colonial Printer, Journalist, and Minister."

86. *Autobiography*, 68.

87. Ibid., 119.

88. This is in the only extant copy of *The Antigua Gazette*, dated April 12, 1755, and in the possession of AAS.

89. "Rules Proper to Be Observed in Trade," *PG*, February 20, 1750; "Advice to a Young Tradesman, Written by an Old One," July 21, 1748, in *PBF*, 3:308.

90. *Poor Richard*, 1755, in *PBF*, 5:474.

91. *Poor Richard*, 1733, ibid., 1:316.

92. *Autobiography*, 108; BF to Benjamin Vaughan, October 24, 1788, in *WrBF*, 9:675–76. Franklin was particularly active in advocating virtuous conduct for young men. See e.g. his essays "Advice to a Young Tradesman," July 21, 1748, in *PBF*, 3:304–8; "How to Get Riches," 1749, ibid., 349–50; "Rules Proper to be Observed in Trade," *PG*, February 20, 1750; "Father Abraham's Speech," 1758, in *PBF*, 7:340–50.

7. The Political Imperative of the Pennsylvania German Partnerships

1. "Articles of Agreement with David Hall," January 1, 1748, in *PBF*, 3:265. There is no documentary evidence Hall protested Franklin's financing of Lancaster and

Philadelphia printing houses, but since the two men worked together and saw each other regularly, it is unlikely such an objection would be in writing. Hall probably objected, though, in much the same polite manner as he did the following decade, when he suspected Franklin helped finance William Goddard's *Pennsylvania Chronicle* in 1767 as a rival to Hall's *Pennsylvania Gazette*. Hall informed Franklin of his rumored silent partnership in Goddard's printing business, but added, "this, I will never allow myself to believe, having still, as I always had, the highest Opinion of your Honour." However, he also reminded Franklin of the terms of the partnership contract, even though it had expired the previous year (DH to BF, January 27, 1767, in *PBF,* 14:17). For Franklin's involvement with Goddard's paper, see John J. Zimmerman, "Benjamin Franklin and the *Pennsylvania Chronicle*."

2. BF to Cadwallader Colden, September 29, 1748, in *PBF,* 3:318.

3. *Autobiography,* 111, 119.

4. BF to Jane Mecom, November 4, 1787, in *WrBF,* 9:621.

5. "Observations on My Reading History in Library," May 9, 1731, in *PBF,* 1:193; *Poor Richard,* 1753, ibid., 4:405. For how Franklin expressed his political views in his almanac, see Conner, *Poor Richard's Politicks.*

6. BF to Henry Laurens, February 12, 1784, in *WrBF,* 9:169–70; "Observations on My Reading History in Library," May 9, 1731, in *PBF,* 1:193; BF to Thomas Cushing, June 10, 1771, ibid., 18:124.

7. *Autobiography,* 120.

8. BF to Peter Collinson, December 29, 1754, in *PBF,* 5:453.

9. Aaron Spencer Fogleman, *Hopeful Journeys: German Immigration, Settlement, and Political Culture in Colonial America, 1717–1775;* Farley Grubb, "The Market Structure of Shipping German Immigrants to Colonial America," 40–41. On ship arrivals and number of passengers, see Gary B. Nash, "Slaves and Slaveowners in Colonial Philadelphia," 227–28n. Taking a broader view, another scholar noted that from 1727 to 1775 there were 317 German immigrant voyages, with most bound for Philadelphia. See Marianne S. Wokeck, "The Flow and Composition of German Immigration to Philadelphia, 1727–1775," 260–61.

10. Marianne S. Wokeck, "German and Irish Immigration to Colonial Philadelphia," 128–43.

11. "Petition to the Governor and Representatives of Pennsylvania," 1734, Bucks County Papers, HSP; Thomas Penn to Richard Peters, March 9, 1754, Thomas Penn Letterbook, AAS.

12. "Petition to the Governor and Representatives of Pennsylvania," 1734; BF to Peter Collinson, [1753?], in *PBF,* 5:158.

13. A. G. Roeber, *Palatines, Liberty, and Prosperity: German Lutherans in Colonial British America.* For the argument that most eighteenth-century immigrants and laborers had little interest in politics, see Billy G. Smith, *The "Lower Sort": Philadelphia's Laboring People, 1750–1800.*

14. Carl Bridenbaugh, ed., *Gentleman's Progress: The Itinerarium of Dr. Alexander Hamilton, 1744,* 30. On Pennsylvania party politics at midcentury, see James H. Hutson, *Pennsylvania Politics, 1746–1770.*

15. [William Smith], *A Brief State of the Province of Pennsylvania . . .*, 27–28.

16. James Hamilton to Thomas Penn, November 8, 1750, Penn Papers, HSP.

17. BF to Peter Collinson, May 9, 1753, in *PBF,* 4:484.

18. Norman S. Cohen, "The Philadelphia Election Riot of 1742," 306–19.

19. Conrad Weiser, "To my Bretheren the Germans," October 2, 1748, Maria Dickinson Logan Papers, HSP. On Weiser's role as a leader among German pacifists, see Paul A. W. Wallace, *Conrad Weiser: Friend of Colonist and Mohawk.*

20. *Plain Truth,* November 17, 1747, in *PBF,* 3:198, 202–3; *Autobiography,* 110.

21. *Autobiography,* 111.

22. "A Dialogue Between X, Y and Z Concerning the Present State of Affairs in Pennsylvania," *PG,* December 8, 1755.

23. Richard Peters to Thomas Penn, January 31, 1757, in *PBF,* 7:110–11n; *Plain Truth,* ibid., 3:201.

24. *Plain Truth,* November 17, 1747, ibid., 203.

25. Christopher Sauer, *Klare und Gewisse Wahrheit; Zeugneusse der Wahrheit.*

26. [Germantown] *Pensylvanische Berichte,* December 16, 1747. Literature on Sauer is extensive. See e.g. Donald F. Durnbaugh, "Christopher Sauer, Pennsylvania-German Printer," 316–40; idem, "Was Christopher Sauer a Dunker?" 383–91; idem, "The Sauer Family: An American Printing Dynasty," 31–40; Longenecker, *The Christopher Sauers;* Anna Kathryn Oller, "Christopher Saur, Colonial Printer: A Study of the Publications of the Press, 1738–1758;" Felix Reichmann, *Christopher Sower, Sr.;* Oswald Seidensticker, *The First Century of German Printing in America, 1728–1830;* William R. Steckel, "Pietist in Colonial Pennsylvania: Christopher Sauer, Printer, 1738–1758." Sauer and his printing descendants used several surname variations. They used "Saur" for German readers and "Sower" or "Sauer" for English readers. The anglicized version the printing family most often used was "Sauer," and it is used here for that reason.

27. BF to Peter Collinson, May 9, 1753, in *PBF,* 4:485; "Observations Concerning the Increase of Mankind," 1751, ibid., 234.

28. Peter Collinson to BF, August 20, 1753, ibid., 5:21.

29. BF to Peter Collinson, [1753?], ibid., 158–60. On the plan to furnish free education to Germans, see Whitfield Bell, "Benjamin Franklin and the German Charity Schools," 381–87; William Frederic Worner, "The Charity School Movement in Lancaster, 1755," 1–11.

30. Louis Timothee, "To all German Inhabitants of the Pennsylvania Province," *Philadelphische Zeitung,* May 6, 1732, in *PBF* 1:230–31. The title means "Philadelphia Newspaper."

31. Louis Timothee, "To the Reader," *Philadelphische Zeitung,* June 24, 1732, in *PBF* 1:233–34. A year before Timothee and Franklin's venture, Andrew Bradford began publishing an almanac, *Der Teutsche Pilgrim,* for the Pennsylvania Germans. It too met with little success, ceasing probably 1733.

32. "Agreement Between Louis Timothee and Directors of the Library Company," November 14, 1732, in *PBF,* 1:250–52; "Articles of Agreement with Louis Timothee," November 26, 1733, ibid., 339–42.

33. Longenecker, *The Christopher Sauers,* 59. Sauer changed the newspaper's name, which means "High-Dutch Pennsylvania Recorder of Events," to *Pensylvanische Berichte,* or "Pennsylvania Reporter," in 1746.

34. Ebenezer Hazard to Isaiah Thomas, June 5, 1809, Book Trades Collection, AAS.

35. Christopher Sauer to Henry Ehrenfried Luther, October 11, 1740, in Durnbaugh, "Christopher Sauer, Pennsylvania-German Printer," 329.

36. BF to Peter Collinson, May 9, 1753, in *PBF,* 4:483.

37. BF to Peter Collinson, [1753?], ibid., 5:160; BF to Peter Collinson, May 9, 1753, ibid., 4:485.

38. BF to Peter Collinson, May 9, 1753, ibid., 483–84.

39. Brigham, *History and Bibliography of American Newspapers,* 2:918, 954, 963; Seidensticker, *First Century of German Printing in America,* 35–38; Thomas, *History of Printing in America,* 442–43; Carl Wittke, *The German-Language Press in America,* 23–24.

40. *Pensylvanische Berichte,* May 16, 1748. Showing he was no Sauer truckler, Armbruster published a German translation of Franklin's "Plain Truth." See *PBF,* 3:184n.

41. BF to Abiah Franklin, April 12, 1750, in *PBF,* 3:474.

42. *PG,* August 22, 1751. "Fama" means "rumor" or "news." The identity of Franklin's German translator for the half-English, half-German newspaper is unknown. It may have been printer Gotthard Armbruster or his brother Anton, who worked with Franklin several years later. As this newspaper was published three years after Franklin's retirement from printing, his partner was likely a German and a printer. The Armbruster brothers' activities during the brief lifespan of the *Zeitung,* Franklin's third German-language newspaper, are unknown.

43. *Poor Richard,* 1753, in *PBF,* 4:405–6; *Autobiography,* 93. No partnership contract among Franklin, Holland, and Miller has survived, but three decades later, Franklin specifically listed the two men as printing partners. See BF to Francis Childs, February 8, 1785, in *WoBF,* 11:8–9.

44. "Notice to Subscribers," [Lancaster] *Hoch Teutsche und Englishe Zeitung,* January 25, 1752, in *PBF,* 4:259–60. For more on Franklin's familiarity with and interest in Lancaster, see George Heiges, "Benjamin Franklin in Lancaster County," 1–26.

45. Brigham, *History and Bibliography of American Newspapers,* 2:875; Thomas, *History of Printing in America,* 422, 447.

46. "Memorandum of Agreement with Samuel Holland," June 14, 1753, in *PBF,* 4:506–7; "From Samuel Holland: Bond," June 14, 1753, ibid., 507–8.

47. BF to Edward Shippen, February 14, 1754, ibid., 5:199.

48. Ibid. On Dunlap, see Turnbull, "William Dunlap," 143–65.

49. *PG,* February 19, 1754.

50. William Dunlap to ?, ca. 1754, HSP, in *PMHB* 22 (1898): 372–73.

51. Thomas, *History of Printing in America,* 386–87; Turnbull, "William Dunlap," 145–46.

52. BF to Peter Collinson, May 9, 1753, in *PBF,* 4:484–85. Despite their appearance of unity, religious differences among German immigrants occasionally led to violence. See Aaron Spencer Fogleman, "Jesus Is Female: The Moravian Challenge in the German Communities of British North America," 295–332.

53. William Smith, *A Brief History of the Rise and Progress of the Charitable Scheme . . . for the Relief and Instruction of Poor Germans.* On educational opportunities offered to German immigrants, see Elizabeth Lewis Pardoe, "Poor Children and Enlightened Citizens: Lutheran Education in America, 1748–1800."

54. BF to Peter Collinson, May 9, 1753, in *PBF,* 4:485; BF to Peter Collinson, [1753], ibid., 5:158–60; Bell, "Benjamin Franklin and the German Charity Schools," 381–83; Worner, "Charity School Movement in Lancaster," 1–5.

55. *Autobiography,* 111.

56. Henry Melchior Muhlenberg to the Society for the Relief and Instruction of Poor Germans, August 9, 1754, in *PBF,* 5:418–19, 21.

57. *Pensylvanische Berichte,* February 16, 1755. For other examples of Sauer's opposition, see e.g. *Pensylvanische Berichte,* June 15, July 1, 1754.

58. Henry Melchior Muhlenberg to the Society for the Relief and Instruction of Poor Germans, August 3, 1754, in *PBF,* 5:419, 21.

59. Henry Melchior Muhlenberg to the Society for the Relief and Instruction of Poor Germans, August 3, 1754, ibid., 418–19; Thomas, *History of Printing in America,* 381–82. Thomas errs by presuming the Society began as early as 1740 and financed Crellius's press.

60. BF to Peter Collinson, May 29, 1754, in *PBF,* 5:333. For more on his views of the immigrants, see John Frantz, "Franklin and the Pennsylvania Germans," 21–34.

61. William Smith to Thomas Penn, April 10, 1755, Penn Official Correspondence, HSP.

62. Smith, *A Brief History . . . ;* Thomas, *History of Printing in America,* 382. For another example of instructive material issued by Franklin and Armbruster, see the book *Das Leben Gottes in der Seele des Menschen, or The Life of God in the Soul of Man,* 1756.

63. [William Smith], *A Brief State of the Province of Pennsylvania . . . ;* idem, *A Brief View of the Conduct of Pennsylvania. For the Year 1755.*

64. BF, "Observations Concerning the Increase of Mankind," 1755, in *PBF,* 4:234. For the "Palatine Boor" epithet's effect on Franklin's reputation, see Philip Gleason, "Trouble in the Colonial Melting Pot," 3–17.

65. BF to Deborah Franklin, June 10, 1758, in *PBF,* 8:93. On Armbruster's debt to Franklin, see e.g. Anton Armbruster to BF, June 13, 1763, ibid., 10:289; "Chattel Mortgage and Inventory," October 29, 1765, ibid., 12:342–45. Franklin and Smith were amicable allies in designing and implementing the Society, but squabbles over provincial politics and printed scurrility made them bitter enemies. See Ralph Ketcham, "Benjamin Franklin and William Smith: New Light on an Old Philadelphia Quarrel," 142–69. Their disaffection contributed to Franklin's desire to distance himself from the Society.

66. BF to Peter Collinson, November 5, 1756, in *PBF,* 7:13; BF to Sarah Franklin,

November 8, 1764, ibid., 11:449. On Franklin's role as a colonial agent, see Bruce I. Granger, "Franklin as Press Agent in England," 21–32.

67. BF to Richard Jackson, September 1, 1764, in *PBF,* 11:329. For more on the 1764 election, see J. Philip Gleason, "A Scurrilous Colonial Election and Franklin's Reputation," 68–84; Hutson, *Pennsylvania Politics,* 170–77; Benjamin H. Newcomb, *Franklin and Galloway: A Political Partnership,* 71–104.

68. BF to Richard Jackson, October 11, 1764, in *PBF,* 1:397. According to Franklin, the number of voters was fewer than four thousand, so more than one thousand opposing votes from Germans would have been pivotal in the election.

69. BF to Joseph Galloway, February 17, 1759, in *PBF,* 7:374. On the Penn proprietorship's final years, see Lorett Treese, *The Storm Gathering: The Penn Family and the American Revolution.*

70. Turnbull, "William Dunlap"; Thomas, *History of Printing in America,* 384.

71. Anton Armbruster to BF, November 12, 1785 (quotation); April 26, 1786; June 26, 1788, Franklin Papers, APS.

72. For Miller, see Willi Paul Adams, "The Colonial German-Language Press and the American Revolution," 151–228.

73. For the argument that Germans did not begin to assimilate until the early nineteenth century, see Steven M. Nolt, *Foreigners in Their Own Land: Pennsylvania Germans in the Early Republic.* For the view that Sauer "contributed a great deal to the preservation of German culture in Pennsylvania through the two hundred years since his death," see Oller, "Christopher Saur," 164.

8. Franklin Plants a Printer in His Native New England

1. *Autobiography,* 119.

2. BF, "Opinions and Conjectures concerning the Properties and Effects of the Electrical Matter, arising from Experiments and Observations Made in Philadelphia, 1749," in *PBF,* 4:9–34; *Poor Richard,* 1753, ibid., 408–9. For Franklin's experiments, see Michael B. Schiffer and Carrie L. Bell, *Draw the Lightning Down: Benjamin Franklin and Electrical Technology in the Age of Enlightenment.* For a skeptical view, see Tom Tucker, *Bolt of Fate: Benjamin Franklin and His Electric Kite Hoax.*

3. "From Harvard College: Degree of Master of Arts," July 25, 1753, in *PBF,* 5:16–17; "From Yale College: Degree of Master of Arts," September 12, 1753, ibid., 58.

4. *Autobiography,* 130. Franklin errs here by noting that the Yale College degree came first.

5. BF to William Strahan, October 27, 1753, in *PBF,* 5:82. For Connecticut's early printing history, see Jarvis Means Morse, *Connecticut Newspapers in the Eighteenth Century.* For the colony's growth and importance, see Richard L. Bushman, *From Puritan to Character and the Social Order in Connecticut, 1690–1765;* Bruce H. Mann, *Neighbors and Strangers: Law and Community in Early Connecticut;* Harold Selesky, *Fighting Colonists: War and Society in Connecticut, 1635–1775.*

6. *Autobiography,* 11, 18–20, 119.

7. BF to Peter Collinson, August 27, 1755, in *PBF,* 6:171; BF to Richard Jackson, October 7, 1755, ibid., 217.

8. Deed from Samuel Mix, November 8, 1753, ibid., 5:109–10; BF to Thomas Darling and Nathan Whiting, January 1, 1754, ibid., 187; Nathan Whiting to BF, January 16, 1754, ibid., 188–89.

9. JP to Jared Ingersoll, March 16, 1767, James Parker Papers, YB.

10. BF to Thomas Darling and Nathan Whiting, January 1, 1754, in *PBF,* 5:187.

11. William Strahan to DH, May 9, 1754, David Hall Papers, APS; BF to William Strahan, November 4, 1754, in *PBF,* 5:439; BF to Thomas Darling and Nathan Whiting, November 25, 1754, ibid., 440.

12. "An humble Address to the PUBLICK," May 30, 1766, in McAnear, "James Parker versus John Holt," part 1, 77–95; Dyer, *Biography of James Parker,* 56.

13. BF to William Strahan, August 8, 1754, in *PBF,* 5:422.

14. BF to William Strahan, October 27, 1753, ibid., 82; BF to William Strahan, November 29, 1753, ibid., 121. For the Franklins' Rhode Island printing operation, see Margaret Lane Ford, "A Widow's Work: Ann Franklin of Newport, Rhode Island," 15–26; Thomas, *History of Printing in America,* 315–16, 325.

15. BF to Jane Mecom, June 28, 1756, in *PBF,* 6:463–65; BF to Thomas Darling and Nathan Whiting, November 25, 1754, ibid., 5:440–41. Mecom remained in Antigua until 1756, after which he undertook a series of failed publishing ventures. See Chapter 6.

16. BF to Thomas Darling and Nathan Whiting, November 25, 1754, in *PBF,* 5:440–41.

17. JP to BF, June 11, 1766, ibid., 13:301–2. Two years earlier, as a strategic maneuver, Franklin had asked Parker to operate a printing house in Williamsburg, Virginia. Parker reluctantly agreed, but his services were never needed. See JP to BF, October 27, 1764, ibid., 11:415–17.

18. Alexander Colden to JP, July 28, 1755, ibid., 6:113–14; Dyer, *Biography of James Parker,* 47–60.

19. *Connecticut Gazette,* April 12, 1755.

20. Ibid., February 7, 1756.

21. Ibid., May 10, 1755.

22. Ibid., April 12, 1755.

23. Ibid., June 21, 1755.

24. Ibid., November 22, June 21, August 16, 1755.

25. JP to BF, June 11, 1766, in *PBF,* 13:301; Beverly McAnear, "James Parker versus William Weyman," 10n, 15–16.

26. *Connecticut Gazette,* June 12, 1756; September 24, 1757.

27. JP to BF, June 11, October 25, 1766, in *PBF,* 13:302–7, 472–75; *Connecticut Gazette,* June 21, 1760.

28. Morse, *Connecticut Newspapers,* 4, 9; Thomas, *History of Printing in America,* 305. Green was a member of an extensive colonial printing family. See Timothy Green to Isaiah Thomas, August 8, 1792, Isaiah Thomas Papers, AAS; Sidney E.

Berger, "Innovation and Diversity Among the Green Family of Printers, 2–20";
Kiessel, "The Green Family."

29. BF to Jane Mecom, May 30, 1757, in *PBF,* 7:223.

30. Thomas, *History of Printing in America,* 141–42, 394.

31. BF to Jane Mecom, January 9, 1760, in *PBF,* 9:19; Jane Mecom to Deborah
Franklin, March 17, 1760, in Carl Van Doren, ed., *The Letters of Benjamin Franklin
& Jane Mecom,* 74.

32. BF to Jane Mecom, November 11, 1762, in *PBF,* 10:153; BF to William
Strahan, December 19, 1763, ibid., 406.

33. BF to William Strahan, December 19, 1763, ibid., 406; JP to BF, June 11,
1766, ibid., 13:307.

34. John Balfour to BF, September 2, 1765, ibid., 12:25–52.

35. Declaration of James Parker, September 18, 1766, James Parker Papers, YB;
New Haven Grand Jury to Justice of the Peace Jared Ingersoll, April 14, 1766, James
Parker Papers, YB. On Mecom's debts, see JP to BF, November 6, 1765, in *PBF,*
12:355.

36. *Connecticut Gazette,* February 19, 1768.

37. JP to BF, June 11, 1766, in *PBF,* 13:302.

38. BF to Jared Ingersoll, December 19, 1763, ibid., 10:402–3; McAnear, "James
Parker versus John Holt," part 1, 77–95.

39. JP to BF, October 27, 1764, in *PBF,* 11:416; *Poor Richard,* 1755, ibid., 5:474.

9. Renegade Second-Generation Printers

1. *Autobiography,* 108.

2. William Strahan to DH, June 22, 1745, David Hall Papers, APS; DH to BF,
December 15, 1759, in *PBF,* 8:448–49. BF concurred with Strahan's assessment,
writing in his memoirs that Hall was "a very able, industrious & honest Partner"
(*Autobiography,* 119).

3. *South-Carolina Gazette,* March 30, 1747; March 12, 1750. For more on
Timothy's imbroglios and editorial practices, see Smith, "Impartiality and Revolutionary Ideology," 511–26.

4. Peter Timothy to BF, June 8, 1755, in *PBF,* 6:69; Isaiah Thomas, *History of
Printing in America,* 569.

5. JP to BF, December 22, 1766, in *PBF,* 13:534. On Parker, see Dyer, *Biography of
James Parker.*

6. BF to William Strahan, July 29, 1747, in *PBF,* 3:165; Power of Attorney to
James Parker, November 5, 1764, ibid., 11:441.

7. Dyer, *Biography of James Parker,* passim.

8. Power of Attorney to James Parker, November 5, 1764, in *PBF,* 11:441.

9. *South-Carolina Gazette,* May 5, 1750; March 4, 1751.

10. Ibid., February 12, 26, 1753; June 25, 1753.

11. Peter Timothy to BF, June 14, 1754, in *PBF,* 5:343.

12. BF to Jane Mecom, ca. June 1748, ibid., 3:301–4; BF to Edward and Jane Mecom, September 14, 1752, ibid., 4:356–57.

13. Griffith Jones to BF, October 6, 1763, ibid., 10:343–45; Thomas Cumming to BF, October 7, 1763, ibid., 347.

14. JP to BF, October 25, 1766, ibid., 13:476; JP to BF, April 23–24, 25, May 10, 1770, ibid., 17:130–33, 140–41.

15. "An APPEAL to the Publick of New-York," February 23, 1759, in McAnear, "James Parker versus William Weyman," 1–23.

16. Ibid., 3.

17. Ibid.; Alfred Lawrence Lorenz, *Hugh Gaine: Colonial Printer-Editor's Odyssey to Loyalism,* 7–8.

18. "An APPEAL to the Publick of New-York," 3–5; Lorenz, *Hugh Gaine,* 8. Gaine's brother's conduct toward the black slaves was surely a key reason Parker ejected him. In addition to whatever moral objections he had, Parker also knew of New York's midcentury racial tension, which led to a violent slave rebellion in 1741. See T. J. Davis, *A Rumor of Revolt: The "Great Negro Plot" in Colonial New York.* Davis asserted New York's slave population was second only to Charles Town's in 1741.

19. *New-York Gazette, Revived in the Weekly Post-Boy,* June 15, 1752; "An APPEAL to the Publick of New-York," 5–6.

20. JP to BF, August 8, 1765, in *PBF,* 12:230. On Parker's gout, see e.g. JP to BF, November 6, December 20, 1765, ibid., 12:355, 408–9.

21. "An APPEAL to the Publick of New-York," 6–8.

22. Ibid, 8–9; *New-York Gazette: or, Weekly Post-Boy,* March 15, 1756; Dyer, *Biography of James Parker,* 64–66. Evidence of how Parker conveyed to Franklin that he lost the government printing contract and Franklin's response has, regrettably, not survived. While he was New York's printer, Parker also attempted to obtain the New Jersey printing contract. "I have had repeated Applications, from Mr. Parker, to appoint him the King's Printer, for this Province; but I shall not do it, unless you are willing, to resign it," New Jersey's governor wrote to the colony's incumbent printer, William Bradford (Jonathan Belcher to William Bradford, October 29, 1754, Franklin Papers, APS).

23. *New-York Gazette: or, Weekly Post-Boy,* October 4, December 20, 27, 1756; April 18, October 17, 1757. For colonial stamp taxes, see Mack Thompson, "Massachusetts and New York Stamp Acts," 253–58.

24. "A Letter to a Gentleman in the City of New-York," November 2, 1759, in McAnear, "James Parker versus New York Province," 329.

25. *New-York Gazette, Revived in the Weekly Post-Boy,* May 4, 11, 1752; BF to Cadwallader Colden, May 14, 1752, in PBF, 4:310–12.

26. Charles Hardy to William Denny, Gratz Collection, HSP; Paul Leicester Ford, ed., *The Journals of Hugh Gaine, Printer,* 2:3.

27. *Weyman's New-York Gazette,* August 27, September 24, 1759; Parker's *New-York Gazette: or, Weekly Post-Boy,* August 6, September 3, 17, 24, 1759; "An APPEAL to the Publick of New-York," 10–11. Parker's pledge to end the journalistic

squabbling appeared in Parker's *New-York Gazette: or, Weekly Post-Boy*, October 8, 1759.

28. McAnear, "James Parker versus William Weyman," 15–16; JP to BF June 11, 1766, in *PBF*, 13:303.

29. McAnear, "James Parker versus William Weyman," 16–19; JP to BF, July 15, 1766, in *PBF*, 13:344.

30. JP to BF, November 24, 1767, January 21, 1768, in *PBF*, 14:322, 15:27; McAnear, "James Parker versus William Weyman," 19–23; Dyer, *Biography of James Parker*, 115–16.

31. JP to BF, July 15, 1766, in *PBF*, 13:344; Lorenz, *Hugh Gaine*, 54–55.

32. [New York] *Independent Reflector*, August 30, 1753.

33. Ibid.; *New-York Weekly Mercury*, September 3, 1753.

34. Cadwallader Colden to Thomas Gage, May 31, 1775, in *Cadwallader Colden Letter Books*, 2:414.

35. *New-York Gazette and Weekly Mercury*, December 30, 1776.

36. Thomas, *History of Printing in America*, 472–73; Philip Freneau, "Hugh Gaine's Life," in F. L. Pattee, ed., *The Poems of Philip Freneau*, 201–8.

37. JP to BF, October 27, November 23, 1764; June 11, 1766, in *PBF*, 11:413–14, 470, 13:301; JP to Jared Ingersoll, April 30, 1768, Ingersoll Papers, NHC; McAnear, "James Parker versus John Holt," part 1, 81.

38. JP to Jared Ingersoll, April 6, 1767, James Parker Papers, YB; McAnear, "James Parker versus John Holt," part 1, 87.

39. John Holt to Jared Ingersoll, May 19, 1768, Ingersoll Papers, NHC; John Holt, Appeal to Connecticut General Assembly, May 1768, Document 110, NHC.

40. JP to BF, March 22, 1765, in *PBF*, 12:89–91; JP to BF, August 8, 1765, ibid., 227–29; Anthony Todd to BF and John Foxcroft, March 12, 1763, ibid., 10:221.

41. JP to BF, May 6, 1766, ibid., 13:263–64; JP to Jared Ingersoll, November 6, 1768, Ingersoll Papers, NHC.

42. John Holt to JP, October 9, 1768, Ingersoll Papers, NHC; JP to Jared Ingersoll, December 29, 1768; July 2, 1769, ibid.; Beverly McAnear, "James Parker versus John Holt," part 2, 209–11. Indeed, Parker suspected Holt was trying to postpone a settlement until one of them died. He told Ingersoll that Holt was trying to delay a trial "In hopes my Death or his own, may set his Family free, and hide his Faults" (JP to Ingersoll, December 29, 1768, Ingersoll Papers, NHC).

43. JP to BF, November 11, 1766, in *PBF*, 13:493.

44. JP to James Balfour, March 4, 1769, Franklin Papers, APS; Mary Parker to BF, August 12, 1770, in *PBF*, 17:204.

45. Power of Attorney to Deborah Franklin, April 4, 1757, in *PBF*, 7:169.

46. JP to BF, October 25, 1766, ibid., 13:476.

47. JP to Jared Ingersoll, July 2, 1767, Ingersoll Papers, NHC; BF to Richard Jackson, June 25, 1764, in *PBF*, 11:237.

48. *Autobiography*, 108; John Holt to JP, October 9, 1768, Ingersoll Papers, NHC.

49. JP to Jared Ingersoll, July 2, 1769, Ingersoll Papers, NHC; JP to BF, June 11, July 1, November 11, 1766, in *PBF*, 13:309, 327, 492. For other examples of Parker's

belief in justice through law, see JP to Jared Ingersoll, September 18, 1766; April 9, October 11, 1767; January 16, December 29, 1768; June 15, 1769, Ingersoll Papers, NHC. Parker's temper cost him a printing contract with the College of New Jersey, later known as Princeton University. The school's president wrote to Holt, "I had much rather deal with you, than with an honest Man of his odd Humour" (Samuel Davies to John Holt, January 21, 1761, Rush Papers, HSP).

50. For BF's advice on appropriate journalistic responses to the Stamp Act, see e.g. BF to DH, June 8, August 9, 1765, in *PBF,* 12:171–72, 233–34.

51. John Holt to William Goddard, February 26, 1778, Book Trades Collection, AAS. For an analysis of this letter, see Charles W. Wetherell, "'For These or Such Like Reasons': John Holt's Attack on Benjamin Franklin."

52. John Holt to the New York State Senate and Assembly, February 10, 1783, Miscellaneous Manuscripts Collection, N-YHS.

53. BF to Jane Mecom, July 10, 1764, in *PBF,* 11:258. On Franklin's political defeat amid bitter accusations in the press of greed and immorality, see Gleason, "A Scurrilous Colonial Election and Franklin's Reputation."

10. The Franklin Network and the Stamp Act

1. William Strahan to DH, September 19, 1764, David Hall Papers, APS.

2. For comparison, the annual national budget at the time was eight million pounds sterling. See Larry L. Gerlach, *Prologue to Independence: New Jersey in the Coming of the American Revolution,* 92–93. On the American Stamp Act, see Fred Anderson, *Crucible of War: The Seven Years' War and the Fate of Empire in British North America, 1754–1766,* 641–728; John L. Bullion, *A Great and Necessary Measure: George Grenville and the Taxation of America, 1763–1765;* Robert Middlekauff, *The Glorious Cause: The American Revolution, 1763–1789,* 70–93; Edward S. Morgan and Helen M. Morgan, *The Stamp Act Crisis: Prologue to Revolution.*

3. *New-York Weekly Mercury,* December 20, 1756; *New-York Gazette: or, Weekly Post-Boy,* October 4, December 20, 27, 1756; April 18, October 17, 1757.

4. "A Letter to a Gentleman in the City of New-York," November 2, 1759, quoted in McAnear, "James Parker versus New York Province," 323.

5. "To the Printer of the London Chronicle," December 30, 1758, in *PBF,* 8:215; *Poor Richard,* 1758, ibid., 7:341.

6. Thompson, "Massachusetts and New York Stamp Acts," 253–58; Bullion, *A Great and Necessary Measure,* 25–26.

7. "The Stamp Act," in Henry Steele Commager, ed., *Documents of American History,* 53–55; Bullion, *A Great and Necessary Measure,* 64–65, 104–5. On Grenville, see Philip Lawson, "George Grenville and America: The Years of Opposition, 1765 to 1770."

8. William Johnson to Cadwallader Colden, September 13, 1765, Miscellaneous Manuscripts Collection, N-YHS; Jared Ingersoll to T. W., July 6, 1764, in *Mr. Ingersoll's Letters Relating to the Stamp-Act.*

9. *PG,* May 16, 1765; "Scheme for Supplying the Colonies with a Paper Currency,"

February 11–12, 1765, in *PBF,* 12:47–60; Thomas Pownall and BF to George Grenville, February 12, 1765, ibid., 60–61; Verner W. Crane, "Benjamin Franklin and the Stamp Act," 56–57.

10. BF to James Galloway, October 11, 1766, in *PBF,* 13:449.

11. William Strahan to DH, July 8, 1765, David Hall Papers, APS.

12. BF to DH, September 14, 1765, in *PBF,* 12:267; BF to Charles Thomson, July 11, 1765, ibid., 207–8.

13. Charles Thomson to BF, September 24, 1765, ibid., 279–80.

14. John Endecott to Edward Hyde, Earl of Clarendon, November 8, 1664, Collection of Original Letters Relating to the American Colonies, JCB. A generation later, New Englanders engaged in a bloodless uprising known as the "Glorious Revolution" of 1689 to secure greater rights of governmental self-determination. For a pamphlet that fueled the revolt, see Ian K. Steele, "Origins of Boston's Revolutionary Declaration of 18 April 1689," 75–81.

15. JP to BF, October 10, 1765, in *PBF,* 12:310.

16. E. Carther to [?], November 2, 1765, Miscellaneous Manuscripts Collection, N-YHS.

17. John Watts to Moses Franks, November 9, 1765, John Watts Letterbook, N-YHS; John Watts to General Robert Monckton, November 22, 1765, ibid. On New York civil disturbances, see Edward Countryman, *A People in Revolution: The American Revolution and Political Society in New York, 1760–1790.* Whig leaders orchestrated some mob actions while others were spontaneous, but most symbolically vented grievances through attacks on property, not persons. On early American civil disorders, see Arthur M. Schlesinger, "Political Mobs and the American Revolution, 1765–1776," 244–50; Thomas P. Slaughter, "Crowds in Eighteenth-Century America: Reflections and New Directions," 3–14. In mob behavior, outrage and anger spread like a virus. Members may suspend self-evaluation, adopting the group's behavior, which is often directed by its most vigorous members. See Gustave LeBon, *The Crowd;* Neal E. Miller and John Dollard, *Social Learning and Imitation.* This point is exemplified by Major General Thomas Gage's observation about Boston rioters who ransacked and destroyed numerous houses: "People then began to be terrified at the spirit they had raised, to perceive that popular fury was not to be guided, and each individual feared he might be the next victim to their rapacity" (Thomas Gage to Henry Seymour Conway, September 23, 1765, Stamp Act Papers, Bancroft Transcript, LC).

18. JP to BF, December 24, 1767, in *PBF,* 14:347. For how the colonial press attacked the Stamp Act and galvanized public opinion against it, see Arthur M. Schlesinger, *Prelude to Independence: The Newspaper War on Britain, 1764–1776,* 67–84. For how the tax affected printers, see Francis G. Walett, "The Impact of the Stamp Act on the Colonial Press," 157–69.

19. *New-Hampshire Gazette,* October 31, 1765; [Hartford] *Connecticut Courant,* October 28, 1765.

20. Nicholas Brown to Esek Hopkins, December 30, 1764, Brigantine Sally Papers, JCB.

21. Joseph Galloway to BF, January 13, 1766, in *PBF,* 13:36.

22. *Boston Gazette,* August 12, 1765.

23. John Hughes to BF, September 12, 1765, in *PBF,* 12:266; Jared Ingersoll to Richard Jackson, November 3, 1765, Ingersoll Papers, NHC. Crowds often compelled stamp distributors to sign statements pledging not to enforce the tax. See e.g. Affidavit of John Hughes, October 7, 1765, Society Collection, HSP.

24. Zachariah Hood to BF, September 23, 1765, in *PBF,* 12:278; John Hughes to BF, September 8, 1765, ibid., 264; BF to Hughes, August 9, 1765, ibid., 235.

25. BF to DH, February 14, 1765, ibid., 65–66; BF to John Hughes, August 9, 1765, ibid., 235.

26. BF to DH, June 8, August 9, 1765, ibid., 65–66, 171–72, 233–34; DH to BF, June 20, June 22, 1765, ibid., 189–90.

27. DH to BF, October 14, 1765, ibid., 319–20.

28. BF to DH, September 14, 1765, ibid., 268; BF to DH, April 8, 1759, ibid., 8:317.

29. BF to Deborah Franklin, June 10, 1758, in *PBF,* 8:92; [Benjamin Franklin], *A Narrative of the Late Massacres in Lancaster County . . .*

30. William Strahan to DH, August 19, 1765, Society Collection, APS. Hall had apparently mentioned his plethora of competitors in a letter to Strahan earlier that summer and in one to Franklin in December 1758, both of which are lost. "The Country is increasing and Business must increase with it," Franklin responded. "We are pretty well establish'd, and shall probably with God's Blessing and a prudent Conduct always have our Share. The young ones will not be so likely to hurt us as one another" (BF to DH, April 8, 1759, in *PBF,* 8:319).

31. DH to William Strahan, September 6, 1765, Society Collection, APS; DH to Henry Unwin, May 19, 1765, David Hall Papers, APS.

32. DH to BF, September 6, 1765, in *PBF,* 12:258.

33. *PG,* October 31, November 7, 1765. Hall's reluctant patriotism during the Stamp Act crisis is discussed in Robert D. Harlan, "David Hall and the Stamp Act," 13–37; Robert Hurd Kany, "David Hall: Printing Partner of Benjamin Franklin," 180–96.

34. *South-Carolina Gazette,* October 19, 31, 1765; Peter Timothy to BF, September 3, 1768, in *PBF,* 15:202. Ironically, Crouch was Timothy's brother–in–law. See Thomas, *History of Printing in America,* 571. On Timothy's activities and how they affected his reputation, see Randolph, "End of Impartiality," 702–9; Smith, "Impartiality and Revolutionary Ideology," 522–24.

35. *Connecticut Gazette,* November 1, 1765; JP to BF, April 25, June 14, August 8, September 22, 1765, in *PBF,* 12:111, 175, 230, 277; Dyer, *Biography of James Parker,* 75–76.

36. *Connecticut Gazette,* November 1, 1765.

37. *New-York Gazette: or, Weekly Post-Boy,* November 7, 1765; JP to BF, November 11, 1766, in *PBF,* 13:474; *New-York Journal,* May 29, 1766.

38. *New-York Gazette and Weekly Mercury,* January 28, May 20, June 17, November 18, December 23, 1765.

39. DH to BF, October 14, 1765, in *PBF,* 12:320; [Philadelphia] *Pennsylvanischer Staatsbote,* October 28, 1765. On German printers and the Stamp Act, see Adams, "The Colonial German-Language Press and the American Revolution," 181–93.

40. Ralph Frasca, "'At the Sign of the Bribe Refused': The *Constitutional Courant* and the Stamp Tax, 1765," 21–39.

41. *Providence Gazette; and Country Journal,* October 6, 1764; Thomas, *History of Printing in America,* 315–16, 321; "William Goddard's Additions to Thomas' *History of Printing,*" in Clarence S. Brigham, *Journals and Journeymen: A Contribution to the History of Early American Newspapers,* 105. On Goddard, see Ward L. Miner, *William Goddard, Newspaperman.* Thomas is also a useful source, as he and Goddard were close friends.

42. *Providence Gazette; and Country Journal,* January 12, 1765.

43. Ibid., May 4, 1765; Miner, *William Goddard,* 46–48.

44. *Providence Gazette; and Country Journal,* May 11, 1765. On Sarah, see Susan Henry, "Sarah Goddard, Gentlewoman Printer," 23–30.

45. [Woodbridge, New Jersey] *The Constitutional Courant,* September 21, 1765.

46. The newspapers included the *New-York Gazette: or, Weekly Post-Boy,* May 13, 1754; *New-York Mercury,* May 13, 1754; *Boston Gazette,* May 21, 1754; *Boston News-Letter,* May 23, 1754. For a history of the uses of Franklin's emblem, see Lester C. Olson, "Benjamin Franklin's Pictorial Representations of the British Colonies in America: A Study in Rhetorical Iconology," 18–42.

47. *Constitutional Courant,* September 21, 1765. The identities of "Philoleutherus" and "Philopatriae" are discussed in Frasca, "At the Sign of the Bribe Refused,'" 35–36.

48. *Constitutional Courant,* September 21, 1765.

49. Ibid.

50. Ibid.

51. Frasca, "'At the Sign of the Bribe Refused'"; Thomas, *History of Printing in America,* 524–25.

52. Edmund Burke, ed., *Annual Register for 1765,* 50–51.

53. [London] *Public Ledger,* November 16, 1765, reprinted in the *Pennsylvania Journal,* February 20, 1766.

54. Quoted in Schlesinger, *Prelude to Independence,* 74.

55. *New-York Gazette: or, Weekly Post-Boy,* April 27, 1752; BF to Cadwallader Colden, May 14, 1752, in *PBF,* 4:310–12.

56. Cadwallader Colden to BF, October 1, 1765, in *PBF,* 12:287–88. On Colden, see Alfred Hoermann, *Cadwallader Colden: A Figure of the American Enlightenment.* Colden's son Alexander was the oblivious New York postmaster. See JP to BF, December 20, 1765, in *PBF,* 12:410.

57. Cadwallader Colden to Henry Seymour Conway, [1765], in *Cadwallader Colden Letter Books,* 2:45.

58. Thomas Gage to Henry Seymour Conway, September 23, November 4, November 8, 1765, Stamp Act Papers, Bancroft Transcript, LC.

59. W. Blair to Mark Baskett, December 21, 1765, Stamp Act Papers, Bancroft

Transcript, LC; William Strahan to DH, January 11, 1766, David Hall Letters, HSP; BF to Joseph Galloway, January 16, 1766, Franklin Papers, HSP.

60. "Examination before the Committee of the Whole of the House of Commons," February 13, 1766, in *PBF,* 13:124–62.

61. Ibid., 142–43, 48.

62. Henry Seymour Conway to Governors of Various Provinces in America, March 31, 1766, Stamp Act Papers, Bancroft Transcript, LC; Anderson, *Crucible of War,* 705–7.

63. George Whitefield to Peter Van Burgh Livingston, February 27, 1766, Collections, CHS; Benadam Gallup to Hannah Avery Gallup, May 24, 1766, State Archives, CSL.

64. *The Pennsylvania Chronicle, And Universal Advertiser,* March 23, 1767, reprinted in *PBF,* 13:182–84. Late in life, Franklin acknowledged authorship of this essay. See BF to Jane Mecom, November 26, 1788, in *WrBF,* 9:685.

65. Samuel Wharton to BF, October 13, 1765, in *PBF,* 12:315–17; Deborah Franklin to BF, September 22, 1765, ibid., 12:271.

66. "Examination before the Committee of the Whole of the House of Commons," February 13, 1766, ibid., 124–28; Charles Thomson to BF, May 21, 1766, ibid., 13:278.

67. JP to BF, November 11, 1766, ibid., 13:494; "An Essay discovering the Authors and Promoters of The Memorable Stamp Act," in Supplement to the *Pennsylvania Journal,* September 18, 1766.

68. BF to Joseph Galloway, November 8, 1766, in *PBF,* 13:487–88. Franklin was attempting to quote himself. In 1757, he wrote, "Act uprightly, and despise Calumny; Dirt may stick to a Mud Wall, but not to polish'd Marble" (*Poor Richard,* 1757, ibid., 7:85).

11. Rebellion and Network Loyalties

1. James Pemberton to BF, May 5, 1766, in *PBF,* 13:261; DH to BF, September 6, 1765, ibid., 12:259. On political damage to Franklin's reputation in 1764, see Gleason, "A Scurrilous Colonial Election and Franklin's Reputation," 68–84.

2. Supplement to the *Pennsylvania Journal,* September 18, 1766; Joseph Galloway to BF, June 7, 1766, in *PBF,* 13:295; BF to DH, September 14, 1765, ibid., 12:268. Several years earlier, when Franklin's reputation was attacked by political opponents, he wrote to Galloway, "the Cannon and Small Arms" of his political adversaries "consist of great and little Calumnies and Falshoods" (BF to Joseph Galloway, June 10, 1758, ibid., 8:96–97).

3. *Poor Richard,* 1750, in *PBF,* 3:454.

4. "The Casuist," *PG,* July 3, 1732; BF to DH, September 14, 1765, in *PBF,* 12:267.

5. BF to Peter Collinson, August 27, 1755, in *PBF,* 6:171; BF to Richard Jackson, September 1, 1764, ibid., 11:329.

6. BF to Joseph Galloway, April 11, 1757, in *PBF,* 7:179; Henton Brown and John Fothergill to James Pemberton, April 8, 1766, Pemberton Papers, HSP.

7. BF to Daniel Wister, September 27, 1766, in *PBF,* 13:429.

8. Franklin network members printed many articles and essays designed to rebuild Franklin's wounded reputation. For Hall, see e.g. *PG,* February 25; March 6, 27; April 10; May 1, 8, 15, 1766. For Peter Timothy, see e.g. *South-Carolina Gazette,* June 16, 1766. For Goddard, see e.g. *Pennsylvania Chronicle,* February 2, 9, 16, 23, March 9, 23, 1767. For evidence Miller printed laudatory Franklin articles (now lost) in *Der Wochentliche Philadelphische Staatsbote* newspaper, see Joseph Galloway to BF, June 7, 1766, in *PBF,* 13:295–96; BF to Daniel Wister, September 27, 1766, ibid., 429.

9. *PG,* September 18, 25, 1766; DH to William Strahan, August 19, 1766, David Hall Papers, APS; "Examination before the Committee of the Whole of the House of Commons," in *PBF,* 19:124–62.

10. BF to Joseph Galloway, April 11, 1757, in *PBF,* 7:179. On Franklin's political labors in England, see David T. Morgan, *The Devious Dr. Franklin, Colonial Agent.*

11. BF to William Strahan, December 19, 1763, in *PBF,* 10:407; BF to Mary Stevenson, September 14, 1767, ibid., 14:253.

12. BF, "The Interest of Great Britain Considered," 1760, in *PBF,* 9:87, 90; "The Albany Plan of Union," July 10, 1754, ibid., 5:387.

13. BF to John Ross, May 14, 1768, in *PBF,* 15:129. For the moral dilemma of rebellion versus acquiescence to authority, see John Thomas Scott, "On God's Side: The Problem of Submission in American Revolutionary Rhetoric," 111–22.

14. BF to ?, November 28, 1768, in *PBF,* 15:273. Franklin made the same point again four years later. See BF to Peter Timothy, November 8, 1772, ibid., 19:362.

15. "Homespun," January 2, 1766, in *PBF,* 13:7–8; "Pacificus Secundus," January 2, 1766, ibid., 5–6; "A Traveller," May 20, 1765, ibid., 12:134–35. For Franklin's journalistic essays in England, see Verner W. Crane, ed., *Benjamin Franklin's Letters to the Press, 1758–1775.*

16. "Rules by Which a Great Empire May Be Reduced to a Small One," September 11, 1773, in *PBF,* 20:389–99; "A Method of Humbling Rebellious American Vassals," May 21, 1774, ibid., 21:220–22.

17. BF to William Franklin, October 6, 1773, in *PBF,* 20:437.

18. "N.N.," December 28, 1765, ibid., 12:414.

19. "A Friend to Both Countries," April 9, 1767, ibid., 14:102–7; "To the Printer," n.d., Franklin Papers, APS.

20. BF to DH, September 14, 1765; June 10, 1758, in *PBF,* 12:68, 8:98.

21. DH to BF, September 6, 1765, ibid., 12:258. On Franklin's partners during the Revolution, see Ralph Frasca, "'The Glorious Publick Virtue So Predominant in Our Rising Country': Benjamin Franklin's Printing Network During the Revolutionary Era," 21–37.

22. *PG,* April 17, 1766; June 2, July 7, 1768; July 20, 27, August 3, October 5, 1769.

23. William Franklin to BF, November 13, 1766, in *PBF,* 13:500.

24. Peter Timothy to BF, September 3, 1768, ibid., 15:200–201; *Considerations on the Impropriety of Exporting Rice to Great-Britain.*

25. *South-Carolina Gazette,* March 26, 1772; November 8, 1773; Peter Timothy to BF, August 24, 1772, BF to Peter Timothy, November 3, 1772, in *PBF,* 19:283–84, 362.

26. Peter Timothy to "The General," August 16, 17, 1778, Miscellaneous Manuscripts Collection, N-YHS; Peter Timothy to BF, June 12, 1777, in *PBF,* 24:155. "The General" to whom Timothy reported may have been Benjamin Lincoln, who surrendered Charleston to the British in 1780, or Mordecai Gist. See "Articles of Capitulation," May 12, 1780, Revolution Collection, LC; William Pierce to Mordecai Gist, November 15, 1782, Gist Papers, MDHS. For the war in the south, see David Lee Russell, *The American Revolution in the Southern Colonies.*

27. JP to BF, September 22, 1765, in *PBF,* 12:277; *New-York Gazette: or, Weekly Post-Boy,* January 22, February 5, March 19, 1770.

28. *New-York Gazette and Weekly Mercury,* December 16, 1776; Lorenz, *Hugh Gaine,* 107–17. For New York's strong British influence, see Patricia U. Bonomi, "New York: The Royal Colony," 5–24.

29. Docket, New York Court of General Sessions, June 17, 1783, Miscellaneous Manuscripts Collection, N-YHS; Thomas, *History of Printing in America,* 472–73. Gaine's biographer offered a different interpretation. He claimed Gaine switched sides for financial reasons, as printing in British-occupied New York provided a better income for his family than printing a rebel newspaper in Newark. See Lorenz, *Hugh Gaine,* 114–17.

30. John Holt to Jared Ingersoll, November 3, 1767, Ingersoll Papers, NHC.

31. *New-York Journal,* January 8, 1775; Thomas Greenleaf to the New York State Legislature, December 10, 1788, Book Trades Collection, AAS.

32. William Franklin to BF, November 13, 1766, in *PBF,* 13:498–502; William Goddard, *The Partnership: or the History of the Rise and Progress of the Pennsylvania Chronicle,* 1–5; Miner, *William Goddard,* 52–110. For the proprietorship issue, see Newcomb, *Franklin and Galloway,* 136–60. On Goddard's role in the *Constitutional Courant,* see Frasca, "'At the Sign of the Bribe Refused.'"

33. William Franklin to BF, November 13, 1766, in *PBF,* 13:500–501; Goddard, *The Partnership,* 6–10.

34. DH to BF, January 27, 1767, in *PBF,* 14:16–18; BF to DH, April 14, 1767, ibid., 126–28;

35. *Pennsylvania Chronicle,* March 16, April 6, 1767; July 4, 1768; Goddard, *The Partnership,* 5–19.

36. William Franklin to BF, May 10, 1768, in *PBF,* 15:121.

37. Goddard, *The Partnership,* 5–16, 22–63; *Pennsylvania Chronicle,* September 23, 1771; February 24, April 27, May 11, 25, July 13, 1772.

38. BF to Joseph Galloway, December 2, 1772, in *PBF,* 19:419; Newcomb, *Franklin and Galloway,* 217–25.

39. BF to William Franklin, January 30, 1772, in *PBF,* 19:51. William wrote, "Enclosed is a Piece just published (and said to be written) by Goddard, with a View

of prejudicing Mr. Galloway at the next Election" (William Franklin to BF, August 3, 1771, ibid., 18:196).

40. *Pennsylvania Chronicle,* November 27, 1773; Miner, *William Goddard,* 109–12, 137–40.

41. [Baltimore] *Maryland Journal,* February 2, 1774; Miner, *William Goddard,* 112–36; Wallace B. Eberhard, "Press and Post Office in Eighteenth-Century America: Origins of a Public Policy," 148–49.

42. [Boston] *Massachusetts Spy,* March 17, 24, 1774.

43. William Goddard to Isaiah Thomas, April 15, 1811, Isaiah Thomas Papers, AAS; Miner, *William Goddard,* 131–35, 147–48; Rich, *History of the United States Post Office to the Year 1829,* 48–49.

44. BF to Richard Bache, February 17, 1774, in *PBF,* 21:101; BF to Silas Deane, August 27, 1775, ibid., 22:183–84; Richard Bache to BF, February 5, 1777, ibid., 23:279–80. While apprenticed to James Parker, Goddard assisted him with postal duties when Parker served as comptroller of the British post under Franklin. See Miner, *William Goddard,* 113.

45. Edmund C. Burnett, ed., *Letters of Members of the Continental Congress,* 4:494–95; John C. Fitzpatrick, ed., *The Writings of George Washington,* 5:350.

46. William Goddard to Isaiah Thomas, April 15, 1811, Isaiah Thomas Papers, AAS; Rich, *History of the United States Post Office,* 49.

47. John Holt to William Goddard, February 26, 1778, Book Trades Collection, AAS.

48. William Goddard to Isaiah Thomas, April 15, 1811, Isaiah Thomas Papers, AAS.

49. Thomas, *History of Printing in America,* 322.

50. BF to William Strahan, December 19, 1763, in *PBF,* 10:407; BF to Joseph Galloway, February 25, 1775, ibid., 21:509. For the effects of the war in Britain, see Stephen Conway, *The British Isles and the War of American Independence.*

51. In the first installment of his "The Busy-Body" essays, Franklin decided to "erect my Self into a Kind of *Censor Morum*" whose job it was to publicly commend virtue and censure vice ("The Busy-Body," in *American Weekly Mercury,* February 4, 1729).

52. BF, "Cause of the American Discontents," January 5–7, 1768, in *PBF,* 15:13; BF to Lord Howe, July 20, 1776, ibid., 22:520. For Franklin's opinion that riots in America "give great Advantage against us to our Enemies," see BF to Thomas Cushing, October 6, 1774, ibid., 21:327.

12. The Moral Reform of a Scurrilous Press

1. *Poor Richard,* 1753, in *PBF,* 4:405.

2. *The Scribler,* 8; *Pennsylvania Journal,* October 26, 1764. For other political attacks on Franklin's character, see Ketcham, "Benjamin Franklin and William Smith"; Miles, "American Image of Benjamin Franklin."

3. BF to Sarah Franklin, November 8, 1764, in *PBF,* 11:449; BF to Robert Morris, July 26, 1781, ibid., 35:311–12.

4. BF to Louis Le Veillard, June 8, 1788, in *WrBF,* 9:657.

5. BF to Joseph Priestley, February 8, 1780, in *PBF,* 31:456; BF to Richard Price, February 6, 1780, ibid., 453.

6. See e.g. "Comparison of Great Britain and America as to Credit, in 1777," ibid., 24:508–14; "Information to Those Who Would Remove to America," 1782, in *WrBF,* 8:603–14. For the link between virtue and a republic, see Peter Berkowitz, *Never a Matter of Indifference: Sustaining Virtue in a Free Republic.*

7. "Dialogue Between Franklin and the Gout," October 22, 1780, in *WrBF,* 8:154–62. Privately, Franklin claimed "disease was intended as the Punishment of Intemperance, Sloth, and other Vices; and the Example of that Punishment was intended to promote and strengthen the opposite Virtues" (BF to John Fothergill, March 14, 1764, in *PBF,* 11:101).

8. "The Morals of Chess," in *PBF,* ca. 1779, 29:755; "Information to Those Who Would Remove to America," 1782, in *WrBF,* 8:605–6.

9. *Autobiography,* 72.

10. Benjamin Vaughan to BF, January 31, 1783, in *Autobiography,* 185–89; Abel James to BF, 1782, ibid., 184–85; *Autobiography,* 72.

11. BF to the Duc de La Rochefoucauld, October 22, 1788, in *WrBF,* 9:665. For Franklin's aims in writing his memoirs, see Paul M. Zall, *Franklin on Franklin.*

12. BF to Samuel Johnson, August 23, 1750, in *PBF,* 4:41.

13. BF to Francis Hopkinson, December 24, 1782, in *WrBF,* 8:647.

14. "To the Editors of the *Pennsylvania Gazette,*" 1788, ibid., 9:639–42.

15. BF to Francis Hopkinson, December 24, 1782, in *WrBF,* 8:648.

16. "To the Printer of the *Evening Herald,*" n.d., in *WrBF,* 9:627; "To the Editors of the *Pennsylvania Gazette,*" 1788, ibid., 9:639–42.

17. "Apology for Printers," *PG,* June 10, 1731.

18. *Autobiography,* 95; "On Ill-Natured Speaking," *PG,* July 12, 1733.

19. BF to Francis Hopkinson, December 24, 1782, in *WrBF,* 8:648. For pamphlets' role as the primary repository of controversial writings that did not involve immediate public concerns, see Bernard Bailyn, *Pamphlets of the American Revolution, 1750–1776.*

20. *Autobiography,* 94–95.

21. [Boston] *The Columbian Centinel,* June 21, 1797; *Autobiography,* 95.

22. BF to Deborah Franklin, June 22, 1767, in *PBF,* 14:193; BF to DH, April 14, 1767, ibid., 127. For Franklin's chance to be a partner in another Philadelphia newspaper, see John J. Zimmerman, "Benjamin Franklin and the *Pennsylvania Chronicle,*" 351–64.

23. Mary Parker to BF, August 12, 1770, in *PBF,* 17:204.

24. Deborah Franklin to BF, November 16, 1773, ibid., 19:373; Richard Bache to BF, January 4, 1773, ibid., 20:6.

25. Thomas, *History of Printing in America,* 569.

26. Ibid., 390, 397, 483, 495, 580–81; BF to Richard Bache, March 3, 1773, in *PBF,* 20:88.

27. "Account with the Estate of James Franklin, Junior," April 4, 1763, in *PBF*, 10:238–41; Thomas, *History of Printing in America*, 315–17, 325.

28. John Lawrence and William Smith to BF, July 19, 1776, in *PBF*, 22:517–18; Jane Mecom to BF, August 15, 1778, ibid., 27:257; Jane Mecom to BF, February 14, 1779, ibid., 28:541.

29. Dwight L. Teeter Jr., "John Dunlap: The Political Economy of a Printer's Success," 3–9, 55; Turnbull, "William Dunlap."

30. Anton Armbruster to BF, November 12, 1785; April 26, 1786; June 26, 1788, Franklin Papers, APS. Other network members sought money from Franklin. In 1768 Samuel Franklin Parker, James Parker's ne'er-do-well son, tried unsuccessfully to borrow from Franklin. See JP to BF, October 17, 24, 1768, in *PBF*, 15:232–33, 241. Ann Franklin's son-in-law and printing partner Samuel Hall succeeded, though he appears never to have repaid the debt. Seven years later, Franklin was still trying to collect. In a letter to his sister, he likened Hall to "a whimsical man in Pennsylvania, of whom it was said that it being against his Principle to pay Interest, and against his Interest to pay the Principal, he paid neither one nor t'other" (Jonathan Williams Sr. to BF, September 19, 1771, ibid., 18:219–20; BF to Jane Mecom, January 13, 1772, ibid., 19:28).

31. Richard Bache to BF, January 4, 1773, in *PBF*, 20:5. For more on Armbruster's debt to Franklin, see BF to Richard Bache, October 7, 1772, ibid., 19:315; Anton Armbruster to BF, June 13, 1763, ibid., 10:289; Anton Armbruster Chattel Mortgage and Inventory, October 29, 1765, ibid., 12:342–45.

32. On Bache's life and journalism, see Richard N. Rosenfeld, *American Aurora: A Democratic-Republican Returns;* Jeffery A. Smith, *Franklin & Bache: Envisioning the Enlightened Republic;* James Tagg, *Benjamin Franklin Bache and the Philadelphia Aurora.*

33. BF to Richard Bache, June 2, 1779, *PBF*, 29:600. For Passy, see Luther S. Livingston, *Franklin and His Press at Passy*, 6–16, 78–80.

34. BF to William Strahan, July 4, 1744, in *PBF*, 2:410; BF to Elizabeth Partridge, October 11, 1779, in *PBF*, 30:514.

35. [Boston] *Massachusetts Gazette*, September 7, 1769; Wroth, *Colonial Printer*, 98–101.

36. David Bemis to the Massachusetts Legislature, October 1785, Book Trades Collection, AAS.

37. BF to William Strahan, December 4, 1781, in *PBF*, 36:193; Benjamin Franklin Bache to Richard and Sarah Bache, May 11, 1785, Society Collection, HSP. For American papermaking, see Dard Hunter, *Papermaking: The History and Technique of an Ancient Craft*. On Didot, see Albert J. George, *The Didot Family and the Progress of Printing*.

38. BF to Richard Bache, November 11, 1784, in *WrBF*, 9:279; BF to Madame Brillon, April 19, 1788, ibid., 644.

39. BF to Mary Hewson, September 7, 1783, in *WrBF*, 9:89; BF to Catherine Greene, March 2, 1789, ibid., 10:4.

40. [Washington] *National Intelligencer*, October 27, 1830; *Burlington Sentinel*,

October 15, 1830; John Jay to Francis Childs, May 11, 1783, in Henry P. Johnston, ed., *The Correspondence and Public Papers of John Jay*, 3:45–46.

41. John Jay to John Dunlap, July 10, 1779, Jay Papers, Columbia University.

42. John Jay to Francis Childs, December 20, 1784, Franklin Papers, APS. On Jay's career, see Walter Stahr, *John Jay: Founding Father;* Phil Webster, *Can a Chief Justice Love God? The Life of John Jay.* On the treaty for which he is known, see Joseph Charles, "The Jay Treaty: The Origins of the American Party System," 581–630; Jerald A. Combs, *The Jay Treaty: Political Battleground of the Fathers;* Todd Estes, "Shaping the Politics of Public Opinion: Federalists and the Jay Treaty Debate," 393–422.

43. John Jay to Francis Childs, May 11, 1783, in Johnston, ed., *Papers of John Jay,* 3:45. On government printing contracts as subsidy, see Boorstin, *The Americans,* 324–40. For a Jacksonian printer who defied his party and was punished with the loss of government printing, bankrupting him, see Robert K. Stewart, "Jacksonians Discipline a Party Editor: Economic Leverage and Political Exile," 591–99.

44. John Jay to Francis Childs, May 11, 1783, in Johnston, ed., *Papers of John Jay,* 3:45. Jay likely erroneously referred to "Robinson" when he meant Alexander and James Robertson, Loyalist printers who published the *Royal American Gazette* in New York under British auspices until the departure of British troops in 1783. See Thomas, *History of Printing in America,* 476–77.

45. BF to Francis Childs, February 8, 1785, in *WoBF,* 11:8–9.

46. *Poor Richard,* 1733, 1738, in *PBF,* 1:315, 2:194.

47. *Poor Richard,* 1754, ibid., 5:185. For Franklin's concepts of virtue, see Norman S. Fiering, "Benjamin Franklin and the Way to Virtue," 199–223; David M. Larson, "Franklin on the Nature of Man and the Possibility of Virtue," 118.

48. Thomas, *History of Printing in America,* 386–87, 393–94; *Autobiography,* 60; "To the Editors of the *Pennsylvania Gazette,*" 1788, in *WrBF,* 9:639.

49. BF to Francis Childs, February 8, 1785, in *WoBF,* 11:9.

50. [New York] *Daily Advertiser,* March 16, 1785, December 12, 1789; Frank L. Mott, *American Journalism: A History,* 115–16. The date of the *Daily Advertiser's* inaugural issue is estimated, based on the earliest extant issue, number 14, dated March 16, 1785. Three other newspapers started as weeklies, then converted to daily publication. One of them, the first daily in New York, was the *New-York Morning Post, and Daily Advertiser.* It switched from semiweekly status to daily on February 23, 1785—just one week before Childs's newspaper.

51. James E. Cronin, ed., *The Diary of Elihu Hubbard Smith,* 77, 126–27.

52. By 1800, twenty of the twenty-four daily newspapers published in the United States denoted their commerce function by using the word "Advertiser" in their titles. The percentage declined in the early nineteenth century as newspapers became increasingly reliant on political parties for income. See Alfred M. Lee, *The Daily Newspaper in America,* 59.

53. Francis Childs to BF, April 3, 1787, Society Collection, HSP; BF to Childs, May 8, 1787, *WrBF,* 9:580.

54. *Daily Advertiser,* May 2, 9, August 10, 1786. Although its roots extend to the

eighteenth century, the American business press was slow to develop. Now it represents more than half of the magazines published in the United States. See Kathleen L. Endres, "Ownership and Employment in Specialized Business Press," 996–98; Carol Smith, "Taking Stock, Placing Orders: A Historiographic Essay on the Business History of the Newspaper."

55. *Daily Advertiser,* March 16, 1785.

56. Ibid., September 23, 1785.

57. Ibid., May 11, 13, 1786. Franklin understood that "the Mob hate Instruction, and the Generality would never read beyond the first Line of my Lectures, if they were usually fill'd with nothing but wholesome Precepts and Advice." He thus sought to "humour them" by weaving moral lessons into satirical essays ("The Busy-Body, No. 4," *American Weekly Mercury,* February 25, 1729).

58. See e.g. *Daily Advertiser,* September 20–22, 1785.

59. *Daily Advertiser,* May 2, 11, 1786.

60. Ibid., May 30, September 24, 1785.

61. Ibid., September 20, 22, 1785.

62. Ibid., December 10, 16, 1785; [Francis Childs], *Letters, being the whole of the Correspondence between the Hon. John Jay, Esquire, and Mr. Lewis Littlepage.* For Littlepage's obsequious pursuit of Jay's patronage, see Lewis Littlepage to BF, February 12, 1780, in *PBF,* 31:476–77.

63. Lambert Cadwalader to John Cadwalader, January 29, 1786, Cadwalader Papers, HSP.

64. *South-Carolina Gazette,* November 21, 1754; July 8, 1755. Timothy also used the term "well-recommended" to mean he expected payment when accepting new apprentices. See Chapter 2.

65. *New-York Journal,* March 22, 1770; [Philadelphia] *Aurora,* March 11, 1795.

66. On Jay's payment to Childs, see Frank Monaghan, *John Jay: Defender of Liberty,* 452.

67. "Apology for Printers," *PG,* June 10, 1731, in *PBF,* 1:195. Franklin explained his indebtedness in his memoirs. See *Autobiography,* 65–66, 69–70.

68. *Autobiography,* 95.

69. BF to John Jay, October 2, 1780, in *PBF,* 33:356.

70. Francis Childs to BF, March 18, 1786; February 27, 1787, Society Collection, HSP.

71. April 3, 1787, Society Collection, HSP; BF to Francis Childs, May 8, 1787, in *WrBF,* 9:580. For other letters in which Childs complained of the types, see Francis Childs to BF, April 18, 28, June 16, 1786, ibid. Nearly two years later, Childs remained dissatisfied, bemoaning "the amazing quantities of imperfections" (Francis Childs to BF, January 8, 1788, Society Collection, HSP).

72. BF to Francis Childs, October 15, 1786; April 27, 1789, Society Collection, HSP. Franklin made the same point earlier about the need for punctuality in repaying America's pecuniary debt to France. See BF to Charles Thomson, April 16, 1784, *WrBF,* 9:192; BF to Samuel Mather, May 12, 1784, ibid., 9:210.

73. "Franklin's Last Will and Testament," July 17, 1788, in *WrBF,* 10:496.

74. BF to Francis Childs, March 10, 1790, ibid., 10:86.

75. *Daily Advertiser,* July 2, 1789; Francis Childs to BF, August 24, 1786, Society Collection, HSP.

76. Alexander Hamilton to Rufus King, July 25, 1792, in Harold C. Syrett, ed., *The Papers of Alexander Hamilton,* 12:100. "Beckley" was John Beckley, clerk of the House of Representatives and a close political ally of Jefferson.

77. Jonathan Dayton to Alexander Hamilton, August 26, 1792, in Syrett, ed., *Papers of Alexander Hamilton,* 12:275.

78. BF to Mary Hewson, October 30, 1785, in *WrBF,* 9:474. Bache was to have received his college degree in July 1787, but the Constitutional Convention delayed the graduation four months. Bache finally graduated in a class of eight on November 22. See BF to Francis Childs, May 8, 1787, Society Collection, HSP; Smith, *Franklin & Bache,* 90.

79. BF to Elizabeth Partridge, November 25, 1788, *WrBF,* 9:683; BF to Jan Ingenhousz, October 24, 1788, ibid., 671; BF to Benjamin Vaughn, November 2, 1789, ibid., 10:49–50.

80. BF to Benjamin Vaughn, November 2, 1789, *WrBF,* 10:49–50; BF to George Washington, September 16, 1789, ibid., 10:41.

81. *Autobiography,* 68; Tagg, *Benjamin Franklin Bache,* 56–71.

82. Benjamin Franklin Bache, *Proposals for Publishing a News-Paper, to be Entitled The Daily Advertiser.*

83. Robert Morris to Benjamin Franklin Bache, July 28, 1790, Bache Papers, APS.

84. [Philadelphia] *General Advertiser,* October 1, 1790. Bache believed he was ready to commence newspaper publishing well before the autumn of 1790, and resented that Franklin had not let him start an independent printing operation sooner. See Benjamin Franklin Bache to Margaret Markoe, June 23, 1790, in Tagg, *Benjamin Franklin Bache,* 76.

85. Benjamin Franklin Bache to Joseph Chambers, September 14, 1796, David Chambers Papers, AAS; *General Advertiser,* March 8, 1792.

86. *General Advertiser,* January 16, 1792; November 10, 1790.

87. Ibid., December 1, 1791; Jane Mecom to Margaret Bache, December 2, 1790, Gratz Collection, HSP.

88. [Philadelphia] *Aurora and General Advertiser,* November 8, 1794.

89. The affronts to which Bache objected included Federalist efforts to skewer Franklin's posthumous reputation and the Congressional dismissal of his father, Richard Bache, as postmaster without offering a reason. For the former, see [Philadelphia] *Gazette of the United States,* February 23, 1793; Cobbett, *Porcupine's Works,* 1:40, 4:32–33; Nian-Sheng Huang, *Benjamin Franklin in American Thought and Culture,* 32–36. For the latter, see Richard Bache to George Washington, April 21, 1789, in W. W. Abbot, ed., *The Papers of George Washington: Presidential Series,* 2:95–96. For the claim that boredom motivated Bache's partisanship, see Jeffrey L. Pasley, *The Tyranny of Printers: Newspaper Politics in the Early American Republic,* 83.

90. *Aurora,* November 8, 1794; March 6, 1797; March 4, 1796; [Benjamin

Franklin Bache], *Remarks Occasioned by the Late Conduct of Mr. Washington as President of the United States; Letters from General Washington to Several of His Friends, In June and July, 1776.* For Bache's attack on Adams, see Arthur Scherr, "'Vox Populi' versus the Patriot President: Benjamin Franklin Bache's Philadelphia *Aurora* and John Adams (1797)," 503–21.

91. *Aurora,* March 5, 1797.

92. Elias Boudinot to John Bayard, December 7, 1795, Edward Everett Papers, MHS; *Aurora,* August 18, 1798.

93. John Adams to Benjamin Rush, April 12, 1809, Adams, ed., *Works of John Adams,* 9:619.

94. *General Advertiser,* November 10, 1790.

95. "An Account of the Supremest Court of Judicature in Pennsylvania, viz., The Court of the Press," [Philadelphia] *Federal Gazette,* September 12, 1789, in *WrBF,* 10:36–37.

96. Ibid., 38–39.

97. *Aurora,* April 6, December 9, 1797; August 9, 10, 1798; *Gazette of the United States,* August 9, 1798. For the "culture" of honor and combat prevalent in the era, see Joanne B. Freeman, *Affairs of Honor: National Politics in the New Republic.*

98. *Aurora,* April 6, 1787, August 10, 1798.

99. Mathew Carey, *Autobiography,* 39.

100. Philadelphia's population in 1798 was fifty-five thousand, but about forty thousand fled to the countryside. Thus, the fever killed nearly a fourth of those who stayed in the city. See John T. Scharff and Thompson Westcott, *History of Philadelphia, 1609–1884,* 2:1629–31. For an eyewitness narrative of the 1798 epidemic, see Thaddeus Brown, *An Address in Christian Love, to the Inhabitants of Philadelphia; on the Awful Dispensation of the Yellow Fever, in 1798;* Philadelphia College of Physicians, *Facts and Observations Relative to the Nature and Origin of the Pestilential Fever . . .*

101. Benjamin Franklin Bache to Richard and Sarah Bache, September 2, 1798, Society Collection, HSP. For the effects of the comparable 1793 Philadelphia epidemic, see J. H. Powell, *Bring Out Your Dead: The Great Plague of Yellow Fever in Philadelphia in 1793.* For firsthand accounts of the 1799 epidemic, see Charles Brockden Brown, *Arthur Mervyn; or, Memoirs of the Year 1793;* Mathew Carey, *A Short Account of the Malignant Fever, Lately Prevalent in Philadelphia.*

102. *Daily Advertiser,* January 25, 1796.

103. [Washington] *National Intelligencer,* October 27, 1830; *Burlington Sentinel,* October 15, 1830. Childs solicited powerful friends to obtain federal appointments, such as the post of American ambassador to Great Britain. For one such example, see Francis Childs to Rufus King, August 9, 1800, Rufus King Papers, N-YHS.

104. For Franklin's early editorial philosophy, see "Apology for Printers," *PG,* June 10, 1731.

105. "An Account of the Supremest Court of Judicature," in *WrBF,* 10:38, 40; BF to ?, November 25, 1786, ibid., 9:549.

Conclusion: God, Humanity, and Franklin's Legacy

1. *Poor Richard*, 1738, in *PBF*, 2:194.

2. "To the Printer of the Evening Herald," ca. 1787, in *WrBF*, 9:627.

3. BF to Samuel Elbert, December 16, 1787, ibid., 626; "The Interest of Great Britain Considered," 1760, in *PBF*, 9:65.

4. BF to Joseph Priestley, June 7, 1782, in *PBF*, 37:444.

5. BF to Louis Le Veillard, October 24, 1788, in *WrBF*, 9:673.

6. Franklin's essays about editorial practices included "To the Printer of the *Evening Herald*," ca. 1787, ibid., 11:397–98; "To the Editors of the *Pennsylvania Gazette*," 1788, ibid., 413–16; and "An Account of the Supremest Court of Judicature in Pennsylvania, viz., the Court of the Press," *Federal Gazette*, September 12, 1789, ibid., 12:129–34.

7. BF to Louis Le Veillard, October 24, 1788, ibid., 9:673.

8. BF to Madame Anne-Louise Brillon, April 19, 1788, ibid., 644; BF to Miss Flainville, October 23, 1788, ibid., 667.

9. BF to Benjamin Vaughan, November 9, 1779, in *PBF*, 31:58; BF to Benjamin Vaughn, October 24, 1788, in *WrBF*, 9:676; *Autobiography*, 95.

10. BF to Louis Le Veillard, September 5, 1789, in *WrBF*, 10:35. In Bache's newspaper, a medical practitioner using the pseudonym "A Friend to Candor and Mankind" noted that "in opium, we have the means of sometimes removing, and always abating the violence of pain arising from spasm," but added that opium is inappropriate for treatment of the gout, rheumatism, or pleurisy ([Philadelphia] *Aurora*, March 29, 1796).

11. *Autobiography*, 205; *PG*, April 21, 1790; [Benjamin Franklin Bache] to [Margaret Markoe], May 2, 1790, Bache Papers, APS.

12. Ezekiel Price to Stephen Collins, September 27, 1790, National and Local Historical Figures Papers, NHC; John Pemberton to Joseph Row, April 28, 1790, Miscellaneous Manuscripts, HSP; Thomas Jefferson to Samuel Smith, August 22, 1798, in Albert Ellery Bergh, ed., *The Writings of Thomas Jefferson*, 10:55.

13. [Rutland] *The Herald of Vermont*, June 25, 1792.

14. [Philadelphia] *The American Museum*, April 1790, 212; *Boston Gazette*, August 9, 1790.

15. Moses Bagg, *The Pioneers of Utica*; J. H. Battle, ed., *The History of Columbia and Montour Counties, Pennsylvania*, 25–26.

16. C[harles] Sumner to Theodore Parker, October 5, 1856, Theodore Parker Papers, MHS.

17. *New York Daily Times*, September 19, 1856, 1; [New York] *Century Illustrated Magazine* 41 (December 1890): 197.

18. "A Very Brief and Very Comprehensive Life of Ben: Franklin, Printer," Collections, NYSL. For additional insight into the formation of Franklin's posthumous reputation, see Gilbert Chinard, "The Apotheosis of Benjamin Franklin," 440–73; Huang, *Benjamin Franklin in American Thought and Culture*; Miles, "American Image of Benjamin Franklin."

19. David Hume to BF, May 10, 1762, in *PBF,* 10:81–82; John Adams to Benjamin Rush, April 4, 1790, in Biddle, ed., *Old Family Letters,* 55.

20. BF to Sarah Bache, June 9, 1779, in *PBF,* 29:613; *Autobiography,* 78–80; BF to Madame Anne-Louise Brillon, April 19, 1788, in *WrBF,* 9:644.

21. "Franklin's Last Will and Testament," July 17, 1788, in *WrBF,* 10:493.

22. Edward Connery Lathem, *Chronological Tables of American Newspapers, 1690–1820.* The eight network newspapers in 1755, and their printers, were: *Connecticut Gazette,* John Holt and James Parker; *Maryland Gazette,* Jonas Green; *New-York Gazette: or, Weekly Post-Boy,* James Parker; *New-York Mercury,* Hugh Gaine; *Pennsylvania Gazette,* David Hall and BF; *Philadelphische Zeitung,* Anton Armbruster and BF; *South-Carolina Gazette,* Peter Timothy; *Antigua Gazette,* Benjamin Mecom. Jonas Green had worked as a journeyman for Franklin, and later in his employ as a postmaster. See Jonas Green to BF, July 25, 1747, in *PBF,* 3:153–54n; BF to Deborah Franklin, November 22, 1757, ibid., 7:277.

23. Eddy, *Account Books,* 52.

24. *Autobiography,* 20.

25. "Articles of Agreement with David Hall," January 1, 1748, in *PBF,* 3:263–67; *Autobiography,* 119.

26. *Poor Richard,* 1752, in *PBF,* 4:248; *Poor Richard,* 1758, ibid., 7:344.

27. JP to BF, June 14, 1765, ibid., 12:176. Responsibility for the disappointing conduct of certain network members, e.g. Lewis Jones and Benjamin Mecom, does not lie entirely with Parker. Franklin arranged for the most troublesome workers to serve their apprenticeships with Parker. See Griffith Jones to BF, October 6, 1763, ibid., 10:343–45; BF to Edward and Jane Mecom, ca. 1744–45, ibid., 2:448.

28. John Holt to William Goddard, February 26, 1778, Book Trades Collection, AAS; BF to Thomas Ringgold, November 26, 1761, in *PBF,* 9:388; BF to Deborah Franklin, November 22, 1757, ibid., 7:277. On Green's employment in Franklin's shop, see Jonas Green to BF, July 25, 1747, ibid., 3:153–54n.

29. "From Jonathan Williams: Account," October 1763, in *PBF,* 10:358n; Martin Howard to BF, November 17, 1764, ibid., 11:461; Jonathan Williams to BF, September 19, December 13, 1771, ibid., 18:219, 264.

30. Jane Mecom to BF, February 14, 1779, ibid., 28:541–42.

31. [Boston] *Continental Journal,* July 7, 1785; [Boston] *Massachusetts Centinel,* June 22, 1785; [Hartford] *Connecticut Courant,* November 20, 1786.

32. BF to John Lathrop, May 31, 1788, in *WrBF,* 9:651.

33. BF to Benjamin Vaughan, July 26, 1784, ibid., 243; BF to Joseph Priestley, June 7, 1782, in *PBF,* 37:444.

34. Thomas, *History of Printing in America,* 370.

35. Thomas Jefferson to Judge William Johnson, June 12, 1823, in Bergh, ed., *Writings of Thomas Jefferson,* 15:448. James Madison made a similar claim. See Madison to John G. Jackson, December 27, 1821, in Gaillard Hunt, ed., *The Writings of James Madison,* 9:74.

36. Stewart Macaulay asserts that "alternative institutions" are more influential in shaping behavior than civil laws, and "the law" is often not an integral regulator of

how society operates. Indeed, such extralegal institutions sometimes subvert the law. Macaulay identified these as "private governments," such as trade associations and networks. "Much of what we could call governing is done by groups that are not part of the institutions established by federal and state constitutions," he wrote. "We live in a world of legal pluralism. Private governments, social fields, and networks administer their own rules and apply their own sanctions to those who come under their jurisdiction" (Stewart Macaulay, "Private Government," 445, 502. See also idem, "Law and the Behavioral Sciences: Is There any 'There' There?" 149–87).

37. *New-York Gazette: or, Weekly Post-Boy,* April 27, May 4, 11, 1752; BF to Cadwallader Colden, May 14, 1752, in *PBF,* 4:310–11. For this essay, see Alfred Owen Aldridge, "Franklin's Deistical Indians," 398–410.

38. JP to BF, April 23–24, 1770, in *PBF,* 17:130–32.

39. BF to DH, September 14, 1765, ibid., 12:268; DH to BF, October 14, 1765, ibid., 319.

40. JP to BF, March 22, 1765, October 25, 1766, ibid., 89–91, 13:476.

41. Peter Timothy to BF, August 24, 1772, ibid., 19:283–84; BF to Peter Timothy, November 3, 1772, ibid., 362.

42. *Boston News-Letter,* August 9, 1753; BF to Thomas Clap, August 20, 1753, in *PBF,* 5:21–22; Alexander Colden to JP, July 28, 1755, in *PBF,* 6:113–14.

43. BF to Francis Childs, February 8, 1785, in *WoBF,* 11:8–9.

44. *PG,* April 20, 1758. Franklin believed the postal riders were underpaid. See BF to DH, April 8, 1759, in *PBF,* 8:318. On the postal system's importance to early American newspaper circulation, see Richard B. Kielbowicz, "The Press, Post Office, and Flow of News in the Early Republic"; idem, "Newsgathering by Printers Exchanges Before the Telegraph," 42–48.

45. *PG,* October 23, 1729; *Autobiography,* 94; Louis Timothee, "To all German Inhabitants of the Pennsylvania Province," *Philadelphische Zeitung,* May 6, 1732, in *PBF,* 1:230–31; [Newburyport, Mass.] *Essex Journal and Merrimack Packet,* March 1, 1775.

46. [New London, Conn.] *The Bee,* June 14, 1797; *The Hartford Gazette,* January 13, 1794; [Providence] *The American Journal,* March 18, 1779. For another example, see [Keene, N.H.] *The Rising Sun,* August 11, 1795. Allan Pred linked the flow of information during the early republic to the flow of commerce and noted that information traveled more quickly between major cities and seaports. See Allan R. Pred, *Urban Growth and the Circulation of Information: The United States System of Cities, 1790–1840.*

47. [Stonington, Conn.] *Journal of the Times,* October 10, 1798; Mathew Carey to Samuel Hall, July 14, 1788, Gardiner Collection, HSP; [Boston] *The Royal American Magazine,* January, 1774. Franklin's papers and business records contain numerous references to the *Poor Richard* almanac and its distribution. See e.g. Eddy, *Account Books;* Ledger "D" in *PBF,* 2:233–34; *Poor Richard,* 1748, ibid., 3:262n.

48. Jonathan Trumbull to BF, May 30, 1778, in *PBF,* 26:547; Simon-Pierre Fournier, February 10, 1779, ibid., 28:505; BF to Richard Bache, June 2, 1779, ibid., 29:599; Richard Bache to BF, October 22, 1778, ibid., 27:599–600.

49. BF to Elizabeth Partridge, November 25, 1788, in *WrBF*, 9:684.

50. Mark S. Granovetter, "The Strength of Weak Ties," 1360–80; idem, "The Strength of Weak Ties: A Network Theory Revisited," 105–30.

51. John R. Anderson, *Shepard Kollock: Editor for Freedom*; Richard F. Hixson, *Isaac Collins: A Quaker Printer in 18th Century America*.

52. *Autobiography*, 108.

53. Ibid.

54. "Information to Those Who Would Remove to America," 1782, in *WrBF*, 8:612.

55. Franklin enumerated moral goals at the age of twenty, when he wrote a "Plan of Conduct" while at sea. It called for frugality, honesty, sincerity, industriousness, patience, and avoidance of foolish diversions. Years later, Franklin wrote of the plan, "It is the more remarkable, as being form'd when I was so young, and yet being pretty faithfully adhered to quite thro' to old Age" ("Plan of Conduct," 1726, in *PBF*, 1:99–100; *Autobiography*, 52).

56. See e.g. Milton M. Klein, ed., *The Independent Reflector*, 57, 336–42; Alan Dyer, *A Biography of James Parker, Colonial Printer*, 31–39, 41–43.

57. *Autobiography*, 108.

58. Botein, "'Meer Mechanics' and an Open Press," 152–60; Thomas, *History of Printing in America*, 179, 182; Wetherell, "Brokers of the Word," 122–56.

59. *Autobiography*, 108. The lucrative nature of the partnerships was one—but not the foremost—of Franklin's motivations. For example, his partnership with David Hall yielded an average of 467 pounds sterling annually, more than twice the salary of Pennsylvania's chief justice. See Esmond Wright, *Franklin of Philadelphia*, 52.

60. BF to Ezra Stiles, March 9, 1790, in *WrBF*, 10:84; BF to Joseph Huey, June 6, 1753, in *PBF*, 4:506.

61. *Autobiography*, 88–89. For the connection between Franklin's printing and his religious faith, see Ralph Frasca, "Benjamin Franklin's Journalism," 60–72.

62. "A Lecture on the Providence of God in the Government of the World," n.d., in *WoBF*, 9:247; *Poor Richard*, 1740, in *PBF*, 2:252.

63. BF to Ezra Stiles, March 9, 1790, in *WrBF*, 10:84; BF to William Strahan, August 19, 1784, ibid., 9:262; "Motion for Prayers in the Convention," June 28, 1787, ibid., 600–601.

64. *Autobiography*, 80; BF to Madame Lavoisier, October 23, 1788, in *WrBF*, 9:668. In one of BF's many uses of Biblical references, he paraphrased Jesus' parable about the sower and the seed from Matt. 4:1–9, advising a correspondent, "When we can sow good Seed, we should however do it" (BF to Alexander Small, September 28, 1787, in *WrBF*, 9:615).

65. "Last Will and Testament," June 22, 1750; April 28, 1757, in *PBF*, 3:481–82, 7:204–5.

66. "A Comparison of the Conduct of the Ancient Jews and of the Anti-Federalists in the United States of America," 1788, in *WrBF*, 9:702; BF to Alexander Small, September 28, 1787, ibid., 615.

67. BF to [Thomas Paine], July 3, 1786, ibid., 520–22.

68. BF to Samuel Elbert, December 16, 1787, ibid., 626; BF to Richard Price, June 13, 1782, in *PBF,* 37:472.

69. BF to Jan Ingenhousz, June 21, 1782, in *PBF,* 35:550.

70. "An Account of the Supremest Court of Judicature in Pennsylvania, viz., The Court of the Press," [Philadelphia] *Federal Gazette,* September 12, 1789, in *WrBF,* 10:38.

71. BF to Richard Price, June 13, 1782, in *PBF,* 37:472–73.

*B*ibliography

Primary Sources

Newspapers

Connecticut

[Hartford] *Connecticut Courant*
The Hartford Gazette
[New Haven] *Connecticut Gazette*
[New London] *The Bee*
[Stonington] *Journal of the Times*

District of Columbia

[Washington] *National Intelligencer*

Maryland

[Annapolis] *Maryland Gazette*
[Baltimore] *Maryland Journal*

Massachusetts

[Boston] *Continental Journal*
Boston Gazette

[Boston] *Massachusetts Centinel*
[Boston] *Massachusetts Gazette*
[Boston] *Massachusetts Spy*
[Boston] *New-England Courant*
Boston News-Letter
[Boston] *Publick Occurrences, Both Forreign and Domestick*
[Boston] *The Columbian Centinel*
[Boston] *Weekly Rehearsal*
[Newburyport] *Essex Journal and Merrimack Packet*

New Hampshire

[Keene] *The Rising Sun*
[Portsmouth] *New-Hampshire Gazette*

New Jersey

[Woodbridge] *The Constitutional Courant*

New York

Mott and Hurtin's New-York Weekly Chronicle
[New York] *Daily Advertiser*
New York Daily Times
New-York Evening Post
New-York Gazette
New-York Gazette: or, Weekly Post-Boy
New-York Gazette, Revived in the Weekly Post-Boy
New-York Gazette and Weekly Mercury
[New York] *Independent Reflector*
New-York Journal
New-York Weekly Mercury
Parker's New-York Gazette: or, Weekly Post-Boy
Weyman's New-York Gazette

Pennsylvania

[Germantown] *Pensylvanische Berichte*
[Lancaster] *Hoch Teutsche und Englishe Zeitung*

[Philadelphia] *American Weekly Mercury*
[Philadelphia] *Aurora*
[Philadelphia] *Aurora and General Advertiser*
[Philadelphia] *Gazette of the United States*
[Philadelphia] *General Advertiser*
[Philadelphia] *Independent Gazetteer*
[Philadelphia] *Pennsylvania Chronicle*
[Philadelphia] *Pennsylvania Gazette*
[Philadelphia] *Pennsylvania Journal*
[Philadelphia] *Pennsylvania Packet*
[Philadelphia] *Pennsylvanischer Staatsbote*
Philadelphische Zeitung
[Philadelphia] *Porcupine's Gazette*
[Philadelphia] *Universal Instructor in all Arts and Sciences, and Pennsylvania Gazette*

Rhode Island

Providence Gazette
Providence Gazette; and Country Journal
[Providence] *The American Journal*

South Carolina

[Charles Town] *South-Carolina Gazette*

Vermont

Burlington Sentinel
[Rutland] *The Herald of Vermont*

Virginia

[Williamsburg] *Virginia Gazette*

West Indies

The Antigua Gazette

Magazines

[Boston] *The Royal American Magazine*
[New York] *Century Illustrated Magazine*
[Philadelphia] *The American Museum*

Diaries and Autobiographies

Bridenbaugh, Carl, ed. *Gentleman's Progress: The Itinerarium of Dr. Alexander Hamilton, 1744.* Chapel Hill: University of North Carolina Press, 1948.

Butterfield, Lyman H., ed. *Diary and Autobiography of John Adams.* 4 vols. Cambridge: Belknap Press of Harvard University Press, 1961–62.

Carey, Mathew. *Autobiography.* Brooklyn, N.Y.: Eugene L. Schwab, 1942.

Cronin, James E., ed. *The Diary of Elihu Hubbard Smith.* Philadelphia: American Philosophical Society, 1973.

Donne, John. *Devotions Upon Emergent Occasions (1624).* Edited by John Sparrow. Cambridge, England: Cambridge University Press, 1929.

Ford, Paul Leicester, ed. *The Journals of Hugh Gaine, Printer.* New York: Dodd, Mead & Company, 1902. Reprint, New York: Arno, 1970.

Lemay, J. A. Leo, and P. M. Zall, eds. *The Autobiography of Benjamin Franklin: A Genetic Text.* Knoxville: University of Tennessee Press, 1981.

Mather, Cotton. *A Christian at His Calling . . .* Boston: B. Green and F. Allen for Samuel Sewall Jr., 1701.

———. "Diary of Cotton Mather, 1709–24," August 24, December 10, 1721, *Massachusetts Historical Society Collections* 7th series, 8 (part 2 1912), 639, 663.

Thomas, M. Halsey, ed. *The Diary of Samuel Sewall, 1674–1729.* 2 vols. New York: Farrar, Straus & Giroux, 1973.

Published Collected Correspondence

Abbot, W. W., ed. *The Papers of George Washington: Presidential Series.* Charlottesville: University Press of Virginia, 1987.

Adams, Charles Francis, ed. *The Works of John Adams.* Boston: Little, Brown, 1850–56.

Bergh, Albert Ellery, ed. *The Writings of Thomas Jefferson.* 20 vols. Washington: Thomas Jefferson Memorial Association, 1904–5.

Biddle, Alexander, ed. *Old Family Letters.* Philadelphia: Lippincott, 1892.

Bigelow, John, ed. *The Works of Benjamin Franklin.* 12 vols. New York: Knickerbocker, 1904.

Boyd, Julian P., et al., eds. *The Papers of Thomas Jefferson.* 28 vols. to date. Princeton, N.J.: Princeton University Press, 1950–.

Burnett, Edmund C., ed. *Letters of Members of the Continental Congress.* 8 vols. Washington: Carnegie Institution, 1921.

Butterfield, Lyman H., ed. *Letters of Benjamin Rush.* 2 vols. Princeton: Princeton University Press, 1951.

Cadwallader Colden Letter Books. New York: New-York Historical Society Collections, 1876–77.

Chalmers, George, ed. *Political Annals of the Present United Colonies, From Their Settlement to the Peace of 1763.* London: Printed for the Author by J. Brown, 1780.

Dunlap, William. "Letter of William Dunlap, Printer," ca. 1754, HSP, in *PMHB* 22 (1898).

Fitzpatrick, John C., ed. *The Writings of George Washington.* Washington, D.C.: Government Printing Office, 1932.

Ford, Paul Leicester, ed. *The Writings of Thomas Jefferson.* 12 vols. New York: G. P. Putnam's Sons, 1892–99.

Hunt, Gaillard, ed. *The Writings of James Madison.* 9 vols. New York: G. P. Putnam's Sons, 1900–1910.

Johnston, Henry P., ed. *The Correspondence and Public Papers of John Jay.* New York: G. P. Putnam's Sons, 1890–93. Reprint, New York: Burt Franklin, 1970.

Labaree, Leonard W., ed. *Royal Instructions to British Colonial Governors, 1670–1776.* New York: Appleton-Century, 1935.

Labaree, Leonard W., et al., eds. *The Papers of Benjamin Franklin.* 37 vols. to date. New Haven: Yale University Press, 1959–.

Letters and Papers of Cadwallader Colden. New York: New-York Historical Society, 1918–37.

Lint, Gregg L., et al., eds. *Papers of John Adams.* 13 vols. Cambridge: Belknap Press of Harvard University Press, 1977–.

Morris, Richard B. *John Jay: The Winning of the Peace—Unpublished Papers, 1780–1784.* New York: Harper & Row, 1980.

Simonson, Harold P., ed. *Selected Writings of Jonathan Edwards.* New York: Ungar, 1970.

Smyth, Albert Henry, ed. *The Writings of Benjamin Franklin.* 10 vols. New York: Macmillan, 1905–7. Reprint, New York: Haskell House, 1970.

Sparks, Jared, ed. *The Works of Benjamin Franklin.* Boston: Tappan, Whittemore and Mason, 1836–40.

Syrett, Harold C., ed. *The Papers of Alexander Hamilton.* 27 vols. New York: Columbia University Press, 1961–87.

Van Doren, Carl, ed. *The Letters of Benjamin Franklin & Jane Mecom.* Princeton: Princeton University Press, 1950.

Other Published Primary Sources

Acts and Laws of Rhode Island. Newport: James Franklin, 1730.

Aristotle. *The Nichomachean Ethics.* Translated by H. Rackham. Cambridge: Harvard University Press, 1926.

Bache, Benjamin Franklin. *Proposals for Publishing a News-Paper, to be Entitled The Daily Advertiser.* Philadelphia: Benjamin Franklin Bache, 1790.

[Bache, Benjamin Franklin.] *Remarks Occasioned by the Late Conduct of Mr. Washington as President of the United States.* Philadelphia: Benjamin Franklin Bache, 1797.

Brown, Charles Brockden. *Arthur Mervyn; or, Memoirs of the Year 1793.* Philadelphia: David McKay, n.d.

Brown, Thaddeus. *An Address in Christian Love, to the Inhabitants of Philadelphia; on the Awful Dispensation of the Yellow Fever, in 1798.* Philadelphia: Robert Aitken, 1798.

Burke, Edmund, ed. *Annual Register for 1765.* 3d ed. London: Lackington, Allen, 1802.

Carey, Mathew. *A Short Account of the Malignant Fever, Lately Prevalent in Philadelphia.* Philadelphia: Mathew Carey, 1794.

[Childs, Francis.] *Letters, being the whole of the Correspondence between the Hon. John Jay, Esquire, and Mr. Lewis Littlepage.* New York: Francis Childs, 1786.

Cobbett, William. *Porcupine's Works.* 12 vols. London: William Cobbett, 1801.

Commager, Henry Steele, ed. *Documents of American History.* New York: Appleton-Century-Crofts, 1968.

Considerations on the Impropriety of Exporting Rice to Great-Britain. Charleston: Peter Timothy, 1775.

Crane, Verner W., ed. *Benjamin Franklin's Letters to the Press, 1758–1775.* Chapel Hill: University of North Carolina Press, 1950.

Emmons, Nathanael. *The Dignity of Man.* New York: Printed by J. Buel for Cornelius Davis, 1798.

[Franklin, Benjamin.] *A Narrative of the Late Massacres in Lancaster County . . .* Philadelphia: Anton Armbruster, 1764.

Goddard, William. *The Partnership: or the History of the Rise and Progress of the Pennsylvania Chronicle.* Philadelphia: William Goddard, 1770.

Howell, Thomas Bayly, comp. *A Complete Collection of State Trials to 1783*. London, 1816–28.

Letters from General Washington to Several of His Friends, In June and July, 1776. Philadelphia: Federal Press, 1795.

Mather, Cotton. *Bonifacius: An Essay Upon the Good . . .* Boston: B. Green for S. Gerrish, 1710.

Miller, Samuel. *A Brief Retrospect of the Eighteenth Century*. 2 vols. New York: T. and J. Swords, 1803. Reprint, New York: Burt Franklin, 1970.

Moxon, Joseph. *Mechanick Exercises on the Whole Art of Printing*. 2d ed. Edited by Herbert Davis and Harry Carter. London: Oxford University Press, 1962.

Mr. Ingersoll's Letters Relating to the Stamp-Act. New Haven: Samuel Green, 1766.

[Parker, James.] *A Letter to the Gentleman in the City of New-York*. New York: James Parker, 1759.

Pattee, F. L., ed. *The Poems of Philip Freneau*. Princeton: Princeton University Press, 1902.

Philadelphia College of Physicians. *Facts and Observations Relative to the Nature and Origin of the Pestilential Fever . . .* Philadelphia: Printed for Thomas Dobson, 1798.

Records of the Colony of Rhode Island and Providence Plantations, in New England. 10 vols. Providence: Knowles, Anthony, 1859.

Richardson, Samuel. *The Apprentice's Vade Mecum*. London: Samuel Richardson, 1734. Reprint, Los Angeles: The Augustan Reprint Society, 1975.

Sauer, Christopher. *Klare und Gewisse Wahrheit*. Germantown: Sauer, 1747.

Smith, William. *A Brief History of the Rise and Progress of the Charitable Scheme . . . for the Relief and Instruction of Poor Germans*. Philadelphia: Franklin & Hall, 1755.

[———.] *A Brief State of the Province of Pennsylvania . . .* London: anonymous, 1755.

[———.] *A Brief View of the Conduct of Pennsylvania. For the Year 1755*. London: anonymous, 1756.

The Scribler. Philadelphia: Anthony Armbruster, 1764.

Thomas, Isaiah. *The History of Printing in America*. Edited by Marcus A. McCorison. New York: Weathervane, 1970.

[Williamson, Hugh.] *What Is Sauce for a Goose Is Also Sauce for a Gander*. Philadelphia, 1764.

Zeugneusse der Wahrheit. Germantown: Sauer, 1747.

Secondary Sources

Books

Alexander, James. *A Brief Narrative of the Case and Trial of John Peter Zenger.* 2d ed. Cambridge: Belknap Press of Harvard University Press, 1972.

Anderson, Fred. *Crucible of War: The Seven Years' War and the Fate of Empire in British North America, 1754–1766.* New York: Knopf, 2000.

Anderson, John R. *Shepard Kollock: Editor for Freedom.* Chatham, N.J.: Chatham Historical Society, 1975.

Bagg, Moses. *The Pioneers of Utica.* Utica, N.Y.: Curtiss & Childs, 1877.

Bailyn, Bernard. *Pamphlets of the American Revolution, 1750–1776.* Cambridge: Harvard University Press, 1965.

Battle, J. H., ed. *The History of Columbia and Montour Counties, Pennsylvania.* Chicago: A. Warner, 1887.

Beall, Otho T., Jr., and Richard H. Shryock. *Cotton Mather: First Significant Figure in American Medicine.* Baltimore: The Johns Hopkins Press, 1954.

Beckles, Hilary, and Verene Shepherd, eds. *Caribbean Slave Society and Economy.* New York: New Press, 1993.

Berkowitz, Peter. *Never a Matter of Indifference: Sustaining Virtue in a Free Republic.* Palo Alto: Stanford University Press, 2003.

Biographical Dictionary of the American Congress, 1774–1971. Washington, D.C.: U.S. Government Printing Office, 1971.

Black, Jeremy. *The English Press in the Eighteenth Century.* Philadelphia: University of Pennsylvania Press, 1987.

Boorstin, Daniel. *The Americans: The Colonial Experience.* New York: Random House, 1958.

Brands, H. W. *The First American: The Life and Times of Benjamin Franklin.* New York: Random House, 2000.

Breitweiser, Mitchell Robert. *Cotton Mather and Benjamin Franklin: The Price of Representative Personality.* Cambridge, England: Cambridge University Press, 1984.

Bridenbaugh, Carl. *Cities in the Wilderness: The First Century of Urban Life in America, 1625–1742.* New York: Ronald, 1938.

Brigham, Clarence S. *History and Bibliography of American Newspapers, 1690–1820.* Worcester: American Antiquarian Society, 1947.

———. *Journals and Journeymen: A Contribution to the History of Early American Newspapers.* Philadelphia: University of Pennsylvania Press, 1950.

Bullion, John L. *A Great and Necessary Measure: George Grenville and the*

Taxation of America, 1763–1765. Columbia: University of Missouri Press, 1982.

Bushman, Richard L. *From Puritan to Character and the Social Order in Connecticut, 1690–1765.* Cambridge: Harvard University Press, 1967.

Butler, Ruth L. *Doctor Franklin, Postmaster General.* Garden City, N.Y.: Doubleday, 1928.

Campbell, James. *Recovering Benjamin Franklin.* Chicago: Open Court, 1999.

Capp, Bernard. *English Almanacs, 1500–1800: Astrology and the Popular Press.* Ithaca, N.Y.: Cornell University Press, 1979.

Clapham, John. *A Concise Economic History of Britain.* Cambridge, England: Cambridge University Press, 1951.

Clowse, Converse D. *Economic Beginnings in Colonial South Carolina, 1670–1730.* Columbia: University of South Carolina Press, 1971.

Cobbett, William, ed. *Cobbett's Parliamentary History of England . . .* London: William Cobbett, 1806–20.

Coclanis, Peter A. *The Shadow of a Dream: Economic Life and Death in the South Carolina Low Country, 1670–1920.* New York: Oxford University Press, 1989.

Cohen, Hennig. *The South Carolina Gazette.* Columbia: University of South Carolina Press, 1953.

Combs, Jerald A. *The Jay Treaty: Political Battleground of the Fathers.* Berkeley: University of California Press, 1970.

Commission on Freedom of the Press. *A Free and Responsible Press.* Chicago: University of Chicago Press, 1947.

Conner, Paul W. *Poor Richard's Politicks: Benjamin Franklin and His New American Order.* New York: Oxford University Press, 1965.

Conway, Stephen. *The British Isles and the War of American Independence.* New York: Oxford University Press, 2000.

Cook, Elizabeth Christine. *Literary Influences in Colonial Newspapers, 1704–1750.* New York: Columbia University Press, 1912.

Countryman, Edward. *A People in Revolution: The American Revolution and Political Society in New York, 1760–1790.* Baltimore: Johns Hopkins University Press, 1981.

Cundall, Frank. *A History of Printing in Jamaica from 1717 to 1834.* Kingston: Institute of Jamaica, 1935.

Davies, Margaret Gay. *The Enforcement of English Apprenticeship, 1563–1642.* Cambridge: Harvard University Press, 1956.

Davis, Richard Beale. *Intellectual Life in the Colonial South, 1585–1763.* Knoxville: University of Tennessee Press, 1978.

Davis, T. J. *A Rumor of Revolt: The "Great Negro Plot" in Colonial New York.* New York: Free Press, 1985.

DeArmond, Anna Janney. *Andrew Bradford, Colonial Journalist.* Newark: University of Delaware Press, 1949.

Douglas, Paul H. *American Apprenticeship and Industrial Education.* New York: Columbia University Press, 1921.

Duniway, Clyde Augustus. *The Development of Freedom of the Press in Massachusetts.* New York: Longmans, Green, 1906.

Dunlop, O. Jocelyn, and Richard Denman. *English Apprenticeship and Child Labour: A History.* London: T. Fisher Unwin, 1912.

Dunn, Richard S., and Gary B. Nash. *Sugar and Slaves: The Rise of the Planter Class in the English West Indies, 1624–1713.* Chapel Hill: University of North Carolina Press, 2000.

Dyer, Alan. *A Biography of James Parker, Colonial Printer.* Troy, N.Y.: Whitston, 1982.

Eddy, George Simpson. *Account Books Kept by Benjamin Franklin: Ledger "D," 1739–1747.* New York: Columbia University Press, 1929.

Eldridge, Larry. *A Distant Heritage: The Growth of Free Speech in Early America.* New York: New York University Press, 1994.

Fay, Bernard. *Franklin: The Apostle of Modern Times.* Boston: Little, Brown, 1929.

Febvre, Lucien, and Henri-Jean Martin. *The Coming of the Book.* London: NLB, 1976.

Fogleman, Aaron Spencer. *Hopeful Journeys: German Immigration, Settlement, and Political Culture in Colonial America, 1717–1775.* Philadelphia: University of Pennsylvania Press, 1996.

Foner, Eric. *Tom Paine and Revolutionary America.* New York: Oxford University Press, 1976.

Ford, Paul Leicester. *Who Was the Mother of Franklin's Son?* New Rochelle, N.Y.: Walpole, 1932.

Ford, Worthington C. *Broadsides, Ballads &c. Printed in Massachusetts, 1639–1800.* Boston: Massachusetts Historical Society, 1922.

Fowler, David C. *A Literary History of the Popular Ballad.* Durham, N.C.: Duke University Press, 1968.

Frank, Joseph. *The Beginnings of the English Newspaper, 1620–1660.* Cambridge: Harvard University Press, 1961.

Freeman, Joanne B. *Affairs of Honor: National Politics in the New Republic.* New Haven: Yale University Press, 2001.

Gaspar, David B. *Bondsmen and Rebels: A Study of Master-Slave Relations in Antigua.* Durham, N.C.: Duke University Press, 1993.

George, Albert J. *The Didot Family and the Progress of Printing.* Syracuse, N.Y.: Syracuse University Press, 1961.

Gerlach, Larry L. *Prologue to Independence: New Jersey in the Coming of the American Revolution.* New Brunswick, N.J.: Rutgers University Press, 1976.

Goodenough, Florence L. *Anger in Young Children.* Minneapolis: University of Minnesota Press, 1931.

Greene, Jack P., et al., eds. *Money, Trade, and Power: The Evolution of Colonial South Carolina's Plantation Society.* Columbia: University of South Carolina Press, 2000.

Hall, Max. *Benjamin Franklin and Polly Baker: The History of a Literary Deception.* Chapel Hill: University of North Carolina Press, 1960.

Haythornthwaite, Philip J. *The Colonial Wars Source Book.* London: Arms & Armour, 1996.

Hixson, Richard F. *Isaac Collins: A Quaker Printer in 18th Century America.* New Brunswick, N.J.: Rutgers University Press, 1968.

Hoermann, Alfred. *Cadwallader Colden: A Figure of the American Enlightenment.* Westport, Conn.: Greenwood, 2002.

Huang, Nian-Sheng. *Benjamin Franklin in American Thought and Culture, 1790–1990.* Philadelphia: American Philosophical Society, 1994.

———. *Franklin's Father Josiah: Life of a Colonial Boston Tallow Chandler, 1657–1745.* Philadelphia: American Philosophical Society, 2000.

Hudak, Leona M. *Early American Women Printers and Publishers, 1639–1820.* Metuchen, N.J.: Scarecrow, 1978.

Hunter, Dard. *Papermaking: The History and Technique of an Ancient Craft.* 2d ed. New York: Knopf, 1957.

Hutson, James H. *Pennsylvania Politics, 1746–1770.* Princeton, New Jersey: Princeton University Press, 1972.

Isaacson, Walter. *Benjamin Franklin: An American Life.* New York: Simon & Schuster, 2003.

Kielbowicz, Richard B. *News in the Mail: The Press, Post Office, and Public Information, 1700–1860s.* New York: Greenwood, 1989.

Klein, Milton M., ed. *The Independent Reflector.* Cambridge: Belknap Press of Harvard University Press, 1963.

Lathem, Edward Connery. *Chronological Tables of American Newspapers, 1690–1820.* Barre, Mass.: American Antiquarian Society, 1972.

Laws, G. Malcolm, Jr. *The British Literary Ballad.* Carbondale: Southern Illinois University Press, 1972.

LeBon, Gustave. *The Crowd.* New York: Viking, 1960.

Lee, Alfred M. *The Daily Newspaper in America.* New York: Macmillan, 1937.

Lemay, J. A. Leo. *Ebenezer Kinnersley: Franklin's Friend.* Philadelphia: University of Pennsylvania Press, 1964.

———. *The Canon of Benjamin Franklin, 1722–1776.* Newark: University of Delaware Press, 1986.

Lenman, Bruce P. *Britain's Colonial Wars, 1688–1783.* Harlow, England: Longman, 2000.

Leonard, Thomas C. *The Power of the Press: The Birth of American Political Reporting.* New York: Oxford University Press, 1986.

Levy, Leonard W. *Emergence of a Free Press.* New York: Oxford University Press, 1985.

———. *Freedom of Speech and Press in Early American History: A Legacy of Suppression.* New York: Harper & Row, 1963.

Livingston, Luther S. *Franklin and His Press at Passy.* New York: Grolier Club, 1914.

Lockridge, Kenneth A. *Literacy in Colonial New England: An Enquiry into the Social Context of Literacy in the Early Modern West.* New York: Norton, 1974.

Longenecker, Stephen L. *The Christopher Sauers: Courageous Printers Who Defended Religious Freedom in Early America.* Elgin, Ill.: Brethren Press, 1981.

Lopez, Claude-Anne. *Mon Cher Papa: Franklin and the Ladies of Paris.* Rev. ed. New Haven: Yale University Press, 1990.

Lopez, Claude-Anne, and Eugenia Herbert. *The Private Franklin: The Man and His Family.* New York: Norton, 1975.

Lorenz, Alfred Lawrence. *Hugh Gaine: Colonial Printer-Editor's Odyssey to Loyalism.* Carbondale: Southern Illinois University Press, 1972.

Mann, Bruce H. *Neighbors and Strangers: Law and Community in Early Connecticut.* Chapel Hill: University of North Carolina Press, 2001.

Martin, Robert W. T. *The Free and Open Press: The Founding of American Democratic Press Liberty, 1640–1800.* New York: New York University Press, 2001.

Maslen, K. I. D. and J. Lancaster. *The Bowyer Ledgers: The Printing Accounts of William Bowyer, Father and Son, Reproduced on Microfiche, with a Checklist of Bowyer Printing, 1699–1777.* New York: Bibliographical Society of America, 1991.

Mayo, Bernard. *Henry Clay, Spokesman of the New West.* Boston: Houghton Mifflin, 1937.

McCrady, Edward. *The History of South Carolina Under the Royal Government, 1719–1776.* New York: Macmillan, 1899.

McMurtrie, Douglas C. *A History of Printing in the United States.* 4 vols. New York: Bowker, 1936.

———. *Early Printing on the Island of Antigua.* Evanston, Ill.: privately printed, 1943.

———. *The First Printing in Dominica.* London: privately printed, 1932.

Middlekauff, Robert. *The Glorious Cause: The American Revolution, 1763–1789.* New York: Oxford University Press, 1982.

Miller, Neal E., and John Dollard. *Social Learning and Imitation.* New Haven: Yale University Press, 1941.

Miner, Ward L. *William Goddard, Newspaperman.* Durham, N.C.: Duke University Press, 1962.

Monaghan, Frank. *John Jay: Defender of Liberty.* New York: Bobbs-Merrill, 1935.

Morgan, David T. *The Devious Dr. Franklin, Colonial Agent.* Macon, Ga.: Mercer University Press, 1996.

Morgan, Edward S., and Helen M. Morgan. *The Stamp Act Crisis: Prologue to Revolution.* Chapel Hill: University of North Carolina Press, 1953.

Morgan, Kenneth, and Maurice Kirby, eds. *Slavery, Atlantic Trade and the British Economy, 1660–1800.* Cambridge, England: Cambridge University Press, 2001.

Morris, Richard B. *Government and Labor in Early America.* New York: Columbia University Press, 1946.

Morse, Jarvis Means. *Connecticut Newspapers in the Eighteenth Century.* New Haven: Yale University Press, 1935.

Mott, Frank L. *American Journalism: A History.* 3d ed. New York: Macmillan, 1962.

———. *A History of American Magazines, 1741–1850.* Cambridge: Harvard University Press, 1930.

Nash, Gary B. *The Urban Crucible.* Cambridge: Harvard University Press, 1979.

Nef, John U. *Industry and Government in France and England, 1540–1640.* Ithaca, N.Y.: Cornell University Press, 1964.

Newcomb, Benjamin H. *Franklin and Galloway: A Political Partnership.* New Haven: Yale University Press, 1972.

Nolt, Steven M. *Foreigners in Their Own Land: Pennsylvania Germans in the Early Republic.* University Park: Pennsylvania State University Press, 2002.

Nord, David Paul. *Communities of Journalism: A History of American Newspapers and Their Readers.* Urbana: University of Illinois Press, 2001.

Oswald, John Clyde. *Benjamin Franklin, Printer.* New York: Doubleday, Page, 1917.

Pactor, Howard S., comp. *Colonial British Caribbean Newspapers: A Bibliography and Directory.* New York: Greenwood, 1990.

Pasley, Jeffrey L. *The Tyranny of Printers: Newspaper Politics in the Early American Republic.* Charlottesville: University of Virginia Press, 2001.

Pottinger, David T. *The French Book Trade in the Ancien Regime.* Cambridge: Harvard University Press, 1958.

Powell, J. H. *Bring Out Your Dead: The Great Plague of Yellow Fever in Philadelphia in 1793.* Philadelphia: University of Pennsylvania Press, 1949.

Pred, Allan R. *Urban Growth and the Circulation of Information: The United States System of Cities, 1790–1840.* Cambridge: Harvard University Press, 1973.

Reichmann, Felix. *Christopher Sower, Sr.* Philadelphia: Carl Schurz, 1943.

Rich, Wesley E. *The History of the United States Post Office to the Year 1829.* Cambridge: Harvard University Press, 1924.

Roeber, A. G. *Palatines, Liberty, and Prosperity: German Lutherans in Colonial British America.* Baltimore: Johns Hopkins University Press, 1993.

Rorabaugh, W. J. *The Craft Apprentice: From Franklin to the Machine Age in America.* New York: Oxford University Press, 1986.

Rosenfeld, Richard N. *American Aurora: A Democratic-Republican Returns.* New York: St. Martin's, 1997.

Russell, David Lee. *The American Revolution in the Southern Colonies.* Jefferson, N.C.: MacFarland, 2000.

Salinger, Sharon V. *"To Serve Well and Faithfully": Labor and Indentured Servants in Pennsylvania, 1682–1800.* Cambridge, England: Cambridge University Press, 1987.

Sandiford, Keith A. *The Cultural Politics of Sugar: Caribbean Slavery and Narratives of Colonialism.* Cambridge, England: Cambridge University Press, 2000.

Scharff, John T., and Thompson Westcott. *History of Philadelphia 1609–1884.* 3 vols. Philadelphia: L. H. Everts, 1884.

Schiffer, Michael B., and Carrie L. Bell. *Draw the Lightning Down: Benjamin Franklin and Electrical Technology in the Age of Enlightenment.* Berkeley: University of California Press, 2003.

Schlesinger, Arthur M. *Prelude to Independence: The Newspaper War on Britain, 1764–1776.* New York: Knopf, 1971.

Seavey, Ormond. *Becoming Benjamin Franklin: The Autobiography and the Life.* University Park: Pennsylvania State University Press, 1988.

Seidensticker, Oswald. *The First Century of German Printing in America, 1728–1830.* Philadelphia: Schaefer & Koradi, 1893.

Selesky, Harold. *Fighting Colonists: War and Society in Connecticut, 1635–1775.* New Haven: Yale University Press, 1989.

Siebert, Frederick S. *Freedom of the Press in England, 1476–1776.* Urbana: University of Illinois Press, 1952.

Siebert, Frederick S., Theodore Peterson, and Wilbur Schramm. *Four Theories of the Press.* Urbana: University of Illinois Press, 1956.

Sirmans, M. Eugene. *Colonial South Carolina: A Political History, 1663–1763.* Chapel Hill: University of North Carolina Press, 1966.

Smith, Billy G. *The "Lower Sort": Philadelphia's Laboring People, 1750–1800.* Ithaca, N.Y.: Cornell University Press, 1990.

Smith, Jeffery A. *Franklin & Bache: Envisioning the Enlightened Republic.* New York: Oxford University Press, 1990.

———. *Printers and Press Freedom: The Ideology of Early American Journalism.* New York: Oxford University Press, 1988.

Stahr, Walter. *John Jay: Founding Father.* London: Hambledon and London, 2005.

Steele, Ian K. *The English Atlantic, 1675–1740: An Exploration of Communication and Community.* New York: Oxford University Press, 1986.

Stuart, I. L., ed. *History of Franklin County, Iowa.* Vol. 1. Chicago: S. J. Clarke, 1914.

Tagg, James. *Benjamin Franklin Bache and the Philadelphia Aurora.* Philadelphia: University of Pennsylvania Press, 1991.

Treese, Lorett. *The Storm Gathering: The Penn Family and the American Revolution.* Mechanicsburg, Pa.: Stackpole, 2002.

Tucker, Tom. *Bolt of Fate: Benjamin Franklin and His Electric Kite Hoax.* New York: Public Affairs, 2003.

Van Doren, Carl. *Benjamin Franklin.* New York: Viking, 1938.

Wade, Richard C. *The Urban Frontier: The Rise of Western Cities, 1790–1830.* Cambridge: Harvard University Press, 1959.

Waldrup, Carole Chandler. *More Colonial Women: 25 Pioneers of Early America.* Jefferson, N.C.: MacFarland, 2004.

Wallace, John William. *An Old Philadelphian: Colonel William Bradford, the Patriot Printer of 1776.* Philadelphia: Sherman, 1884.

Wallace, Paul A. W. *Conrad Weiser: Friend of Colonist and Mohawk.* New York: Russell & Russell, 1971.

Walters, Kerry S. *Benjamin Franklin and His Gods.* Urbana: University of Illinois Press, 1999.

Ward, Harry M. *"Unite or Die:" Intercolony Relations, 1690–1763.* Port Washington, N.Y.: Kennikat, 1971.

Warner, Michael. *The Letters of the Republic: Publication and the Public Sphere in Eighteenth-Century America.* Cambridge: Harvard University Press, 1990.

Webster, Phil. *Can a Chief Justice Love God? The Life of John Jay.* Bloomington, Ind.: Authorhouse, 2002.

Williams, Samuel Cole. *History of the Lost State of Franklin.* Rev. ed. Philadelphia: Porcupine Press, 1974.

Winslow, Ola Elizabeth. *Samuel Sewall of Boston.* New York: Macmillan, 1964.

Winston, Sanford. *Illiteracy in the United States.* Chapel Hill: University of North Carolina Press, 1930.

Wittke, Carl. *The German-Language Press in America.* Lexington: University of Kentucky Press, 1957.

Wolf, Edwin, II. *"At the Instance of Benjamin Franklin": A Brief History of the Library Company of Philadelphia, 1731–1976.* Philadelphia: Library Company of Philadelphia, 1976.

Wright, Esmond. *Franklin of Philadelphia.* Cambridge: Belknap Press of Harvard University Press, 1986.

————, ed. *Benjamin Franklin: His Life as He Wrote It.* Cambridge: Harvard University Press, 1990.

Wroth, Lawrence C. *The Colonial Printer.* New York: Grolier, 1931. Rev. ed. Charlottesville: University of Virginia Press, 1964.

Zall, Paul M. *Franklin on Franklin.* Lexington: University Press of Kentucky, 2000.

Book Chapters

Adams, Willi Paul. "The Colonial German-Language Press and the American Revolution." In *The Press & the American Revolution.* Edited by Bernard Bailyn and John B. Hench. Worcester, Mass.: American Antiquarian Society, 1980.

Eberhard, Wallace B. "Press and Post Office in Eighteenth-Century America: Origins of a Public Policy." In *Newsletters to Newspapers: Eighteenth-Century Journalism.* Edited by Donovan H. Bond and W. Reynolds McLeod. Morgantown: School of Journalism, West Virginia University, 1977.

Granger, Bruce I. "Franklin as Press Agent in England." In *The Oldest Revolutionary: Essays on Benjamin Franklin.* Edited by J. A. Leo Lemay. Philadelphia: University of Pennsylvania Press, 1976.

Granovetter, Mark S. "The Strength of Weak Ties: A Network Theory Revisited." In *Social Structure and Network Analysis.* Edited by Peter V. Marsden and Nan Lin. Beverly Hills: Sage, 1982.

Lemay, J. A. Leo. "The Text, Rhetorical Strategies, and Themes of 'The Speech of Miss Polly Baker.'" In *The Oldest Revolutionary: Essays on Benjamin Franklin.* Edited by J. A. Leo Lemay. Philadelphia: University of Pennsylvania Press, 1976.

Macaulay, Stewart. "Private Government." In *Law and the Social Sciences.* Edited by Leon Lipson and Stanton Wheeler. New York: Russell Sage, 1986.

Mancall, Peter C., et al. "Conjectural Estimates of Economic Growth in the Lower South, 1720–1800." In *History Matters: Essays on Economic Growth, Technology, and Demographic Change.* Edited by Timothy W. Guinnane, et al. Palo Alto: Stanford University Press, 2004.

Menzel, Emil W., Jr. "General Discussion of the Methodological Problems Involved in the Study of Social Interaction." In *Social Interaction Analysis: Methodological Issues.* Edited by Michael E. Lamb, et al. Madison: University of Wisconsin Press, 1979.

Nickels, Cameron C. "Franklin's Poor Richard's Almanacs: 'The Humblest of his Labors.'" In *The Oldest Revolutionary: Essays on Benjamin Franklin.* Edited by J. A. Leo Lemay. Philadelphia: University of Pennsylvania Press, 1976.

Skemp, Sheila. "Family Partnerships: The Working Wife, Honoring Deborah Franklin." In *Benjamin Franklin and Women.* Edited by Larry E. Tise. University Park: Pennsylvania State University Press, 2000.

Smith, Willam. "An Introduction to the Study of Rhetoric." In Dennis Barone, "An Introduction to William Smith and Rhetoric at the College of Philadelphia." *Proceedings of the American Philosophical Society* 134, no. 2 (1990): 111–60.

Stiverson, Cynthia A., and Gregory A. Stiverson. "The Colonial Retail Book Trade: Availability and Affordability of Reading Material in Mid-Eighteenth Century Virginia." In *Printing and Society in Early America.* Edited by William L. Joyce, et al. Worcester, Mass.: American Antiquarian Society, 1983.

Walett, Francis G. "The Impact of the Stamp Act on the Colonial Press." In *Newsletters to Newspapers: Eighteenth-Century Journalism.* Edited by Donovan H. Bond and W. Reynolds McLeod. Morgantown: School of Journalism, West Virginia University, 1977.

Journal Articles

Aldridge, Alfred Owen. "Franklin's Deistical Indians." *Proceedings of the American Philosophical Society* 94 (August 1950): 398–410.

Baker, Ira L. "Elizabeth Timothy: America's First Woman Editor." *Journalism Quarterly* 54 (Summer 1977): 280–85.

Baker, Jennifer Jordan. "Franklin's Autobiography and the Credibility of Personality." *Early American Literature* 35, no. 3 (2000): 274–93.

Barone, Dennis. "An Introduction to William Smith and Rhetoric at the College of Philadelphia." *Proceedings of the American Philosophical Society* 134, no. 2 (1990): 111–60.

Bell, Whitfield. "Benjamin Franklin and the German Charity Schools." *Proceedings of the American Philosophical Society* 99, no. 6 (1955): 381–87.

Berger, Sidney E. "Innovation and Diversity Among the Green Family of Printers." *Printing History* 12, no. 1 (1990): 2–20.

Blake, John B. "The Inoculation Controversy in Boston: 1721–22." *New England Quarterly* 25 (December 1952): 489–506.

Blasi, Vincent. "The Checking Value in First Amendment Theory." *American Bar Foundation Research Journal* (Summer 1977): 521–649.

Bloore, Stephen. "Samuel Keimer: A Footnote to the Life of Franklin." *PMHB* 54 (July 1930): 255–87.

Bonomi, Patricia U. "New York: The Royal Colony." *New York History* 82 (Winter 2001): 5–24.

Bosco, Ronald A. "'He that best understands the World, least likes it': The Dark Side of Benjamin Franklin." *PMHB* 111 (October 1987): 525–54.

Botein, Stephen. "'Meer Mechanics' and an Open Press: The Business and Political Strategies of Colonial Printers." *Perspectives in American History* 9 (1975): 127–225.

Brown, Jerald E. "'It Facilitated the Correspondence': The Post, Postmasters and Newspaper Publishing in Colonial America." *Retrospection* 2, no. 1 (1989): 1–15.

Burnard, Trevor. "Inheritance and Independence: Women's Status in Early Colonial Jamaica." *WMQ* 48 (January 1991): 91–113.

Burton, John D. "'The Awful Judgements of God Upon the Land': Smallpox in Colonial Cambridge, Massachusetts." *New England Quarterly* 74 (September 2001): 495–506.

———. "John Adams and the Problem of Virtue." *Journal of the Early Republic* 21 (Fall 2001): 393–412.

Carlson, C. Lennart. "Samuel Keimer: A Study in the Transit of English Culture to Colonial Pennsylvania." *PMHB* 61 (October 1937): 357–86.

Carr, Lois Green, and Lorena S. Walsh. "The Planter's Wife: The Experience of White Women in Seventeenth-Century Maryland." *WMQ* 34 (October 1977): 542–71.

Charles, Joseph. "The Jay Treaty: The Origins of the American Party System." *WMQ* 12 (October 1955): 581–630.

Chinard, Gilbert. "The Apotheosis of Benjamin Franklin." *Proceedings of the American Philosophical Society* 99, no. 6 (1955): 440–73.

Christensen, Merton A. "Franklin on the Hemphill Trial: Deism versus Presbyterian Orthodoxy." *WMQ* 10 (July 1953): 422–40.

Clark, Charles E., and Charles Wetherell. "The Measure of Maturity: The *Pennsylvania Gazette,* 1728–1765." *WMQ* 46 (April 1989): 279–303.

Coclanis, Peter. "The Lightning-Rod Man: Franklin of Philadelphia." *Business History Review* 61 (Winter 1987): 615–22.

Cohen, Norman S. "The Philadelphia Election Riot of 1742." *PMHB* 92 (July 1968): 306–19.

Crane, Verner W. "Benjamin Franklin and the Stamp Act." *Transactions of the Colonial Society of Massachusetts* 82 (February 1934): 56–77.

Cundall, Frank. "The Press and Printers of Jamaica Prior to 1820." *Proceedings of the American Antiquarian Society* 26 (October 1916): 290–412.

de Wetering, Maxine. "A Reconsideration of the Inoculation Controversy." *New England Quarterly* 58 (March 1985): 46–67.

Duffy, John. "Eighteenth Century Carolina Health Conditions." *Journal of Southern History* 18 (August 1952): 289–302.

———. "Yellow Fever in Colonial Charleston." *South Carolina Historical Magazine* 52 (October 1951): 189–97.

Durnbaugh, Donald F. "Christopher Sauer, Pennsylvania-German Printer." *PMHB* 82 (July 1958): 316–40.

———. "The Sauer Family: An American Printing Dynasty." *Yearbook of German-American Studies* 23 (1988): 31–40.

———. "Was Christopher Sauer a Dunker?" *PMHB* 93 (July 1969): 383–91.

Eames, Wilberforce. "The Antigua Press and Benjamin Mecom, 1748–1765." *Proceedings of the American Antiquarian Society* 38 (October 1928): 303–48.

Endres, Kathleen L. "Ownership and Employment in Specialized Business Press." *Journalism Quarterly* 65 (Winter 1988): 996–98.

Estes, Todd. "Shaping the Politics of Public Opinion: Federalists and the Jay Treaty Debate." *Journal of the Early Republic* 20 (Fall 2000): 393–422.

Evans, William B. "John Adams' Opinion of Benjamin Franklin." *PMHB* 92 (April 1968): 220–38.

Fiering, Norman S. "Benjamin Franklin and the Way to Virtue." *American Quarterly* 30 (Summer 1978): 199–223.

Fogleman, Aaron Spencer. "Jesus Is Female: The Moravian Challenge in the German Communities of British North America." *WMQ* 60 (April 2003): 295–332.

Ford, Margaret Lane. "A Widow's Work: Ann Franklin of Newport, Rhode Island." *Printing History* 12, no. 2 (1990): 15–26. ·

Frantz, John. "Franklin and the Pennsylvania Germans." *Pennsylvania History* 65 (Winter 1998): 21–34.

Frasca, Ralph. "'At the Sign of the Bribe Refused': The *Constitutional Courant* and the Stamp Tax, 1765." *New Jersey History* 107 (Fall–Winter 1989): 21–39.

———. "Benjamin Franklin's Journalism." *Fides et Historia* 29 (Winter/Spring 1997): 60–72.

———. "Benjamin Franklin's Printing Network." *American Journalism* 5, no. 3 (1988): 145–58.

———. "From Apprentice to Journeyman to Partner: Benjamin Franklin's Workers and the Growth of the Early American Printing Trade." *PMHB* 114 (April 1990): 229–48.

———. "'The Glorious Publick Virtue So Predominant in Our Rising Country': Benjamin Franklin's Printing Network During the Revolutionary Era." *American Journalism* 13 (Winter 1996): 21–37.

Fry, Jennifer Reed. "'Extraordinary Freedom and Great Humility': A Reinterpretation of Deborah Franklin." *PMHB* 127 (April 2003): 167–96.

Gayle, Charles Joseph. "The Nature and Volume of Exports from Charleston, 1724–1774." *Proceedings of the South Carolina Historical Association* (1937): 25–33.

Gleason, J. Philip. "A Scurrilous Colonial Election and Franklin's Reputation." *WMQ* 18 (January 1961): 68–84.

Gleason, Philip. "Trouble in the Colonial Melting Pot." *Journal of American Ethnic History* 20 (Fall 2000): 3–17.

Granovetter, Mark S. "The Strength of Weak Ties." *American Journal of Sociology* 78, no. 6 (1979): 1360–80.

Greene, Jack P. "Society and Economy in the British Caribbean during the Seventeenth and Eighteenth Centuries." *American Historical Review* 79 (December 1974): 1499–1517.

Grubb, Farley. "The Market Structure of Shipping German Immigrants to Colonial America." *PMHB* 111 (January 1987): 27–48.

Harlan, Robert D. "David Hall and the Stamp Act." *The Papers of the Bibliographical Society of America* 61 (1967): 13–37.

Hecht, Arthur. "Pennsylvania Postal History of the Eighteenth Century." *Pennsylvania History* 30 (October 1963): 420–42.

Heiges, George. "Benjamin Franklin in Lancaster County." *Journal of the Lancaster County Historical Society* 61, no. 1 (1957): 1–26.

Henry, Susan. "Sarah Goddard, Gentlewoman Printer." *Journalism Quarterly* 57 (Spring 1980): 23–30.

Jehlen, Myra. "'Imitate Jesus and Socrates': The Making of a Good American." *South Atlantic Quarterly* 89 (Summer 1990): 501–24.

Jorgenson, Chester E. "A Brand Flung at Colonial Orthodoxy: Samuel Keimer's *Universal Instructor in All Arts and Sciences.*" *Journalism Quarterly* 12 (September 1935): 272–77.

Kenny, Robert W. "James Ralph: An Eighteenth-Century Philadelphian in Grub Street." *PMHB* 64 (April 1940): 218–42.

Ketcham, Ralph. "Benjamin Franklin and William Smith: New Light on an Old Philadelphia Quarrel." *PMHB* 88 (April 1964): 142–69.

Kielbowicz, Richard B. "Newsgathering by Printers Exchanges Before the Telegraph." *Journalism History* 9 (Summer 1982): 42–48.

———. "The Press, Post Office, and Flow of News in the Early Republic." *Journal of the Early Republic* 3 (Fall 1983): 255–80.

Kiessel, William C. "The Green Family: A Dynasty of Printers." *The New England Historical and Genealogical Register* 54 (April 1950): 81–93.

King, Marion R. "One Link in the First Newspaper Chain: The *South Carolina Gazette.*" *Journalism Quarterly* 9 (Spring 1932): 257–68.

Kloppenburg, James T. "The Virtues of Liberalism: Christianity, Republicanism, and Ethics in Early American Political Discourse." *Journal of American History* 74 (June 1987): 9–33.

Larson, David M. "Franklin on the Nature of Man and the Possibility of Virtue." *Early American Literature* 10 (Fall 1975): 118.

Lawson, Philip. "George Grenville and America: The Years of Opposition, 1765 to 1770." *WMQ* 37 (October 1980): 561–76.

Lemay, J. A. Leo. "Franklin's Suppressed 'Busy-Body.'" *American Literature* 37 (November 1965): 307–11.

Leonard, Thomas. "Recovering 'Wretched Stuff' and the Franklins' Synergy." *The New England Quarterly* 72 (September 1999): 444–55.

Macaulay, Stewart. "Law and the Behavioral Sciences: Is There any 'There' There?" *Law and Policy* 6 (April 1984): 149–87.

McAnear, Beverly. "James Parker versus John Holt," part 1. *Proceedings of the New Jersey Historical Society* 59 (April 1941): 77–95.

———. "James Parker versus John Holt," part 2. *Proceedings of the New Jersey Historical Society* 59 (July 1941): 198–212.

————. "James Parker versus New York Province." *New York History* 22 (1941): 321–30.

————. "James Parker versus William Weyman." *Proceedings of the New Jersey Historical Society* 59 (January 1941): 1–23.

McMurtrie, Douglas C. "The Green Family Printers." *Americana* 26 (July 1932): 364–75.

Miles, Richard D. "The American Image of Benjamin Franklin." *American Quarterly* 9 (Summer 1957): 117–43.

Minkema, Kenneth P. "Old Age and Religion in the Writings and Life of Jonathan Edwards." *Church History* 70 (December 2001): 674–704.

Morgan, David T. "Benjamin Franklin: Champion of Generic Religion." *Historian* 62 (Summer 2000): 723–29.

Nash, Gary B. "Slaves and Slaveowners in Colonial Philadelphia." *WMQ* 90 (April 1973): 225–56.

Newcomb, Theodore. "An Approach to the Study of Communication Acts." *Psychological Review* 60 (November 1953): 393–404.

Oldham, Ellen M. "Early Women Printers of America." *The Boston Public Library Quarterly* 10 (January 1958): 6–26.

Olsen, Alison. "The Zenger Case Revisited: Satire, Sedition, and Political Debate in Eighteenth-Century America." *Early American Literature* 35, no. 3 (2000): 223–45.

Olson, Lester C. "Benjamin Franklin's Pictorial Representations of the British Colonies in America: A Study in Rhetorical Iconology." *Quarterly Journal of Speech* 73 (February 1987): 18–42.

Pardoe, Elizabeth Lewis. "Poor Children and Enlightened Citizens: Lutheran Education in America, 1748–1800." *Pennsylvania History* 68 (Spring 2001): 162–201.

Rabban, David A. "The Ahistorical Historian: Leonard Levy on Freedom of Expression in Early American History." *Stanford Law Review* 37 (February 1985): 795–856.

Randolph, J. Ralph. "The End of Impartiality: *South-Carolina Gazette*, 1763–75." *Journalism Quarterly* 49 (Winter 1972): 702–9, 720.

Rogers, Deborah D. "The Commercialization of Eighteenth-Century Literature." *Clio* 18 (Winter 1989): 171–78.

Rosemont, Henry. "Benjamin Franklin and the Philadelphia Typographical Strikers of 1786." *Labor History* 22 (Summer 1981): 398–429.

Salley, A. S. "The First Presses of South Carolina." *Proceedings and Papers of the Bibliographical Society of America* 2 (1907–8): 28–69.

Scherr, Arthur. "'Vox Populi' versus the Patriot President: Benjamin Franklin

Bache's Philadelphia *Aurora* and John Adams (1797)." *Pennsylvania History* 62 (Fall 1995): 503–21.

Schlesinger, Arthur M. "Political Mobs and the American Revolution, 1765–1776." *Proceedings of the American Philosophical Society* 99, no. 4 (1955): 244–50.

Scott, John Thomas. "On God's Side: The Problem of Submission in American Revolutionary Rhetoric." *Fides et Historia* 34 (Winter/Spring 2002): 111–22.

Shalhope, Robert E. "Republicanism and Early American Historiography." *WMQ* 39 (April 1982): 334–56.

———. "Toward a Republican Synthesis: The Emergence of an Understanding of Republicanism in American Historiography." *WMQ* 29 (January 1972): 49–80.

Shilstone, Eustace M. "Some Notes on Early Printing Presses and Newspapers in Barbados." *The Journal of the Barbados Museum and Historical Society* 26 (November 1958): 27–29.

Slaughter, Thomas P. "Crowds in Eighteenth-Century America: Reflections and New Directions." *PMHB* 115 (January 1991): 3–14.

Smith, Billy G. "The Material Lives of Laboring Philadelphians, 1750 to 1800." *WMQ* 38 (April 1981): 163–202.

Smith, Carol. "Taking Stock, Placing Orders: A Historiographic Essay on the Business History of the Newspaper." *Journalism Monographs* 132 (April 1992).

Smith, Jeffery A. "Impartiality and Revolutionary Ideology: Editorial Policies of the *South-Carolina Gazette,* 1732–1775." *Journal of Southern History* 49 (November 1983): 511–26.

Steele, Ian K. "Origins of Boston's Revolutionary Declaration of 18 April 1689." *New England Quarterly* 62 (March 1989): 75–81.

———. "Time, Communications, and Society: The English Atlantic, 1702." *Journal of American Studies* 8 (April 1974): 1–21.

Stephens, Mitchell. "Sensationalism and Moralizing in 16th and 17th Century Newsbooks and News Ballads." *Journalism History* 12 (Autumn–Winter 1985): 92–95.

Stewart, Robert K. "Jacksonians Discipline a Party Editor: Economic Leverage and Political Exile." *Journalism Quarterly* 66 (Autumn 1989): 591–99.

Swan, Bradford F. "A Checklist of Early Printing on the Island of Antigua." *Papers of the Bibliographical Society of America* 50 (3d quarter 1956): 285–92.

Teeter, Dwight L., Jr. "John Dunlap: The Political Economy of a Printer's Success." *Journalism Quarterly* 52 (Spring 1975): 3–8, 55.

Thompson, E. P. "Time, Work-Discipline, and Industrial Capitalism." *Past and Present* 38 (December 1967): 56–97.

Thompson, Mack. "Massachusetts and New York Stamp Acts." *WMQ* 26 (April 1969): 253–58.

Tolles, Frederick B. "Benjamin Franklin's Business Mentors: The Philadelphia Quaker Merchants." *WMQ* 2 (April 1945): 60–69.

Turnbull, Mary D. "William Dunlap, Colonial Printer, Journalist, and Minister." *PMHB* 103 (April 1979): 143–65.

Wehtje, Myron F. "The Ideal of Virtue in Post-Revolutionary Boston." *Historical Journal of Massachusetts* 17 (Winter 1989): 67–83.

Weintraub, Karl J. "The Puritan Ethic and Benjamin Franklin." *Journal of Religion* 56 (July 1976): 223–37.

Wendel, Thomas. "The Keith-Lloyd Alliance: Factional and Coalition Politics in Colonial Pennsylvania." *PMHB* 92 (July 1968): 289–305.

Wetherell, Charles W. "'For These or Such Like Reasons': John Holt's Attack on Benjamin Franklin." *Proceedings of the American Antiquarian Society* 88 (part 2 1978): 251–75.

Wilson, C. Edward. "The Boston Inoculation Controversy: A Revisionist Interpretation." *Journalism History* 7 (Spring 1980): 16–19, 40.

Winton, Calhoun. "The Colonial South Carolina Book Trade." *Proofs* 2 (1972): 71–87.

Wokeck, Marianne S. "The Flow and Composition of German Immigration to Philadelphia, 1727–1775." *PMHB* 105 (July 1981): 249–78.

———. "German and Irish Immigration to Colonial Philadelphia." *Proceedings of the American Philosophical Society* 133 (June 1989): 128–43.

Worner, William Frederic. "The Charity School Movement in Lancaster, 1755." *Papers of the Lancaster County Historical Society* 42, no. 1 (1938): 1–11.

Wright, Esmond. "'The fine and noble china vase, the British Empire': Benjamin Franklin's 'Love-Hate' View of England." *PMHB* 111 (October 1987): 435–64.

Yodelis, Mary Ann. "Who Paid the Piper? Publishing Economics in Boston, 1763–1775." *Journalism Monographs* 38 (February 1975).

Young, Alfred F. "George Robert Twelves Hewes (1742–1840): A Boston Shoemaker and the Memory of the American Revolution." *WMQ* 38 (October 1981): 561–623.

Zimmerman, John J. "Benjamin Franklin and the *Pennsylvania Chronicle*." *PMHB* 81 (October 1957): 351–64.

Unpublished Sources

The Benjamin Franklin Tercentenary Commission, www.benfranklin300.com

Ferro, David L. "Selling Science in the Colonial American Newspaper: How the Middle Colonial American General Periodical Represented Nature, Philosophy, Medicine, and Technology, 1728–1765." Ph.D. diss., Virginia Polytechnic Institute and State University, 2001.

Kany, Robert Hurd. "David Hall: Printing Partner of Benjamin Franklin." Ph. D. diss., Pennsylvania State University, 1963.

Oller, Anna Kathryn. "Christopher Saur, Colonial Printer: A Study of the Publications of the Press, 1738–1758." Ph.D. diss., University of Michigan, 1963.

Steckel, William R. "Pietist in Colonial Pennsylvania: Christopher Sauer, Printer, 1738–1758." Ph.D. diss., Stanford University, 1949.

Wetherell, Charles W. "Brokers of the Word: An Essay in the Social History of the Early American Press, 1639–1783." Ph.D. diss., University of New Hampshire, 1980.

Index